AUTOMATIC RM 037

Caliber CRMA1
Power reserve: circa 50 hours
Baseplate and bridges made of titanium
Rotor with variable geometry
Free sprung balance with variable inertia
Newly developed gear teeth profile
Oversize date display
Function selector
Newly designed flat head movement screws
and spline screws in grade 5 titanium
New patented crown construction
Balance: CuBe, 4 arms, 4 setting screws,
Inertia moment 7.5 mg·cm^2, angle of lift 50°
Frequency: 28,800 vph (4 Hz)
Microblasted anglage
Microblasted sinks
Microblasted milled section
Titalyt® treatment for the baseplate and DLC treatment for the bridges

WATCHES XIII INTERNATIONAL®

THE ORIGINAL ANNUAL OF THE WORLD'S FINEST WRISTWATCHES

First published in the United States in 2012 by

TOURBILLON INTERNATIONAL
A MODERN LUXURY MEDIA COMPANY

11 West 25th Street, 8th Floor
New York, NY 10010
Tel: +1 (212) 627-7732 Fax +1 (312) 274-8418
www.modernluxury.com/watches

In association with RIZZOLI INTERNATIONAL PUBLICATIONS, INC.

300 Park Avenue South, New York, NY 10010

ISBN: 978-0-8478-3750-2

PRINTED IN ITALY

COVER: TOURBILLON 14 DAYS (VACHERON CONSTANTIN)

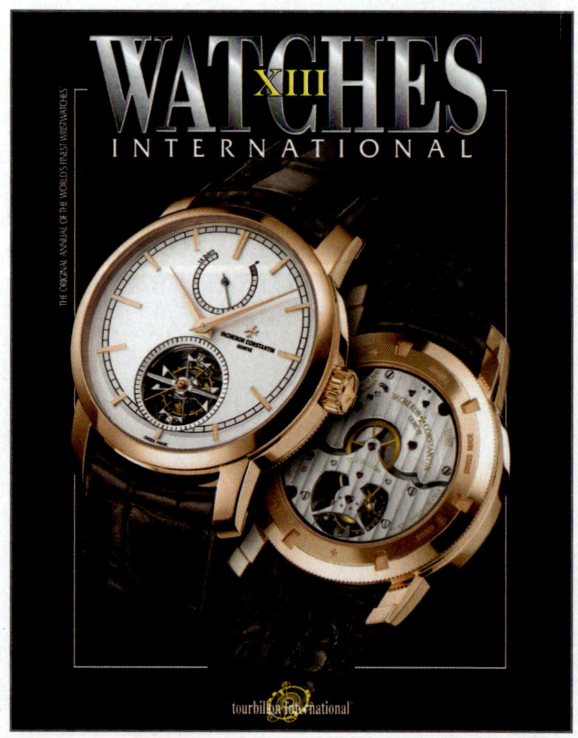

1B 1735
BLANCPAIN
MANUFACTURE DE HAUTE HORLOGERIE
L-evolution Collection
Tourbillon Grande Date
7-day power reserve
Tourbillon large date
Power reserve on the oscillating weight
Ref. 8822-15B30-53B
www.blancpain.com
BLANCPAIN BOUTIQUES ABU DHABI · BEIJING · CANNES · DUBAI · EKATERINBURG · GENEVA · HONG KONG · MACAU · MADRID · MANAMA
MOSCOW · MUMBAI · MUNICH · NEW YORK · PARIS · SEOUL · SHANGHAI · SINGAPORE · TAIPEI · TOKYO · ZURICH

CHANEL
J12
AUTOMATIC
SWISS
MADE

The Time is Now

I have a confession to make. I am not an expert on luxury timepieces, but I am definitely a watch enthusiast. With each years' edition, I find more and more detail to appreciate in the watches I do collect and more watches to add to my wish list. After one year of partnering with Modern Luxury Media, I am proud to not only introduce the lucky 13th edition of *Watches International*, but also the inaugural issue of *Watches International Chinese Edition Volume I*.

Throughout the last decade we have been committed to delivering an encyclopedic tome of great timepieces. We've worked tirelessly to acquaint consumers and collectors with watches that are perfectly conceived, technically brilliant, visually stunning, precisely engineered, and ready to be worn and displayed. After all, a luxury watch is more than a time-telling instrument; it is a status statement.

Along with this printed issue, we provide all content digitally and, most importantly, in app format for the iPad, too. With more than 40,000 Tourbillon International apps downloaded in this digital age, we understand the importance of allowing our elite global audience to view this content anywhere, anytime.

Luxury timepieces have stood the test of time themselves. Even in this era of rapid technological growth we still find great satisfaction in horology and craftsmanship. Whether it is a watch's weight on the wrist, the allure of a favorite brand, or the ability to pass a special timepiece along to the next generation, ultimately, it's the pure pleasure of distinction.

Please enjoy this issue.

Michael Dickey

RALPH LAUREN
THE 867 WATCH
18K ROSE GOLD
SQUARE MODEL
ULTRATHIN CASE
MANUAL WINDING
MANUFACTURE MOVEMENT
131 COMPONENTS
40-HOUR POWER RESERVE
SWISS MADE
RALPHLAURENWATCHES.COM

cellini

cellini

New York City is not for the faint of heart. The streets teem with the most successful people in the world, and the city is notoriously tough on those who don't measure up. This is the environment in which Cellini Jewelers has thrived for more than 30 years, exceeding expectations in the world's most demanding city with an unsurpassed selection of rare timepieces and sublime jewelry, all presented by a gracious staff of experts dedicated to consummate service.

AHEAD OF HIS TIME

Leon Adams, Cellini's founder and president, has always been passionate about *haute horlogerie*. It led him to open his first boutique inside the Hotel Waldorf-Astoria in 1977, and a second on Madison Avenue a decade later.

Cellini opened at the dawn of the current horological renaissance, a time when fine mechanical watches were scarce commodities. By offering an extensive array of hard-to-find timepieces, Cellini struck a chord with collectors, who visited the stores to see watches they could not find anywhere else in the United States.

Through the years, Cellini's reputation grew along with its collection, which was the first in the U.S. to include brands like Audemars Piguet, A. Lange & Söhne, Roger Dubuis and Maîtres du Temps. Today, Cellini covers the spectrum of *haute horlogerie* as an authorized dealer for more than two dozen of the world's best known and most exotic watchmakers. Its phenomenal range appeals to all types of enthusiasts, from budding aficionados in search of their first fine timepiece, to savvy collectors who prize Cellini's unrivaled selection of rare watches.

DB28

This titanium version of De Bethune's DB28 is part of Cellini Jeweler's unsurpassed selection of mechanical timepieces from the world's best known and most exotic watchmakers.

EXPLORING OPULENCE

For those who treasure the natural beauty of jewelry, both of Cellini's boutiques reflect a deep appreciation for all things precious. Freestanding glass cabinets gleam with imaginatively designed, impeccably crafted jewelry creations organized by gemstone.

Diamonds of all colors populate one area, while another is reserved for the vibrant fire reflecting from their white counterparts. Nearby, a rich assortment of gems and pearls—assembled through the years from sources around the world—are used to make glamorous showpieces that feature everything from Burmese rubies and Kashmir sapphires to South Sea pearls and alexandrite, the exceedingly rare Russian gem whose color changes in natural light.

For exceptional glamour, nothing outshines a bespoke setting. Cellini's team of gemologists, designers and craftsmen combine their expertise and artistry to transform these precious gems into jewelry tailored exclusively to your personal style, whether you are looking for a unique engagement ring or a one-of-a-kind necklace.

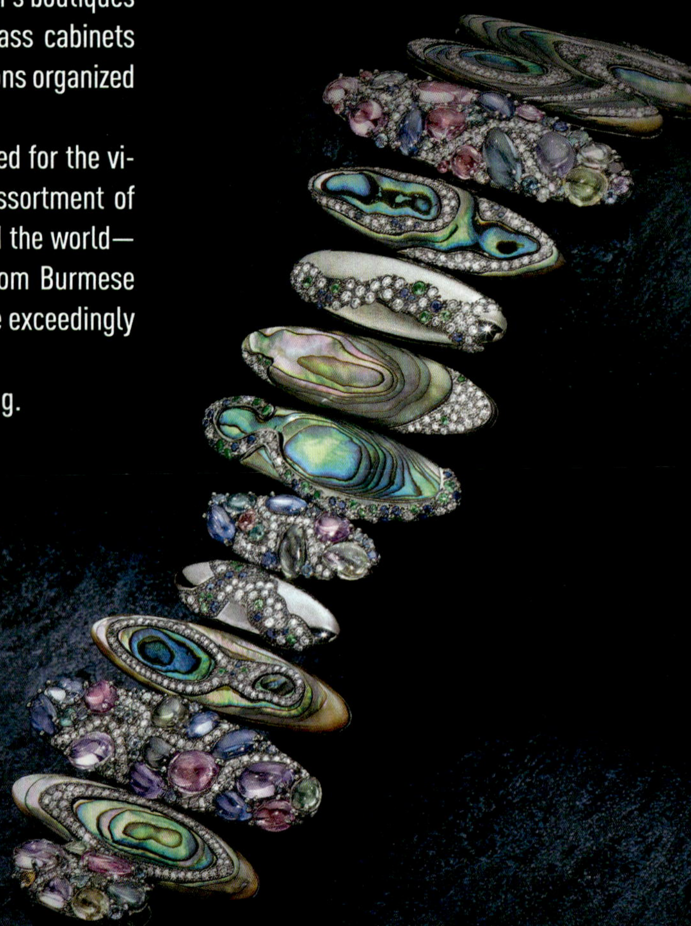

ABALONE SHELL BRACELET

One-of-a-kind with diamonds, sapphires, tourmalines and tsavorites in 18-karat gold.

SKELETON DOUBLE FLYING TOURBILLON
(Roger Dubuis)

KING POWER AYRTON SENNA
(Hublot)

TWENTY-8-EIGHT REGULATOR A.S.W HORIZONS
(DeWitt)

CALIBRE DE CARTIER MULTIPLE TIME ZONE
(Cartier)

BRANDS CARRIED

- A. Lange & Söhne
- Audemars Piguet
- Bell & Ross
- Cartier
- Chopard
- De Bethune
- DeWitt
- Franck Muller
- Girard-Perregaux
- Guy Ellia
- H. Moser & Cie.
- Hublot
- IWC
- Jaeger-LeCoultre
- Jean Dunand
- Ludovic Ballouard
- Maîtres du Temps
- Panerai
- Parmigiani
- Piaget
- Richard Mille
- Roger Dubuis
- Ulysse Nardin
- Vacheron Constantin
- Zenith

EXCEEDING EXPECTATIONS

But the merchandise is far from the only reason the most discerning connoisseurs opt for Cellini. A knowledgeable staff at both locations provides impeccable service before, during and after a purchase.

Cellini's horological specialists live and breathe watches, and draw upon this wealth of knowledge to help each watch lover find the perfect fit. For those enchanted instead by shimmering works of art, Cellini's jewelry experts put a world of exquisite beauty at your fingertips. The experience they provide puts the emphasis on the client's needs.

Sophisticated horology, irresistible jewels, inviting venues and a dedicated staff—it's no wonder that after nearly three and a half decades Cellini continues to be one of the most respected and successful boutiques of its kind. In this wildly competitive city, where storefronts, skylines and styles change as often as the weather, Cellini's longevity is a testament to the power of an irreplaceable experience.

DIAMOND & SAPPHIRE EARRINGS
Breathtaking heart-shaped diamond earrings edged with sapphires.

CELLINI JEWELERS

Hotel Waldorf-Astoria • 301 Park Avenue at 50th Street • New York, NY 10022 - Tel 212 751 9824

509 Madison Avenue at 53rd Street • New York, NY 10022 - Tel 212 888 0505

800-CELLINI • www.CelliniJewelers.com

HUBLOT
THE ART OF FUSION

Jean-Claude Biver, Chairman of the Board & Ricardo Guadalupe, CEO

"Cathedral" Minute Repeater Tourbillon and column wheel Chronograph

This achievement is realized in 100% carbon fiber, including its movement bridges.

"More watchmaking, more mastery, more innovation, more daring, more fusion!" This was the encouragement that Jean-Claude Biver, Chairman of the Board of Hublot, gave the new Complications department that reinforced the Hublot Manufacture in 2010. Hublot presents a minute repeater watch featuring two "cathedral" type gongs, a tourbillon and column wheel chronograph, with carbon fiber bridges, all in a carbon fiber case. This is a perfect illustration of "fusion" between great watchmaking tradition and the technology of the future. It is a timepiece whose sophisticated mechanism, featuring three major haute horology complications particularly prized by connoisseurs and collectors, but revisited in a contemporary spirit: the main particularity lies in the fact that the three complications are visible from the dial side. Besides carbon fiber, the case is also fashioned from materials such as titanium and rubber—a perfect illustration of Hublot's characteristic Art of Fusion. From a design point of view, the minute repeater bolt is ingeniously integrated into the King Power case middle, just like the chronograph control pushbutton subtly integrated into the watch's crown. The minute repeater, activated by a lever situated between 8 and 10 o'clock, sounds the hours, quarter-hours and minutes. Its two "cathedral" gongs (one for hours and the other for minutes) are double the length of a regular gong. The whole design aims for a very uncomplicated overall effect for a piece of this level. The manual-winding mechanical movement boasts a five-day power reserve. The hour and minute indicator is situated centrally, for a conventional readout. The flying tourbillon—with suspended cage—is situated at 6 o'clock, and features an unusual structure of very high quality: indeed, the cage rotates without a ball bearing, and has a Swiss lever escapement.

Succumbing to temptation

In this period when the economic situation is hardly favorable, decency should perhaps prevent us from mentioning it. Nonetheless, we cannot help admitting that this is a time for rejoicing. A fresh wind is blowing through the world of haute horology, which—although it will of course always face occasional downturns—is overall in excellent health. So what lies behind the growing enthusiasm it is generating?

Firstly, the emerging countries, which inevitably wish to attain the same standard of living as the world's major economic powers. These include China, which, having explored the world of fashion, fragrances and accessories, is showing ever-increasing awareness of watchmaking culture. With tens of millions of potential customers, the Middle Empire is single-handedly capable of ensuring the prosperity of haute horology. It is also in a bid to respond to Chinese enthusiasts' thirst for knowledge that Watches International is now also published in their language.

Luxury is no longer reserved for a wealthy clientele wishing to confirm its belonging—or accession—to a certain social class. The strong media coverage of luxury we have seen over the past decades has fostered growing interest among a discerning public. Customers are no longer looking so much for luxury labels worn specifically to express socio-professional success, but instead for beautiful and useful objects that feature technical characteristics and meet precise objectives they have set for themselves. Whether exceptional, episodic or habitual, the acquisition of an haute horology timepiece now conveys an aspiration to comfort, aesthetic elegance and technological perfection.

The choice of carefully selected materials, the perpetuation of extremely demanding production processes, the development of subtle and complex mechanical movements, a creative craftsmanship approach combining inventiveness and expertise: all these factors combine to endow watches with that rare quality of being equally beautiful inside and out. Creating them involves rigorous work performed by artists with golden hands actively cultivating the noble essence of time-honored artistic crafts. Isn't treating oneself to a luxury watch a way of saluting the human genius that presided over its creation?

An appreciation of know-how is naturally echoed in the quest for a certain art of living. Alternately precious, sporty and elegant, a watch, more than any other object, inspires dreams—which are indeed the very essence of luxury.

Like a remedy for the prevailing gloom, luxury seems to exercise a cathartic effect. If there is one object that harbors a soul liable to arouse sensual pleasure and deep-felt emotion, a watch certainly fits the bill. Acquiring one is first and foremost about succumbing to temptation.

Increasingly coveted and yet still little known to the public at large, a watch reminds us of our need to live in an enchanted world. And in this respect, its future is quite certainly full of promise.

Caroline Childers

GPHG
2011
Best Men's Watch Prize
HERMÈS
PARIS
Le temps suspendu

arije

PARIS • LONDON • CANNES

Arije, in Paris, is more than a boutique, more than just a showcase, and more than one of the most welcoming smiles of Parisian horology: It is a secret. It is a private mystery that is shared amongst friends. Arije is also an address that we would love to keep to ourselves, but that we can't resist sharing with others.

It is a gentle environment, in a unique space that knows how to make time stand still, precisely because it speaks of the language of time, and of the objects that convey it.

Arije, in all honesty, is frankly *somewhere else*, despite the doors that open onto the "golden triangle" of the Avenue George-V. Arije is also present on the famous "Croisette" in Cannes, in the Grand Hôtel du Cap-Ferrat, and in the heart of London's Sloane Street. These noble and exclusive sites for exceptional timepieces offer horological and jewelry enthusiasts a chance to admire approximately 40 eminently prestigious brands.

If there is a secret within the secret, it is the constant focus on respecting other people's sensibilities, regardless of cultural codes and standards: here, almost every language is spoken, and in all cases the language of the heart. This is the hallmark of Arije.

One might say that Arije has the most niche international clientele of watches and jewelry. It is hard to judge, discretion being the watchword in this field, but it is undoubtedly one of the most select that Paris (or anywhere else for that matter) has to offer.

JUMBO CHRONO LIMITED EDITION
(Guy Ellia)

arije
Cartier
Cartier
ROGER DUBUIS

Arije is a byword among devotees of fine objects, who know how to trust the eye and the choices of a house that demonstrates great maturity and a wealth of expertise in its vision of brands, of watches, and of those who create them.

This pervasively elegant and refined atmosphere provides a perfect setting to write, to tell and to experience for a special moment in time, a beautiful story surrounding a particular watch or a jewelry creation.

This is such a rare occurrence within the world of international luxury that has become so systematic and full of stereotypes that one is left to wonder if people don't simply find their way back to Carla Chalouhi's boutique as much for these shared values as for its rare pieces, limited editions or exclusive offerings...

Of course, Arije would not be Arije without the spirit and efforts of its CEO, Carla Chalouhi. The daughter of Arije's founder and herself a cosmopolitan businesswoman with her finger on the pulse of the watch industry, Carla is at the heart of it all; she is the woman behind the watches.

MILLENARY 4101
(Audemars Piguet)

CRAZY FLOWER
(Breguet)

ZEITWERK LUMINOUS
(A. Lange & Söhne)

PATRIMONY TRADITIONNELLE WORLD TIME
(Vacheron Constantin)

PORTUGUESE GRAND COMPLICATION
(IWC)

ROTONDE DE CARTIER ASTROREGULATEUR
(Cartier)

BRANDS CARRIED

A. Lange & Söhne**
Audemars Piguet***
Baume & Mercier**
Bell & Ross*
Blancpain*
Breguet*
Cartier***
Chanel*
Chaumet*
Chopard*
Dior*
Ebel*
Franck Muller*
Girard-Perregaux***
Glashütte Original*
Guy Ellia***
Harry Winston**
Hautlence*
Hublot*
IWC***
Jaeger-LeCoultre*
Jaquet Droz*
Montblanc*
Omega*
Panerai*
Parmigiani***
Piaget**
Pierre Kunz*
Roger Dubuis***
Rolex*
TAG Heuer*
Tudor*
Ulysse Nardin**
Vacheron Constantin*
Van Cleef & Arpels**
Zenith**

* Paris
* London
* Cannes

OYSTER PERPETUAL YACHT MASTER II
(Rolex)

ARIJE

PARIS
50 rue Pierre Charron - Tel +33 (0) 1 47 20 72 40
30 avenue George V - Tel +33 (0) 1 49 52 98 88

LONDON
165 Sloane Street - Tel +44 (0) 20 7752 0246

CANNES
50 boulevard de la Croisette - Tel +33 (0) 4 93 68 47 73

SAINT-JEAN-CAP-FERRAT
Grand-Hôtel du Cap-Ferrat • 71 boulevard du Général de Gaulle - Tel +33 (0) 4 93 76 50 24

www.arije.com
contact: shop@arije.com

«JUMBO CHRONO»

Tomorrow is another day

It was back in October 2011, in Dubai. The Swatch Group had organized an event there for one of its brands. Marc A. Hayek—CEO of Blancpain, Breguet and Jaquet Droz—was on the platform. A journalist put to him the question on everyone's mind: what are the prospects for 2012?

Whether because of the nervous state of the markets, the ills befalling the euro or the utterly uncertain economy, 2012 has become the new terra incognita. It crystallizes all kinds of expectations. "2010 was a record year," responded Hayek. "Demand exceeded our production capacities. 2011 is a year of panic in many respects. However, if we were playing a waiting game, do you think we would have launched a new watch in this superlative city?"

The response was considered a definitive answer, and also as a kind of a barometer. Swatch Group is the world's leading watch group, as well as the third largest luxury group behind LVMH and Richemont. Its word is often considered gospel on the markets. At the turn of the year, forecasters no longer know which compass to trust; Europe and the United States are despondent because of the crimson red state of their debts. All eyes are turned towards the emerging countries, but their purchasing power is not enough to gauge which way the wind is really blowing

One day in 2008, the crisis swept away everything in its path: growth, confidence, dividends. After spending two years making up the lost ground, watchmakers have enjoyed two prosperous years in 2010 and 2011, setting a new record. Plunging back into crisis would mean having their wings clipped in mid-flight. The coming year will bring tricky challenges. While the media in general are past masters in the art of propagating the current depressed climate, let's do just the opposite. Let's trust in the Swiss watch industry's ability to rebound. It is indeed indispensable to believe in it. For almost 30 years, it has been all-conquering and displays an infinite number of qualities. The list is a long one. The industry harbors countless possibilities for evolution, and is building manufacturing facilities.

In the mid-1980s, the quartz revolution almost destroyed it. A man at that time adopted a strategy based on an in-depth restructuring of the production system, convinced of the certainty of the possible renewal of mechanical horology. A renewal paradoxically rendered possible by the success of Swatch, which then enabled the industry to focus on marketing and to orchestrate the big comeback of fine watchmaking onto the world scene. He never gave up. That man was the grandfather of Blancpain's CEO, Nicolas G. Hayek.

Michel Jeannot

BVLGARI
BVLGARI
Gérald Genta
CAL 7722
OCTO BI-RETRO STEEL CERAMIC
ELECTED WATCH OF THE YEAR 2010 BY A SWISS PROFESSIONAL JURY
ATLANTA • BAL HARBOUR • BEVERLY HILLS • BOCA RATON • CHEVY CHASE
CHICAGO • DALLAS • HONOLULU • HOUSTON • LAS VEGAS • NEW YORK
SAN FRANCISCO • SCOTTSDALE • SHORT HILLS • SOUTH COAST PLAZA • BULGARI.COM
m
MONTRE
DE L'ANNEE
2010

ULTIMATE DISCRETION
PIAGET
PIAGET ALTIPLANO
The world's thinnest automatic watch
White gold case, 5.25 mm thick
The world's thinnest automatic movement
Piaget Manufacture Calibre, 2.35 mm thick

WATCHES XIII INTERNATIONAL®

THE ORIGINAL ANNUAL OF THE WORLD'S FINEST WRISTWATCHES

TOURBILLON INTERNATIONAL
A MODERN LUXURY MEDIA COMPANY
ADMINISTRATION, ADVERTISING SALES, EDITORIAL, BOOK SALES

11 West 25th Street, 8th Floor • New York, NY 10010
Tel: +1 (212) 627-7732 Fax: +1 (312) 274-8418

Caroline Childers
PUBLISHER

Michel Jeannot
EDITOR IN CHIEF

EDITORS Samson Crouhy, Claire Loeb, Elise Nussbaum
ART DIRECTOR Mutsumi Hyuga
CONTRIBUTING EDITORS Fabrice Eschmann, Gregory Pons
TRANSLATIONS Susan Jacquet
COORDINATION Caroline Pita

VICE PRESIDENT OF PRODUCTION Meg Eulberg
VICE PRESIDENT OF MANUFACTURING Sean Bertram
VICE PRESIDENT OF AUDIENCE DEVELOPMENT Eric Holden
DIRECTOR OF INFORMATION TECHNOLOGY Scott Brookman
SALES ADMINISTRATOR Ralph Gago

WEB DISTRIBUTION
www.modernluxury.com/watches

PHOTOGRAPHY
Photographic Archives
Property of Tourbillon International, a Modern Luxury Media Company

---

MODERN **LUXURY MEDIA**

Lew Dickey
CHIEF EXECUTIVE OFFICER

Michael Dickey
PRESIDENT

EXECUTIVE VICE PRESIDENT AND CO-CHIEF OPERATING OFFICER John Dickey
EXECUTIVE VICE PRESIDENT AND CO-CHIEF OPERATING OFFICER Jon Pinch
CHIEF FINANCIAL OFFICER JP Hannan
GENERAL COUNSEL Richard Denning

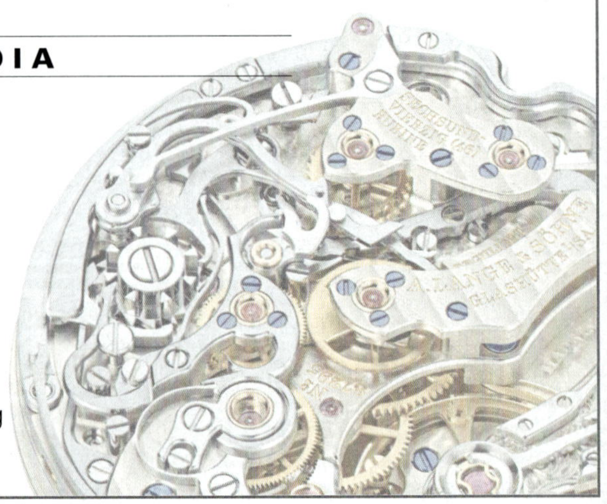

MASTER GRANDE TRADITION TOURBILLON À QUANTIÈME PERPÉTUEL
Jaeger-LeCoultre Calibre 987

GREG SIMONIAN
Westime President

Westime

Los Angeles
Beverly Hills
La Jolla

For the best selection of prestigious watches in Southern California, collectors from around the world head to Westime. Its three boutiques—in West Los Angeles, Beverly Hills and La Jolla—present more than 50 of the most sought-after watch brands in surroundings that reflect California's famous laid-back elegance.

Since its opening 25 years ago, Westime Los Angeles's spacious showroom at the Westside Pavilion has proudly displayed a wide selection of fine timepieces for serious collectors and casual shoppers alike. With the help of experienced staff members who speak more than 12 different languages combined, this is the place where any shopper can discover up-and-coming Swiss watch brands, find watches that complement the hottest fashion trends, or inspect one-of-a-kind grand complication timepieces in the privacy of a VIP viewing room.

Westime Beverly Hills is a multi-story jewel box of a boutique on one of the world's most celebrated shopping streets: Rodeo Drive. Here customers will discover limited edition watches that won't be seen in any other watch store. It's not unusual to meet a master watchmaker from Switzerland in the boutique, who makes his own regular pilgrimage to Westime to greet important clients. Throughout the year, the boutique stages watch auction previews for serious connoisseurs, as well as light-hearted parties that introduce the world of watches to new shoppers in a fun way.

ROYAL OAK OFFSHORE CHRONOGRAPH CARBON
(Audemars Piguet)

Late last year, Westime La Jolla debuted in one of California's most exclusive seaside destinations. The new boutique, located north of San Diego, symbolizes Westime's commitment to introducing the new masters of haute horlogerie to a discriminating clientele. Young, independent watch brands, including Richard Mille, Urwerk, Greubel Forsey, Ikepod and De Bethune, are available in the region for the first time at Westime La Jolla. And of course, the best traditional watch brands—from Zenith to Ulysse Nardin—are thoughtfully represented in the newest Westime location.

Westime's expansion continues this year. In 2012, Westime's flagship Los Angeles store will relocate to a 6,500-square-foot building on Sunset Boulevard, in West Hollywood. The two-level open space will not only showcase an extensive selection of watches, but also an ever-changing line-up of exquisitely crafted accessories, artwork, objects and amenities. Curated by Westime Founder John Simonian and President Greg Simonian, the collections, design, services and décor will transform the new flagship from a place to shop, into a destination where one appreciates the finest things in life at his or her own pace.

Even as it grows, Westime remains a family-owned and -operated business that succeeds by nurturing personal relationships with watchmakers, customers and charitable organizations in its communities.

WESTIME

LOS ANGELES
10800 West Pico Blvd., #197 • Los Angeles, CA 90064 - Tel 310 470 1388 • Fax 310 475 0628

BEVERLY HILLS
254 North Rodeo Drive • Beverly Hills, CA 90210 - Tel 310 271 0000 • Fax 310 271 3091

LA JOLLA
1227 Prospect Street • La Jolla, CA 92037 - Tel 858 459 2222

www.westime.com

OCTA UTC
(F. P. Journe)

KING POWER BLACK MAGIC
(Hublot)

LM1
(MB&F)

RM 004
SPLIT SECONDS CHRONOGRAPH
(Richard Mille)

BRANDS CARRIED

Alpina
Audemars Piguet
Baume & Mercier
Bell & Ross
Blancpain
Breitling
BRM
Buben & Zörweg
Bulgari
Chopard
Concord
De Bethune
DeWitt
Dior
Dottling
Ebel
FP Journe
Franck Muller
Frédérique Constant
Girard-Perregaux
Giuliano Mazzuoli
Glashütte Original
Graham-London
Greubel Forsey
H. Moser
Hamilton
Harry Winston
Hublot
Ikepod
Jacob & Co
Longines
Ludovic Ballouard
MB&F
Milus
Nixon
Omega
Pierre Kunz
Richard Mille
RogueDZN
Roland Iten
Romain Jerome
Shamballa
TAG Heuer
Tiffany & Co.
Tissot
Ulysse Nardin
URWERK
Vertu
Zenith

Summary

RICHARD MILLE

LONGINES

HUBLOT
4000M

PATEK PHILIPPE
GENEVE

TO BREAK THE RULES, YOU MUST FIRST MASTER THEM.
THE UNIQUE ASYMMETRIC STYLING OF THE AUDEMARS PIGUET MILLENARY COLLECTION HAS TRANSFORMED THE WAY DESIGN ENGINEERS DEVELOP CALIBRES. THIS TRI-DIMENSIONAL MOVEMENT COMBINES PERFORMANCE AND CHRONOMETRY WITH HAUTE HOROLOGY MICRO-DETAILING.
IN THE TRANSVERSAL BALANCE-BRIDGE, OPTIMUM SHOCK-RESISTANCE IS COMBINED WITH THE ELEGANCE OF THE CÔTES DE GENÈVE WAVE-FORM FINISHING. THE PERFECT SYMBIOSIS OF ENGINEERING, DESIGN AND CRAFTSMANSHIP, AND A CLASSIC EXPRESSION OF THE PHILOSOPHY OF LE BRASSUS.
AUDEMARS PIGUET
MILLENARY 4101
IN PINK GOLD. SELFWINDING MANUFACTURE MOVEMENT.
AUDEMARS PIGUET
Le Brassus

L'INTRANSIGEANT

Web Site Directory

A. LANGE & SÖHNE	www.alange-soehne.com
ALPINA	www.alpina-watches.com
AUDEMARS PIGUET	www.audemarspiguet.com
BELL & ROSS	www.bellross.com
BLANCPAIN	www.blancpain.com
BREGUET	www.breguet.com
BUBEN & ZÖRWEG	www.buben-zorweg.com
BVLGARI	www.bulgari.com
CARL F. BUCHERER	www.carl-f-bucherer.com
CARTIER SA	www.cartier.com
CHANEL	www.chanel.com
CHAUMET	www.chaumet.com
CHRISTOPHE CLARET	www.claret.ch
DE GRISOGONO	www.degrisogono.com
DEWITT	www.dewitt.ch
DIOR HORLOGERIE	www.diorhorlogerie.com
FRANCK MULLER	www.franckmullerusa.com
FRÉDÉRIQUE CONSTANT SA	www.frederique-constant.com
GIRARD-PERREGAUX	www.girard-perregaux.ch
GLASHÜTTE ORIGINAL	www.glashuette-original.com
GRAHAM-LONDON	www.graham-london.com
GREUBEL FORSEY	www.greubelforsey.com
GUY ELLIA	www.guyellia.com
H. MOSER & CIE.	www.h-moser.com
HAMILTON WATCHES	www.hamiltonwatch.com
HARRY WINSTON SA	www.harrywinston.com
HERMÈS	www.hermes.com
HUBLOT	www.hublot.com
IWC	www.iwc.com
JACOB & CO.	www.jacobandco.com
JAEGER-LECOULTRE	www.jaeger-lecoultre.com
JAQUET DROZ SA	www.jaquet-droz.com
LONGINES	www.longines.com
LOUIS VUITTON	www.louisvuitton.com
MONTBLANC MONTRE	www.montblanc.com
PANERAI	www.panerai.com
PATEK PHILIPPE	www.patek.com
PIAGET	www.piaget.com
RALPH LAUREN	www.ralphlauren.com
RAYMOND WEIL SA	www.raymond-weil.com
REBELLION TIMEPIECES	www.rebellion-timepieces.com
RICHARD MILLE	www.richardmille.com
ROGER DUBUIS	www.rogerdubuis.com
ROLEX	www.rolex.com
STÜHRLING ORIGINAL	www.stuhrling.com
TAG HEUER	www.tagheuer.com
URWERK	www.urwerk.com
VACHERON CONSTANTIN	www.vacheron-constantin.com
VAN CLEEF & ARPELS	www.vancleef-arpels.com
ZENITH	www.zenith-watches.com

RELATED SITES

BASELWORLD	www.baselworld.com
SIHH	www.sihh.ch

AUCTION HOUSES

CHRISTIE'S	www.christies.com
SOTHEBY'S	www.sothebys.com

LOUIS VUITTON
TACHYMETRE
LOUIS VUITTON
AUTOMATIQUE
SWISS MADE
Tambour Voyagez
Automatic chronograph with tachymeter function, manufactured in Louis Vuitton's watchmaking workshops in Switzerland
Sold exclusively in Louis Vuitton stores and on louisvuitton.com.

www.dior.com

Dior
AUTOMATIC
VIII
SWISS MADE

RAYMOND WEIL
GENEVE
PRECISION
IS MY INSPIRATION
raymond-weil.com | maestro collection
Vh1 SAVE THE MUSIC foundation
Music Education = Brainpower
PROUD SUPPORTER
vh1savethemusic.com

In 1839 Vacheron Constantin created several machines, among them the famous pantograph, a mechanical device which meant that for the first time in history principal watchmaking components could be reproduced with total precision, raising the quality of its timepieces once again. This invention carried the brand into the future and would revolutionise Swiss watchmaking.

Faithful to the history for which it is renowned, Vacheron Constantin undertakes to maintain, repair and restore all watches it has produced since its foundation: a sign of excellence and confidence which still today gives the manufacture its reputation.

Patrimony Contemporaine Perpetual Calendar
Pink-gold case, ultra-slim mechanical movement with automatic winding, calibre 1120 QP, moon phase.
Reference: 43175/000R-9687

FOUNDED IN 1755, ON AN ISLAND
IN LAKE GENEVA. AND STILL THERE.
VACHERON CONSTANTIN
GENEVE
GENEVE

Juan-Carlos Torres

CEO of Vacheron Constantin

THE HUMANITY OF HAUTE HOROLOGY

Masterfully guided by Juan-Carlos Torres, Vacheron Constantin is experiencing remarkable success, notably in the United States and China. To cope with this strong demand, the brand is substantially investing in production facilities and projects a doubling of its workforce, a decision that matches the manufacture's philosophy of combining strong human resources with audacious innovation.

"Vacheron Constantin has grown strongly, everywhere," notes Juan-Carlos Torres, the brand's CEO. This growth has entailed an impressive increase of 55% in the United States, along with a Chinese market to which "our entire production could be devoted if we so wished. This is why we have decided to maintain the existing product and production strategy, while increasing our means," explains Torres.

To keep pace with its current success, the manufacture is making considerable investments this year in its production sites of Plan-les-Ouates and Le Brassus, in Switzerland's Vallée du Joux in the Jura Mountains. The objective? To increase the number of watches produced annually from 19,000 to 33,000, all the while preserving and further nurturing the very essence of the brand.

In parallel, Vacheron Constantin will strengthen its distribution network in several markets, including by opening proprietary boutiques in Macau, Seoul, Paris, Taiwan, Los Angeles and São Paulo, as well as a fourth store in Hong Kong.

"I DON'T ADD MACHINES, I ADD WORKSHOPS"

To increase the capacity of production, Torres does not follow the path of excessive industrialization. He instead builds on the foundations of the success and the reputation of this ancient manufacture, founded in Geneva in 1755: namely, its strong attachment to ancestral techniques, particularly hand craftsmanship. "The development strategy of hand-made crafts will be further reinforced," he points out, "because I don't add machines, I add workshops made up of professionals. This is why we are going to double our collective team in Switzerland in the years to come, rather than undertake excessive mechanization of production." These human skills are duly fostered at each level, as the manufacture is equally committed to its internal training program and is accordingly doubling its number of apprentices.

"Human quality can be both seen and felt in a watch."

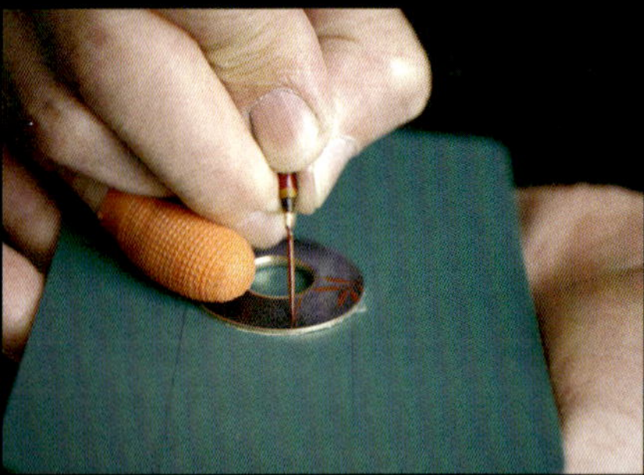

SYMBOLIQUE DES LAQUES

The future of the manufacture is already clearly expressed in the models presented in 2011, representing a tribute to the horological arts. At the heart of the Vacheron Constantin workshops, a Métiers d'Art unit that brings together virtuoso exponents of their crafts, is a gathering of artisans gifted with talents that are both remarkable in themselves and extremely rare. There, Vacheron Constantin perpetuates traditional expertise through dedicated collections, such as the Masques series of 2007, and the Symbolique des Laques line introduced in 2010. The brand also achieved a world first for the Only Watch charity auction held in September 2011. The dial of the Colombes watch features the alliance of four separate decorative techniques: engraving, guilloché, gem setting, and enameling. This timepiece, inspired by M.C. Escher's technique of repetition of forms, heralded the birth of a new collection: Métiers d'Art – Perspectives d'Art. In doing so, the manufacture innovated by developing a new style of guillochage. Beyond the repeating motifs, the craftsman creates veritable drawings, which are all miniature works of art.

Uniting these same competencies, the one-of-a-kind Métiers d'Art – Chagall & l'Opéra de Paris piece flirted with the limits of achievability, as the engraver needed fairy-like fingers to sculpt the gold while preserving the dial's grand feu enameling miniature artwork.

In 2011, Vacheron Constantin additionally unveiled two pieces that are part of its Atelier Cabinotiers project, launched in 2006 and never before seen in the field of horology. Devoted to the creation of custom-built, one-of-a-kind pieces of exceptional craftsmanship, the project provides absolute exclusivity and complete personalization. A single hand, for example, revolves around the Philosophia's dial! And as if to free its owner from the frenzied race for precision, only the hours are displayed. If needed, a minute repeater comprising three gongs provides a precise indication of time. Representing the ultimate complication, a tourbillon sets the final touch to this masterpiece...

Vladimir, the second one-off piece born in the Atelier Cabinotiers, marries high-flying technique and artistic craftsmanship, with the hand-decoration of each of the movement's 891 components, and the bas-relief engraving adorning the case. The heart of the watch houses 17 complications, making it, following four years of development, one of the most complicated watches on the market.

TRADITION, THE ROOT OF TECHNICAL INNOVATION

Building on past achievements to propel them even farther is the trademark of Vacheron Constantin. As early as 1930, the House, in collaboration with Louis Cottier, became one of the earliest manufactures to develop watches with world-time displays. At last year's Salon International de la Haute Horologie, the brand unveiled the Patrimony Traditionnelle Heures du Monde. Thirty-seven time zones, including half zones and even quarter zones, are displayed on the dial. This timepiece is the only one to date to boast such a complete and comprehensive display, a prowess that notably earned it the second prize of *Montres Passion* magazine's Watch of the Year competition. Endowed with a rich heritage, Vacheron Constantin proves its willingness to reinterpret tradition through the glorious spectrum of technical innovation.

The year 2012 began with the presentation of the exceptional Patrimony Traditionnelle 14-Day Tourbillon, featuring an impressive record-setting power reserve for this complication, combined with the absolute purity of a round and sober case. In fact, the new Vacheron Constantin 2260 caliber beating at the heart of the Patrimony Traditionnelle 14-Day Tourbillon is simply unrivaled in the industry. And that isn't all: this new arrival in the Patrimony Traditionnelle line is the first

Vacheron Constantin timepiece to be officially recognized as meeting the new criteria of the Geneva Seal, thereby already making it a collector's piece.

UPDATING THE GENEVA SEAL FOR THE GOOD OF THE INDUSTRY

Vacheron Constantin also took part in redefining the criteria of the Geneva Seal. To celebrate the distinction's 125th anniversary, it was revised to become "more understandable and more attuned to customer expectations." The requirements are now applied not only to the movement, but also to the finished watch. Through its active participation in the new definition of the Geneva Seal, Vacheron Constantin has expressed its pronounced interest in our shared horological heritage and its determination to be a driving force in the pursuit of excellence.

In 2012, Vacheron Constantin's agenda is expressed through the consolidation of its lines and products, the enlargement of its offering, and the investments it is making, which encompass the production facilities of Plan-les-Ouates and Le Brassus, as well as human resources. Torres explains: "The necessary concern for these three elements is driven not by financial reasons, but most importantly by a need for quality!" The soul of Vacheron Constantin, linked to its expertise in hand-craftsmanship, is thus beating more vibrantly than ever. And if the timepieces may serve as stages for extraordinary complications and virtuosity, the brand well knows how to demonstrate an intelligent simplicity, while truly focusing on the long term.

PATRIMONY TRADITIONNELLE HEURES DU MONDE

TOGETHER, WE'RE BUILDING HIS FUTURE

Since Andre Agassi retired from professional tennis, he hasn't stopped pursuing excellence. Founding and inspiring the Andre Agassi Foundation for Education and the Andre Agassi College Preparatory Academy. To give underprivileged children a chance to receive an education, learn a trade and build a life.

Longines is happy to help. It funded the Longines Scholarship Fund for Agassi Prep Graduates. Allowing gifted and motivated youngsters to learn a trade with a future, at the N.G. Hayek Watchmaking School

Elegance is an attitude
Andre Agassi
LONGINES®
The Longines Saint-Imier Collection
www.longines.com

Walter von Känel

President of Longines

180 YEARS OF EXPERTISE AND ELEGANCE

Longines belongs to that rare breed of Swiss watchmakers whose production has been uninterrupted since their founding. In 2012, the company celebrates a significant anniversary against a backdrop of commercial success and internationally recognized prestige.

If one asks Walter von Känel to describe the brand he has helmed since 1988, his response is clear: "Longines is above all a Swiss brand that makes the most of a long history and thus an excellent reputation. Longines is also a company that has been able to make the transition between two eras: the first saw the market adapt to technique, and the second has seen technique adapt to the market. In addition, Longines is a family business that has successively undergone several mergers to finally, in 1984, become a member of the Swatch Group, the largest watch group in the world." Besides these historical realities, von Känel also points out other particularities of the brand: "Longines is a leader in its price category—watches between 800 and 4,000 CHF—and it is especially recognized for an excellent price to quality ratio." Thus painted in broad strokes by von Känel, Longines's current reality is heir to a long tradition.

The history of Longines is rooted in a region of Switzerland that is both quiet and rugged: the Bernese Jura. Far from the crowded centers of trading cities, in the heart of a valley filled with fields and pine trees, the company's buildings, vast and white, stand out from the Saint-Imier landscape. They still stand on the spot where the first movements and first watches came from the workshops, in a grassy area called Les Longines—a name that became a brand.

IN CHINA SINCE 1867

Today, Longines is on every continent and in some countries for over a century, such as China, where it has been since 1867, or India, since 1878. A member of the Swatch Group, the industry's largest group, Longines is one of the group's treasures, and remains one of the top-selling brands.

Its current success is due to 180 years of history, founded on the will to achieve technically impeccable watches, and to an obvious consistency that has become a part of its era. As evidence, one need only recall Longines's slogan, "Elegance is an attitude," coined 15 years ago. Known by all watch lovers, it embodies the brand's soul and serves as an axis for all communication.

Native son, colonel in the Swiss Army, politician and history buff, von Känel directs the destiny of the company. He joined it in 1969, then rose through the ranks until he took the helm in 1988. It is to his vision and his experience that the brand owes the experience of belonging to a trio of multi-line brands at the heart of the Swatch Group: along with Tissot and Omega, Longines offers strong, cohesive collections, in all registers, from classic to sporty, including ladies' collections and an emphasis on horological tradition.

Longines is also one of the few brands to possess its own museum with archives of all its production books, collections of vintage models and advertisements of yesteryear—a priceless heritage. Numerous publications, written by historians and researchers, regularly emphasize this patrimony, as well as that of the region in which it is based.

FACTORY 1866

AGASSIZ-FRANCILLONS

EXCELLENCE FROM THE BEGINNING

In 1832, businessman Auguste Agassiz laid the foundation for what would become Longines. The entrepreneur debuted his horological career by partnering with a small establishment in the town of Saint-Imier, naming the business "Agassiz & Compagnie." At the time, production of watch components was divided among several producers, usually families, each one specialized in a type of piece or operation. The administrators of Agassiz & Compagnie had the task of ordering and repairing the correct pieces in the proper quantities, commissioning their assembly and ensuring their sale. The business already enjoyed an excellent reputation, at home and abroad, when Agassiz handed over the reins to his nephew Ernest Francillon.

Looking to optimize and increase production, in 1866 Francillon acquired two lots on the land the people called "Longines." There he converted a building that would allow him to bring together several workers under the same roof. During the same period, he hired the young engineer Jacques David, whose mission was to invent machines capable of perfecting and optimizing the fabrication of watches. Within the context of global industrialization and the growing strength of mass production, Francillon's wager paid off handsomely. In 1876, he was proven right at the Universal Exposition in Philadelphia, where the increased degree of industrialization in America's horological industry would act as a catalyst for Swiss watchmakers. They raced to develop the same streamlined production methods. Longines, however, already had a head start in the subject.

FIRST REGISTERED WATCH BRAND

At the turn of the 20th century, Longines pursued industrialization and further increased its capacities of production and development. Wristwatch calibers entered the scene, though most production focused on pocket watch movements. Under the leadership of the technical director of the time, Alfred Pfister, Longines developed oval and even rectangular movements to satisfy the demands of the day. In 1911, the Longines manufacture already counted more than 1,100 workers and the brand's watches were sold all over the world. Though the years of war that followed were slow ones for watch sales, the engineers at Longines indefatigably continued their research.

ANNE AND CHRLES LINDBERGH, 1933.

CHARLES LINDBERGH
ATLANTIC VOYAGE WATCH

SPECIALIST IN TIMEKEEPING

Meanwhile, since around 1878, Longines has developed its expertise in complicated calibers, beginning with the chronograph, which became a specialty of the brand. Equipped with a 30-minute totalizer, the 19CH caliber boasted accuracy to one fifth of a second. The necessity of measuring short times grew dramatically with the rise of athletic competitions, for which Longines naturally provided chronographs. The complication would soon become a trademark of the brand, and the best advertising it could have to attract the attention of a large audience. The company built its success on the timekeeping quality of its products in particular. Longines won no fewer than ten grand prizes and 28 gold medals at the International and Universal Expositions, up until the 1929 Barcelona International Exposition.

Longines also developed instruments specially designed for the needs of pilots and navigators. The brand also timed, in 1927, the first nonstop trans-Atlantic flight (from New York to Paris), performed by Charles Lindbergh—33 hours and 30 minutes long. Upon his return, the adventurer sketched plans for an hour angle wristwatch that allowed the wearer to calculate one's exact longitude by correlating the information with the other flight instruments. Awarded several prizes, the watch enjoyed great success among aviators, and the brand still offers it in an updated version.

ALWAYS CUTTING EDGE

Longines's role as timekeeper of sporting events meant that it had to systematically integrate the latest technological developments into its products. Besides watches, which remained its stock in trade, the brand developed a true technological savoir-faire, as well as instruments designed to keep time during competitions. Longines engineers innovated with their use of electricity, then with optical systems such as the camera trigger that led to the first photo finishes. Since 1949, Longines has demonstrated its mastery of the development, perfecting and construction of quartz watches, still within a sporting framework.

Over time, the systems invented by the brand gained widespread popularity, measuring untold numbers of competitions, from Formula 1, to the Tour de France, to many horse races, among other athletic or technical exploits. Technological transfers happened even in the brand's own workshops, and in 1969 the company launched the Ultra Quartz, its first quartz caliber designed for the wristwatch.

Today, Longines carries on its long tradition in sporting timekeeping. It is associated with numerous competitions in varied disciplines, such as the French Open, the Alpine Ski World Cup and rhythmic and artistic gymnastics at the International Gymnastics Federation, as well as awarding a special Longines prize at the Archery World Cup. Not to mention the numerous prestigious horse races under the aegis of Longines, such as the Kentucky Derby, the Prix de Diane Longines, the Dubai World Cup, the Royal Ascot, the Melbourne Cup Carnival, the Longines Singapore Gold Cup and the Grand Prix Longines Lydia Tesio.

Longines is also an official partner and timekeeper for many equestrian events, such as most of the CSIO Nations Cup show jumping competitions as well as the various competitions organized by the Arab Equestrian League.

BOLLYWOOD ACTRESS AISHWARYA RAI BACHMAN.

EXCLUSIVE CALIBERS

Longines has never flagged in its tireless research and development efforts, and constantly comes up with new calibers, as it proved in its 2009 presentation of the exclusive Column-Wheel Chronograph caliber. This development is part of Longines's strategy to use mechanical movements developed exclusively for Longines by ETA (a member of the Swatch Group). Other fruits of these exclusive projects include the calibers that beat at the hearts of the watches in The Longines Master Collection Retrograde.

Today, Longines's catalog is structured along four collections: Elegance, Watchmaking Tradition, Sport and Heritage. Each one is divided into several lines.

The Elegance collection features the Longines DolceVita, the Longines PrimaLuna and of course La Grande Classique de Longines, the company's top seller. "For the last 22 years, La Grande Classique de Longines has met with overwhelming success," says von Känel. "Our fans in Asia especially like it. Often they are purchased in pairs, with one for the husband and another, with a smaller diameter, for the wife."

COLUMN-WHEEL CHRONOGRAPH

DOLCEVITA

LONGINES MASTER COLLECTION RETROGRADE

LONGINES EVIDENZA

The Watchmaking Tradition collections—including The Longines Master Collection and Longines evidenza—feature the most complicated models, for example The Longines Master Collection Retrograde with four retrograde hands. This highly horological collection treats the exclusive developments with the highest esteem by offering exceptional mechanisms.

The Sport collection has three lines. HydroConquest is devoted to the marine universe and stands out for its use of rotating bezels and an impressive water resistance. The refined Conquest line unites technique, athleticism and elegance. The Longines Admiral aims to be the most chic, most prestigious watch of the sport world.

Finally, the Heritage collection reflects the precious horological tradition upon which Longines can pride itself.

Ensconced in an area of the market at a price point between 800 and 4,000 CHF, Longines gives pride of place to mechanical calibers, which represent about 60% of the production. The 180th anniversary that Longines celebrates in 2012 also finds worthy commemoration in the presentation of a new exclusive caliber, as well as models in limited editions.

HYDROCONQUEST

Elegance is an attitude
Kate Winslet
www.longines.com

LONGINES®
The Longines Saint-Imier Collection

Philippe Merk

CEO of Audemars Piguet

Wolfgang Sickenberg

Director of Sales at Audemars Piguet

SPORTY ELEGANCE: 40 YEARS OF THE ROYAL OAK

WOLFGANG SICKENBERG

Audemars Piguet celebrates, in 2012, the 40th anniversary of its emblematic model, the Royal Oak. Presented in 1972 at BaselWorld, its avant-garde design drove many to forecast a shipwreck. Forty years later, the Royal Oak has become a global legend! The celebration that awaits will bring several surprises: upon reaching the age of reason, the Royal Oak will, in 2012, be more demure and more strictly horological.

Appointed as the head of Audemars Piguet in January of 2009, Philippe Merk already has the brand under his skin. Supported by his right-hand man Wolfgang Sickenberg, he has a very clear vision for the oldest family-owned watchmaking house: to expand its unique horological expertise in every collection. On the eve of a transitional year—the 40th birthday of the Royal Oak—the two men are committed to showcasing the virtues of the Manufacture's timepieces, as well as the men and women who develop them, thereby providing a more complete understanding of the house.

If you had to explain to a novice, in a few words, what Audemars Piguet means, what would you tell him?

Philippe Merk: It is the oldest watch manufacturer still owned by the founding family (or families in this case). This temporal dimension is essential, since it gives us genuine legitimacy in our field. Audemars Piguet is also a spirit of independence, free from all trends and fashions: the expertise that we have developed over the centuries will still be relevant in the coming centuries. Audemars Piguet is all of this: tradition, but also innovation. It's a fantastic driving force!

And if you had to explain Audemars Piguet to an economist?

PM: The group consists of 1,100 people, of which 800 are in Switzerland. We produce 30,000 watches annually with sales in excess of 500 million Swiss francs.

EXTRA-THIN ROYAL OAK

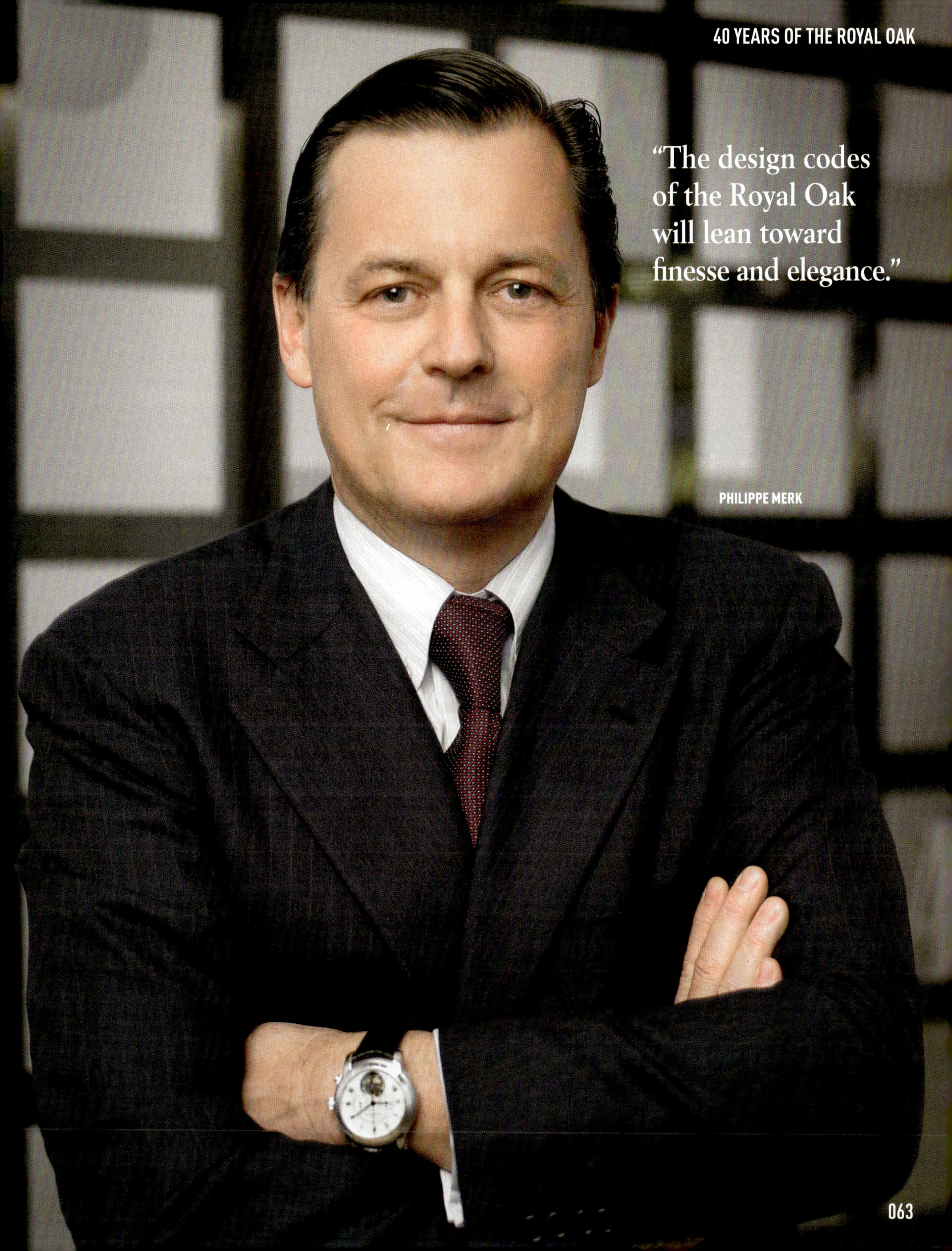

"The design codes of the Royal Oak will lean toward finesse and elegance."

PHILIPPE MERK

TOURBILLON GMT
ROYAL OAK CONCEPT

ROYAL OAK CHRONOGRAPH

How are the sales of Audemars Piguet divided between regions?

Wolfgang Sickenberg: Our balance is quite nice: 35% in Europe, 40% in Asia, 20% in the Americas, while the Middle East makes up the remainder. This is a situation that works well for us; we are a globally appreciated brand.

Is China important to you at this time?

WS: Greater China, with Hong Kong and Taiwan, as well as Singapore and Korea, where a lot of Chinese people reside, represent a large portion of our worldwide sales. Once we take into account the Chinese who buy in Europe, this becomes our leading clientele.

EQUATION OF TIME
ROYAL OAK

It seems today that demand is insatiable...

WS: One must be careful: certain countries are clearly overheating; others work well because they are supported by an international clientele—such as Switzerland. We must continue to be present everywhere, to be close to the client.

Despite all of this, are you expecting, in terms of production, to see significant growth this year?

PM: We were relatively spared by the crisis, during which the collapse was not disastrous for us. Picking up from there was quite easy, again seeing positive growth in 2011.

WS: The difficulty is to be on time with the right quantity of the right product. At Audemars Piguet, we don't have a problem of quantity maximization, we simply need to maintain a stable balance: too many watches, and the value of the brand diminishes; too few, and the consumer, who is more demanding than ever, won't wait.

Is it easy to communicate the "substance" that a brand such as yours offers?

WS: It's important to give people the time to discover all the subtleties and details of a brand like Audemars Piguet. It is our responsibility to effectively communicate, to the marketplace, the differences between industrial results and hand-crafted finishing. With the euphoria that we have experienced over the last ten years, we may have forgotten to put that in the forefront. We have returned to these values with a complete marketing strategy that leans in that direction. It won't be the only axis, but it will be an important one.

Let's then discuss the Royal Oak, which celebrates its 40th anniversary in 2012...
PM: We have planned an itinerary of exhibitions that will travel to the world's key cities, as well as other activities in the form of slightly more local events that will find their way onto the program.
WS: The primary theme emphasis will be placed on Audemars Piguet, and within that, the 40 years of the Royal Oak, which has become a legendary icon in itself. The Royal Oak is almost as famous as Audemars Piguet. This is of course an enormous success, but we would like to give the brand renewed precedence over the timepiece.

Is the image of the Royal Oak too strong?
PM: Finding a better balance in our product portfolio is indeed one of our goals. We were obviously thrilled with reactions that followed the launch of the Millenary, with its very special and unusual shape. While we are able to produce such timepieces, we are equally convinced that with classical watches, we can do much more!

How do you integrate the very sporty Royal Oak within this strategy for the future?
PM: By further differentiating the Royal Oak and Royal Oak Offshore. The forthcoming design codes of the Royal Oak will lean more toward finesse and elegance.
WS: We would like to make the Royal Oak, not a classical watch, but a watchmaking classic. Fundamentally, it is a timepiece born from the sports world. Today however, in comparison to the Offshore, it has lost a bit of the extreme image that it had 40 years ago. We are therefore going to revise it so that it can regain its original aesthetic: same size, same logo placement, etc.

It's a return to authentic values...
PM: It's necessary. We must once again be inspired by the object!
WS: Audemars Piguet is fortunate to possess several platforms of communication: with the Offshore, we can move towards the future; with the Jules Audemars, we connect with tradition; the Millenary has a resolutely contemporary quality. We can be in the past, the present and the future. We aren't going to abandon timely relevance, the "success story" that we are enjoying today in the company of our ambassadors. We are simply going to restore the overall balance: less lifestyle and more horology. For example, we have invested a lot in our industrial capabilities these last few years, but we haven't highlighted this aspect as much as we should.

Audemars Piguet has stood out over the last few years by its audacity. Are you becoming less non-conformist?
WS: I wouldn't put it that way. We are going to better explore certain avenues, such as proprietary research by Audemars Piguet. The AP escapement, for example, which has perhaps not received all the recognition that it deserves: it was our desire to initially use it on a very small scale. But in the future, it is an extraordinary challenge to grow its production from around thirty to possibly 30,000! Now that is audacious!

ROYAL OAK AUTOMATIC

Peter Stas

President and CEO of Frédérique Constant

EXPANDING THE RANGE

A leading player in the midrange arena, the Frédérique Constant brand is experiencing growing success, having sold 120,000 watches in 2011. The numbers are enough to reaffirm the initial strategic decision of its Dutch founding directors, Peter and Aletta Stas, to focus the manufacture's energy on classical luxury at an affordable price. This concept is so valuable that the couple chose to launch, or re-launch, two additional brands rather than diversify their collections. Alpina, with its sporty collections, and Ateliers deMonaco, operating in the very high end of the segment, define the present range of the Frédérique Constant group.

Peter Stas's rise to success is certainly a beautiful story. Born in Holland, the lover of Swiss watches founded his brand in 1988. By combining the given name of his wife's great-grandmother, Frédérique, with that of his own great-grandfather, Constant, he created a title that "sounded nicely Genevan," as co-founder and Chief Operating Officer Aletta Stas likes to point out. Living in Switzerland since 1997, the couple has never ceased to enhance their company. More than 20 years into the brand's history, the founding spouses maintain the status of majority shareholders with a 95% ownership of the firm they created—an independence that Aletta and Peter Stas are not nearly ready to relinquish.

You founded Frédérique Constant in 1988. What was your career path before that date?

I acquired a Masters degree in economics in Rotterdam, before moving to New York to work for a consulting firm for two years. I then joined Philips as Product Marketing Manager, first in Holland, then in the Far East, where I stayed for six years. In 1988, my wife and I founded the Frédérique Constant brand. But it was a part-time endeavor, as I hadn't left Philips at the time. We produced prototypes and received our first order in 1991, from Japan. It took us a year to honor it, between Holland, the Far East, and Switzerland.

Where did your desire to create a watchmaking brand come from?

I've always loved watches. I loved to window-shop during my family vacations in Switzerland. But above all, I love to create, to build something different. I wouldn't have wanted to work in finance, for example; I needed a product. I learned a lot with Philips in terms of investment, technology, and innovation.

TOURBILLON MANUFACTURE SILICIUM

"Frédérique Constant sales grew by 25% in 2011!"

When did you decide to relocate to Geneva?
We had a watch assembly partner in Geneva. But in 1997, we had a couple of issues with quality, which drove us to the decision to move there. We began in a small space, before expanding to $100m^2$, then 1,000. Since 2006, finally, we've been operating in our $3,200m^2$ facility.

How many watches did you sell in 2011?
Approximately 120,000 pieces, or a growth of 25% in relation to 2010.

Frédérique Constant was the first brand, in 1994, to incorporate an aperture in the dial, as a means of revealing a portion of the movement. How did this idea come to you?
At the time, right after the quartz crisis, nobody displayed the movement from the top, only from the caseback. We wanted to re-explain the mechanics to our clients. Today, nearly everybody has copied us...

You never patented this innovation?
No, and I regret that a little.

Revealing the inner workings of the movement is clearly close to your heart. In 2010, you launched the Junior collection, with a 38mm model for boys. In 2011, you released a feminine version. Why this line?
You're right, it has to do with helping young people discover the beauty of horology. In 2010, my son was 14 years old. Several people asked me: "Why not produce a wristwatch for him?" We gifted the first model to one of his friends. The response was such that we turned it into a complete collection.

How successful has it been?
In 2010, we sold 8,000 pieces for boys, and in 2011, 5,000 for girls.

At the summit of the pyramid, you also developed a tourbillon. Your positioning is however one of affordable luxury. Isn't such a timepiece, with grand feu enamel and a silicon escapement, sold for 50,000 Swiss francs, outside of that realm?
This tourbillon equips one of our two in-house made base movements, in this instance the FC-930 Heart Beat Manufacture caliber. Such a regulating organ fits nicely within our open-heart concept. But above all, we had the internal competencies to accomplish it. It's a way of showcasing our engineers' know-how.

How many have you sold?
Eighty the first year, and 60 per year since.

Is it your grandest complication?
Yes, the FC-930 caliber was launched in 2004 after three years in development. We have interpreted it since in several versions—manual-winding, automatic, moonphase with date, tourbillon and GMT. In 2009, we presented the Maxime Manufacture FC-700. It currently exists in three variations—automatic, hand-indicated date, and power reserve. More versions will be launched in the near future.

Are all components manufactured in house?
No. The jewels and balance springs, for example, are outsourced.

FRÉDÉRIQUE CONSTANT JUNIOR

HEART BEAT
MANUFACTURE GMT AUTOMATIC

Where do you acquire your balance springs?
From Nivarox at the moment, a Swatch Group company.

Are you very dependent on Swatch Group for the delivery of your movements?
At the moment, Swatch Group only delivers 2,000 movements per year to us. But we're in the process of developing, together with Sellita and Ronda, two movement makers that are independent of the group, a strategy designed to increase our own independence.

What portion of your production consists of mechanical watches?
We currently produce 50% mechanical watches, which adds up to 70% of our total sales.

You also founded, in 2009, the Ateliers deMonaco brand, installed in the prestigious principality. Why?
We had the opportunity to create some special movements: perpetual calendar, tourbillon, minute repeater. But such models, worth between 40,000 and 200,000 euros, did not fit the identity of the Frédérique Constant brand. We therefore sought the acquisition of an existing brand, to no avail. Creating one seemed like the only solution, but many already existed in Geneva. Monaco is one of the greatest centers of luxury in the world—a unique place. Following two years of negotiating with authorities, we were able to set up there. The production, made in Monaco, is presently very exclusive, with only 60 to 70 pieces per year.

Where do the movements come from?
A portion of the components is produced here in Geneva.

Your Geneva-based headquarters house a third brand, Alpina...
Alpina has existed since 1883; we bought it in 2002. This acquisition represents the same logic: we wanted to release sporty models, which didn't find their place within the DNA of the very classical Frédérique Constant collections. We deemed it quite important to preserve a coherent design identity across the entire brand.

How many Alpina models did you sell in 2011?
Around 8,000, a growth of 250% for the year. But it must be said that Alpina was somewhat affected by the 2009 crisis. Our objective is to reach 25,000 annually.

You recently inaugurated a Frédérique Constant boutique in Taiyuan, the capital of the Chinese province of Shanxi. Where will the next one be opened?
We already have two in Hong Kong, one in Seoul, and one in Saudi Arabia. The next boutique will be in Europe.

In Switzerland, in Geneva?
Not yet, the rent is so expensive!

Is China an important market for you?
Very important. We have roughly 100 points of distribution in China, including seven in Taiyuan. It was self-evident for us to open our first mono-brand boutique in that city. It's a beautiful high-end 1,400ft^2 space.

What does China represent in terms of sales?
Around 15% of our revenue.

Is it your number one market?
No. That's Europe, with Germany, France, Switzerland and the Benelux (Belgium, Netherlands, Luxembourg) at the head of the pack. Together, these markets represent 38% of the sales. Next is Asia at 32%, then the United States and Russia. We have a very good overall balance.

Have you established a growth ceiling for yourselves?
No. We are presently distributed in 2,700 points of sale worldwide, and I think that we can increase that number to 3,000 or 3,500. That's a reasonable growth.

MAXIME MANUFACTURE
AUTOMATIC SILICIUM

de GRISOGONO
GENEVE
de GRISOGONO
GENEVE
SWISS MADE
meccanico dG
LIMITED EDITION OF 10 PIECES
Grand Prix d'Horlogerie de Genève
Public Prize · 2009
THE FIRST MECHANICAL WATCH IN THE WORLD WITH A DUAL ANALOGUE AND DIGITAL DISPLAY
MECCANICO dG IN TITANIUM WITH BLACK PVD COATING, HANDWINDING MECHANICAL MOVMENT
WITH DUAL TIME AND MECHANICAL DIGITAL SECOND TIME ZONE
www.degrisogono.com

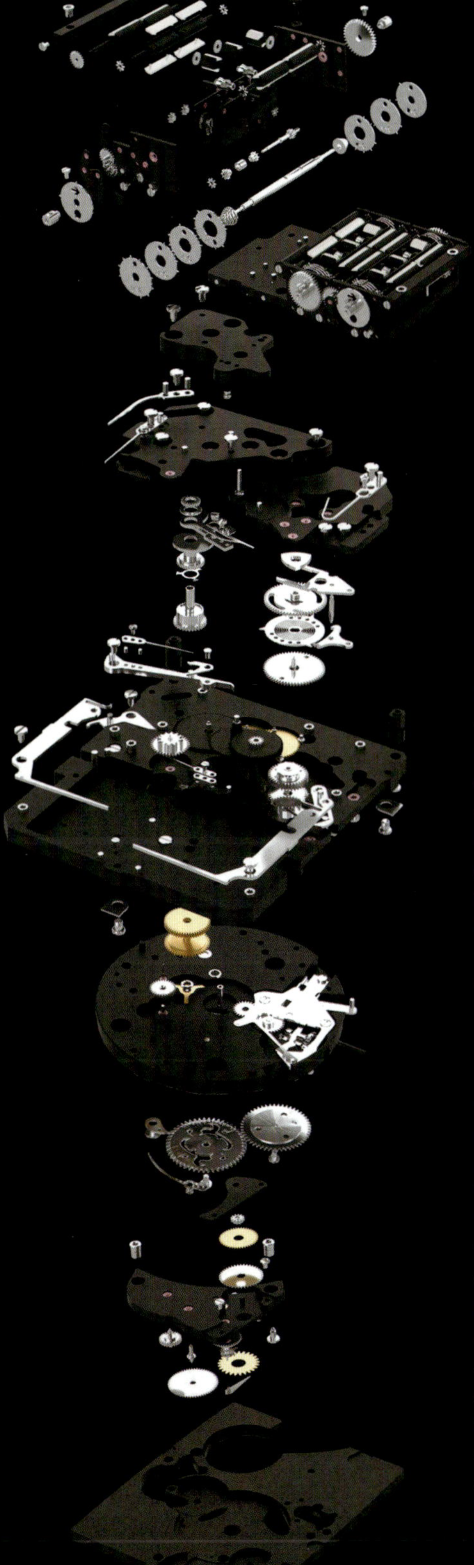

With its double analogue and mechanical digital display, this watch from de Grisogono asserts itself as one of the most exceptional contemporary haute horlogerie models. Its highly sophisticated movement called for years of development, but this marvel of precision is not reserved exclusively for connoisseurs of horological techniques. The accurate and constantly repeated choreography performed by its gear trains, cams and microsegments generates extraordinary emotion and fascinating poetry that can be sensed by everyone. This majestic performance is set off to its best advantage within a case featuring imposing yet elegant lines.

The heart of the watch beats to the tune of **a hand-wound mechanism composed of 651 parts**, all hand-assembled by the company's most skilled and experienced watchmakers. The analogue display of the hours and minutes is located in the upper part of the dial, while the lower area features a mechanical digital display indicating a second time zone. The latter reveals tens of hours, single hours, tens of minutes and single minutes thanks to the action of mobile microsegments driven by a set of **23 cams** combined with gears plus a triggering/synchronisation device. The vertical segments are 4.55 mm high and the horizontal ones have a display length of 1.80 mm. Each segment has four faces: two visible faces opposite each other with coloured inserts and two invisible faces, also opposite. One or more segments rotate 90° to turn one time indication into the next.The jump is instantaneous, while anywhere from 1 to 12 segments move, depending on the time being displayed.

Each year, the digital function is activated 518,400 times and sets 285 million parts into motion.

This exceptional movement lends its full value to this timepiece that is inventing a new watchmaking language. Limited edition of 10 pieces.

SPORTS AND

HOROLOGY:

A SYMBIOTIC RELATIONSHIP

From the necessity of handling the first sporting contests to today's thousandth-of-a-second performance timing operations, sports and horology have maintained a faithful relationship throughout the centuries, so much so that today, the former has become one of the latter's main channels of communication of the latter.

When it comes to sports, there are two schools of historiographic thought. For some, sports are a phenomenon that has always existed, evolving into different forms over the course of centuries. Supporting this point of view, one might recall passages from the epic of Gilgamesh, written in Babylon in the 13th and 12th centuries BC, that describe sporting activities of the era, such as wrestling or boxing. As for the Egyptians, they also practiced foot racing, fencing with staffs, archery and aquatic sports. However, these two cultures were also pioneers in time measurement, using astronomical observations. Could it be a coincidence? Could it also be a coincidence that the Greeks, the brilliant inventors of the Olympic Games—synonymous with truces in the incessant conflicts between city-states—found a place in their pantheon for Chronos, the god of time and destiny?

In any case, emphasizes Dominique Fléchon, historian and expert at the Geneva-based Fondation de la Haute Horlogerie, "over the course of the evolution of civilizations, sports appear to be an almost universal phenomenon, as too is time measurement." This assertion is certainly not contradicted by the second school of thought on the history of sports. But the partisans of this theory prefer to date the genesis of sport as we know it today to a precise moment in history and a particular historical context, that of the social elite in England in the middle of the Industrial Revolution, in the 19th century. "There is a very neat break between modern sports and those of antiquity: the notion of a record and thus a performance," writes historian Philippe Lyotard. The idea of record and performance express a vision of the world that is profoundly different between the Greeks and the moderns. The culture of the body is different. For Greeks, this culture was ritual, of religious inspiration; for the moderns, the body is a productive machine."

Bell & Ross
Bell & Ross
POWER RESERVE
SWISS MADE

"Faster, Higher, Stronger"

The term of "sport" has undergone a similar evolution. Its root is the Old French "desport," meaning "diversion, physical or mental pleasure" in the 12th and 13th centuries. The word then crossed the English Channel and became simply "sport," losing its connotation of leisure and referring only to physical activities. The German language adopted the word in this new definition in 1831, three years after its first recorded use in France. At this point, the confrontation between individuals, the main value of sport until this point, was "supplanted by the quest for performance, which opened the door to horological timekeeping," continues Dominique Fléchon. "In other words, the art of sport and the art of horology both constitute a form of expression framed by a set of defined, considered and progressive rules. Precision, perfection, elegance, beauty, purity, quality, exclusivity—in a word, standards—these are the common values that have always been common to sport and horology, both of which are synonyms for excellence."

By approaching physical and intellectual limits, and even seeking to surpass them, the athlete must honor the Olympic motto, "Citius, altius, fortius" (Faster, higher, stronger), proposed on June 23, 1894 by Pierre de Fredy, Baron of Coubertin, at the Congress that founded the International Olympic Committee (IOC). The very term "faster" naturally implies a method of measurement. Under these conditions, it is no wonder that the two fields have since experienced a similar trajectory. From the first athletic exploits of the 20th century to the spectacular sports we have today, Swiss horology has constantly affirmed its presence in this world dedicated to speed and precision, with major technological breakthroughs at stake. The goal is not only to be able to respond to ever-more demanding chronometric necessities required by the evolution of athletic competitions, but also to equip timepieces with technical features indispensable to long-haul adventurers, the extreme sportsmen and women who have always fascinated the masses.

Milla Jovovich
&co
JACOB&CO
jacobandco.com 212.719.5887
48 East 57th Street, New York, NY

Mobilizing its energy reserves.

HIGH
HIGH CHARGE LOW
CARL F. BUCHERER
28
MON
EvoTec

To the Skies

ORVILLE AND WILBUR WRIGHT

ALBERTO SANTOS-DUMONT

"In the 20th century, activities spanning the dividing line between sports and adventure, such as astronautics, aviation, parachuting, mountain-climbing and diving, would not have been able to develop without the watch, which assured the safety of those who participated in these activities," explains Fléchon. The development of aviation offers a perfect example of the unconditional support offered by Swiss watch manufacturers to the early pilots. The Wright brothers, who accomplished their first flight in Kitty Hawk, North Carolina, in 1907, had equipped their aircraft with a "watch-instrument," fixed to the knee for maximum visibility. During the same period, all of Paris was transfixed by the exploits of Alberto Santos-Dumont, Brazilian aviation pioneer, for whom his friend Louis Cartier created in 1904, and at his request, one of the very first wristwatches, commercialized seven years later, in order to allow him to read the time without letting go of the plane's controls. In a world populated almost exclusively by pocket watches, this was a true breakthrough.

PANERAI.COM
LUMINOR
PANERAI
GMT
12
pm
am
20
10
8 DAYS
REG.
T.M.

1000
MIKROTIMER
TAG HEUER
1/1000th PRECISION
CHRONOGRAPH
SWISS MADE
BEATS PER HOUR
1000
TAG HEUER
TAGHeuer
SWISS AVANT-GARDE SINCE 1860

WEEMS SYSTEM OF NAVIGATION

The measurement of time represents a crucial parameter for both pilots and sailors in getting their bearings or synchronizing a change of course. Whereas modern electronic devices fulfill these functions with diabolical precision, at the time it was still necessary to dream up the necessary mechanical "instruments." In this vein, the Longines manufacture created a true marvel in exploring one of aeronautics' most fertile paths: positioning. In 1929, the brand presented the Weems, named after the American naval officer known for inventing the "Weems System of Navigation," which incorporated time measurement as a central element. This timepiece was distinguished by a mobile central subdial activated by a crown, which allowed the wearer to synchronize the watch with a radio signal, to the nearest second. Charles Lindbergh, the first pilot to make a nonstop solo flight between New York and Paris, took up this idea for his Angle Horaire watch, which was designed with the help of Longines and patented in 1935. Thanks to the new indications positioned on the bezel and the dial, the pilot now possessed an instrument capable of accurately giving one's position—an instrument that would also be developed by manufactures such as IWC, Jaeger-LeCoultre, A. Lange & Söhne and Vacheron Constantin.

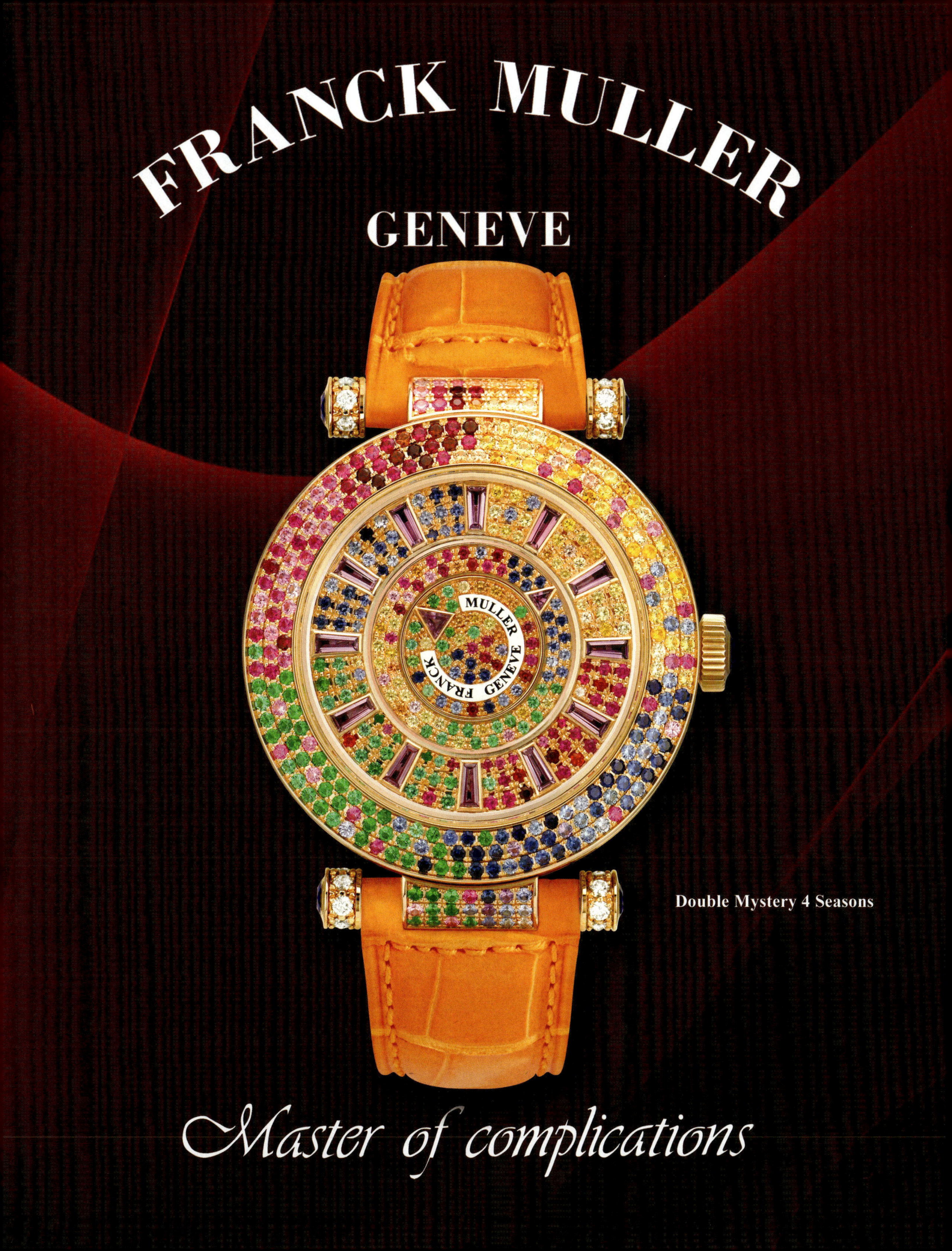
FRANCK MULLER
GENEVE
MULLER
FRANCK
GENEVE
Double Mystery 4 Seasons
Master of complications

Foundational Challenges for Modern Horology

It is also to Longines that we owe the first flyback chronograph movement, a function that allows the wearer to start the chronograph seconds hands and reset it to zero, before instantly restarting a measurement. This was an indispensable function for calculating waiting times when circling before landing, for example. In the field of aeronautics, Breitling was also an early leader, offering timepieces equipped with a slide rule using an exterior graduated bezel that turned alongside a fixed scale printed on the periphery of the dial. Utilizing such a timepiece facilitated ten or so different calculations, including multiplication, division, fuel consumption, rate of ascent or descent, average speed and distance conversion. This was a must-have, as shown by the Navitimer produced in the early 1950s.

NAVITIMER
(Breitling)

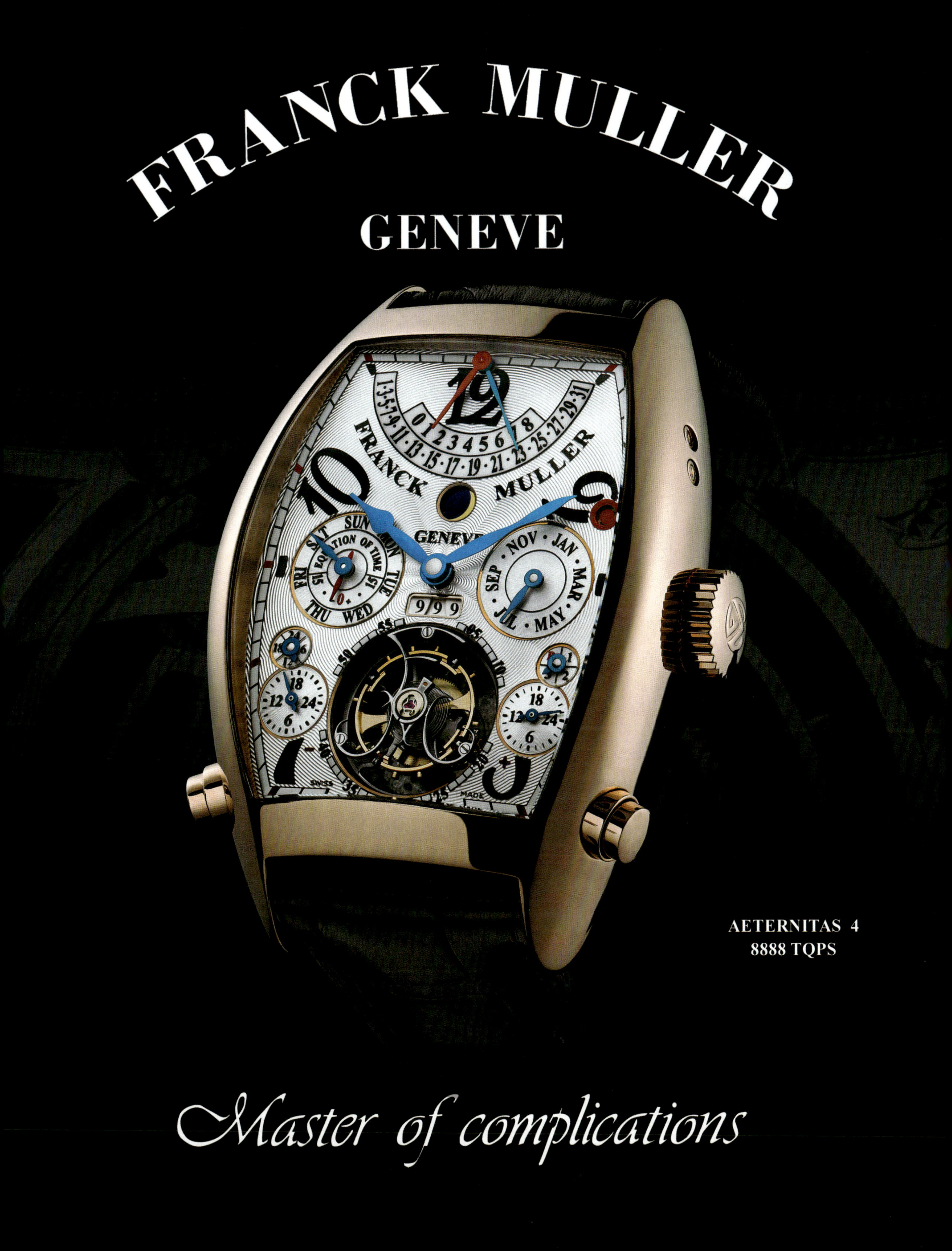
FRANCK MULLER
GENEVE
AETERNITAS 4
8888 TQPS
Master of complications

Extreme Environments

However, aviation was not everything. The conquest of the Arctic and the Antarctic in 1911 and 1908 respectively, Mercedes Gleitz's swim across the English Channel in 1927, the Kon-Tiki epic between Peru and the Polynesian Islands, the summiting of Annapurna by Maurice Herzog and Louis Lachenal in 1950, followed by that of Everest three years later by Edmund Hillary and Tenzing Norgay, not to mention the space race of the 1960s—all represented challenges for watchmakers, who spent the first half of the 20th century laying the groundwork for modern horology. For explorers, watchmakers developed extremely technical watches, equipped with barometers, altimeters, thermometers and compasses, as well as protection against magnetic fields, an aspect of which Favre-Leuba was to make a specialty with its Bivouac.

MASTER COMPRESSOR EXTREME LAB2
(Jaeger-LeCoultre)

HARRY WINSTON
SWISS
AUTOMATIC
08

On the High Horse

For lovers of high-impact sports prior to the 1929 invention of unbreakable sapphire crystal, watchmakers designed anti-shock protective mechanisms such as the era's aperture-display watches or the essential Reverso from Jaeger-LeCoultre, a 1931 timepiece born from a challenge set by a British polo player in India.

REVERSO 1931
(Jaeger-LeCoultre)

Glashütte Original – 165 years of German watchmaking art.*

Senator Diary

* 165 ans d'art horloger. – La Senator Diary. Une première mondiale. Quel moment dans les semaines à venir sera le plus important pour vous? Pensez-y! Maintenant, réglez la date et l'heure du jour choisi, remontez l'alarme et vous pouvez retourner à votre activité. 600 composants manufacturés s'occuperont du reste. Découvrez plus de details et informations sur www.glashuette-original.com. Téléchargez notre application iPhone „GO Diary" sur l'Apple Store. Manufacturé en Allemagne. Liste des revendeurs.

Glashütte
ORIGINAL

HANDMADE IN GERMANY*

The Senator Diary. A world first. Which moment in the weeks ahead will mean the most to you? Think about it. Now, set the date and the time of day, wind the alarm and get back to work. 600 handcrafted mechanical and manually finished components will take care of the rest. Find out more at www.glashuette-original.com. Download our new iPhone Application in the App store.*

Boutique Glashütte Original · 25, rue du Faubourg Saint-Honoré · 75008 PARIS · Tel +33 (0)1 53 43 08 80

Glashütte Original Printemps · Printemps Haussmann – Espace Luxe · 64, boulevard Haussmann · 75009 PARIS · Tél +33 (0)1 42 82 78 91

Retailer list*: Tel +33 (0)1 53 81 22 68 · www.glashuette-original.com

Conquest of the Deep

FIRST OYSTER 1926
(Rolex)

For divers, watchmakers would also have to solve the tricky problem of water resistance, most notably with a 1926 Rolex patent for a case and crown with perfect water resistance, the famous Oyster. As with aviation, this marked the beginning of a thrilling adventure, synonymous with rivalry among all the watchmakers to equip underwater sports enthusiasts with ever more effective instruments. Modern-day diving watches conform to strict standards that establish the criteria the watches must fulfill, for reasons of safety. They must guarantee water resistance of at least 100m (10atm) and perfect readability of the indications in the dim light of the aquatic depths, as well as including a one-way rotating bezel to calculate dive times. The watches must also be resistant to shocks and magnetic fields, and mounted on a strap with proven sturdiness.

These demands now represent a set of prerequisites that could pass for a simple exercise of style among watch brands, as they have piled achievement upon achievement in the field of diving watches. Several watchmakers have built their reputations in this field over decades, with models that have become true watchmaking icons. Rolex is of course the leader in this field; besides the Oyster in 1926, it has also given us the Submariner (1953) and the Sea-Dweller (1971).

SEA-DWELLER
(Rolex)

DEWITT
CLASSICAL AUDACITY
PHANTOM
Tourbillon Différentiel
Full Titanium
Limited Edition
Grand Prix d'Horlogerie de Genève
First Prize for Innovation
Dewitt America - For information and catalog +1 305 572 9812 - info@dewittamerica.com
www.dewitt.ch

LUMINOR POWER RESERVE AUTOMATIC
(Panerai)

TRIBUTE TO FIFTY FATHOMS AQUA LUNG
(Blancpain)

Other horologers have followed suit and made their own advancements, such as Panerai's Luminor (1950), Blancpain's Fifty Fathoms (1953), Breitling's Superocean (1957), Jaeger-LeCoultre's Memovox Deep Sea (1959) and Polaris (1963), Girard-Perregaux's Sea Hawk Deep Diver (1965), IWC's Aquatimer (1967), Omega's Ploprof (1971) and TAG Heuer's Aquaracer (1985).

All of this naturally entails landmark collaborations between watchmakers and frogmen, professionals involved in projects on the high seas and brilliant scientists. Of course, it also entails a race to the bottom of the sea, with watches resistant to ever-lower depths. Rolex once again merits a mention for pushing the envelope in 1960 by descending a timepiece down to 11,000m below sea level in the Mariana Trench, affixed to the bathyscaphe of Professor Piccard on his Trieste mission. Though this model was designed to prove the technical mastery of the manufacture, it also inspired other big names of the day to exceed the limitations of the genre, producing commercially available watches capable of resisting depths of several thousand meters—all equipped with a helium valve to prevent them from opening up like an oyster during the decompression stage. The latest achievement to date: after 18 months of development, the Oceanographic 4000 Titanium from Hublot tested resistant to 4,000m under the water.

OCEANOGRAPHIC 4000 TITANIUM
(Hublot)

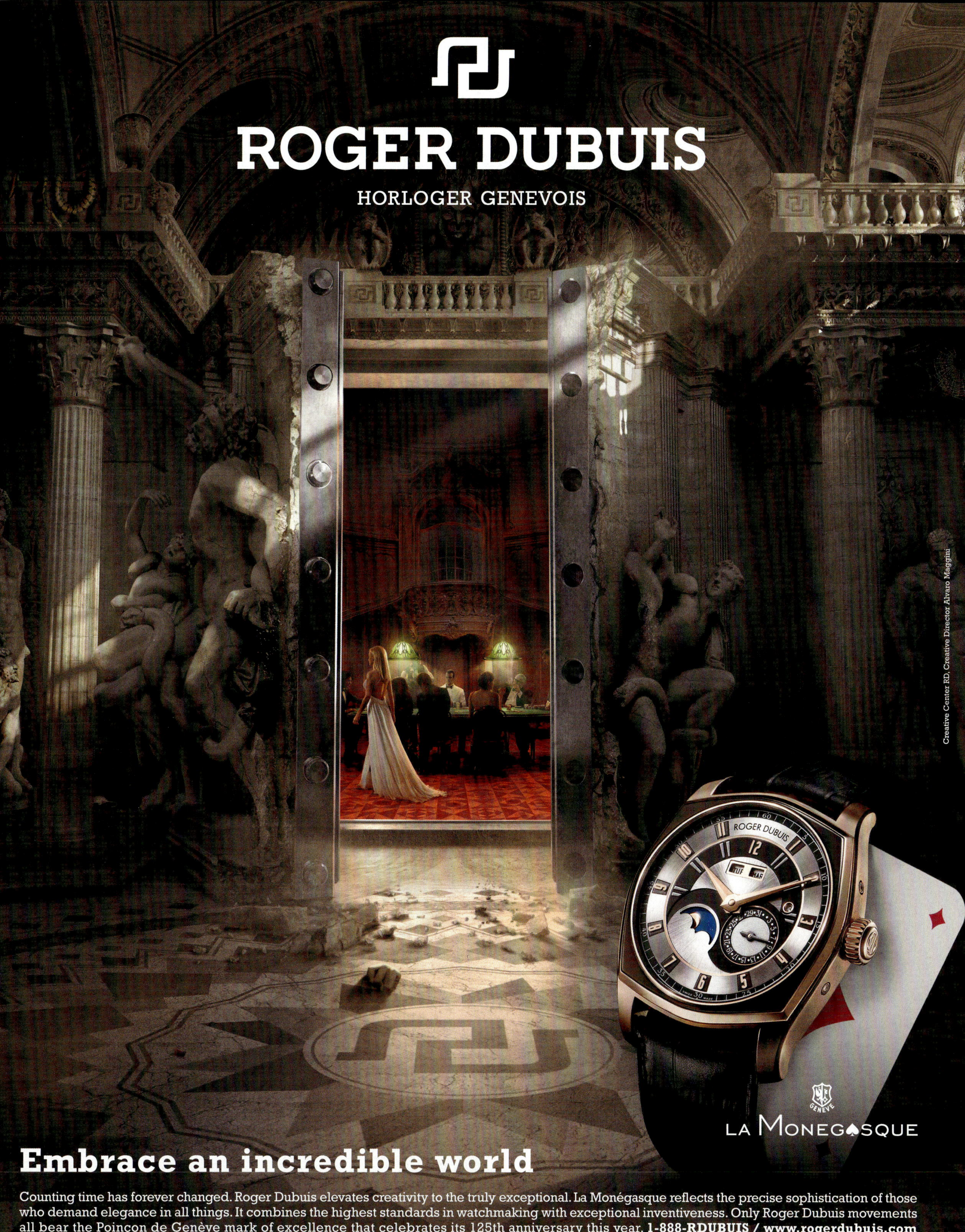
ROGER DUBUIS
HORLOGER GENEVOIS
Creative Center RD, Creative Director Alvaro Maggini
ROGER DUBUIS
GENÈVE
LA MONEGASQUE
Embrace an incredible world
Counting time has forever changed. Roger Dubuis elevates creativity to the truly exceptional. La Monégasque reflects the precise sophistication of those who demand elegance in all things. It combines the highest standards in watchmaking with exceptional inventiveness. Only Roger Dubuis movements all bear the Poinçon de Genève mark of excellence that celebrates its 125th anniversary this year. 1-888-RDUBUIS / www.rogerdubuis.com

The Art of Mechanics

The world of the automobile has also been a powerful driving force for watch designers, with obvious parallels between the two universes—the obsession with design and attention to the last detail ties in naturally with a similar quest for mechanical perfection. At the end of the First World War, the return to the roads of Bugatti, Lancia, Hispano-Suiza and Delage inspired Georges Schären of Mido. The latter watch brand's early success was due to timepieces whose contours clearly evoked the shapes of the radiators on these high-powered cars. A new fashion was born, to which brands such as Patek Philippe, Tiffany, Vacheron Constantin and Cartier would make huge contributions, responding to the needs of an ever-growing population of drivers. Rotating crowns, rounded or tilted cases, or those designed specifically to be worn on the edge of the wrist now appeared to facilitate reading the time according to the particular ergonomics of an activity that would soon become a sport in its own right.

The symbiotic relationship fully matured with the advent of chronograph wristwatches in the 1930s, and subsequently with the launch of the automatic chronograph movement with micro-rotor in 1969—an accomplishment achieved simultaneously by Zenith, with its famous El Primero caliber, and Heuer and Breitling, based on caliber 11. For the flying aces of the era, it was now possible to calculate their performances to the tenth of a second. In this sense, as in the world of diving watches, horologers have never stopped pushing the limits of their watches, proving themselves with constant achievements that have grown even more impressive over the last decade.

EL PRIMERO 1969
(Zenith)

ZENITH
SWISS WATCH MANUFACTURE
SINCE 1865
EL PRIMERO by Zenith, inventor of the
high-frequency self-winding chronograph
EL PRIMERO
CHRONOMASTER OPEN
ZENITH, THE PIONEER SPIRIT SINCE 1865
www.zenith-watches.com

A Motor on the Wrist

TAG Heuer offers an excellent example of the advancements of the chronograph. After having been in the vanguard of the 1930s with the Mikrograph, the very first mechanical sporting counter accurate to 1/100th of a second, and then, in the 1970s, with its Carrera and Monaco lines—the latter well-promoted by the film *Le Mans* in which Steve McQueen sported one on his wrist—the House achieved a tour de force with the successive presentation at the BaselWorld Watch & Jewelry Show, several years in a row, of watches that have greatly impressed the community of aficionados. After the Mikrotimer in 2002, the first wristwatch chronograph with a quartz movement accurate to 1/1000th of a second, and the Sixty-Nine in 2003, a reversible watch with one quartz and one mechanical movement, the company showed up in 2004 with its Monaco V4, whose drive-belt transmission and linear weight were inspired by automobile motors. The year 2005 saw the launch of the Calibre 360, the first mechanical wristwatch chronograph accurate to 1/1000th of a second. At BaselWorld 2011, TAG Heuer presented the Mikrotimer Flying 1000, the first mechanical wristwatch chronograph in the world capable of measuring and displaying 1/1000ths of a second.

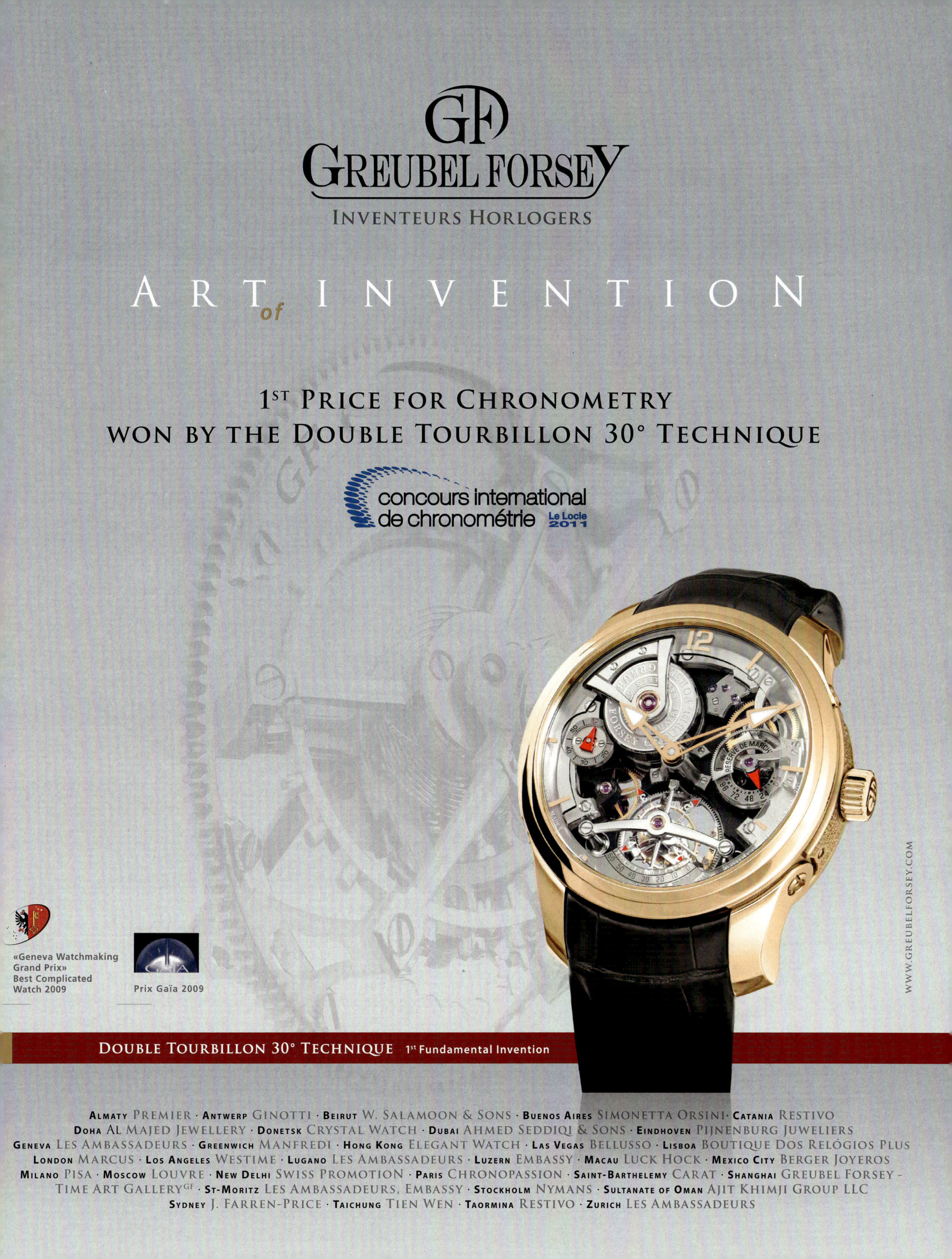
GREUBEL FORSEY
INVENTEURS HORLOGERS
ART of INVENTION
1ST PRICE FOR CHRONOMETRY
WON BY THE DOUBLE TOURBILLON 30° TECHNIQUE
concours international de chronométrie Le Locle 2011
«Geneva Watchmaking Grand Prix» Best Complicated Watch 2009
Prix Gaïa 2009
WWW.GREUBELFORSEY.COM
DOUBLE TOURBILLON 30° TECHNIQUE 1st Fundamental Invention
ALMATY PREMIER · ANTWERP GINOTTI · BEIRUT W. SALAMOON & SONS · BUENOS AIRES SIMONETTA ORSINI · CATANIA RESTIVO
DOHA AL MAJED JEWELLERY · DONETSK CRYSTAL WATCH · DUBAI AHMED SEDDIQI & SONS · EINDHOVEN PIJNENBURG JUWELIERS
GENEVA LES AMBASSADEURS · GREENWICH MANFREDI · HONG KONG ELEGANT WATCH · LAS VEGAS BELLUSSO · LISBOA BOUTIQUE DOS RELÓGIOS PLUS
LONDON MARCUS · LOS ANGELES WESTIME · LUGANO LES AMBASSADEURS · LUZERN EMBASSY · MACAU LUCK HOCK · MEXICO CITY BERGER JOYEROS
MILANO PISA · MOSCOW LOUVRE · NEW DELHI SWISS PROMOTION · PARIS CHRONOPASSION · SAINT-BARTHELEMY CARAT · SHANGHAI GREUBEL FORSEY - TIME ART GALLERY GF · ST-MORITZ LES AMBASSADEURS, EMBASSY · STOCKHOLM NYMANS · SULTANATE OF OMAN AJIT KHIMJI GROUP LLC
SYDNEY J. FARREN-PRICE · TAICHUNG TIEN WEN · TAORMINA RESTIVO · ZURICH LES AMBASSADEURS

This passion for automotive mechanics is not the sole prerogative of TAG Heuer, not by a long shot. Many horologers have in fact created tight bonds with the big names of the universe in which speed is second nature. Since 1988, Chopard has sponsored the legendary Mille Miglia race, which was reborn as a showcase for the power of vintage cars; Girard-Perregaux, a pioneer in the field, had an early partnership with Ferrari that lasted ten years and was later taken up by Panerai and then Hublot; Breitling partnered with Bentley and Audemars Piguet with Maserati; Jaeger-LeCoultre, with a rich history in the automobile sector, notably for its Jaeger counters, collaborated with Aston Martin; Oris entered the world of Formula 1 alongside the AT&T Williams racing team; while Hublot—associated with Morgan Motor Company on the occasion of the British manufacturer's 100th anniversary—has recently become the official watchmaker of the Formula 1 circuit.

CHRISTOPHE CLARET
SWISS
MADE
Baccara
Lucky Number

OLYMPIC GAMES, BEIJING 2008

The Unequalled Olympic Games

At the 2008 Olympic Games, held in Beijing, official timekeeper Omega deployed over 450 technicians at different sites, supported by one thousand specially trained local volunteers, to see to 450 tons of equipment and maintain 70 notice boards for the public and the 322 auxiliary boards for each discipline, all connected by 175km of cable and fiber optics. In 1932, the year in which Omega was the first company to be entrusted with all the timing of the Games, just 30 chronographs were enough to cover all the competitions! Such a use of resources in Beijing was not coincidental, as the Olympic Games occupies such a dominant place in the world of sport—just as it has in the world of chronometry since 1896, date of the first modern Olympic Games. Though the title of official timekeeper has always been highly coveted, as it carries an extraordinary visibility, it has only been granted to a handful of brands, namely Longines, Heuer, Omega, Seiko, Swatch and Swiss Timing, a subsidiary of the Swatch Group—all of which have entered an unbridled technological race.

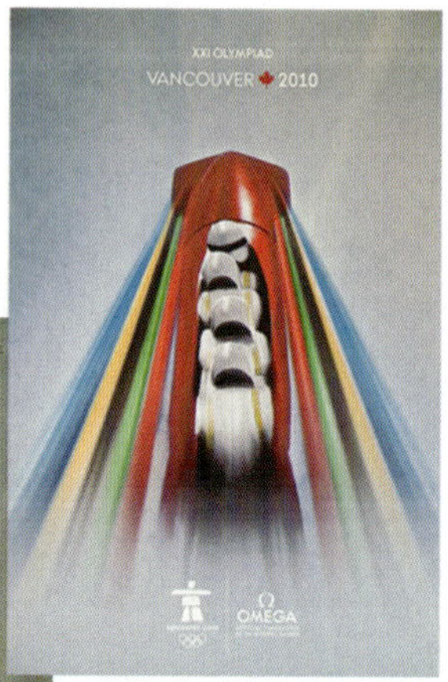

Though Heuer had already patented a chronograph mechanism accurate to 1/50th of a second in 1916, and though the manual chronographs of the 1920s, accurate to 1/10th of a second, were already reliable enough to be used in sporting competitions, the Olympic records would only be measured to 1/5th of a second until 1932, thanks to chronographs from Heuer (timekeeper of the Games in Antwerp (1920), Paris (1924) and Amsterdam (1920)), and from Longines, which was already present at the Athens Games (1896) and has acted as timekeeper 14 times since the Oslo Games (1952). Longines produced a technological breakthrough in 1912, the "broken wire" automatic timing system: the athlete broke a wire stretched on the starting line, triggering an electric signal that started a chronometer with electromagnetic controls. It was also Longines that perfected a pocket-watch chronograph in 1928, accurate to 1/100th of a second.

CHAUMET
PARIS
Creating watches for 200 years
12
CHAUMET
PARIS
SWISS MADE
Dandy
chaumet.com

A Platinum Anniversary

Is it any wonder that the love story between sports and horology is approaching its platinum anniversary? If anything, it is becoming even more intense, as modern watchmakers raise high the colors of sports clubs and associations, turn star athletes into brand ambassadors and sponsor international sporting events—in the process gaining a visibility of which they could never have dreamed half a century ago. It is no surprise, in such circumstances, that a number of the greatest athletes are linked to the most prestigious horological brands. For example, Loïck Peyron, the multi-titled French yachtsman, is Corum's sailing advisor.

LOÏCK PEYRON

[CHRONOFIGHTER]
OVERSIZE GMT BLACK STEEL
GRAHAM
GMT
CHRONOFIGHTER
OVERSIZE
SWISS MADE
GRAHAM
LONDON
HANDCRAFTED IN SWITZERLAND
WWW.GRAHAM-LONDON.COM

Tennis, Anyone?

Tennis player Roger Federer, third-ranked in the world, is tied to Rolex, while Rafael Nadal, second-ranked, wears a Richard Mille watch that was specially designed for him and Novak Djokovic, the first-ranked tennis player in the world, has just signed with Audemars Piguet.

Prestigious Partnerships

The golf legend Greg Norman has joined forces with Omega. Bode Miller, triple gold-medal-winner in skiing at the Vancouver Olympic Games (2010) has a partner in Hublot. Bulgari is quite taken with the famous New Zealand rugby team the All Blacks. The Formula 1 racing driver Lewis Hamilton wears the colors of TAG Heuer, and Danica Patrick, first woman to win an Indy Car race, wears those of Tissot. As for Jaeger-LeCoultre, it has thrown its lot in the world of polo in a nod to the Reverso watch...

And the list goes on. As Jasmine de Boccard explains in her study, *Athletic Sponsorship in the World of Luxury Watchmaking*, "luxury and sport have a lot in common, as they share the same values: elegance, precision, purity and high standards. That is why luxury businesses have increasingly turned to the world of sport, making it one of their primary tools of communication." This observation is clearly true for the watchmaking Houses, who are continually revising and evolving their approach. "In sports, as in haute horology," says Dominique Fléchon, "nothing is ever permanently won. The values common to the two endeavors are a constant influence and inspiration for both fields."

ENDURER CHRONOSPRINT ALL BLACKS SPECIAL EDITION
(Bvlgari)

Alpina
GENEVE
AUTOMATIC
CHRONOGRAPH
Alpina
GENEVE
AVIATIONCOLLECTION
The Alpina Startimer Pilot timepieces.
A collection of limited editions, developed
in close collaboration with Cessna Aircraft and PrivatAir.
ALPINA WATCH INTERNATIONAL SA · T 1-877-61-WATCH · www.alpina-watches.com

The Era of New Materials

In this line of thought, it is impossible to ignore the latest developments in an industry that is, of course, the heir to a long tradition, but nonetheless turned toward the technologies of the future. These technologies include the use of futuristic materials such as those stemming from high-tech fields such as the aerospace industry. "We must live in the future," declares Jean-Claude Biver, Chairman of the Board of Hublot, which recently unveiled the King Power Cathedral Minute Repeater Tourbillon Column-Wheel Chronograph entirely in carbon—a world first. "But using these high-tech materials must add a real value to the watch, an advantage over using traditional materials." This advantage might reside in a lighter timepiece, better shock resistance, anti-corrosive or –allergenic properties, or improved accuracy due to the absence of lubrication in the heart of the movement, which has notably been achieved with the expert use of silicon components.

Richard Mille, after having developed its RM 035 expressly for Rafael Nadal, now offers the timepiece in a version whose certified Chronofiable® skeletonized movement weighs just 4.3g, with a case in magnesium-aluminum. The brand also developed the RM 038, conceived especially for golfer Bubba Watson. This tourbillon watch, designed for the extreme conditions of this sport, is equipped with bridges and a bottom plate in titanium for maximum lightness, shock-resistance and comfort. Panerai, for its part, has used an electrochemical process to develop a composite material made of aluminum and ceramic, which boasts extreme lightness and hardness. The brand inaugurated its use of this new material with the Panerai Luminor Marina Composite 1950 3 Days Automatic.

KING POWER CATHEDRAL MINUTE REPEATER TOURBILLON COLUMN-WHEEL CHRONOGRAPH
(Hublot)

LUMINOR MARINA COMPOSITE 1950 3 DAYS AUTOMATIC
(Panerai)

"CREATE THE WORLD'S
ULTIMATE TIME MEASURING
DEVICE, BY FAR!"
REBELLION
REBELLION T-1000 THE TIME MACHINE
REBELLION®
SWISS EXCLUSIVE TIMEPIECES

Audemars Piguet has become a specialist in forged carbon—another material that stands out for its resistance and lightness—integrated for the first time into watches designed in homage to Alinghi, two-time winner of the America's Cup yachting race. Using its savoir-faire in production, the manufacture perfected a system allowing it to produce carbon fiber dials and cases that are submitted to a pressure of 4,267 pounds per square foot at very high temperatures. This advance, among many others, reveals much about the evolution of horological research. Emmanuel Vuille, CEO of Greubel Forsey, sums it up: "horology has developed a scientific culture that calls on chemistry, physics and other branches of science, whereas previously it had relied mostly on artisanal skills and techniques."

ROYAL OAK OFFSHORE CHRONOGRAPH
(Audemars Piguet)

HAMILTON
THE AMERICAN BRAND SINCE 1892
HB-ZEF
KHAKI
FLIGHT TIMER
SWISS MADE
WWW.HAMILTONWATCH.COM

Timing Competitions

Such technical feats are a far cry from Milo of Croton, one of the most celebrated Greek athletes and a wrestling champion at not only the Olympic Games, but also the Pythian, Nemean and Isthmian Games. Nevertheless, the competitive spirit remains the same, the same one that has always pushed men to outdo each other—and themselves—in athletic disciplines, aided in this endeavor by those who measure time. The timekeepers have established their own competitions, such as the chronometry or timing contest that took place in Geneva as early as 1772. Neuchâtel Observatory, which has assessed and rated the accuracy of Swiss watches since 1860, would take up the idea in 1866, while in Besançon, France, such chronometric tests would debut in 1885. The arrival of wristwatches would only reinforce this spirit of competition between horologers, who would continue to vie with each other on this type of product from 1945 onwards. Unfortunately, the 1970s arrival of quartz, a technology that would shatter the standards of horological precision, would seem to sound the death knell for this sort of competition.

EQUATION IN 18K GOLD
(Breguet)

NEUCHÂTEL OBSERVATORY

190 YEARS AGO
A MAN BET ON HORSES AND CHANGED WATCHMAKING FOREVER.
In 1821, at a horse race in Paris, Nicolas Rieussec successfully tested his revolutionary invention that allowed time to be recorded to an accuracy of a fifth of a second. The chronograph was born. A tribute to a visionary man, the Montblanc Nicolas Rieussec Chronograph Automatic is centred on the essence of his invention, the rotating disc technique. Monopusher chronograph, MB R200 self-winding manufacture movement, second time zone, 30 min. and 60 sec. rotating disc counters. Crafted in the Montblanc Manufacture in Le Locle, Switzerland. MONTBLANC. A STORY TO TELL.
MONT BLANC
® Montblanc®

A Race Against Time

The passion for mechanical precision timing would not disappear with the temporary hegemony of electronic timekeeping—far from it. Thus, in 2009 these competitions would reappear with the launch of a new Chronométrie International Timing Competition under the aegis of the Besançon Observatory, the Swiss Official Chronometer Testing Institute (COSC) and the Haute École de l'Arc in the Jura. After a hard-fought struggle, Jaeger-LeCoultre took the two first prizes in the competition with the two models it had entered: the Master Tourbillon in first place, followed by the Gyrotourbillon 2. In the "Independents" category, watchmaker René Addor took honors for his Calibre Papillon with an 11-day power reserve. In announcing the results, the chairman of the Organization Committee, Claude-Henri Chabloz stated, "The mechanical watch has not drawn its last breath. The new techniques of design and production, and new materials encourage those watchmakers who are keen on science and mad about precision to develop new calibers that give an avant-garde image to the new mechanical horology. The quest for accuracy and precision constitutes an exciting challenge, which the new generation of watchmakers is eager to take on."

The athletes can rest assured that there will always be a watchmaker to time their exploits—even if they only play on Sundays.

MASTER TOURBILLON
(Jaeger-LeCoultre)

GYROTOURBILLON 2
(Jaeger-LeCoultre)

WATCHES
INTERNATIONAL

Kiss, Kiss, dar-leeng,
where do you want to go?
the Frenchway travel
we do it...with passion

A. LANGE & SÖHNE
GLASHÜTTE I/SA

THE CLARITY OF PERFECTION

In combining the most revered complications in haute horology with designs that pronounce the innovative ingenuity of the brand, A. Lange & Söhne declares ambiguity to be a thing of the past.

The tenth masterpiece to be added to the manufacture's most famous watch family, the Lange 1 Tourbillon Perpetual Calendar, makes a firm statement as to the synergic possibilities between sophisticated technology and optimal clarity. Thanks to the off-centered configuration of the hour and minute circle on the right side of the silver dial, the calendar is neatly executed on a plane of its own. While the moonphase, retrograde day, leap-year aperture, and date are immediately recognized, the last indicator of this instantaneously changing calendar marks a world-first of inventive poignancy. Freeing the dial of conventional clutter, the manufacture's caliber designers have armed this timepiece with an unprecedented rotating peripheral month ring. Equipped with a pointing indicator beneath the leap-year aperture at 6 o'clock, this unique innovation features slots of variable length to account for each month's respective duration.

Only needing to be advanced by one day—on March 1, 2100—the Lange 1 Tourbillon Perpetual Calendar's self-winding L082.1 caliber boasts a platinum centrifugal mass that permits an exceptional winding efficiency of the 50-hour power reserve.

Due to the brand's devotion to dial-side clarity, the technically immaculate tourbillon is invisible on the watch face, and is instead to be admired intimately through the sapphire crystal caseback.

LANGE 1 TOURBILLON PERPETUAL CALENDAR
This 41.9mm masterpiece boasts a 624-component hand-decorated movement.

LANGE 1 TIME ZONE LUMINOUS

With its 72-hour power reserve and luminous indications, this world-time watch provides complete horological guidance for the distinguished frequent flyer.

The German manufacture extends its expertise of the world-time concept to the darkness of night. With the Lange 1 Time Zone Luminous in white gold with luminous indications, the house presents a timepiece whose guidance radiates anywhere, anytime. With the ease of a pushbutton, the peripheral cities ring rotates in increments of 15º, immediately adjusting the position of the subsidiary hour hand. While both subdials display hours, minutes, and individual day/night indicators with their rhodiumed-gold luminous hands, the larger local time counter features a small seconds function, and is complemented by an external digital date. In an ingenious demonstration of watchmaking expertise, a synchronization mechanism allows an effortless swapping of the two dials' time zones.

Housed within a 41.9mm white-gold case with an argenté dial, the L031.1 caliber joins with the timepiece's brilliant luminosity to deliver global horological reliability by day and by night, wherever the spirit of time may guide its owner.

Echoing the harmonious dial design that made its predecessor famous, the Datograph Up & Down stands alone within the shine of its 41mm platinum case. Favoring, first and foremost, the virtues of the brand's exemplary flyback chronograph expertise, the timepiece's exquisite L951.6 hand-wound movement, visible through the sapphire crystal caseback, provides mechanical accuracy of the highest order. Offering a bright contrast from the depth of the black dial, the 30-minute counter at 4 o'clock boasts a precise jumping minute for optimal legibility. In addition to the large date at 12 o'clock, this newest manufacture Datograph features a discreet 6 o'clock indicator for its extended 60-hour power reserve.

With three innovatively designed timepieces driven by feats of technical exceptionalism, A. Lange & Söhne conquers the vital challenge of decisive timekeeping clarity.

DATOGRAPH UP & DOWN

Confirming the manufacture's devotion to timekeeping excellence, this remarkable chronograph features a flyback function and precise jumping minute.

LANGE 1 TOURBILLON PERPETUAL CALENDAR — REF. 720.025

Movement: automatic-winding Lange L082.1 caliber; Ø 34.1mm, thickness: 7.8mm; 50-hour power reserve; 624 components; 68 jewels (including one diamond endstone); 21,600 vph; decorated and assembled by hand; precision-adjusted in five positions; plates and bridges made of untreated German silver; central element of the unidirectional winding rotor in 21K gold; platinum centrifugal mass; hand-engraved intermediate-wheel and tourbillon cocks; lever escapement; shock-resistant balance with eccentric poising weights; superior-quality balance spring manufactured in-house.

Functions: off-centered hours and minutes; small seconds; tourbillon with patented stop-seconds mechanism; perpetual calendar with large date, day of week, month, and leap year cycle; day/night indication; moonphase.
Case: platinum; Ø 41.9mm, thickness: 12.2mm; crown for winding the watch and setting the time; recessed pushbutton for collectively advancing all calendar indications or for individually correcting the month, day of the week, and moonphase; sapphire crystal caseback.
Dial: solid silver and rhodié; rhodium-gold hands.
Strap: black hand-stitched crocodile; platinum Lange deployant buckle.
Note: limited to 100 pieces.
Also available: 18K pink gold with hand-stitched red-brown crocodile strap.

LANGE 1 TIME ZONE LUMINOUS — REF. 116.039

Movement: manual-winding Lange L031.1 caliber; Ø 34.1mm, thickness: 6.7mm; 72-hour power reserve; 417 components; 54 jewels; 21,600 vph; decorated and assembled by hand; precision-adjusted in five positions; twin mainspring barrel; plates and bridges made of untreated German silver; four screwed gold chatons; balance cock and intermediate-wheel cock engraved by hand; lever escapement; shock-resistant Glucydur screw balance, Nivarox® balance spring; whiplash precision index adjuster with patented beat adjustment mechanism.

Functions: home time with day/night indicator (hours, minutes, small seconds with stop seconds); large date for home time; zone time (hours, minutes) with day/night indicator and city ring; power reserve indicator.
Case: 18K white gold; Ø 41.9mm, thickness: 11mm; crown for winding the watch and setting the time; pushbutton for switching the outsize date; pushbutton for advancing the city ring; antireflective sapphire crystal caseback.
Dial: solid silver and argenté; applied rhodium-gold with luminescent coating; rhodium-gold hands with luminescent coating; blued steel.
Strap: black hand-stitched crocodile; 18K white-gold Lange prong buckle.

DATOGRAPH UP & DOWN — REF. 405.035

Movement: manual-winding Lange L951.6 caliber; Ø 30.6mm, thickness: 7.9mm; 60-hour power reserve; 451 components; 46 jewels; 18,000 vph; decorated and assembled by hand; precision-adjusted in five positions; plates and bridges made of untreated German silver; four screwed gold chatons; hand-engraved balance cock; shock-resistant balance with eccentric poising weights; superior-quality balance spring manufactured in-house; precision beat adjustment system with lateral setscrew and whiplash spring.

Functions: hours, minutes; small seconds with stop seconds; large date; flyback chronograph with precise jumping; power reserve indicator.
Case: platinum; Ø 41mm, thickness: 13.1mm; crown for winding the watch and setting the time; two pushers for operating the chronograph, one pusher for rapid correction of the large date; sapphire crystal caseback.
Dial: solid silver and black; rhodium-gold and steel hands.
Strap: blue-gray hand-stitched crocodile; platinum Lange prong buckle.

GRAND LANGE 1 — REF. 117.021

Movement: manual-winding Lange L095.1 caliber; Ø 34.1mm, thickness: 4.7mm; 72-hour power reserve; 397 components; 42 jewels; 21,600 vph; decorated and assembled by hand; precision-adjusted in five positions; plates and bridges made of untreated German silver; seven screwed gold chatons; hand-engraved balance cock; lever escapement; shock-resistant screw balance; superior-quality balance spring manufactured in-house; precision beat adjustment system with lateral setscrew and whiplash spring.

Functions: off-centered hours and minutes; small seconds with stop seconds; large date; power reserve indicator.
Case: 18K yellow gold; Ø 40.9mm, thickness: 8.8mm; sapphire crystal caseback.
Dial: solid silver and champagne; 18K yellow-gold hands.
Strap: medium brown hand-stitched crocodile strap; 18K yellow-gold Lange prong buckle.
Also available: 18K pink gold; solid silver and argenté dial; 18K pink-gold hands; red-brown hand-stitched crocodile strap; 18K pink-gold OR platinum Lange prong buckle; solid silver and rhodié dial; rhodium-gold hands; black hand-stitched crocodile strap; platinum Lange prong buckle.

SAXONIA THIN — REF. 211.026

Movement: manual-winding Lange L093.1 caliber; Ø 28mm, thickness: 2.9mm; 72-hour power reserve; 167 components; 21 jewels; 21,600 vph; decorated and assembled by hand; precision-adjusted in five positions; plates made of untreated German silver; balance cock engraved by hand; lever escapement; shock-resistant screw balance; superior-quality balance spring manufactured in-house.
Functions: hours, minutes.
Case: 18K white gold; Ø 40mm, thickness: 5.9mm; crown for winding the watch and setting the time; sapphire crystal caseback.
Dial: solid silver and argenté; rhodium-gold hands.
Strap: black hand-stitched crocodile; 18K white-gold Lange prong buckle.
Also available: 18K pink-gold case with brown hand-stitched crocodile strap and 18K pink-gold Lange prong buckle.

1815 — REF. 233.021

Movement: manual-winding Lange L051.1 caliber; 55-hour power reserve; 21 jewels; 21,600 vph; 188 components; decorated and assembled by hand; precision-adjusted in five positions; three-quarter plate made of untreated German silver; balance cock engraved by hand; five screwed gold chatons; shock-resistant Glucydur screw balance; Nivarox balance spring; whiplash precision index adjuster with patented beat adjustment mechanism.
Functions: hours, minutes; small seconds with stop functions.
Case: 18K yellow gold; Ø 40mm, thickness: 8.9mm; crown for winding the watch and setting the time; sapphire crystal caseback.
Dial: solid silver and champagne; blued steel hands.
Strap: medium brown hand-stitched crocodile; 18K yellow-gold Lange prong buckle.
Also available: other dial and case combinations.

LANGE 1 — REF. 101.032

Movement: manual-winding Lange L901.0 caliber; 72-hour power reserve; 53 jewels; 21,600 vph; 365 components; decorated and assembled by hand; precision-adjusted in five positions; twin mainspring barrels; patented two-disc large date mechanism; stop seconds mechanism; three-quarter plate made of cross-laminated untreated German silver, damascened with Glashütte ribbing; balance cock engraved by hand; screwed gold chatons; shock-resistant Glucydur screw balance; Nivarox 1 balance spring; whiplash precision index adjuster with patented beat adjustment mechanism.
Functions: off-centered hours and minutes; small seconds with stop seconds; patented large date; up/down power reserve indicator.
Case: 18K pink gold; Ø 38.5mm, thickness: 10mm; antireflective sapphire crystal caseback.
Dial: solid silver and argenté; 18K pink-gold hands.
Strap: black hand-stitched crocodile; 18K pink-gold Lange prong buckle.
Also available: other dial and case combinations.

LANGE 1 DAYMATIC — REF. 320.025

Movement: automatic-winding Lange L021.1 caliber; 50-hour power reserve; 67 jewels; 21,600 vph; 426 components; decorated and assembled by hand; precision-adjusted in five positions; central rotor with centrifugal mass in platinum; balance cock engraved by hand; seven screwed gold chatons; shock-resistant Glucydur balance with eccentric poising weights; superior quality balance spring manufactured in-house; whiplash precision index adjuster with patented beat adjustment mechanism.
Functions: off-centered hours and minutes; small seconds with stop seconds; patented large date; retrograde display.
Case: 18K white gold; Ø 39.5mm, thickness: 10.4mm; crown for winding the watch and setting the time; pushbutton for correcting the date and day displays; sapphire crystal caseback.
Dial: solid silver and argenté; 18K white-gold hands.
Strap: black hand-stitched crocodile; 18K white-gold Lange prong buckle.
Also available: other dial and case combinations.

SAXONIA ANNUAL CALENDAR — REF. 330.026

Movement: automatic-winding Lange L085.1 SAX-0-MAT caliber; 46-hour power reserve; 476 components; 43 jewels; 21,600 vph; decorated and assembled by hand; precision-adjusted in five positions; three-quarter plate made of untreated German silver with integrated three-quarter rotor in 21K gold and centrifugal mass in platinum; reversing and reduction gear with four ball bearings; balance cock engraved by hand; shock-resistant Glucydur screw balance; Nivarox balance spring; whiplash precision index adjuster with patented beat adjustment mechanism.

Functions: hours, minutes; small seconds with stop seconds; zero-reset function; large date at 12; annual calendar: day at 9 and month at 3; moonphase.
Case: 18K white gold; Ø 38.5mm, thickness: 9.8mm; crown for winding the watch and setting the time; sapphire crystal caseback.
Dial: solid silver and argenté; blued-steel hands.
Strap: brown hand-stitched crocodile leather; 18K white-gold Lange prong buckle.
Also available: 18K pink-gold case with brown hand-stitched crocodile strap and 18K pink-gold Lange prong buckle.

LANGE ZEITWERK — REF. 140.029

Movement: manual-winding Lange L043.1 caliber; 36-hour power reserve; 388 components; 66 jewels; 18,000 vph; decorated and assembled by hand; precision-adjusted in five positions; three-quarter plate made of untreated German silver; balance cock engraved by hand; constant-force escapement; shock-resistant Glucydur balance with eccentric poising weights; superior-quality balance spring manufactured in-house with patent-pending attachment system (balance spring clamp); whiplash precision index adjuster with patented beat adjustment mechanism.

Functions: jumping hours and minutes; small seconds with stop seconds.
Case: 18K white gold; Ø 41.9mm, thickness: 12.6mm; crown for winding the watch and setting the time; sapphire crystal caseback.
Dial: solid silver and black; rhodium-gold hands; German silver and rhodium time bridge.
Strap: black hand-stitched crocodile leather; 18K white-gold Lange prong buckle.
Also available: other dial and case combinations.

1815 CHRONOGRAPH — REF. 402.032

Movement: manual-winding Lange L951.5 caliber; 60-hour power reserve; 40 jewels; 306 components; 18,000 vph.
Functions: hours, minutes; small seconds with stop seconds; chronograph: flyback, jumping minutes and 30-minute counter.
Case: 18K pink gold; Ø 39.5mm, thickness: 10.85mm; antireflective sapphire crystal bezel; antireflective sapphire crystal caseback.

Dial: solid silver and black; blued-steel hands; chronograph pushbutton at 2 and 4.
Strap: brown hand-stitched crocodile leather; 18K pink-gold Lange prong buckle.
Also available: 18K white-gold case with black hand-stitched crocodile strap and 18K white-gold Lange prong buckle.

DOUBLE SPLIT — REF. 404.032

Movement: manual-winding Lange L001.1 caliber; Ø 30.6mm, thickness: 9.45mm; 38-hour power reserve; 465 components; 40 jewels; 21,600 vph.
Functions: hours, minutes; small seconds with stop seconds; chronograph: jumping minutes counter and 30-minute rattrapante flyback; power reserve indicator.
Case: 18K pink gold; Ø 43.2mm, thickness: 15.3mm; antireflective sapphire crystal bezel; antireflective sapphire crystal caseback.

Dial: solid silver, chronograph pushbutton at 2 and 4; date pushbutton at 10; two silvered base and black subdials; applied 4N 18K pink-gold Roman numerals; luminous tachometer scale at 3, 9 and 12; 4N 18K pink-gold hour, minute, seconds, power reserve and chronograph hands with SuperLumiNova; blued steel chronograph rattrapante hands with SuperLumiNova.
Strap: brown hand-stitched crocodile leather; 5N 18K pink-gold Lange prong buckle.

RICHARD LANGE — REF. 232.025

Movement: manual-winding Lange L041.2 caliber; 38-hour power reserve; 199 components; 26 jewels; 21,600 vph; decorated and assembled by hand; precision-adjusted in five positions; plates and bridges made of untreated German silver; balance cock engraved by hand; shock-resistant Glucydur balance with off-center poising weights; superior-quality balance spring manufactured in-house with patent-pending attachment system (balance spring clamp); whiplash precision index adjuster with patented beat adjustment mechanism.
Functions: hours, minutes; sweep seconds.
Case: platinum; Ø 40.5mm, thickness: 11mm; antireflective sapphire crystal caseback.
Dial: solid silver; rhodium-gold hands; blued-steel seconds hand.
Strap: hand-stitched black crocodile leather with precious metal; platinum Lange prong buckle.
Also available: 18K pink-gold case with brown hand-stitched crocodile strap with 18K pink-gold Lange prong buckle.

RICHARD LANGE TOURBILLON "POUR LE MERITE" — REF. 760.032

Movement: manual-winding Lange L072.1 caliber; Ø 33.6mm, thickness: 7.6mm; 36-hour power reserve; 351 components; 32 jewels; 21,600 vph; fusée-and-chain transmission; decorated and assembled by hand; precision-adjusted in five positions; three-quarter plate made of untreated German silver; fourth-wheel bridge engraved by hand; shock-resistant Glucydur screw balance with eccentric poising weights; superior-quality balance spring manufactured in-house with patent-pending attachment system (balance spring clamp); whiplash precision index adjuster with patented beat adjustment mechanism.
Functions: hours, minutes; small seconds; one-minute tourbillon with patented stop seconds; pivoting dial segment.
Case: 18K pink gold; Ø 41.9mm, thickness: 12.2mm; crown for winding the watch and setting the time; sapphire crystal caseback.
Dial: solid silver, argenté; pink-gold seconds hand; blued-steel hands.
Strap: red-brown hand-stitched crocodile leather; 18K pink-gold Lange prong buckle.

LANGE ZEITWERK STRIKING TIME — REF. 145.029

Movement: manual-winding Lange L043.2 caliber; Ø 36mm, thickness: 10mm; 36-hour power reserve; 528 components; 78 jewels; 18,000 vph; decorated and assembled by hand; precision-adjusted in five positions; three-quarter plate made of untreated German silver; balance cock engraved by hand; shock-resistant Glucydur screw balance with eccentric poising weights; superior-quality balance spring manufactured in-house with patent-pending attachment system (balance spring clamp); whiplash precision index adjuster with patented beat adjustment mechanism.
Functions: jumping hours and minutes; small seconds with stop seconds; power reserve indicator; acoustic signal at quarter-hours and full hours.
Case: 18K white gold; Ø 44.2mm, thickness: 13.8mm; crown for winding the watch and setting the time; push-button for enabling and disabling the acoustic signal; sapphire crystal caseback.
Dial: solid silver and black; German silver and rhodium time bridge; rhodium-gold hand.
Strap: black hand-stitched crocodile leather; 18K white-gold Lange prong buckle.
Also available: platinum case with black hand-stitched crocodile strap and platinum Lange prong buckle.

SAXONIA DUAL TIME — REF. 385.026

Movement: automatic-winding Lange L086.2 caliber; Ø 30.4mm, thickness: 4.6mm; 72-hour power reserve; 31 jewels; 21,600 vph; 268 components; decorated and assembled by hand; precision-adjusted in five positions; plate made of untreated German silver; balance cock engraved by hand; shock-resistant Glucydur screw balance; superior-quality balance spring manufactured in-house; whiplash precision index adjuster with patented beat adjustment mechanism.
Functions: hours, minutes; small seconds with stop seconds; second time zone with additional hour hand; 24-hour display; day/night indication.
Case: 18K white gold; Ø 40mm, thickness: 9.1mm; crown for winding the watch and setting the time; one pushbutton each for stepping the time forward and backward in one-hour increments; sapphire crystal caseback.
Dial: solid silver and argenté; rhodium-gold hands; blued steel second time zone and 24-hour hand.
Strap: black hand-stitched crocodile leather; white-gold Lange prong buckle.
Also available: 18K pink-gold case with chestnut hand-stitched crocodile strap and 18K pink-gold Lange prong buckle.

Alpina GENEVE

PILOTS TAKE FLIGHT

Alpina's introduction of the Startimer Pilot collection takes the brand back to one of the most illustrious eras of its rich history.

The decade following World War I was for the Genevan watchmaker the beginning of twenty years that would lay the foundation for an aviation heritage that continues to evolve through the present day. For two decades, Alpina gained its fame as a specialized manufacturer and supplier of military pilots' watches. Given the strict and vital requirements for the instruments of these early aviation pioneers, Alpina implemented a set of core principles that remain pivotal nearly a century later.

To meet the needs of aviators, the manufacture produced timepieces of ultimate legibility and precision that possessed anti-magnetism and anti-shock qualities. Alpina founded its proud tradition on the creation of timekeeping instruments that were as robust and clear as they were precise.

The Startimer Pilot collection represents the core values of the Alpina aviation concept with four variations that combine the functionality of a pilot's timepiece with an unassuming elegance. The new range of watches, produced in association with Cessna Aircraft and PrivatAir, links its watches together with a clean design that draws inspiration from Alpina's past and the values of the brand's collaborative partners. The 44mm antireflective satin-finished steel case draws the eye to a matte black dial with oversized white luminous numerals that offers ideal readability through a glare-free sapphire crystal. The Swiss house adds a touch of individuality with the incorporation of its signature red Alpina triangle on the seconds hand. Also, an original securing solution, in which the leather strap closes on the front side of the wrist, not the reverse or lower side, improves overall comfort and adds a reminder of leather straps of the past.

STARTIMER PILOT COLLECTION

Startimer Automatic (left), Startimer Chronograph (center), Startimer Manufacture (right). This pilot concept collection, with movements built in-house, possesses an understated elegance that echoes the values of Alpina's partners, Cessna Aircraft and PrivatAir.

Taking off with the Startimer Automatic's basic three-hand date model of understated distinction, the collection follows with the powerfully designed automatic Startimer Chronograph, which evokes the commanding intricacy of in-flight instrumentation and is powered by the AL-860 caliber.

Next in line is the Startimer Manufacture, which features a date counter at 6 o'clock and the AL-710 caliber. In addition to the black leather strap or metal bracelet options that all four Startimer Pilot variations offer, Alpina also presents the stunning Pilot Manufacture model in 18-karat rose gold. This glamorous model offers an alternative fashionable accent to go with the aeronautic authenticity of the collection.

Finally, the AL-950 caliber powers the iconic Startimer Manufacture Regulator, a watch that combines the historic pilot design with a contemporary regulator layout. A decentralized hour counter at 10 o'clock creates a contrast in numeral size with the date indicator at 6 o'clock, while its positioning completes a balanced design that doesn't rely on evident symmetry and gives the watch a distinctive technical appeal.

The 8,888 limited edition models of the Startimer Pilot collection are each presented in luxurious packaging, alongside a scale model of the Cessna Citation Mustang business jet that adds an aerial dimension to the display of the watch.

Alpina's new Startimer Pilot collection presents four variations on a nearly century-old concept—each one brings a pioneering past to the present, and takes this present to the sky.

STARTIMER MANUFACTURE

With a date display at 6 o'clock, this model is available in glamorous rose gold.

ALPINA STARTIMER PILOT AUTOMATIC — REF. AL-525B4S6

Movement: automatic-winding AL-525 caliber; 38-hour power reserve; 25 jewels; 28,800 vph; black PVD-coated Alpina rotor.
Functions: hours, minutes, seconds; date at 3.
Case: stainless steel; Ø 44mm, thickness: 10.7mm; new round 2-part case; screw-down crown; sapphire crystal; transparent screw-down caseback; water resistant to 10atm.
Dial: black; large white numerals with luminescent coating; white hands with luminescent coating; seconds hand with signature Alpina red triangle.
Strap: black leather; stainless steel folding buckle.
Note: limited edition of 8,888 pieces; delivered in a special gift box with a plane miniature.
Suggested price: $1,150
Also available: metal bracelet.

ALPINA SAILING AUTOMATIC — REF. AL-525LB4V6

Movement: automatic-winding AL-525 caliber; 38-hour power reserve; 25 jewels; 28,800 vph; black PVD-coated Alpina rotor.
Functions: hours, minutes, seconds; date at 3.
Case: stainless steel; Ø 44mm, thickness: 12.6mm; unidirectional turning bezel; sapphire crystal; transparent caseback; water resistant to 20atm.
Dial: black; large white hour markers with luminescent coating; white hands with luminescent coating; seconds hand with signature Alpina white triangle.
Strap: black rubber; stainless steel buckle.
Note: delivered in a special gift box with an Extreme 40 boat miniature.
Suggested price: $1,150
Also available: metal and mesh bracelet.

ALPINA STARTIMER CLASSIC AUTOMATIC — REF. AL-525SCR4S6

Movement: automatic-winding AL-525 caliber; 38-hour power reserve; 25 jewels; 28,800 vph; black Alpina rotor decorated with Côtes de Genève.
Functions: hours, minutes, seconds; date at 3.
Case: stainless steel; Ø 44mm, thickness: 10.7mm; new round 2-part case; screw-down crown; sapphire crystal; transparent screw-down caseback; water resistant to 10atm.
Dial: silver; large rose-gold plated hand-applied Arabic numerals; white hands with luminescent coating; seconds hand with signature Alpina rose-gold triangle.
Strap: brown crococalf; stainless steel Alpina folding buckle.
Suggested price: $995

ALPINA STARTIMER PILOT MANUFACTURE — REF. AL-710B4S6

Movement: automatic-winding AL-710 caliber; 42-hour power reserve; 26 jewels; 28,800 vph; black PVD-coated Alpina rotor.
Functions: hours, minutes, seconds; date at 6.
Case: stainless steel; Ø 44mm, thickness: 13.4mm; new round 2-part case; screw-down crown; sapphire crystal; transparent screw-down caseback; water resistant to 10atm.
Dial: black; large white numerals with luminescent coating; white hands with luminescent coating; seconds hand with signature Alpina red triangle.
Strap: black leather; stainless steel folding buckle.
Note: limited edition of 8,888 pieces; delivered in a special gift box with a plane miniature.
Suggested price: $2,195
Also available: metal bracelet.

ALPINA SAILING CHRONOGRAPH REF. AL-880LS4V6B2

Movement: automatic-winding AL-880 caliber; 46-hour power reserve; 25 jewels; black PVD-coated Alpina rotor.
Functions: hours, minutes, seconds; yacht timer countdown function.
Case: stainless steel; Ø 44mm, thickness: 14.3mm; round 3-part case; screw-down crown; sapphire crystal; transparent screw-down caseback; water resistant to 10atm.
Dial: black; white hands with luminescent coating; seconds hand with signature Alpina red triangle; chronograph counters with red elements.
Strap: black crococalf leather strap with red stitching.
Suggested price: $2,595

ALPINA STARTIMER PILOT CHRONOGRAPH AUTOMATIC REF. AL-860B4S6

Movement: automatic-winding AL-860 caliber; 46-hour power reserve; 25 jewels; 28,800 vph; black PVD-coated Alpina rotor.
Functions: hours, minutes, seconds; chronograph.
Case: stainless steel; Ø 44mm, thickness: 14.7mm; new round 2-part case; screw-down crown; sapphire crystal; transparent screw-down caseback; water resistant to 10atm.
Dial: black; large white numerals with luminescent coating; white hands with luminescent coating; seconds hand with signature Alpina red triangle.
Strap: black leather; stainless steel folding buckle.
Note: limited edition of 8,888 pieces; delivered in a special gift box with a plane miniature.
Suggested price: $2,595
Also available: metal bracelet.

ALPINA STARTIMER CLASSIC CHRONO AUTOMATIC REF. AL-860SCR4S6

Movement: automatic-winding AL-860 caliber; 46-hour power reserve; 25 jewels; 28,800 vph; black Alpina rotor decorated with Côtes de Genève.
Functions: hours, minutes, seconds; chronograph.
Case: stainless steel; Ø 44mm; new round 2-part case; screw-down crown; sapphire crystal; transparent caseback; water resistant to 10atm.
Dial: silver; large rose-gold-plated hand-applied Arabic numerals; white hands with luminescent coating; seconds hand with signature Alpina rose-gold triangle.
Strap: brown crococalf; stainless steel Alpina folding buckle.
Suggest price: $2,450
Also available: black nickel hand-applied Arabic numerals and black leather strap; black nickle with tachometer scale on the dial.

ALPINA SAILING CHRONOGRAPH REF. AL-880LS4V6B2

Movement: automatic-winding AL-880 caliber; 46-hour power reserve; 25 jewels; black PVD-coated Alpina rotor.
Functions: hours, minutes, seconds; yacht timer function.
Case: stainless steel; Ø 44mm; unidirectional turning bezel with compass; sapphire crystal; transparent caseback; water resistant to 30atm.
Dial: white; large white hour markers with luminescent coating; white hands with luminescent coating; Alpina red seconds hand.
Bracelet: mesh.
Note: limited edition of 8,888 pieces; delivered in a special gift box with an Extreme 40 boat miniature.
Suggested price: $2,995
Also available: black dial; black rubber strap and metal bracelet.

AUDEMARS PIGUET

Le Brassus

SIMPLY SOPHISTICATED

New additions to Audemars Piguet's collections have expanded the brand's personality and continue a tradition of excellence.

With the 2011 introduction of two new powerful yet exquisite Royal Oak Offshore chronographs, Audemars Piguet has bolstered the collection's esteemed reputation of sporty, masculine masterpieces. The Selfwinding Royal Oak Offshore Tourbillon Chronograph establishes a perfect union between a sophisticated, powerful design and internal finesse. The new self-winding 2897 Caliber, equipped with a daring combination of tourbillon and chronograph, finds its home within a case whose blend of black materials contributes to the sturdiness of the watch. The mélange of forged carbon, ceramic, and rubber creates a dynamic contrast for a sapphire crystal caseback that, in conjunction with a peripheral oscillating weight, lets the owner in on a hidden symphony of masterful engineering.

The introduction of the Royal Oak Offshore Arnold Schwarzenegger The Legacy Chronograph will be the last of the collaborative collection that has raised millions of dollars for the After-School All-Stars charity. As such, it is fitting that the partners would celebrate this illustrious relationship with a collector timepiece that balances audacity, power and performance. A dedication to the highest level of ceramic finishing, as well as applied numerals crafted in diamond-polished pink gold, makes this watch the picture of rugged elegance.

SELFWINDING ROYAL OAK OFFSHORE TOURBILLON CHRONOGRAPH

ROYAL OAK OFFSHORE ARNOLD SCHWARZENEGGER THE LEGACY CHRONOGRAPH

JULES AUDEMARS SMALL SECONDS

EXTRA-THIN JULES AUDEMARS

JULES AUDEMARS DUAL TIME

JULES AUDEMARS MOON-PHASE CALENDAR

The Jules Audemars collection represents the roots of Audemars Piguet. The tribute to one of its founders recounts a legacy based on a vision of simplicity. While the present proudly appears through pertinent innovations, it is a refusal of all things superfluous and purely ornamental that makes these watches both elegant and graciously modern.

Armed with one of the world's slimmest self-winding movements, the extra-thin Jules Audemars presents a timepiece of lean sophistication. The thinness of the 2120 caliber makes it hard to believe its remarkable performance, achieved with the masterful alliance of multiple high-efficiency mechanisms within a space that few would dare.

The Jules Audemars Small Seconds eschews overstatement, opting for a graceful minimalism that exudes a seductive femininity. A slender bezel emphasizes the ease of the round case and enables a maximum dial opening. The crisp clarity of the silver-toned background makes way for the discreet small seconds subdial at 6 o'clock. Audemars Piguet's ability to capture elegance through understated subtlety gives this watch an air of weightlessness, while its 3090 caliber honors the women who appreciate the sophistication of a mechanical movement.

Staying true to the vision of the collection, the Jules Audemars Dual Time possesses a dial that provides optimal legibility, framed by a sleek bezel for an elegant ensemble. Despite the complexity of a watch equipped with indications of date, power reserve, and second time zone complete with day/night display, this Jules Audemars Dual Time remains understated and refined, maintaining the precious respect for classical aesthetics while providing a timepiece fit for the worldly ways of the modern globetrotter.

The Jules Audemars Moon-Phase Calendar evokes the poetic maritime origins of horology. A decorative fillet surrounds the date, day, and moonphase displays, highlighting these emblems of watchmaking tradition. Yet the beauty of this watch rests equally beneath the dial, thanks to the meticulous production of this ingenious mechanical calendar.

In the Millenary collection, Audemars Piguet presents a watch that indulges the curiosity of the modern watch connoisseur. The Swiss manufacture's Millenary 4101 is a fascinating spectacle staged within the perimeter of a voluptuous oval case. The piece extracts the watch's beating heart from the cavity of the case to reveal the fine mechanism in all its splendor. The watch is powered by the oval 4101 caliber, which boasts an ingenious structural approach that turns the parts upside down, playing a key role in the design of the watch.

Also joining the Millenary collection is the Hand-Wound Millenary Minute Repeater. This watch's three-dimensional architecture reveals the visual delight of its refined movement, including a new escapement and double balance spring. Every aspect of each watch is beautifully finished according to the highest horological standard. Meanwhile, the audible indication of the time acts as an homage to the oldest of all horological complications.

With remarkable additions to three collections that shine in their own distinctive ways, Audemars Piguet demonstrates its continued mastery of the delicate marriage of performance and elegance.

MILLENARY 4101

HAND-WOUND MILLENARY MINUTE REPEATER

SELFWINDING ROYAL OAK — REF. 15300ST.OO.1220ST.01

Movement: automatic-winding proprietary 3120 caliber; thickness: 4.26mm; 60-hour power reserve; 21,600 vph; diamond-engraved beveled bridges; stop balance when setting time; poised balance with inertia blocks; 22K gold oscillating weight with ceramic ball bearings; decorated with the Audemars and Piguet family crests; rhodium-plated, Côtes de Genève decorative pattern and circular graining.
Functions: hours, minutes, seconds; date at 3.

Case: stainless steel; Ø 39mm; screw-down crown; antireflective sapphire crystal and caseback; water resistant to 5atm.
Dial: silver; "Grande Tapisserie" pattern; applied white-gold hour markers; Royal Oak hands with luminescent coating.
Bracelet: stainless steel with AP folding clasp.
Price: available upon request.
Also available: blue or black dial.

SELFWINDING OPENWORKED ROYAL OAK — REF. 15305ST.OO.1220ST.01

Movement: automatic-winding proprietary 3129 caliber; thickness: 4.31mm; 60-hour power reserve; 21,600 vph; poised balance with inertia blocks; bridges and mainplate hand-drawn with a file; polished angles; stop balance when setting time; 22K gold oscillating weight; Côtes de Genève decorative pattern.
Functions: hours, minutes, seconds.
Case: stainless steel; Ø 39mm; 18K white-gold assembly screws; transparent sapphire crystal and caseback; water resistant to 5atm.

Dial: anthracite; eleven applied and faceted 18K white-gold hour markers and Royal Oak hands with luminescent coating.
Bracelet: stainless steel with open-worked AP folding clasp.
Price: available upon request.
Also available: 18K pink-gold case with brown leather strap.

ROYAL OAK CHRONOGRAPH — REF. 25960OR.OO.1185OR.03

Movement: automatic-winding 2385 caliber; thickness: 5.5mm; 40-hour power reserve; 21,600 vph; integrated chronograph movement; column-wheel chronograph mechanism; 18K gold oscillating weight; rhodium-plated, Côtes de Genève decorative pattern and circular graining.
Functions: hours, minutes; small seconds; date at 4:30; chronograph.
Case: 18K pink gold; Ø 39mm; screw-down crown; antireflective sapphire crystal; water resistant to 5atm.

Dial: brown; "Grande Tapisserie" pattern; bi-colored counters; applied 18K pink-gold hour markers; Royal Oak hands with luminescent coating.
Bracelet: 18K pink gold with AP folding clasp.
Price: available upon request.
Also available: silvered dial; silvered dial with yellow-gold bracelet.

SELFWINDING ROYAL OAK EQUATION OF TIME PERPETUAL CALENDAR — REF. 26603OR.OO.D092CR.01

Movement: automatic-winding proprietary 2120/2808 caliber; extra-thin; thickness: 2.45mm; 42-hour power reserve; 19,800 vph; poised balance with inertia blocks; suspended barrel; 22K gold oscillating weight; distinctive features: cams (sunrise and sunset times) and the flange (mean time of solar culmination) can be calibrated to most locations situated between the 56th parallel north and the 46th parallel south; rhodium-plated, Côtes de Genève decorative pattern and circular graining.

Functions: hours, minutes, seconds; sunrise and sunset times; equation of time; perpetual calendar; astronomical moonphase.
Case: 18K pink gold; Ø 39mm; 18K gold assembly screws; antireflective sapphire crystal and caseback.
Dial: silvered; "Grande Tapisserie" pattern; applied 18K pink-gold hour markers and Royal Oak hands with luminescent coating.
Strap: hand-sewn "large square scale" dark brown crocodile leather with 18K pink-gold AP folding clasp.
Price: available upon request.
Also available: silvered dial with black leather strap.

ROYAL OAK OFFSHORE CHRONOGRAPH REF. 26400SO.OO.A002CA.01

Movement: automatic-winding proprietary 3126/3840 caliber; thickness: 4.26mm; 55-hour power reserve; 21,600 vph; poised balance with inertia blocks; diamond-engraved beveled bridges; inverted snailing on the bridges; stop balance when setting time; 22K gold oscillating weight with ceramic ball bearings; Côtes de Genève decorative pattern.
Functions: hours, minutes; small seconds; date at 3; chronograph.
Case: stainless steel; Ø 44mm; black ceramic bezel; screw-down crown and pushbutton; stainless steel pushbutton guards; antireflective sapphire crystal; titanium sapphire crystal caseback; water resistant to 10atm.
Dial: silvered; "Grande Tapisserie" pattern; black counters; applied white-gold hour markers and Royal Oak hands with luminescent coating; black flange.
Strap: black rubber; titanium pin buckle.
Price: available upon request.
Also available: black dial and forged carbon or black dial with 18K pink-gold case.

HAND-WOUND ROYAL OAK OFFSHORE TOURBILLON CHRONOGRAPH REF. 26288OF.OO.D002CR.01

Movement: manual-winding proprietary 2912 caliber; thickness: 10.67mm; 10-day power reserve; 21,600 vph; integrated chronograph movement; column-wheel chronograph mechanism; two barrels; blackened steel bridges; circular-grained motifs; hand-drawn strokes; snailed and small circular-grained barrels bearing the Audemars Piguet signature; Côtes de Genève decorative pattern.
Function: hours, minutes, seconds; tourbillon; chronograph: 30-minute counter at 3.
Case: 18K pink gold; Ø 44mm; forged carbon bezel; black ceramic crown and pushbuttons; assembly polished steel screws; antireflective sapphire crystal and caseback.
Dial: black; snailed and openworked at 6, 9 and 12; applied 18K pink-gold numerals and Royal Oak hands with luminescent coating.
Strap: hand-sewn "large square scale" black crocodile leather with 18K pink-gold AP folding clasp.
Price: available upon request.

SELFWINDING ROYAL OAK OFFSHORE DIVER REF. 15703ST.OO.D002CA.01

Movement: automatic-winding proprietary 3120 caliber; thickness: 4.26mm; 60-hour power reserve; 21,600 vph; diamond-engraved beveled bridges; stop balance when setting time; poised balance with inertia blocks; 22K gold oscillating weight with ceramic ball bearings; decorated with the Audemars and Piguet family crests; rhodium-plated, Côtes de Genève decorative pattern and circular graining.
Functions: hours, minutes, seconds; date at 3; dive-time measurement.
Case: stainless steel; Ø 42mm; polished stainless steel assembly screws; antireflective sapphire crystal; water resistant to 30atm.
Dial: black; "Grande Tapisserie" pattern; inner rotating ring with diving scale; applied white-gold hour markers and Royal Oak hands with luminescent coating.
Strap: black rubber; oversized stainless steel pin buckle.
Price: available upon request.

SELFWINDING LADIE'S ROYAL OAK OFFSHORE DIAMOND-SET CHRONOGRAPH REF. 26048SK.ZZ.D010CA.01

Movement: automatic-winding 2385 caliber; thickness: 5.5mm; 40-hour power reserve; 21,600 vph; integrated chronograph movement; column-wheel chronograph mechanism; 18K gold oscillating weight; rhodium-plated, Côtes de Genève decorative pattern and circular graining.
Functions: hours, minutes; small seconds at 6; date at 4:30; chronograph: 12-hour counter at 9, 30-minute counter at 3 and central seconds hand.
Case: stainless steel; Ø 37mm; set with 32 brilliant-cut diamonds (1.25 carats); stainless steel assembly screws; clad white rubber bezel, crown and pushbuttons; antireflective sapphire crystal; water resistant to 5atm.
Dial: silvered; "Grande Tapisserie" pattern; black numerals and Royal Oak hands with luminescent coating.
Strap: white rubber; stainless steel AP folding clasp.
Price: available upon request.
Also available: black dial with black strap.

SELFWINDING EXTRA-THIN JULES AUDEMARS — REF. 15180OR.OO.A002CR.01

Movement: automatic-winding proprietary 2120 caliber; extra-thin; thickness: 2.45mm; 40-hour power reserve; 19,800 vph; polished bevels; 21K gold oscillating weight; rhodium-plated, Côtes de Genève decorative pattern and circular graining.
Functions: hours, minutes.
Case: 18K pink gold; Ø 41mm; antireflective sapphire crystal and caseback.
Dial: black; applied 18K pink-gold hour markers and hands.

Strap: hand-sewn "large square scale" black crocodile leather with 18K pink-gold AP folding clasp.
Price: available upon request.
Also available: silvered dial with brown strap; silvered dial with 18K white-gold case.

JULES AUDEMARS SMALL SECONDS — REF. 77239OR.ZZ.A088CR.01

Movement: manual-winding proprietary 3090 caliber; thickness: 2.8mm; 48-hour power reserve; 21,600 vph; all parts finely decorated; diamond-engraved beveled bridges; circular-grained mainplate; rhodium-plated beveled bridges, snailed and adorned with Côtes de Genève decorative pattern.
Functions: hours, minutes; small seconds at 6.
Case: 18K pink gold; Ø 33mm; bezel set with 60 brilliant-cut diamonds (0.52 carat); sapphire crystal caseback.
Dial: silvered; applied 18K pink-gold hour markers and hands.
Strap: hand-sewn "large square scale" brown crocodile leather with 18K pink-gold pin buckle.
Price: available upon request.
Also available: 18K white-gold case with black strap.

JULES AUDEMARS DUAL TIME — REF. 26380BC.OO.D002CR.01

Movement: automatic-winding 2329/2846 caliber; thickness: 3.3mm; 38-hour power reserve; 28,800 vph; stop balance when setting time; 21K gold oscillating weight with ceramic ball bearings; circular-grained and beveled mainplate; bridges adorned with Côtes de Genève decorative pattern.
Functions: hours, minutes; date at 2; power reserve indicator on an arc between 9 and 11; dual time zone; day/night display.

Case: 18K white gold; Ø 41mm; antireflective sapphire crystal.
Dial: silvered; applied 18K pink-gold hour markers and hands.
Strap: hand-sewn "large square scale" black crocodile leather with 18K white-gold AP folding clasp.
Price: available upon request.
Also available: 18K pink-gold case with brown strap; 18K pink-gold case with black dial.

SELFWINDING JULES AUDEMARS PERPETUAL CALENDAR — REF. 26390OR.OO.D088CR.01

Movement: automatic-winding proprietary 2120/2802 caliber; extra-thin; thickness: 2.45mm; 40-hour power reserve; 19,800 vph; 21K gold oscillating weight; suspended barrel; rhodium-plated, Côtes de Genève decorative pattern and circular graining.
Functions: hours, minutes; date at 3; days of the week at 9; perpetual calendar; leap-year cycle; moonphase.

Case: 18K pink gold; Ø 41mm; antireflective sapphire crystal and caseback.
Dial: silvered; applied 18K pink-gold hour markers and hands.
Strap: hand-sewn "large square scale" brown crocodile leather with 18K pink-gold AP folding clasp.
Price: available upon request.
Also available: brown dial.

HAND-WOUND JULES AUDEMARS LARGE DATE TOURBILLON REF. 26559OR.OO.D002CR.01

Movement: manual-winding 2909 proprietary caliber; thickness: 6.53mm; 72-hour power reserve; 21,600 vph; poised balance with inertia blocks; manual finishing on bridges and mainplate; polished bevels, grained finishing on top and matte brouillé finishing underneath; Côtes de Genève decorative pattern.
Functions: hours, minutes; large date at 12; tourbillon at 6.
Case: 18K pink gold; Ø 41mm; antireflective sapphire crystal.
Dial: black; applied 18K pink-gold hour markers and hands.
Strap: hand-sewn "large square scale" black crocodile leather with 18K pink-gold AP folding clasp.
Price: available upon request.
Also available: silvered dial with brown leather strap.

HAND-WOUND JULES AUDEMARS CHRONOMETER REF. 26153PT.OO.D028CR.01

Movement: manual-winding proprietary 2908 caliber; thickness: 8.11mm; 90-hour power reserve; 43,200 vph; chronometer with AP escapement, double balance spring; stop balance when setting time; twin-barrel system; white-gold mainplate decorated with a barleycorn pattern; Côtes de Genève decorative pattern.
Functions: hours, minutes; small seconds; power reserve indicator.
Case: 950 platinum; Ø 46mm; sapphire crystal and caseback.
Dial: white enamel; painted black Roman numerals; white-gold small seconds counter with blued steel hand.
Strap: hand-sewn "large square scale" blue crocodile leather with 950 platinum AP folding clasp.
Price: available upon request.

SELFWINDING MILLENARY 4101 REF. 15350OR.OO.D093CR.01

Movement: automatic-winding proprietary 4101 caliber; oval shaped; thickness: 7.46mm; 60-hour power reserve; 28,800 vph; mainplate adorned with horizontal Côtes de Genève on the front and circular-grained on the back; diamond-polished jewel sinks; diamond-polished countersinks and beveled wheel spokes; beveled screw rims and slots; AP monogram; Audemars and Piguet family crests engraved on the oscillating weight; rhodium-plated bridges, beveled, snailed and adorned with horizontal and circular Côtes de Genève decorative pattern and circular graining.
Functions: off-centered hours and minutes at 3; off-centered small seconds at 7.
Case: 18K pink gold; 42x47mm; antireflective sapphire crystal and caseback.
Dial: anthracite silvered; applied 18K pink-gold Roman numerals and hands.
Strap: hand-sewn "large square scale" brown crocodile leather with 18K pink-gold folding clasp.
Price: available upon request.
Also available: stainless steel case with black strap.

HAND-WOUND MILLENARY MINUTE REPEATER WITH AP ESCAPEMENT REF. 26371TI.OO.D002CR.01

Movement: manual-winding proprietary 2910 caliber; oval shaped; thickness: 10.05mm; 165-hour power reserve; 21,600 vph; AP escapement, double balance spring; stop balance when setting time; all parts finely decorated, with hand-polished beveling, interior angles, snailing, hand-drawn file strokes; horizontal Côtes de Genève decorative pattern and circular graining on the mainplate.
Functions: off-centered hours and minutes at 3; off-centered small seconds at 7; minute repeater (repeater slide serving to activate the minute repeater at 7).
Case: titanium; 42x47mm; antireflective sapphire crystal and caseback.
Dial: anthracite; applied 18K pink-gold Roman numerals and hands; silvered small seconds counter.
Strap: hand-sewn "large square scale" black crocodile leather with titanium AP folding clasp.
Price: available upon request.

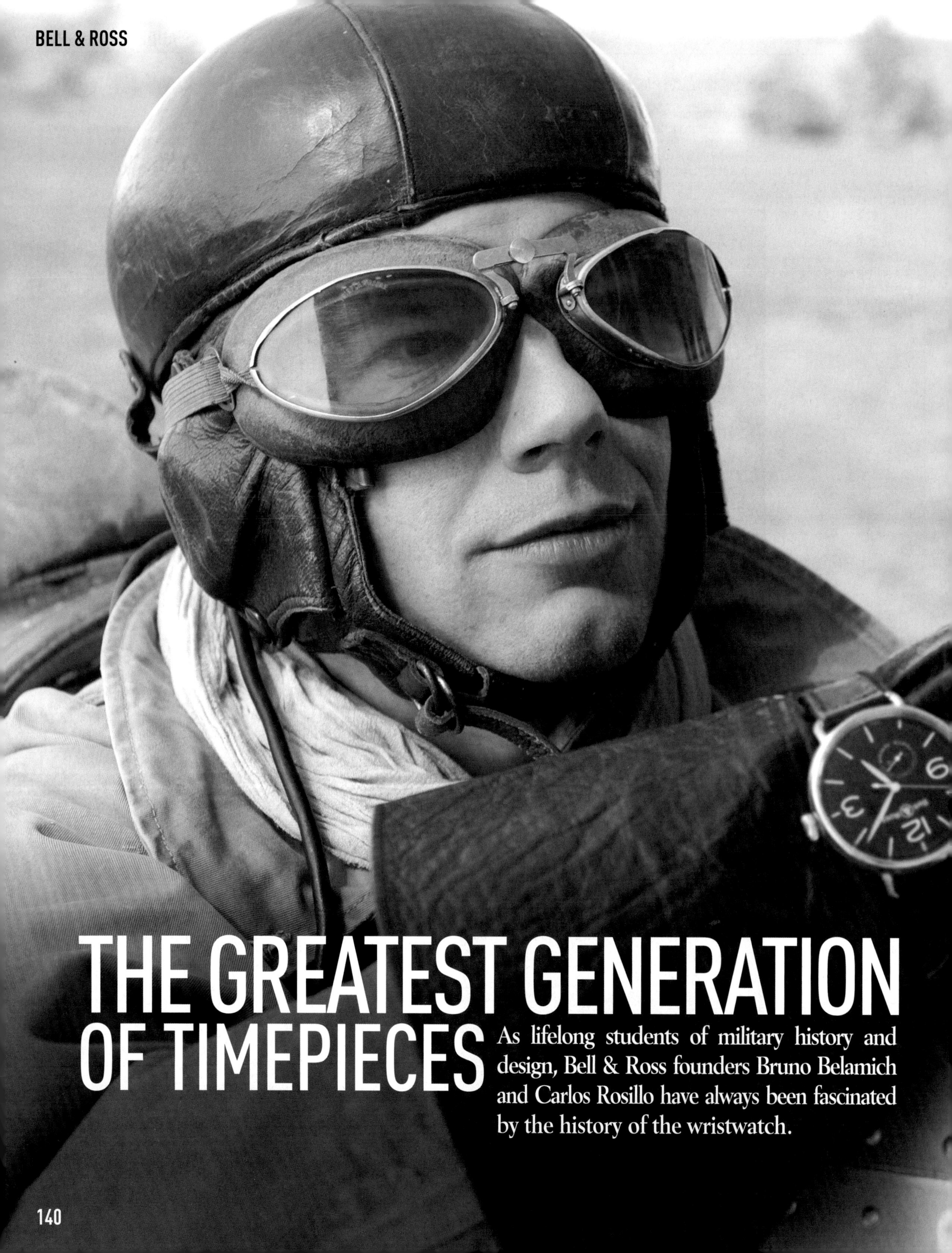

THE GREATEST GENERATION OF TIMEPIECES

As lifelong students of military history and design, Bell & Ross founders Bruno Belamich and Carlos Rosillo have always been fascinated by the history of the wristwatch.

Bell & Ross

TIME INSTRUMENTS

With the brand's latest additions, Bell & Ross has transformed passion into action by adding two "missing links" to its Vintage collection—the PW1 and WW1. "We are delving into the past even more in order to round out our collection," explains Belamich, "and we were looking to reinvent the first models of these wristwatches that appeared on pilots' wrists in the 1920s."

The reimagining of this bygone era is a two-fold process: first, the PW1, whose design is based on the pocket watches that were prevalent at the beginning of the 20th century, followed by the WW1, an adaptation of the first wristwatches used by the military during World War I. The PW1 (Pocket Watch 1) pays tribute to the compact, portable timepieces that were used during those very first years of aviation. Just as the World War I pilots attached handles and straps to their pocket watches in order to keep their hands free during combat, Bell & Ross added horn lugs and a thin, elegant leather strap to a large fob watch case in order to create the Vintage WW1 (Wrist Watch 1). Both of these watches, with their clean, elegant lines and traditional styling, illustrate Bell & Ross's ongoing passion for vintage military watches.

By World War II, wristwatches had become commonplace and were issued to military pilots to be used as tools on their missions. The Vintage Original, Officer and Heritage lines recreate those timepieces of the "Greatest Generation." By combining movement functionality, dial legibility, domed crystals and elegant strap finishes, Bell & Ross has combined the authenticity of vintage watches with the very latest technologies.

With the introduction of the BR02, Bell & Ross transitioned from air to sea by developing a diving watch with a distinctive rounded case. Continuing its focus on extreme professions, these watches, part of Bell & Ross's Marine Collection, meet the demands of deep-sea divers.

The Aviation Collection's iconic BR01 represents the final step in the evolution of the wristwatch. The design of this watch is based on the airplane instrument panels found in cockpits beginning in the 1940s. The square case with its four fastening screws is reminiscent of the method used to affix instruments to the planes' cockpit panels in order to make their installation and removal fast and efficient.

With the addition of the PW1 and WW1 lines, Bell & Ross has achieved its goal of tracing the evolution of the military watch from the pocket to the wrist to the dashboard, and has used military timepiece history to create watch collections well suited to every professional requirement and style.

VINTAGE COLLECTION

Military pilots were the first professionals to consider the wristwatch as a tool to assist them in carrying out their missions. As a tribute to servicemen, particularly pilots, Bell & Ross created the Heritage collection. Its refined lines and style, both classical in its shape and modern in its design, evoke the era of the "Greatest Generation."

Bell & Ross created the Heritage collection by combining the design elements of the 1930s and '40s with the principles of cockpit legibility: a black matte finish to avoid distracting light reflections, the sand color of the hands and numerals which reproduce the patina of vintage watches and the natural leather strap typical of period timepieces.

AVIATION COLLECTION

It all started with a simple idea: to turn a cockpit instrument panel clock into a wristwatch. To create the BR 01 aviation watch, Bell & Ross designers took their inspiration from aeronautical instrumentation, the ultimate reference point for readability, reliability and performance. Available with a variety of functions (chronograph, large date, power reserve, tourbillon...), case materials and finishes (steel, titanium, carbon, gold), and dial colors (white, black, orange, blue...), the BR 01 Instrument watch is no longer exclusively reserved for professional users. It has become an iconic watch, to the great delight of collectors of limited series and fine watches.

MARINE COLLECTION

Water resistant up to 1,000 meters, legible in the darkness of the deep, equipped with a decompression valve and a rotating bezel, unidirectional, notched and calibrated at 60 minutes, the BR 02 watch is a diving instrument perfectly adapted for professional use.

VINTAGE WW1-96 BIG DATE

Movement: manual-winding (ETA 6497).
Functions: hours, minutes, seconds; date at 3.
Case: polished stainless steel; Ø 45mm; antireflective sapphire crystal; water resistant to 3atm.
Dial: galvanic black; sunburst; numerals, markers and hands with photoluminescent coating to optimize nighttime reading.
Strap: black alligator leather; polished stainless steel tongue buckle.
Suggested price: $4,200

VINTAGE WW1-90 BIG DATE AND POWER RESERVE

Movement: manual-winding (SOPROD 9090).
Functions: hours, minutes, seconds; date at 12; power reserve indicator at 6.
Case: polished stainless steel; Ø 45mm; antireflective sapphire crystal; water resistant to 5atm.
Dial: galvanic black; sunburst; numerals, markers and hands with photoluminescent coating to optimize nighttime reading.
Strap: black alligator leather; polished stainless steel tongue buckle.
Suggested price: $5,000

VINTAGE BR 123 ORIGINAL BLACK

Movement: automatic-winding (ETA 2895).
Functions: hours, minutes; small seconds and date at 6.
Case: satin-finished stainless steel; Ø 41mm; antireflective sapphire crystal; water resistant to 10atm.
Dial: black; numerals, markers and hands with photoluminescent coating to optimize nighttime reading.
Strap: black calfskin; satin-finished stainless steel folding buckle.
Suggested price: $2,800
Also available: satin-finished stainless steel case, beige dial and brown calfskin strap.

VINTAGE BR 126 ORIGINAL BLACK CARBON

Movement: automatic-winding (ETA 2894).
Functions: hours, minutes, seconds; date between 4 and 5; chronograph: 30-minute and 60-second counters.
Case: stainless steel with black PVD coating; Ø 41mm; antireflective sapphire crystal; water resistant to 10atm.
Dial: matte black; numerals, markers and hands with photoluminescent coating to optimize nighttime reading.
Suggested price: $4,600
Strap: brown calfskin; stainless steel with black PVD coating tongue buckle.

AVIATION BR 01-92 CERAMIC

Movement: automatic-winding (ETA 2892).
Functions: hours, minutes, seconds.
Case: polished black ceramic; Ø 46mm; antireflective sapphire crystal; water resistant to 10atm.
Dial: galvanic matte black; numerals, markers and hands with photoluminescent coating to optimize nighttime reading.
Strap: black alligator leather.
Suggested price: $5,600
Also available: heavy-duty canvas strap.

AVIATION BR 03-90 BIG DATE AND POWER RESERVE

Movement: automatic-winding (SOPROD 9090).
Functions: hours, minutes, seconds; date at 12; power reserve indicator at 6.
Case: satin-finished stainless steel; Ø 42mm; antireflective sapphire crystal; water resistant to 10atm.
Dial: galvanic matte black; numerals, markers and hands with photoluminescent coating to optimize nighttime reading.
Strap: black rubber.
Suggested price: $5,000
Also available: heavy-duty canvas strap.

AVIATION BR 01-92 RED RADAR

Movement: automatic-winding (ETA 2892); disc display system.
Functions: hours, minutes, seconds.
Case: stainless steel with black PVD coating; Ø 46mm; screw-in crown; red tinted sapphire crystal reinforced with a protective layer; water resistant to 10atm.
Dial: red radar screen; three concentric black discs: hours outside disc, minutes middle disc and seconds central disc.
Strap: black rubber.
Note: limited edition of 999 pieces.
Suggested price: $6,100
Also available: heavy-duty canvas strap.

AVIATION BR 03-92 BLUE CERAMIC

Movement: automatic-winding (ETA 2892).
Functions: hours, minutes, seconds; date between 4 and 5.
Case: matte blue ceramic; Ø 42mm; antireflective sapphire crystal; water resistant to 10atm.
Dial: black; numerals, markers and hands with photoluminescent coating to optimize nighttime reading.
Strap: blue rubber.
Suggested price: $4,500
Also available: heavy-duty canvas strap.

MARINE BR 02-92 CARBON PRO DIAL

Movement: automatic-winding (ETA 2892).
Functions: hours, minutes, seconds; date between 4 and 5; decompression valve for deep-sea diving.
Case: stainless steel with black PVD coating; Ø 44mm; unidirectional interior bezel graduated to 60 minutes with photoluminescent reference point; antireflective sapphire crystal; water resistant to 100atm.

Dial: black; large markers and hands with photoluminescent coating to optimize nighttime reading.
Strap: black heavy-duty canvas strap.
Suggested price: $4,000
Also available: black rubber strap.

MARINE BR 02-94 STEEL

Movement: automatic-winding (ETA 2894).
Functions: hours, minutes, seconds; date between 4 and 5; chronograph: 30-minute and 60-second counters; decompression valve for deep-sea diving.
Case: stainless steel; Ø 44mm; unidirectional interior bezel toothed and graduated to 60 minutes with photoluminescent reference point; screw-in pushpieces, crowns and caseback; antireflective sapphire crystal; water resistant to 50atm.

Dial: black; numerals, markers and hands with photoluminescent coating to optimize nighttime reading.
Strap: black rubber.
Suggested price: $5,400
Also available: black heavy-duty canvas strap.

MARINE BR 02-92 PHANTOM

Movement: automatic-winding (ETA 2892).
Functions: hours, minutes, seconds; date between 4 and 5; decompression valve for deep-sea diving.
Case: stainless steel with black PVD coating; Ø 44mm; unidirectional interior bezel graduated to 60 minutes with photoluminescent reference point; screw-in crowns; antireflective sapphire crystal; water resistant to 100atm.

Dial: black with Clou de Paris pattern; numerals, markers and hands with photoluminescent coating to optimize nighttime reading.
Strap: black rubber.
Suggested price: $4,000
Also available: black heavy-duty canvas strap.

MARINE BR 02-92 STEEL WITH CARBON FIBER DIAL

Movement: automatic-winding (ETA 2892).
Functions: hours, minutes, seconds; date between 4 and 5; decompression valve for deep-sea diving.
Case: stainless steel; Ø 44mm; unidirectional interior bezel graduated to 60 minutes with photoluminescent reference point; screw-in crowns; antireflective sapphire crystal; water resistant to 100atm.

Dial: black with carbon fiber; numerals, markers and hands with photoluminescent coating to optimize nighttime reading.
Strap: black rubber.
Suggested price: $3,500
Also available: black heavy-duty canvas strap.

AVIATION BR 01 TOURBILLON PINK GOLD

Movement: manual-winding BR 01 tourbillon; 120-hour power reserve; carbon fiber mainplates and black-gold tourbillon carriage.
Functions: small hours at 12; central minutes; trust index at 3; power reserve indicator at 9.
Case: satin-polished 18K pink gold; Ø 46mm; screw-in crown; antireflective sapphire crystal; water resistant to 10atm.
Dial: black with carbon fiber; numerals, markers and hands with photoluminescent coating to optimize nighttime reading.
Strap: black rubber.
Note: limited edition of 20 pieces.
Suggested price: $170,000
Also available: black alligator strap.

AVIATION BR 01 TOURBILLON

Movement: manual-winding BR 01 tourbillon; 120-hour power reserve; carbon fiber mainplates and black-gold tourbillon carriage.
Functions: small hours at 12; central minutes; trust index at 3; power reserve indicator at 9.
Case: glass-bead-blasted titanium with virtually unscratchable DLC coating (4,000 Vickers); Ø 46mm; screw-in crown; antireflective sapphire crystal; water resistant to 10atm.
Dial: black carbon fiber; numerals, markers and hands with photoluminescent coating to optimize nighttime reading.
Strap: black rubber.
Note: limited edition of 60 pieces.
Suggested price: $140,000
Also available: black alligator strap.

AVIATION BR 01 TOURBILLON PHANTOM

Movement: manual-winding BR 01 tourbillon; 120-hour power reserve; carbon fiber mainplates and black-gold tourbillon carriage.
Functions: small hours at 12; central minutes; trust index at 3; power reserve indicator at 9.
Case: glass-bead-blasted titanium with virtually unscratchable DLC coating (4,000 Vickers); Ø 46mm; screw-in crown; antireflective sapphire crystal; water resistant to 10atm.
Dial: black with carbon fiber; numerals, markers and hands with photoluminescent coating to optimize nighttime reading.
Strap: black rubber.
Note: limited edition of 18 pieces.
Suggested price: $150,000
Also available: black alligator strap.

AVIATION BR 01 TOURBILLON AIRBORNE

Movement: manual-winding BR 01 tourbillon; 5-day power reserve; carbon fiber plates and bridges; black-gold tourbillon carriage.
Functions: tourbillon; trust index; regulator; power reserve indicator.
Case: titanium with DLC coating; Ø 46mm; titanium screw-in crown; antireflective sapphire crystal; water resistant to 10atm.
Dial: three-dimensional; black photoluminescent coating with mesh-like design.
Strap: black shagreen.
Note: limited edition of 20 pieces.
Suggested price: $150,000

IB
1735
BLANCPAIN

INNOVATION IS A WAY OF LIFE

Drawing from its own horological heritage for a rich source of inspiration, Blancpain remains decisively committed to a pioneering path.

Through a combination of optimal performance, accuracy and stunning finishes, Blancpain once again affirms the legitimacy of the brand's revered status in haute horology. The automatic 4225G caliber boasts a flying tourbillon and a dual-disc large date display, while the finely decorated seven-day power reserve is integrated into the oscillating weight on the back of the movement.

With the creation of its limited edition Villeret Running Equation of Time, the Swiss pioneer reinvents one of the most prestigious timekeeping complications. The equation of time function addresses the variances in the length of a day that result from the 23º irregularity in the earth's orbit. The Villeret Running Equation boasts a secondary blue "running" hand that displays the discrepancy instantly and clearly. Blancpain's innovative complication requires the extraordinary sophistication of the incorporated ellipsoidal cam. In order for the solar hand to be driven in parallel to the civil hand (by the minute-hand gear train) and partially guided by a cam that adds or subtracts the appropriate time, the movement requires two sources of rotation for the secondary hand alone, achieved through an entire differential mechanism made up of free-moving satellite gears that operate in both directions without interfering with the movement of the minute-hand train.

Featuring two equation of time indicators and a porthole into the complexities of the solar system, as well as a perpetual calendar that is smoothly assimilated into the white grand feu enameled cambered dial, this astonishing self-winding timepiece is presented in two exclusive versions in red gold or platinum. With a declaration of time's intricate bond to astronomy, the Villeret Running Equation of Time propels the spirit of the perpetual calendar to a spectacular height of innovation.

VILLERET RUNNING EQUATION OF TIME

Along with its dual equation of time displays, ellipsoidal cam, and perpetual calendar complete with moonphase indication, this limited edition timepiece features a finely decorated gold winding rotor.

TRIBUTE TO FIFTY FATHOMS AQUA LUNG

This diver's watch boasts a water resistance of 300m, or slightly more than 164 fathoms.

Complementing Blancpain's conquest of the planetary orbits, the Tribute to Fifty Fathoms Aqua Lung is a contemporary revival of a timepiece that, in 1953, became the archetype of diver's watches. Originally water resistant to a depth of 50 fathoms (91.45m), the Fifty Fathoms was created to outfit the elite combat diver, upon the request of the French Ministry of Defense. Unable to find an existing watch that could withstand the extreme conditions of underwater missions, Captain Bob Maloubier and Lieutenant Claude Riffaud took their demanding standards to Blancpain. Armed with a revolutionary unidirectional bezel, sturdy construction, and excellent reliability, the Fifty Fathoms gained a celebrated reputation among international Special Forces. Beyond the military field, this trailblazing timepiece became the watch of choice for oceanic explorers of the highest caliber, even chosen to accompany the crew of legendary Jacques Cousteau and Louis Malle for their filming of the classic documentary *The Silent World*. Now resistant to depths of 300m, the automatic-winding Tribute to Fifty Fathoms Aqua Lung displays hours, minutes, seconds, and date on an inspiring black dial, surrounded by the unidirectional rotating bezel that brought its predecessor to fame. Housed within a 45mm brushed-steel case, this elegant take on a Blancpain milestone is powered by the 227-component 1315 caliber with 35 jewels and a 120-hour power reserve.

Whether through its ingenious mastery of the celestial concept, or its revitalization of a legendary heritage, Blancpain never fails to express the relentless spirit of innovation that led the Swiss manufacture to produce 18 new outstanding mechanical movements in just a six-year span.

VILLERET 8 DAY HALF-TIMEZONE — REF. 6661-3631-55B

Movement: automatic-winding 5235DF caliber; Ø 30.2mm, thickness: 7.75mm; 192-hour power reserve; 324 components; 36 jewels.
Functions: hours, minutes; date at 6; day/night indication.
Case: 18K red gold; Ø 42mm, thickness: 13.65mm; sapphire crystal caseback; water resistant to 3atm.
Dial: white Grand Feu enamel.
Strap: brown alligator leather.
Price: available upon request.
Also available: white gold with black leather strap (ref. 6661-1531-55B).

VILLERET RUNNING EQUATION — REF. 6638-3431-55B

Movement: automatic-winding 3863 caliber; Ø 26.8mm, thickness: 5.25mm; 72-hour power reserve; 397 components; 39 jewels.
Functions: hours, minutes; small seconds; perpetual calendar: day at 9, date at 3 and month at 12; retrograde moonphase.
Case: platinum; Ø 42mm, thickness: 11.5mm; under-lug correctors; sapphire crystal caseback; water resistant to 3atm.
Dial: white Grand Feu enamel.
Strap: black alligator leather.
Price: available upon request.
Note: limited edition of 88 pieces.
Also available: red gold with brown leather strap (ref. 6638-3631-55B).

VILLERET CHRONOGRAPHE MONOPOUSSOIR — REF. 6685-3642-55B

Movement: automatic-winding 66CM8 caliber; Ø 32mm, thickness: 7.5mm; 40-hour power reserve; 450 components; 35 jewels.
Functions: hours, minutes; central date hand; day and month at 12; single-pusher chronograph: 12-hour counter at 9, 30-minute counter at 3 and central seconds hand; moonphase.
Case: red gold; Ø 40mm, thickness: 12.98mm; sapphire crystal caseback; water resistant to 3atm.
Dial: stamped opaline.
Strap: brown alligator leather.
Price: available upon request.
Also available: steel with white dial and black strap (ref. 6685-1127-55B).

VILLERET 8 DAY COMPLETE CALENDAR — REF. 6639-3437-55B

Movement: automatic-winding 6639 caliber; Ø 32mm, thickness: 7.6mm; 192-hour power reserve; 325 components; 36 jewels.
Functions: hours, minutes; central date hand; day and month at 12; moonphase.
Case: platinum; Ø 42mm, thickness: 13.07mm; sapphire crystal caseback; water resistant to 3atm.
Dial: black Grand Feu enamel.
Strap: black alligator leather.
Price: available upon request.
Note: limited edition of 88 pieces.
Also available: red gold with black dial and brown leather strap (ref. 6639-3637-55B).

L-EVOLUTION, ONE-MINUTE FLYING SAPPHIRE CARROUSEL REF. 00222-1500-53B

Movement: manual-winding 22T caliber; Ø 33.5mm, thickness: 6.01mm; 120-hour power reserve; 209 components; 43 jewels; sapphire movement; nanotechnology-inspired finish on the upper bridge.
Functions: hour, minutes; tourbillon.
Case: tantalum; Ø 43.5mm, thickness: 13.5mm; white-gold lugs; sapphire crystal caseback; water resistant to 3atm.
Dial: sapphire.
Strap: black alligator leather.
Price: available upon request.
Note: limited edition of 50 pieces.

L-EVOLUTION FLYBACK CHRONOGRAPH REF. 560STC-11B30-52B

Movement: automatic-winding F185 caliber; Ø 26.2mm, thickness: 5.5mm; 40-hour power reserve; 308 components; 37 jewels.
Functions: hours, minutes; small seconds at 6; date at 12; flyback chronograph: 12-hour counter at 9, 30-minute counter at 3 and central seconds hand.
Case: brushed steel; Ø 43.5mm, thickness: 12.8mm; sapphire crystal caseback; water resistant to 10atm.
Dial: black.
Strap: black crocostrap; folding clasp.
Price: available upon request.
Note: limited edition of 275 pieces.

L-EVOLUTION TOURBILLON LARGE DATE REF. 8822-15B30-53B

Movement: automatic-winding 4225G caliber; Ø 27.6mm, thickness: 8.68mm; 168-hour power reserve; 414 components; 46 jewels.
Functions: hours, minutes; date at 6; tourbillon; power reserve indicator on the oscillating weight.
Case: satin-brushed white gold; Ø 43.5mm, thickness: 14.9mm; sapphire crystal caseback; water resistant to 3atm.
Dial: black.
Strap: black alligator leather.
Price: available upon request.
Also available: satin-brushed rose-gold with brown alligator leather strap (ref. 8822-36B30-53B).

TRIBUTE TO FIFTY FATHOMS AQUA LUNG REF. 5015C-1130-52B

Movement: automatic-winding 1315 caliber; Ø 30.6mm, thickness: 5.65mm; 120-hour power reserve; 227 components; 35 jewels.
Functions: hours, minutes, seconds; date at 3.
Case: brushed steel; Ø 45mm, thickness: 15.4mm; unidirectional rotating bezel; sapphire crystal caseback; water resistant to 3atm.
Dial: black.
Strap: black crocostrap; folding clasp.
Price: available upon request.
Note: limited edition of 500 pieces.

Breguet
Depuis 1775

A LEGEND AT WORK

With the simple push of an exquisite crown, Breguet turns haute horology into an affair of instant teleportation.

The Classique Hora Mundi's extraordinary instant-jump time zone display allows the wearer to traverse the globe faster than he can dream of a faraway horizon. A world-first in mechanical watchmaking, the timepiece's 77F0 self-winding caliber, with silicon escapement and balance wheel, possesses an innovative synchronized module that, upon the pre-selection of two cities from the 24-time zone list at 6 o'clock, allows for a single push of the crown at 8 o'clock to instantly, and simultaneously, switch all of the time coordinates from one city to the next. An ingenious revolution of the dual time zone concept, the Hora Mundi's instant-jump system, with reprogrammable mechanical memory wheel, synchronizes every component of the calendar, from the central Breguet hands, to the date at 12 o'clock and the solid-gold hand-engraved day/night indicator at 4 o'clock. The dragging date disc—exposing three consecutive days with the current digit surrounded by a retrograde circle—in conjunction with the gliding seconds hand, expresses the fluid continuity of the passing of one day to the next. In a unique design twist, Breguet offers the choice of three continental dial centers, each intricately crafted with a rose engine to achieve a remarkable wave motif atop the oceanic backdrop.

CLASSIQUE HORA MUNDI

Along with a choice of case in 18-karat red gold or 950 platinum, this unprecedented instant-jump dual time zone wristwatch offers three available continental dials: the Americas, the European and African continents, or Asia and Oceania.

CRAZY FLOWER

The imaginative and perfectly executed mobile mounting of 116 baguette-cut diamonds allows the dazzling bezel to flow freely with the movement of the wrist.

The High Jewelry collection's Crazy Flower cannot help but take its admirer back to the house's late 18th-century Parisian beginnings, where founder Abraham-Louis Breguet fascinated the eccentric royal couple with the exuberant excellence of his mechanical timepieces. Applying the house's daring character to the setting of spectacular diamonds, Breguet creates a shimmering ballet of petals undulating in the wind. Acting as a floral bezel, 116 mobile baguette-cut diamonds gracefully dance to the movement of the wrist that they adorn. Individually numbered and signed Breguet, the Crazy Flower's curved concave dial features eye-catching blue hands and is immaculately paved with 206 inverted and 20 baguette-cut diamonds. Extending its technical mastery to the heart of the 18-karat white-gold case, Breguet powers this triumphant mobile gem-setting masterpiece with the automatic-winding 586 caliber, ensuring that each ripple of the sparkling petals is met by a worthy mechanical oscillation.

If diamonds are the eternal symbol of beauty, haute horology finds its badge in the majestic form of the tourbillon. With the Marine Tourbillon High Jewelry Chronograph, Breguet marries the two emblems in a timepiece that boldly honors the manufacture's own revolutionary 1801 invention. Through an aperture at 12 o'clock, the part-titanium tourbillon carriage with running seconds joins the chronograph's central hand and two totalizers at 3 and 6 o'clock, to form the complementary modules of the watch's 18-karat silvered-gold dial.

Hand-engraved with a rose engine and bejeweled with 132 diamonds, the watch face features applied blue Roman numerals that play off the signature color of the brand's rotating indicators. Further accentuating the tourbillon's luxurious surroundings, the bezel, case middle, lugs, pushbuttons and crown are set with 186 baguette-cut diamonds.

Armed with a legendary heritage and an incessant drive to revolutionize, Breguet unveils three timepieces that deliver astounding excellence, from their inventive conceptions all the way to the luxurious nobility of their design.

MARINE TOURBILLON HIGH JEWELRY CHRONOGRAPH

This exceptional blend of the finest technical finesse and elegant setting of the most brilliant diamonds is powered by the hand-wound 554.4 mechanical movement with silicon escapement and balance spring.

CLASSIQUE HORA MUNDI — REF. 5717BR

Movement: automatic-winding Breguet 77F0 caliber; 55-hour power reserve; 12 lines; 43 jewels; 4Hz frequency; Breguet balance wheel with regulating screws; 18K gold oscillating weight; hand-guilloché; flat balance spring; silicon Swiss straight-line lever escapement; adjusted in six positions.
Functions: hours, minutes, seconds; instant time zone jump with synchronized date, day/night and city indication; moonphase between 3 and 4.

Case: 950 platinum; Ø 44mm; screw-down crown at 3; rounded lugs; pushbutton at 8; sapphire crystal caseback; water resistant to 3atm.
Dial: 18K white gold; wave motif beneath a translucent lacquer; applied chapter ring with Roman numerals; open-tipped blued steel Breguet hands; individually numbered and signed Breguet.
Strap: black alligator leather.
Price: available upon request.
Also available: European or Asian dials; 18K red gold with Asian, American or European dials.

CLASSIQUE 7337 — REF. 7337BR

Movement: automatic-winding 502.3 QSE1 caliber; 45-hour power reserve; 12 lines; 35 jewels; 3Hz frequency; Breguet balance wheel; 18K gold oscillating weight; hand-guilloché; individually numbered and signed Breguet; adjusted in six positions.
Functions: off-centered hours and minutes at 6; small seconds at 5; date at 2; day of the week at 10; age and moonphase at 12.
Case: 18K red gold; Ø 39mm; rounded lugs; sapphire crystal caseback; water resistant to 3atm.

Dial: silvered 18K gold; chapter ring with Roman numerals; guilloché cross-weave basket pattern; open-tipped blued steel Breguet hands; individually numbered and signed Breguet.
Strap: brown alligator leather.
Price: available upon request.
Also available: 18K yellow gold (ref. 7337BA/1E/9V6); 18K white gold (ref. 7337BB/1E/9V6).

CLASSIQUE MOON PHASES — REF. 7787BR

Movement: automatic-winding Breguet 591 DRL caliber; 38-hour power reserve; 11½ lines; 25 jewels; 4Hz frequency; Breguet balance wheel with four adjusting screws; 18K gold oscillating weight; hand-guilloché; flat balance spring; silicon Swiss straight-line lever escapement; adjusted in six positions.
Functions: hours, minutes, seconds; power reserve indicator between 5 and 6; moonphase at 12.

Case: 18K red gold; Ø 39mm; rounded lugs; sapphire crystal caseback; water resistant to 3atm.
Dial: silvered 18K gold; applied chapter ring with Roman numerals; open-tipped blued steel Breguet hands; individually numbered and signed Breguet.
Strap: brown alligator leather.
Price: available upon request.
Also available: 18K white-gold with guilloché dial (ref. 7787BB/12/9V6); 18K red-gold with Grand Feu enamel dial (ref. 7787BR/29/9V6); 18K red-gold with bezel and lugs set with diamonds and Grand Feu enamel dial (ref. 7788BR/29/9V6 DD00).

CLASSIQUE 5177 — REF. 5177BR

Movement: automatic-winding 777Q caliber; 55-hour power reserve; 12 lines; 26 jewels; 4Hz frequency; Breguet balance wheel with four regulating screws; 18K oscillating weight; hand-guilloché; flat balance spring; silicon Swiss straight-line lever escapement; adorned with Côtes de Genève; numbered and signed Breguet; adjusted in six positions.
Functions: hours, minutes, seconds; date at 3.

Case: 18K red gold; Ø 38mm; rounded lugs; sapphire crystal caseback; water resistant to 3atm.
Dial: 18K gold; chapter ring with Roman numerals; open-tipped blued steel Breguet hands; individually numbered and signed Breguet.
Strap: brown alligator leather.
Price: available upon request.
Also available: yellow and white gold dials; grand feu enamel dial (ref. 5177BR/29/9V6).

MARINE TOURBILLON CHRONOGRAPH — REF. 5837PT

Movement: manual-winding 554.4 caliber; 50-hour power reserve; 12 lines; 28 jewels; 3Hz frequency; silicon balance spring and escape-wheel and lever; Breguet balance wheel; individually numbered and signed Breguet; adjusted in six positions.
Functions: hours, minutes; small seconds on the tourbillon at 12; chronograph: 12-hour counter at 6, 30-minute counter at 3 and central seconds hand.
Case: platinum 950; Ø 42mm; sapphire crystal caseback; water resistant to 3atm.
Dial: silvered platinum-coated gold; chapter ring with Roman numerals; hour markers with luminescent coating; open-tipped blued steel Breguet hands with luminescent tips; individually numbered and signed Breguet.
Strap: black rubber.
Price: available upon request.

MARINE LADIES' CHRONOGRAPH — REF. 8827BB

Movement: automatic-winding 550 caliber; 45-hour power reserve; 10½ lines; 47 jewels; 3Hz frequency; 18K gold rotor with hand-guilloché; Swiss straight-line lever escapement; flat balance spring; annular balance wheel; individually numbered and signed Breguet; adjusted in five positions.
Functions: hours, minutes; small seconds and date at 6; chronograph: 12-hour counter at 9, 30-minute counter at 3 and central seconds hand.
Case: 18K white gold; Ø 34.6mm; crown set with a cabochon-cut sapphire; wave-shaped chronograph pushbutton; sapphire crystal caseback; water resistant to 5atm.
Dial: natural mother-of-pearl; chapter ring with Breguet Arabic numerals; Breguet 18K gold hands with luminescent tips; individually numbered and signed Breguet.
Strap: white rubber; 18K gold Marine folding clasp with two gold loops.
Price: available upon request.
Also available: 18K red gold (ref. 8827BR/52/586).

TYPE XX I — REF. 3810TI

Movement: automatic-winding 584Q/1 caliber; 45-hour power reserve; 13¾ lines; 25 jewels; 4Hz frequency; Swiss straight-line lever escapement; flat balance spring; numbered and signed Breguet; adjusted in five positions.
Functions: hours, minutes; small seconds at 9; date at 6; flyback chronograph: 12-hour counter at 6, day/night indicator at 3 and central minute totalizer.
Case: titanium; Ø 42mm; black unidirectional rotating bezel in polished titanium with raised numerals; screw-down crown; rounded lugs; water resistant to 10atm.
Dial: matte black; chapter ring with Breguet Arabic numerals; hands and hour markers with luminescent coating; signed Breguet.
Strap: black calfskin leather.
Note: flyback function: pressing the lower button returns the chronograph to zero and restarts it immediately.
Price: available upon request.
Also available: titanium bracelet (ref. 3810TI/H2/TZ9).

REINE DE NAPLES — REF. 8918BR

Movement: automatic-winding 537/1 caliber; 40-hour power reserve; 8¾ lines; 20 jewels; 3Hz frequency; 18K gold oscillating weight; hand-guilloché; Swiss straight-line lever escapement; flat balance spring; annular balance wheel; numbered and signed Breguet; adjusted in five positions.
Functions: hours, minutes; small seconds at 6.
Case: 18K red gold; 36.5x28.45mm; bezel and flange set with 117 diamonds (0.99 carat); crown set with one diamond (0.26 carat); sapphire crystal caseback; water resistant to 3atm.
Dial: silvered 18K gold; natural white mother-of-pearl inserts; chapter ring with Breguet Arabic numerals; one pear-cut diamond (0.09 carat) at 6; open-tipped Breguet blued steel hands; individually numbered and signed Breguet.
Strap: natural black satin; folding clasp set with 26 diamonds (0.13 carat).
Price: available upon request.
Also available: 18K red gold chain bracelet (ref. 8918BR/58/J20 DOOO); 18K yellow gold (ref. 8918BA/58/864 DOOD); 18K white gold (ref. 8918BB/58/864 DOOD).

TITAN

This state-of-the-art watch-winding safe is on display in a prestigious boutique room in Geneva.

BUBEN&ZŌRWEG

HABITAT FOR HOROLOGY

Just as a fine mechanical wristwatch bridges the gap between timelessness and the precise measure of a moment, Buben & Zörweg sets the stage for that timepiece to astound at all phases of its existence.

With an exquisite level of craftsmanship that echoes the philosophies of sophisticated watchmaking, the masterful designer of watch winders presents solutions for the most distinguished horological collectors. Through advanced winding systems, gracious aesthetics, and safes with the highest protective standards, Buben & Zörweg lets connoisseurs enjoy the full splendor of their prized collections.

Weighing in at an imposing 1,430 pounds, the Titan takes the strongbox concept into the domain of elegant interior design. Fit for the world's most prestigious ambiences with its signature Buben & Zörweg clock, high-end German sound system with Bluetooth and MP3 docking station, and superb workmanship, this heavyweight of watch-winding exhibitors never forgets its primary purpose: security. Endowed with a proven technology in full compliance with the European VDS IV security standard, the Titan boasts the ability to be connected to a home's central alarm system. Once uncovered by pushing aside the extravagantly designed handle, the high-security compact lock's code pad grants entry into a formidable treasure chest of automatic-winding timepieces. A two-sided installation, equipped with an elaborate rotary mechanism, glides forward to reveal a total of 36 Time Mover units, systematically calibrated to wind the watch's mainspring by simulating the motions of a wrist. While a sleep mode is ingeniously integrated to avoid unnecessary wear caused by excessive winding, a state-of-the-art LED lighting system with fading technology sets a graceful atmosphere for the timekeeping stars to shine. With the utmost comprehension of the watch connoisseur's affection for life's finest pleasures, the Titan provides concealed shelves on its upper surface, which are optionally designed as a humidor with an electronic humidification system.

Prestigiously featured in the VIP room of an exclusive Genevan boutique, this masterpiece safe is as much a tasteful addition to a room's refined décor as it is the perfect functional companion to a sophisticated collector.

With its dynamic design crafted in splendid materials, the innovative Mirage demonstrates a brilliant balance of protection and permanent showcase. While 16 of the Mirage's 26 hand-crafted Time Mover units are contained within the secured German VDS I safe in the lower half of the interior, the remaining ten are subject to the viewer's constant admiration through an ingenious two-way mirror in the upper portion of the façade. As the Buben & Zörweg signature clock makes a symbolic and artistic statement as to the object's raison d'être, the intricacies of its visual appeal make it any room's centerpiece. The Mirage's supplementary drawers afford additional storage space for precious items, horological or otherwise, that belong in the company of the beloved collection. Once the owner's inspiration draws him to the timepiece of his choice, he can be sure that it has been optimally maintained and is ready to strut its stuff with full mechanical capacity.

MIRAGE

The Mirage offers its owner two sets of Time Mover units—16 within the German VDS I safe, and ten on display behind a two-way glass mirror.

PHANTOM

Discreet yet highly expressive, the Phantom allows its owner to wind and present his timepieces in any chosen environment—anywhere from a room's centerpiece to the proximity of a bedside table.

Whether elevated on its metallic stand to enhance the modern styling of a room, or intimately showcased on a luxurious desk or tabletop, the Phantom delivers a compact alternative to Buben & Zörweg's more imposing line of secured watch-winding models. Available with exteriors in warm macassar wood or carbon fiber, the Phantom provides Time Mover units for four or eight automatic timepieces. With the push of a button, the high-security lock separates the shell's two hemispheres and exposes the red leather interior within which the desired number of watches are precisely preserved and optimized. To ensure a vibrant exhibition, high-grade LED lighting with fading technology illuminates the enclosed prized collection. As with all Buben & Zörweg Time Mover units, the winders' rotational frequency and direction—left, right or alternating— are adjustable for customized performance.

Joining the Phantom as a winding coffer of reserved dimension, the Revolution merges the collector's passion for watchmaking with his enthusiasm for the stylish interior of luxury automobiles. Framed on a backdrop of the finest leather, the designer's Time Mover units provide a deluxe treatment for either eight or twelve chosen timepieces—or eight Time Mover units and the brand's signature clock. The innovative opening system, even when sealed by its German safety lock, offers an unobstructed visibility of the box's modern aluminum design accentuated by carbon inlays, while the ideal visual ambience, as expected, is enhanced by premier LED lighting.

Genuine works of art designed with exemplary craftsmanship, Buben & Zörweg's watch-winding strongboxes are ingenious answers to the sincere needs of passionate automatic timepiece collectors. Combining stringent security standards, innovative technology, and magnificent artistry, the brand provides a vast range of unique showcases as sophisticated as the precious collections that inhabit them.

REVOLUTION

Exuding a blend of Art Deco and refined craftsmanship, the Revolution is a watch-winding box of unconventional personality.

GRANDE SONNERIE
PERPETUAL CALENDAR

BVLGARI

EMBLEMS OF EXCELLENCE

From its creation in 1884 to the 21st century, Bulgari has had a passionate and long-lasting history with technologically advanced movements and daring style.

Bulgari timepiece creations have always been emblematic of their time, anticipating aesthetic trends. Contemporary and assertive, these horological creations combine sophisticated mechanical movements and unique design for both men's and women's collections. They form an essential part of one of today's most creative world-class luxury watch brands, and testify to Bulgari's powerful and innovative dynamics.

Bulgari has always had a passionate relationship with distinctive jewelry and watch creations for both women and men. This long-lasting history is as intense as ever, thanks to the House's enduring emblems.

For gentlemen, there is no doubt that the Octo collection appears to be the early 21st century's most evocative model. Neither traditional nor merely eccentric, its octagon shape combines a distinctive architecture with high-end manufacture movements offering a wide spectrum of complications, from relatively basic to ultra-sophisticated. From the stylish Endurer Chronosprint to the Grande Sonnerie Perpetual Calendar—one of the most complicated masterpieces of the last year—these uniquely refined creations are designed for the most demanding collectors and connoisseurs. They remain faithful to Bulgari's early engagement with the watch creation process: to offer original, distinctive and high-end masterpieces worthy of the House.

TOURBILLON SAPHIR

DIAGONO CALIBRO 303

Since the turn of the 20th century, Bulgari has distinguished itself with the quality and beauty of its jewelry and timepieces. Bulgari watches from the early days combined the formal purity of the Greco-Roman aesthetic with the peerless technique of the watchmakers chosen to craft these first custom-made creations. The 1960s and '70s saw the first production watches, with a character as unique as ever and a style conceived predominantly for women. Mechanical movements produced by the finest names in the field were combined with the richness of Bulgari jewelry to create timepieces celebrated for both the monocromatic play of the stones and their adherence to the highest standards of Haute Joallerie.

Over the next two decades, Bulgari confirmed its status as a serious watchmaker with the launch of several milestones. It demonstrated its vocation with the creation of a watch destined to become an icon: the Bulgari Bulgari, named for the double logo engraved on the perfectly cylindrical case. Launched in 1977, this model remains today one of the few 20th-century historical models still in production. The '90s confirmed Bulgari's status as an innovative watchmaker with new models and daring combinations of unusual materials such as aluminum and natural rubber—a stylistic evolution that further increased the unmistakable uniqueness of Bulgari watches and helped initiate a trend of unexpected materials within luxury watches. With the new millennium, Bulgari deployed its time-tested savoir-faire to consolidate its position in the field of fine watchmaking by integrating the production processes of the components, establishing an exceptionally qualified centralized manufacturing facility, where the attention devoted to every detail adds new value to a unique aesthetic. This process comes full circle with the I Calibri di Manifattura collection, where the marriage of mechanical excellence and Bulgari style gives rise to a new era.

OCTO GRANDE SONNERIE TOURBILLON

OCTO BI-RETRO STEEL CERAMIC

OCTO BI-RETRO REF. BGOP43BGLDBR

Movement: automatic-winding GG 7722 caliber; Ø 25.6mm, thickness: 5.53mm; 45-hour power reserve; 35 jewels; 28,800 vph; decorated with perlage finishing and specific antique gold finish.
Functions: jumping hours; retrograde minutes and date.
Case: 18K pink gold; Ø 43mm, thickness: 12.35mm; 18K pink-gold beaded crown with onyx cabochon; scratch-resistant antireflective double-sided sapphire crystal; 18K pink-gold satin-finished transparent caseback; water resistant to 10atm.
Dial: black lacquered, cloisonné and guilloché; faceted pink-gold-plated skeleton hour and minute hands.
Strap: black alligator; 18K pink-gold three-blades folding buckle.
Price: available upon request.

OCTO CHRONOGRAPH QUADRI-RETRO STEEL/CERAMIC REF. BGO45BSCLDCHQR

Movement: automatic-winding GG7800 caliber; 38-hour power reserve; 45 jewels; 21,600 vph; potter finishing and antique gold finish.
Functions: jumping hours; retrograde minutes and date; column-wheel chronograph: retrograde 12-hour counter at 9, 30-minute counter at 3 and central seconds hand.
Case: steel; Ø 45mm; ceramic bezel; ceramic cabochon on the crown; transparent sapphire crystal caseback; water resistant to 10atm.
Dial: cloisonné; protected by a scratch-resistant antireflective sapphire crystal.
Strap: alligator leather; triple-blade clasp with safety fastening.
Price: available upon request.

GEFICA HUNTER REF. BGF47BBLMPGMT

Movement: automatic-winding GG 1006 caliber; Ø 25.6mm, thickness: 5.98mm; 45-hour power reserve; 41 jewels; 28,800 vph; decorated with perlage finishing and specific antique gold finish.
Functions: jumping hours; retrograde minutes with central seconds; GMT at 7; moonphase at 4.
Case: sand-blasted bronze and brushed titanium; Ø 46.5mm, thickness: 19.65mm; bronze and titanium crown; domed scratch-resistant antireflective double-sided sapphire crystal; titanium satin-finished transparent caseback; water resistant to 10atm.
Dial: multi-layer concave, black lacquered and satiné; oversized and skeletonized minute hands.
Strap: black alligator; titanium three-blades folding buckle.
Price: available upon request.
Note: limited edition.

ENDURER CHRONOSPRINT ALL BLACKS SPECIAL EDITION REF. BRE56BSBVDCHS/AB

Movement: automatic-winding DR 1306 caliber; 45-hour power reserve; decorated with perlage, Côtes de Genève and chamfering finishing.
Functions: hours, minutes; small seconds at 6; big date at 12; chronosprint function.
Case: stainless steel with black DLC (Diamond Like Carbon) treatment; Ø 56mm; transparent caseback engraved with 1905 All Blacks® logo.
Dial: Maori tattoo pattern.
Strap: black rubber; stainless steel ardillon buckle with black DLC (Diamond like Carbon) treatment.
Price: available upon request.

GRANDE LUNE — REF. BRRP46C14GLDMP

Movement: manual-winding DR 2300 caliber; 40-hour power reserve; decorated with perlage, Côtes de Genève and chamfering finishing.
Functions: hours, minutes; three-armed small seconds at 9; date counter at 5; astronomical moonphase.
Case: 18K pink gold; Ø 46mm; transparent caseback.
Dial: multi-layered lacquer with satiné vertical treatment; hand-applied 18K pink-gold hour markers.
Strap: brown alligator; 18K pink-gold ardillon buckle.
Price: available upon request.

PAPILLON CHONOGRAPH — REF. BRRP46C14GLCHP

Movement: automatic-winding DR 2319 caliber; 38-hour power reserve; decorated with perlage, Côtes de Genève and chamfering finishing.
Functions: jumping hours; papillon minute system; column-wheel chronograph: 12-hour counter at 10, 30-minute counter at 1 and central seconds hand.
Case: 18K pink gold; Ø 46mm; transparent caseback.
Dial: multi-layered lacquer with satiné treatment.
Strap: brown alligator; 18K pink-gold folding buckle.
Price: available upon request.

TOURBILLON SAPHIR — REF. BGGW53GLTBSK

Movement: manual-winding GG 8000 caliber; 70-hour power reserve; sapphire bridges.
Functions: hours, minutes; tourbillon.
Case: 18K white gold; Ø 53mm; sapphire crystal case middle framed on either side by the bezel and back; transparent caseback; patented construction.
Dial: skeletonized sapphire crystal.
Strap: black alligator; 18K white-gold folding buckle.
Price: available upon request.

IL GIOCATORE VENEZIANO — REF. BRRP46GLGV/2

Movement: manual-winding DR 7300 caliber; 48-hour power reserve; decorated with Côtes de Genève and chamfering finishing.
Functions: dice player automaton; minute repeater; hours, minutes.
Case: 18K pink gold; Ø 46mm; five different animations; transparent caseback.
Dial: unique hand-painted 18K gold.
Strap: brown alligator; 18K pink-gold folding buckle.
Price: available upon request.

PATRAVI EVOTEC POWER RESERVE

This model's peripherally mounted rotor operates more efficiently while also revealing the movement.

PATRAVI EVOTEC BIG DATE

A patented Central Dual Adjustment System means that this watch's balances and escapements need to be adjusted only once.

The newly introduced Patravi EvoTec Power Reserve embodies the grandeur of Carl F. Bucherer's expansive vision. Armed with a variation on the aforementioned CFB A1000, this watch presents a distinguished power reserve indication. A scale shaped like the stage of an amphitheater provides the platform for a small red hand to trace a gentle curve beneath an opening in the dial. As the power runs down, the hand, which carries with it a white-coated rack, renders the red surface increasingly visible. The Patravi EvoTec Power Reserve thus creatively and elegantly upholds Carl F. Bucherer's standard for optimal legibility.

Another new release, the Patravi EvoTec Big Date, makes no compromise in the domain of mechanical and technical sophistication. The first-ever reliably functioning peripheral rotor offers an unimpeded view of the CFB A1003 caliber. Whereas central rotors cover half the movement at all times, the challenging development of an oscillating weight mounted on the periphery lets the wearer admire the precisely ticking microcosm through a sapphire crystal on his or her watch's caseback. As with the Patravi EvoTec Power Reserve, this watch features the innovative switching of the big date.

With Smart SimPlexity production methodology guiding the entire process of manufacture, Carl F. Bucherer is able to present these two watches as part of a collection that is sure to delight and fascinate with a marriage of advanced technology and aesthetic refinement.

PATRAVI EVOTEC BIG DATE — REF. 00.10628.03.77.01

Movement: automatic-winding CFB A1003 caliber; Ø 32mm, thickness: 6.3mm; 55-hour power reserve; 33 jewels; peripheral rotor; patented dynamic shock absorber (DSA); patented Central Dual Adjusting System (CDAS), which requires adjustment only once.
Functions: hour, minutes; small seconds at 6; date at 11.
Case: 18K rose gold; 38.54x39.25mm, thickness: 12.9mm; screw-down crown; antireflective sapphire crystal; water resistant to 5atm.

Dial: white mother-of-pearl; 5 FC TW VVS diamond hour markers; six polished 18K rose-gold hour markers.
Strap: black alligator leather; 18K rose-gold folding clasp.
Suggested price: $30,500
Also available: diamond-set bezel, brown water snakeskin strap with 18K rose-gold folding clasp ($37,900).

PATRAVI TRAVEL TEC GMT — REF. 00.10620.03.33.01

Movement: automatic-winding CFB 1901 caliber; Ø 28.6mm, thickness: 7.3mm; 42-hour power reserve; 39 jewels; COSC-certified chronograph.
Functions: hours, minutes; small seconds at 3; date between 4 and 5; chronograph: 12-hour counter at 6, 30-minute counter at 9 and central seconds hand; GMT; three time zones.
Case: 18K rose gold; Ø 46.6mm; screw-down crown; antireflective sapphire crystal; water resistant to 5atm.

Dial: black; nine polished 18K rose-gold hour markers.
Strap: black calfskin leather; 18K rose-gold folding clasp.
Suggested price: $44,000
Also available: stainless steel with calfskin strap and stainless steel folding clasp ($10,900); 18K rose gold on a bracelet ($63,500); various dial and strap combinations.

PATRAVI EVOTEC BIG DATE — REF. 00.10630.08.87.11

Movement: automatic-winding CFB A1003 caliber; Ø 38.5mm, thickness: 11.8mm; 55-hour power reserve; 33 jewels; peripheral rotor; patented dynamic shock absorber (DSA); patented Central Dual Adjusting System (CDAS), which requires adjustment only once.
Functions: hours, minutes; small seconds at 6; date at 11.
Case: stainless steel; Ø 38.5mm, thickness: 11.8mm; set with 64 FC TW VVS diamonds (1 carat); screw-down crown; antireflective sapphire crystal; water resistant to 5atm.

Dial: black Tahitian mother-of-pearl; five FC TW VVS diamond hour markers; seven polished stainless steel hour markers.
Strap: black alligator leather; stainless steel folding clasp.
Suggested price: $19,200
Also available: white dial with brown water snakeskin strap ($16,800); without diamond-set bezel and calfskin leather strap with stainless steel folding clasp ($9,500); 18K rose gold with various strap, dial and diamond combinations.

MANERO BIG DATE POWER — REF. 00.10905.18.13.21

Movement: automatic-winding CFB 1964 caliber; 42-hour power reserve.
Functions: hours, minutes, seconds; date at 12; power reserve indicator in an arc between 5 and 8.
Case: stainless steel; Ø 40mm; antireflective sapphire crystal.
Dial: silver; eleven polished stainless steel hour markers.
Bracelet: stainless steel.

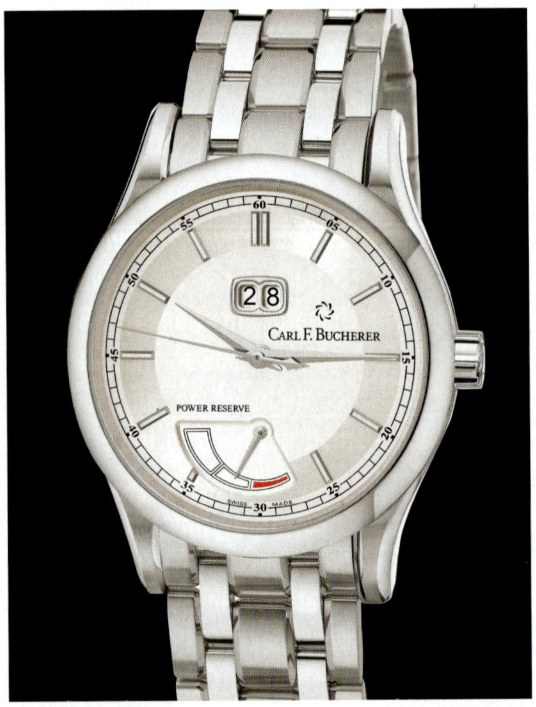

Suggested price: $6,400
Also available: alligator leather strap ($5,800); 18K rose-gold with alligator leather strap and 18K rose-gold folding clasp ($16,600); 18K rose-gold bracelet ($33,800); various strap and diamond combinations.

PATRAVI TRAVEL GRAPH REF. 00.10618.13.33.01

Movement: automatic-winding CFB 1901 caliber; Ø 28.6mm, thickness: 7.3mm; 42-hour power reserve; 39 jewels; bi-directional 24-hour bezel for a third time zone.
Functions: hours, minutes; small seconds at 3; date between 4 and 5; chronograph: 12-hour counter at 6, 30-minute counter at 9 and central seconds hand; GMT; second time zone.
Case: stainless steel; Ø 42mm; black rubber bezel; screw-down crown; antireflective sapphire crystal; water resistant to 5atm.
Dial: black; nine polished stainless steel hour markers.
Strap: black calfskin leather; stainless steel folding clasp.
Suggested price: $7,300
Also available: stainless steel bracelet ($7,900); various dial and strap color combinations.

PATRAVI CALENDAR REF. 00.10629.08.33.01

Movement: automatic-winding CFB A1004 caliber; Ø 32mm, thickness: 6.9mm; 55-hour power reserve; 33 jewels; peripheral rotor; patented dynamic shock absorber (DSA); patented Central Dual Adjusting System (CDAS), which requires adjustment only once.
Functions: hours, minutes; small seconds at 6; day at 9; date at 11; 53 calendar weeks dial indicator.
Case: stainless steel; Ø 42.6mm, thickness: 12.85mm; screw-down crown; antireflective sapphire crystal; water resistant to 5atm.
Dial: black; twelve polished stainless steel hour markers.
Strap: black calfskin leather; stainless steel folding clasp.
Suggested price: $10,900
Also available: 18K rose-gold with silver dial and brown calfskin strap with 18K rose-gold folding clasp ($33,900).

MANERO CHRONO PERPETUAL REF. 00.10906.03.13.01

Movement: automatic-winding CFB 1904 caliber; Ø 30mm, thickness: 7.6mm, 50-hour power reserve; 49 jewels.
Functions: hours, minutes; small seconds at 12; chronograph flyback: 12-hour counter at 6, 30-minute counter at 9 and central seconds hand; perpetual calendar: day, date, month, leap year; moonphase.
Case: 18K rose gold; Ø 42.5mm, thickness: 14.3mm; antireflective sapphire crystal; water resistant to 3atm.
Dial: silver; eight polished 18K rose-gold hour markers.
Strap: brown alligator leather; 18K rose-gold pin buckle.
Suggested price: $52,600
Also available: stainless steel case with alligator leather strap and stainless steel folding clasp ($33,000).

MANERO CENTRAL CHRONO REF. 00.10910.08.13.01

Movement: automatic-winding CFB 1967 caliber; Ø 30mm, thickness: 7.4mm; 42-hour power reserve; 47 jewels.
Functions: hours, minutes; small seconds at 3; date at 6; chronograph: 60-second counter and central minute counter; day/night indicator.
Case: stainless steel; Ø 42.5mm, thickness: 14.24mm; antireflective sapphire crystal; water resistant to 3atm.
Dial: silver; nine polished stainless steel hour markers.
Strap: brown alligator leather; stainless steel folding clasp.
Suggested price: $7,100
Also available: stainless steel case with black dial and black alligator leather strap with stainless steel folding clasp ($7,100).

A FEARLESS HEARTBEAT

With four additions to its Fine Watchmaking Collection, Cartier demonstrates a daring audacity that personifies the brand's extraordinary genius.

Offsetting the imposing diameter of the Calibre de Cartier Astrotourbillon's 47mm case, the extreme lightness of the titanium with which it is constructed is highly symbolic of the watch's most exceptional characteristic. Positioned above the movement, the elongated tourbillon carriage, whose reliance on a specific rotational axis required the redesigning of the entire gear train, orbits the dial's center, completing one full revolution of the watch face every minute. As it does so, the arrow-shaped off-centered balance bridge indicates the seconds against the watch's outermost ring. The hovering quality of the innovative regulator gives the Astrotourbillon a nearly weightless quality that exemplifies Cartier's unique vision of aesthetic functionality. Echoing the complication's harmony of power and intricate precision, the timepiece's case offers a tone of decisive masculinity, enhanced by the delicacy of its perfect finish, and the extra-large XII Roman numeral that dominates the chapter ring.

CALIBRE DE CARTIER ASTROTOURBILLON

The 9451 MC caliber that powers this limited edition timepiece steers the tourbillon carriage into a precise orbit around the dial's center.

CARTIER
45
40
35
30
SWISS MADE

Proving with expressive grace that the space between, is the space that tells the story, the Pasha de Cartier Skeleton Flying Tourbillon, honored with the exclusive Geneva Seal, takes its eponymous complication to a mesmerizing height. With the transparent 9457 MC movement's beveled bridges acting as smoothly integrated Arabic numerals, this entire timepiece boasts a liberated quality of suspension. As the blued-steel diamond-shaped hands revolve above the minimalist architecture of the 42mm white-gold case, the flying tourbillon at 6 o'clock reminds its owner of time's freedom. An uninhibited exhibition of mechanical savoir-faire and hand-finished craftsmanship, the Pasha de Cartier Skeleton Flying Tourbillon is a spectacular exposition of watchmaking purity... of time liberated from space.

Cartier further confirms its obsession with time-telling innovation at the service of functionality, in an world-time wristwatch that grants its owner complete control of the global scope of time. Whereas the Calibre de Cartier Multiple Time Zone's galvanic guilloché upper, exterior, dial identifies traveler time via black transferred Roman numerals, the lower, interior, scale, presents home time in combination with an easily identified day/night indicator on an Arabic numeral hemisphere. With the press of a pivoting pushbutton, the ingenious cities disc, visible in a lateral magnifier on the side of the watch, provides a clear reference to time in any of the 24 reference locations. Of course, the self-winding 9909 MC caliber was bound to feature a spectacular innovation. Offering extraordinary detail to the timepiece's owner, a brilliant aperture between 4 and 8 o'clock demonstrates the time difference between the two selected time zones, as if to grant the beholder entry into the mind of the movement.

PASHA DE CARTIER SKELETON FLYING TOURBILLON

Limited to 100 pieces, this skeletonized work of horological art oscillates of 21,600 vph.

CALIBRE DE CARTIER MULTIPLE TIME ZONE

Expressing two time zones, and conceptually enriched with a scale marking the time difference between them, the Calibre de Cartier Multiple Time Zone makes brilliant use of a limited space.

ROTONDE DE CARTIER ASTRORÉGULATEUR

Each of the 50 individually numbered limited units of this timepiece represent Cartier's bold passion for pushing the envelope.

As a definitive statement of the Parisian watchmaker's elite pioneering status, the Rotonde de Cartier Astrorégulateur ignores convention. While a tourbillon escapement averages out errors to cancel out variations caused by the effects of gravity on the movement's components, the Cartier Manufacture in La Chaux-de-Fonds has targeted the issue at its core. Since a single, stable, center of gravity is necessary to avoid the disturbing effects of the constant gravitational force, the house's master watchmakers have innovatively designed an anti-gravity system centered on the one element, the rotor, that continually returns to an identical place in the vertical plane. By positioning, in the 9800 MC self-winding Astrorégulateur movement, the escapement, oscillator and pendular seconds on the rotor, Cartier achieves a steady gravitational center that carries five times the number of components of a traditional tourbillon carriage. The 55mm niobium-titanium case draws the eye to the galvanic guilloché slate-gray dial that embraces the spectacular mechanical achievement. In a delightful play of color, the sword-shaped blued-steel hands redirect the inspiring hue of the crown's sapphire cabochon. Displaying seconds as a clever two-leveled module, the Rotonde de Cartier Astrorégulateur invites its owner's eyes on a fantastic voyage.

Having pushed the boundaries of horological innovation with the Fine Watchmaking Collection, Cartier takes the time to expand a line of understated wristwatches that exude the delicate refinement of the brand's characteristic elegance. Available in steel, with a bracelet of the same material, and a black or silvered dial, as well as in a gold and steel version with silvered dial, on a gold and steel bracelet, the 42mm Calibre de Cartier features hours, minutes, small seconds and date through an aperture at 9 o'clock. Powered by the manufacture's self-winding 1904-PS MC movement, this timepiece ruptures the splendidly crafted serenity of the dial with its trademark extra-large XII numeral. Handsome, powerful and decisively elegant, these three new variations of the Calibre de Cartier complete their performance with a sapphire crystal caseback that exhibits their mechanical heartbeat.

Accepting change is a testament to an open mind. Executing an innovative revolution is a badge of honor that belongs to the prodigies of each era. With its most recent masterpieces, Cartier leaves no doubt as to its raison d'être in haute horology.

CALIBRE DE CARTIER

The addition of a steel bracelet to this elegant line further accentuates its masculine appeal.

ROTONDE DE CARTIER ASTROREGULATOR REF. CRW1556211

Movement: automatic-winding 9800 MC caliber.
Functions: hours, minutes (with escapement fitted on the oscillating weight to counteract the effects of gravity in vertical positions); tourbillon.
Case: niobium titanium; Ø 50mm; circular-grained titanium crown, set with a sapphire cabochon; sapphire crystal; sapphire crystal caseback; water resistant to 3atm.
Dial: guilloché galvanic and slate-colored; silvered openwork grill with sunburst effect; black transferred Roman numerals; sword-shaped blued steel hands.
Strap: black alligator skin; double-adjustable 18K gold folding clasp.
Note: limited edition of 50 individually numbered pieces.
Suggested price: $485,700
Also available: white-gold bezel with baguette-cut diamonds (limited edition of 10 individually numbered pieces).

CALIBRE DE CARTIER GRANDE COMPLICATION SKELETON REF. CRW7100031

Movement: manual-winding 9436 MC caliber.
Functions: hours, minutes, seconds; day; date; month; power reserve indicator; tourbillon.
Case: platinum; water resistant to 3atm.
Dial: gold; azure-colored counters; gold flange sunburst motif; black transfer Arabic numerals.
Strap: black alligator skin.
Note: limited edition of 25 individually numbered pieces. Skeleton parts are hand-finished, all the bridges are chamfered and the C-bridge is polished to a mirror finish.
Suggested price: $522,500
Also available: white-gold case set with round diamonds, lunette set with baguette-cut diamonds on leather (limited edition of 5 individually numbered pieces).

CALIBRE DE CARTIER ASTROTOURBILLON REF. CRW7100028

Movement: manual-winding astrotourbillon 9451 MC caliber.
Functions: hours, minutes; tourbillon.
Case: titanium; Ø 47mm; heptagonal titanium crown, set with a faceted sapphire; sapphire crystal; sapphire crystal caseback; water resistant to 3atm.
Dial: guilloche; silver-colored upper and lower dial; Roman numerals sector displaying a satin-finish sunburst motif; black transfer Roman numerals.
Strap: black alligator skin; double-adjustable 18K white-gold folding clasp.
Suggested price: $129,000

PASHA DE CARTIER REF. CRW3030013

Movement: manual-winding 9438 MC caliber; 8-day power reserve.
Functions: hours, minutes; tourbillon; chronograph.
Case: 18K white gold; water resistant to 3atm.
Dial: guilloché galvanic, slate-colored; openwork silvered grid sunburst motif; black transfer numerals; arabic numeral 12.
Strap: black alligator skin.
Note: limited edition of 50 individually numbered pieces.
Suggested price: $195,500

CALIBRE DE CARTIER MULTIPLE TIME ZONE — REF. CRW7100025

Movement: automatic-winding 9909 MC caliber.
Functions: hours, minutes; multiple time zones; city name disc; day/night indicators; time difference indicator.
Case: 18K white gold; Ø 45mm; heptagonal 18K gold crown, set with a faceted sapphire; sapphire crystal; sapphire crystal caseback; water resistant to 3atm.
Dial: upper dial: galvanic guilloché, slate-gray color, silvered openwork grill with sunburst effect and black transferred Roman numeral; lower dial: silvered with black transferred Arabic numerals; sword-shaped blued steel hands; blued day/night and multiple time zone hands.
Strap: brown alligator skin strap; double-adjustable 18K gold folding clasp.
Note: individually numbered movement.
Suggested price: $56,000
Also available: 18K rose gold on brown alligator skin strap ($52,500).

CALIBRE DE CARTIER — REF. CRW7100040

Movement: automatic-winding 1904 MC caliber.
Functions: hours, minutes; small seconds at 6; date at 3.
Case: 18K rose gold; heptagonal crown set with sapphire crystal; water resistant to 3atm.
Dial: chocolate; outer rail-track minute circle with four luminescent dots; six pink transferred Roman numerals; XII and brown transferred hour markers; small seconds counter with sun-like satin finish; pink gilded and luminescent sword-shaped hands.
Bracelet: rose-gold.
Suggested price: $38,000
Also available: silvered, snailed opaline dial (same price).

BALLON BLEU EXTRA FLAT — REF. CRW6920059

Movement: manual-winding 430 MC caliber.
Functions: hours, minutes.
Case: 950/1000 platinum; water resistant to 3atm.
Dial: blue sun-like finish; twelve Roman numerals; rhodiumized steel sword-shaped hands.
Strap: blue alligator.
Note: limited edition of 99 individually numbered pieces.
Suggested price: $35,900
Also available: 18K white gold, 12 zones flinqué silvered dial ($24,000); 18K pink gold, 12 zones flinqué silvered dial ($22,500).

DELICES DE CARTIER (LARGE) — REF. CRW8100011

Movement: quartz 157.
Functions: hours, minutes.
Case: 18K rose gold; water resistant to 3atm.
Dial: silvered lacquered; flinqué external décor; twelve black Roman numerals; blued steel sword-shaped hands.
Strap: pinkish beige toile brossée (fabric).
Suggested price: $13,600
Also available: small model.

LE CIRQUE ANIMALIER DE CARTIER CALOPSITTE REF. CRHP100406

Movement: quartz 056.
Functions: hours, minutes.
Case: 18K rose gold; water resistant to 3atm.
Dial: 18K rose gold and white mother-of-pearl set with round diamonds; 18K rose-gold steel stained sword-shaped hands.
Strap: pinkish beige toile brossée (fabric).
Note: limited edition of 100 individually numbered pieces.
Suggested price: $180,000
Also available: 18K white gold, dragon decor with dark gray strap ($141,000); 18K white gold, turtle decor with beige strap ($180,000); gecko decor with light gray strap ($180,000).

SANTOS 100 MEDIUM MODEL REF. CRHP100411

Movement: automatic-winding 076 caliber.
Functions: hours, minutes.
Case: 18K rhodiumized white gold; water resistant to 10atm.
Dial: 18K white gold; hummingbird motif in champlevé enamel; mother-of-pearl marquetry; pink sapphires; 18K rhodiumized white-gold sword-shape hands.
Strap: white pearlescent alligator.
Note: limited edition of 50 individually numbered pieces.
Suggested price: $95,000

TOURBILLON AND CROCODILE WATCH FLYING TOURBILLON REF. CRHP100414

Movement: manual-winding 9458 MC caliber; Geneva Seal certified.
Functions: hours, minutes; flying tourbillon.
Case: 18K white gold; water resistant to 3atm.
Dial: 18K white gold; dark purple mother-of-pearl; 18K rhodiumized white-gold crocodile set with round diamonds; two emerald eyes; 18K white-gold lilies set with round diamonds and translucent red and green enamel; blued steel sword-shaped hands.
Strap: dark gray toile brosée.
Suggested price: $254,000

BALLON BLEU DE CARTIER REF. CRWE9004Z3

Movement: automatic-winding Cartier 076 caliber.
Functions: hours, minutes, seconds.
Case: medium model; 18K yellow gold; Ø 36.5mm; set with round diamonds (1.22 carats); 18K yellow-gold fluted crown set with a cabochon sapphire; water resistant to 3atm.
Bracelet: 18K yellow gold.
Price: available upon request.
Also available: 18K white gold; 18K rose gold; stainless steel; stainless steel and 18K yellow gold; on a strap; without diamonds in Ø 28mm and Ø 42mm.

BAIGNOIRE — REF. WB520005

Movement: manual-winding 430 caliber; Cartier workshop-crafted.
Functions: hours, minutes.
Case: large model; 18K rose gold set with round diamonds; 44x32mm; 18K rose-gold octagonal crown set with a diamond; sapphire crystal; water resistant to 3atm.
Dial: silvered opaline; guilloché and lacquered; 12 black Roman numerals; sword-shaped blued steel hands.
Strap: toile brossée; 18K rose-gold ardillon buckle.
Price: available upon request.
Also available: 18K yellow gold or 18K white gold; on a bracelet; in smaller size.

TORTUE PERPETUAL CALENDAR — REF. CRW1580045

Movement: automatic-winding 9422 MC caliber; Cartier workshop-crafted.
Functions: hours, minutes; perpetual calendar; retrograde day display; month and leap year in a counter at 12.
Case: 18K rose gold; 18K rose-gold octagonal crown set with faceted sapphire; mineral crystal; sapphire crystal caseback; water resistant to 3atm.
Dial: white silvered guilloché; black transfer Roman numerals; apple-shaped hour and minute hands.
Strap: brown alligator skin; 18K rose-gold double-adjustable deployant buckle.
Price: available upon request.

SANTOS-DUMONT SKELETON — REF. CRW2020052

Movement: manual-winding 9612 MC caliber; Cartier workshop-crafted.
Functions: hours, minutes; skeleton bridges in the shape of Roman numerals.
Case: titanium and black ADLC coating; blackened titanium crown; black faceted spinel; sapphire crystal; sapphire crystal caseback; water resistant to 3atm.
Dial: skeleton; rhodium-plated brass sword-shaped hands.
Strap: black alligator skin; 18K white-gold and ADLC coating.
Price: available upon request.
Also available: white gold.

PASHA DE CARTIER SKELETON FLYING TOURBILLON — REF. CRW3030021

Movement: manual-winding 9457 MC caliber; Cartier workshop-crafted; Geneva seal certified.
Functions: hours, minutes; flying tourbillon with display at seconds via C-shaped tourbillon carriage; skeleton bridge in shape of Arabic numerals.
Case: 18K white gold; Ø 42mm; 18K white-gold fluted crown with a sapphire cabochon; sapphire crystal; sapphire crystal caseback; water resistant to 3atm.
Dial: skeleton; blued-steel lozenge-shaped hands.
Strap: black alligator skin; 18K white-gold adjustable deployant buckle.
Note: individually numbered and limited to 100 pieces.
Price: available upon request.

CHANEL

AUDACITY AND EXPERTISE

Prestigious watchmaker and jeweler, CHANEL combines audacity with watchmaking expertise and mastery of high jewelry.

J12: THE WATCHMAKING ICON OF THE 21ST CENTURY

Gabrielle Chanel inverted the types and functions of her creations, transforming their meaning and value, creating cult objects from this art of counterpoint, such as the N°5 perfume and "2.55" bag. Inspired by the nautical world and born at the dawn of the third millennium, the J12 is another example of this and an icon of 21st-century watchmaking. Ahead of its time, this watch transformed ceramic into precious material, revolutionizing watchmaking codes and combining inalterable robustness with timeless CHANEL elegance.

The first "intense black" model was launched in 2000 and was followed by a white model in 2003. The J12 represents night and day, strength and elegance, mystery and clarity, masculinity and femininity. It has become a true mechanical talisman!

In 2011, CHANEL used a new material to invent a new color for the J12 Chromatic. This sensual and intense innovation was achieved by adding titanium to ceramic, producing its color and lightness. Its unique shine is then achieved by using a polishing process with diamond powder.

PREMIERE: THE ULTIMATE FEMININE TIMEPIECE

Getting straight to the essential is one of the keys to the code of CHANEL. It is not surprising that CHANEL's first watch, launched in 1987, was baptized "Première": it was both logical and fundamental to a new tradition. The shape of the Première reflects both a heritage and a message.

Its case evokes the characteristic geometry of Place Vendôme—a rectangle with cut-off corners—where the famous bronze column sits on the Parisian paving, indicating the passage of time like the hand of a sundial. A resemblance can also be found between the octagonal shape of the Première case and the shape of the bottle stopper Gabrielle Chanel chose for her N°5 perfume.

This silhouette, with its indescribable power of seduction, paired with gold or steel, diamonds or high-tech ceramic, pearls and interwoven leather, frees itself from the test of time without ever tarnishing its honor. The Première's feminine lines unite, in complete simplicity, CHANEL tradition and its eternally renewed inventiveness.

WATCHMAKING EXPERTISE

Switzerland's La Chaux-de-Fonds has 37,000 inhabitants, and the highest concentration of fine watchmakers and related activities worldwide. It was quite natural that CHANEL's watchmaking facility was set up in the town, the birthplace of Swiss watchmaking. From conception to the final assembly process, CHANEL teams conceive, design, shape, mold, polish, assemble and fit all watch parts, including some components of the mechanical movements housed in the famous J12 high-tech ceramic cases.

INNOVATION AT THE HEART OF TIMEKEEPING

Innovation is at the heart of everything CHANEL undertakes. The guiding principle of this innovation is always the same: swim against the tide, reverse the roles of the objects created, divert them from their normal functions to give them a hitherto unknown use. The same is true in the watch world.

CHANEL's first innovation was to transform ceramic into a precious material and thus overturn the codes of timekeeping. The second innovation, after the intense black of the first J12, was the introduction of a white watch, thus inaugurating a new trend. The third innovation was the creation, with the J12 Chromatic, of a totally new and unique color, once again transforming the art of ceramics. However, there is another innovation that may be less visible, but is certainly not any less striking—the use of ceramic in the actual watch functions.

CHANEL's first incursion into this new domain dates back to 2005 with the presentation of the J12 Tourbillon, whose movement plate was made in ceramic for the very first time. CHANEL's second venture of integrating ceramic into the heart of the mechanical movement is the J12 Calibre 3125. The Haute Horlogerie timepiece is equipped with the CHANEL-AP3125—a self-winding mechanical movement custom-made by Audemars Piguet exclusively for CHANEL—which pairs a rotor in black high-tech ceramic with a segment in rhodium-plated 22K yellow gold mounted on high-tech ceramic ball bearings.

With the successful results of its incursion into the land of Haute Horlogerie and its experience with the tourbillon, CHANEL decided to push even further into unusual watchmaking by proposing a mechanical complication that would be both innovative and original. This resulted in the J12 Rétrograde Mystérieuse, created and realized in collaboration with the manufacturer Renaud & Papi, a specialist in avant-garde movement development. As Giulio Papi explains from his vantage point as a master watchmaker, the key to CHANEL's watchmaking innovations is the crossroads of the case and the movement, where form, design, function, and motorization are interlinked, where the allure and the elegance of a design can find their most successful mechanical expression—or where the mechanical can find its perfect form.

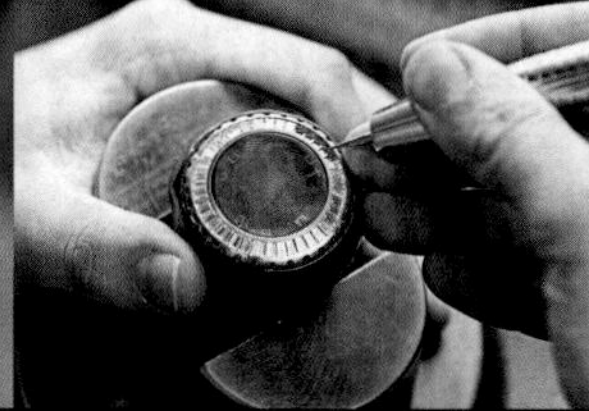

CHANEL invents a new color

The new J12 Chromatic is exemplary of the creative approach taken by CHANEL, one that favors, above all, research and innovation. The J12 Chromatic was born from CHANEL's desire to invent a color and give ceramic a tint that has never been seen before. This determination is at the heart of the brand's incessant quest to offer the greatest comfort possible to the wearer of the watch, to assure the timeless quality of the piece, and to give it a very special brilliance.

The choice of ceramic perfectly meets these criteria. From an ergonometric point of view, ceramic is a warm material that takes the temperature of the wrist. Its hardness gives it an exceptional longevity, protects it from scratches and dents, and maintains its particular brilliance. However, the ceramic developed specifically and exclusively for the J12 Chromatic possesses even greater qualities. Incorporating titanium, it is lighter and more resistant than traditional ceramic. Above all, it has a sparkle unlike anything else. The Chromatic color shimmers with a varying intensity and density according to the ambient light. Material, color, and sheen are inextricably linked. It passes from a stormy sky to a shimmering ocean, becoming a mirror or a reflection of the depths. The color is intense and changeable, vibrant and warm.

Success in obtaining such a unique color is certainly a question of time: four years for research and development, and two years for industrializing this timepiece. This does not even count the very special polishing techniques that had to be developed. It is also a question of paying very special attention to details. Specific galvanic treatments were thus developed to give the dial the tint that matches the Chromatic tones. The same careful considerations were given to the decoration of the dial, which features vertical brushing at the center, stamping around the edge, applied indexes and rhodium-plated hands. The bezel, made in titanium ceramic, bears a satin finish that contrasts with and accentuates the evocative power and subtlety of the J12 Chromatic's reflections.

Seven models have been designed for the launch of the J12 Chromatic: a 33mm version with a quartz movement; 38mm and 41mm versions with automatic mechanical movement; two versions set with round diamonds; and two models with baguette-cut diamonds set in a radial design. The latter diamond-set watches open new horizons as the sparkle of the diamonds mixed with the special brilliance of the titanium ceramic is unlike anything seen up to now.

J12 CHROMATIC

J12 RETROGRADE MYSTERIEUSE — REF. H2557

Movement: manual-winding CHANEL RMT-10 caliber; 10-day power reserve.
Functions: hours, minutes; tourbillon; retrograde minute hand.
Case: white high-tech ceramic and 18K white gold; Ø 47mm; twelve inserts on the bezel; retractable vertical crown; dual-face sapphire crystal and caseback with anti-reflective coating; water resistant to 3atm.
Dial: digital minute counter; perforated skeleton hands.
Bracelet: white high-tech ceramic; 18K white-gold triple-folding buckle.
Also available: black high-tech ceramic.
Note: unique piece.

J12 JEWELRY — REF. H2920

Movement: automatic-winding; 42-hour power reserve; COSC-certified chronograph.
Functions: hours, minutes; small seconds at 3; date; chronograph: 30-minute counter and central seconds hand.
Case: 18K white gold; Ø 41mm; set with 65 baguette-cut diamonds (7.12 carats); bezel set with 48 baguette-cut diamonds (4.85 carats); crown and pushbutton set with one brilliant-cut diamond (0.25 carat); water resistant to 5atm.
Dial: 18K white gold and black high-tech ceramic; set with 10 baguette-cut diamond indicators and 34 trapeze-cut diamond counters (1.76 carats).
Bracelet: 18K white gold and black high-tech ceramic set with 404 baguette-cut diamonds (20.3 carats); 18K white-gold triple-folding buckle.
Note: numbered and limited to 12 pieces.

J12 JEWELRY — REF. H2919

Movement: high-precision quartz.
Functions: hours, minutes.
Case: 18K white gold; Ø 29mm; set with 42 diamonds (0.34 carat); bezel set with 112 diamonds (1.18 carats); crown set with 12 diamonds; water resistant to 5atm.
Dial: 18K white gold and black high-tech ceramic; set with 126 diamonds and 12 black diamonds (0.83 carat).
Bracelet: 18K white gold set with 738 diamonds (9.55 carats); 18K white-gold triple-folding buckle.
Also available: Ø 33mm (high-precision quartz movement); Ø 38mm (automatic-winding movement).

PREMIERE JEWELRY — REF. H2437

Movement: high-precision quartz.
Functions: hours, minutes.
Case: 18K white gold; Ø 19.7mm; set with 52 diamonds (0.26 carat); water resistant to 3atm.
Dial: set with 113 diamonds (0.37 carat).
Bracelet: 18K white gold set with 404 diamonds (2.46 carats); 18K white-gold clasp.

J12 WHITE REF. H2572

Movement: high-precision quartz.
Functions: hours, minutes, seconds.
Case: white high-tech ceramic and steel; Ø 29mm; set with 40 diamonds (0.9 carat); screw-down crown; water resistant to 5atm.
Dial: mother-of-pearl; eight diamond hour markers; rhodium-plated hands and numerals.
Bracelet: white high-tech ceramic; steel triple-folding buckle; adjustable standard size.
Also available: black high-tech ceramic.

J12 WHITE REF. H2423

Movement: automatic-winding; 42-hour power reserve.
Functions: hours, minutes, seconds.
Case: white high-tech ceramic and steel; Ø 38mm; screw-down crown; water resistant to 20atm.
Dial: mother-of-pearl; eight diamond hour markers; rhodium-plated hands and numerals.
Bracelet: white high-tech ceramic; steel triple-folding buckle; adjustable standard size.
Also available: Ø 33mm (high-precision quartz movement).

J12 GMT REF. H3103

Movement: automatic-winding; 42-hour power reserve.
Functions: hours, minutes, seconds; date; GMT.
Case: white high-tech ceramic and steel; Ø 38mm; screw-down crown; water resistant to 5atm.
Dial: white lacquered; rhodium-plated hands and numerals; second time zone displayed on the 24-hour flange.
Bracelet: white high-tech ceramic; steel triple-folding buckle; adjustable standard size.
Also available: black and chromatic styles.

J12 WHITE REF. H2981

Movement: automatic-winding; 42-hour power reserve.
Functions: hours, minutes, seconds; date.
Case: white high-tech ceramic and steel; Ø 42mm; unidirectional rotating bezel; screw-down crown; water resistant to 20atm.
Dial: white lacquered; rhodium-plated hands and numerals.
Bracelet: white high-tech ceramic; steel triple-folding buckle; adjustable standard size.
Also available: black high-tech ceramic; Ø 33mm (high-precision quartz movement); Ø 38mm (automatic-winding movement).

J12 CHROMATIC REF. H2913

Movement: automatic-winding; 42-hour power reserve.
Functions: hours, minutes, seconds.
Case: titanium ceramic and 18K white gold; Ø 38mm; set with 34 baguette-cut diamonds (2.5 carats); brilliant-cut diamond crown (0.15 carat); titanium caseback; water resistant to 5atm.
Dial: vertical satin-finish center plate with coiled outer plate; twelve baguette-cut diamond hour markers (0.4 carat); mirror-polished rhodium-plated hands.
Bracelet: titanium ceramic; titanium triple-folding buckle; adjustable standard size.
Also available: Ø 33mm (high-precision quartz movement).

J12 CHROMATIC REF. H2566

Movement: automatic-winding; 42-hour power reserve.
Functions: hours, minutes, seconds.
Case: titanium ceramic and steel; Ø 38mm; set with 54 diamonds (1.4 carat); water resistant to 5atm.
Dial: vertical satin-finish center plate with coiled outer plate; eight diamond hour markers; mirror-polished rhodium-plated hands and numerals.
Bracelet: titanium ceramic; steel triple-folding buckle; adjustable standard size.
Also available: Ø 33mm (high-precision quartz movement).

J12 CHROMATIC REF. H3242

Movement: automatic-winding; 42-hour power reserve.
Functions: hours, minutes, seconds; date.
Case: titanium ceramic and steel; Ø 38mm; unidirectional rotating bezel; screw-down crown; water resistant to 20atm.
Dial: vertical satin-finish center plate with coiled outer plate; twelve diamond hour markers; mirror-polished rhodium-plated hands.
Bracelet: titanium ceramic; steel triple-folding buckle; adjustable standard size.
Also available: Ø 33mm (high-precision quartz movement).

J12 CHROMATIC REF. H2979

Movement: automatic-winding; 42-hour power reserve.
Functions: hours, minutes, seconds; date.
Case: titanium ceramic and steel; Ø 38mm; unidirectional rotating bezel; screw-down crown; water resistant to 20atm.
Dial: vertical satin-finish center plate with coiled outer plate; mirror-polished rhodium-plated hands and numerals.
Bracelet: titanium ceramic; steel triple-folding buckle; adjustable standard size.
Also available: Ø 33mm (high-precision quartz movement) and Ø 41mm (automatic-winding movement).

J12 CALIBRE 3125 REF. H2918

Movement: automatic-winding CHANEL AP 3125 caliber; 60-hour power reserve; black high-tech ceramic and 22K rhodium-plated yellow-gold rotor mounted on high-tech ceramic ball bearings.
Functions: hours, minutes, seconds; date.
Case: matte black high-tech ceramic and 18K yellow gold; Ø 42mm; unidirectional rotating bezel; screw-down crown; sapphire crystal and caseback; water resistant to 5atm.
Dial: black lacquered; 18K yellow-gold hands and numerals.
Bracelet: matte black high-tech ceramic; 18K yellow-gold triple-folding buckle; adjustable standard size.
Also available: black alligator strap.

J12 MARINE REF. H2559

Movement: automatic-winding; 42-hour power reserve.
Functions: hours, minutes, seconds; date; immersion-time indicator.
Case: matte black high-tech ceramic and steel; Ø 42mm; notched unidirectional rotating bezel equipped with a blue high-tech ceramic disc; screw-down crown; sapphire crystal with blue antireflective treatment on the interior and exterior; water resistant to 30atm.
Dial: black lacquered; hour markers, hands and the numeral 12 with luminescent coating.
Strap: matte black rubber; polished and satin-finished steel ardillon buckle.
Also available: black and white styles.

J12 GMT REF. H2012

Movement: automatic-winding; 42-hour power reserve.
Functions: hours, minutes, seconds; date; GMT.
Case: black high-tech ceramic and steel; Ø 42mm; second time zone displayed on the engraved 24-hour bezel; screw-down crown; water resistant to 10atm.
Dial: black lacquered.
Bracelet: black high-tech ceramic; steel triple-folding buckle; adjustable standard size.
Also available: white high-tech ceramic (limited edition).

J12 BLACK REF. H2980

Movement: automatic-winding; 42-hour power reserve.
Functions: hours, minutes, seconds; date.
Case: black high-tech ceramic and steel; Ø 42mm; unidirectional rotating bezel; screw-down crown; water resistant to 20atm.
Dial: black lacquered; rhodium-plated hands and numerals.
Bracelet: black high-tech ceramic; steel triple-folding buckle; adjustable standard size.
Also available: white high-tech ceramic; Ø 33mm (high-precision quartz movement); Ø 38mm (automatic-winding movement).

CHAUMET
PARIS

IMPERIAL TIMEKEEPING

This Parisian maison has upheld the highest standards of watchmaking since 1811—a legacy that began with just one man.

When Marie-Etienne Nitot, a former employee of Aubert (Marie Antoinette's jeweler) caught Napoleon Bonaparte's runaway horse by its bridle, the Emperor expressed his gratitude by appointing the brilliant Parisian as his official imperial jeweler, a gesture that would catapult Nitot straight into the heart of the Imperial Court.

Chaumet's founder became a notable player in Napoleon's ambition to transform France into the European center of creativity, luxury, and fashion. Though Chaumet's first watch appeared in 1811, Marie-Etienne Nitot had made his bejeweled mark on the court years before. In 1802, he produced the Consular sword, on which he mounted the Regent, a 140-carat diamond now on display in the Louvre. Two years later, he designed the jewels for both the Consecration of the Emperor and the Coronation of Empress Josephine. Nitot's adornment of Napoleon extended to that of the women in the Emperor's life, creating luxurious jewelry parures to symbolize the power and splendor of the Empire. In fact, Chaumet continues to honor its first muse, Empress Josephine, with a delicate and elegant collection named after her.

The first watch of Chaumet's luminous history was no less patrician, coming in the form of A Pair of Wristwatches ordered by Eugène de Beauharnais, Prince of Venice, for his wife Princess Augusta of Bavaria, Duchess of Leuchtenberg. This historical timepiece, created in collaboration with the inventor of contemporary watchmaking, Abraham-Louis Bréguet, marked its 200th anniverary in 2011. Two bracelets, one indicating the hours and minutes, the other indicating the date, are to be worn one on each wrist, as was the fashion of the early 19th century. Adorned with pearls and emeralds, the watches are crafted with a yellow-gold mounting whose floral arabesques conjure up an intimate French garden.

The two centuries that mark Chaumet's journey from Napoleon to the present have seen stunning changes in the world, with the jeweler as a common thread. In July 2011, 12 Place Vendôme opened its doors for a celebration of the manufacture's bicentennial. Thirty historical pieces, dating from the First Empire to the 1990s, were exhibited for the first time, mirrored by contemporary creations and accompanied by 300 original drawings unveiled in an exquisite cabinet. The presented pieces, created for the Imperial family, the Duchess de Luynes, President Adolphe Thiers, and many more historical figures, tell the watchmaking story of Chaumet.

In its journey through time, this French house has earned a reputation as an adaptable and trend-setting leader through the eras, mastering everything from Romanticism, to Naturalism, to Art Deco, and even harnessing the exoticism of the Orient. In a physical manifestation of this reputation, Chaumet's townhouse, famously located at 12 Place Vendome, is home to The Grand Salon, an official historic monument—where, it is worth noting, Frédéric Chopin composed and played his last Mazurka, Opus 68 No. 4.

Another continuing thread in Chaumet's journey is its emphasis on savoir-faire. This starts at the center and works its way out, permeating every aspect of the finished watch. Movements are created in collaboration between Chaumet and renowned horologers, continuing a tradition started by Etienne Nitot and Abraham-Louis Breguet and extended to the present day by Chaumet's work with contemporary watchmaking luminaries. Dials boast individualized touches while maintaining perfect readability. Cases blend precious metals in carefully considered shapes, adorned with beautiful finishings. Such expertise in all areas illustrates Chaumet's mission of jewelry savoir-faire dedicated to time. The House bestows upon artistic crafts such as engraving, enameling and stone setting with an obsessive attention to detail that endows each of its pieces with a unique value. This transforms each Chaumet watch into a masterpiece that combines time and art.

1811

Marking its bicentennial in 2011, the Pair of Wristwatches was conceived as a gift to Princess Augusta of Bavaria from her husband, Eugène de Beauharnais.

Chaumet's artistic legacy graces every watch from the House's collections, including the latest models, which perpetuate a proud history. The Attrape-moi... si tu m'aimes collection is as playful as it is stunning, evoking an amorous game of hide-and-seek between a bee and a spider. The bee, in addition to its beautiful detail and poetic charm, serves as a tribute to the Napoleonic emblem sewn on the Emperor's Coronation Robes.

The limited edition of the Attrape-moi LM watch includes just 12 models. The piece displays a black diamond-pavé spiderweb dial inside a diamond-pavé white-gold case. It is decorated with brilliant-cut diamonds, oval cabochon-cut amethyst and blue sapphire, round pink sapphire, blue topaz, and yellow sapphire, with sword-shaped hands and a white-gold bee stylus. A black satin strap with silver bee motif embroidery completes this sharp and passionate exclusive timepiece. The new Attrape-moi... si tu m'aimes unique timepiece creations, with their mother-of-pearl or champlevé enamel casebacks and their high jewelry diamond- and colored sapphire-set bezels and bracelets, perpetuate the House's long tradition of jewelry savoir-faire.

Continuing the theme, Chaumet presents the one-of-a-kind Bee my love watch in white gold and diamonds. This lean yet luxurious watch boasts a bezel set with sapphires. The sapphire crystal glass, curved with 2 angles, offers a magnifying effect, presenting a white mother-of-pearl dial with honeycomb motif set with four diamonds. The rhodium-plated 18-karat white-gold bracelet is set with 46 diamonds and 38 sapphires. With a total of 52 diamonds and 62 sapphires, this watch is a proud illustration of Chaumet's everlasting dedication to jewelry excellence and Parisian fashion through time.

ATTRAPE-MOI... SI TU M'AIMES

The limited edition Attrape-moi LM watch features a diamond pavé spiderweb dial.

BEE MY LOVE

This one-of-a-kind piece is set with a total of 52 diamonds and 62 sapphires.

The Dandy Arty Open Face is a perfect embodiment of Chaumet's attitude toward fashion and horology. Without a superfluous gesture, this stainless steel piece exudes masculine refinement. Hours and minutes tick away in an off-center subdial, an exposed section of the plate decorated with Côtes de Genève engraving, while a wheel-shaped seconds hand makes its revolution in an overlapping circle. Powered by the automatic CP 12V-V movement, the Dandy Arty Open Face offers complications developed by Chaumet in collaboration with the best of Swiss engineers, for those who are passionate about haute horology. A black patent calfskin strap features a stripe evoking the consummate evening outfit for stylish gentlemen: the tuxedo.

Of course, fashion is far from Chaumet's only inspiration. Named after the powerful planing monohull, Class One has been the epitome of the sporty chic style since 1998. In 2011, Chaumet introduced its new Class One Titane Deep collection with colored titanium. The titanium in the case, dial, and buckle is colored by an anodizing treatment. It is then immersed in an electrolysis bath, where a layer of oxide gradually forms. The shade thus develops as the voltage increases, allowing the intensity of the color to be controlled with the utmost precision.

Stronger, yet lighter, than steel, the Titane Deep offers a leap for watchmaking into the ergonomics of the aeronautical and aerospace universe. Both hypoallergenic and highly resistant to corrosion, particularly in water, this watch truly takes the diving watch concept deep into the 21st century. It is available in black, green, purple and Chaumet's signature blue and *lumière* shades. These five colors revive the essential, sophisticated spirit of Class One, giving it a whole new look of contemporary purity. The rubber straps offer the wearer a choice between white and colored for an utterly monochrome effect.

Though two centuries separate the Pair of wristwatches and the Class One Titane Deep, Chaumet's journey, as traced in its bicentennial exhibition, has always rested on the three pillars of jewelry watches, prestigious watchmaking partnerships and technical innovation, all of which were amply demonstrated at the House's bicentennial exhibition and live on in every Chaumet creation.

DANDY ARTY OPEN FACE

This series combines wit and elegance in an edition of just 200 pieces.

CLASS ONE TITANE DEEP

Superior ergonomics and innovatively colored titanium add new depth to the diving watch concept.

CLASS ONE HIGH JEWELLERY — REF. W17590-38J

Movement: automatic-winding; 42-hour power reserve; oscillating weight in white mother-of-pearl Class One pattern.
Functions: hours, minutes, seconds.
Case: rhodium-plated 18K white gold; Ø 39mm; fully paved with 118 caliber-cut white diamonds (12.69 carats); crown set with one rose-cut white diamond cabochon (0.18 carat); 150 brilliant-cut white diamonds (0.73 carat) set on the caseback side; curved sapphire crystal; rhodium-plated 18K white-gold skeleton caseback; water resistant to 3atm.

Dial: 18K white gold; fully paved with 120 caliber-cut white diamonds (4.94 carats); 18K white-gold hour and minute hands with SuperLumiNova; 18K white-gold seconds hand with round tip filled with SuperLumiNova.
Bracelet: rhodium-plated 18K white gold; fully paved with 656 caliber-cut white diamonds (33.62 carats).
Total carats: 52.162 carats (1045 diamonds).
Note: unique piece.
Price: available upon request.

CLASS ONE HIGH JEWELLERY — REF. W17181-38Y

Movement: automatic-winding; 42-hour power reserve; oscillating weight in white mother-of-pearl Class One pattern.
Functions: hours, minutes, seconds.
Case: rhodium-plated 18K white gold; Ø 39mm; fully paved with 108 caliber-cut and baguette-cut white diamonds (10.57 carats), 12 baguette-cut blue sapphires (2.04 carats) and 84 brilliant-cut blue sapphires (0.35 carat); crown set with one rose-cut blue sapphire cabochon (0.7 carat); 52 brilliant-cut white sapphires (0.48 carat) set on the caseback side; curved sapphire crystal; rhodium-plated 18K white-gold skeleton caseback; water resistant to 3atm.

Dial: 18K white gold; Damier pattern; fully paved with 60 caliber-cut diamonds (2.47 carats) and 60 caliber-cut blue sapphires (6.6 carats); 18K white-gold hour and minute hands with SuperLumiNova; 18K white-gold seconds hand with round tip filled with SuperLumiNova.
Strap: white vulcanized rubber; polished rhodium-plated 18K white gold double-folding buckle; fully paved with 26 baguette-cut white diamonds (1.04 carats) and 26 sapphires (3.64 carats).
Total carats: 27.89 carats (194 diamonds, 14.08 carats and 235 blue sapphires, 13.81 carats).
Note: unique piece; additional complimentary blue rubber strap.
Price: available upon request.

CLASS ONE TITANIUM DEEP BLACK — REF. W1722E-33M

Movement: quartz.
Functions: hours, minutes, seconds; date at 6.
Case: grade 2 black titanium; Ø 33mm; unidirectional turning bezel with diamond-set hour markers (36 brilliant-cut diamonds, 0.24 carat); grade 2 black titanium, fluted, double-security screw-in crown; antireflective curved sapphire crystal; grade 2 black titanium caseback engraved with Class One pattern; water resistant to 10atm.

Dial: grade 2 black titanium; 11 diamond hour markers (13 brilliant-cut diamonds, 0.05 carat); applied rhodium-plated Arabic numeral 12 with SuperLumiNova; date window at 6; rhodium-plated hour and minute hands with SuperLumiNova; rhodium-plated seconds hand with round tip filled with SuperLumiNova.
Strap: white vulcanized rubber; stainless steel double-folding buckle with safety pushbuttons and grade 2 black titanium cover.
Note: additional complimentary black vulcanized rubber strap.
Price: available upon request.
Also available: lumière (ref. W1722E-33N); blue (ref. W1722E-33W); purple (ref. W1722E-33Q); green (ref. W1722E-33S).

CLASS ONE WHITE & BLACK — REF. W17224-33E

Movement: quartz.
Functions: hours, minutes, seconds; date at 6.
Case: polished stainless steel; Ø 33mm; white and black lacquered unidirectional turning bezel with five diamond-set hour markers (15 brilliant-cut diamonds, 0.1 carat); polished steel fluted crown; antireflective curved sapphire crystal; screw-down polished caseback engraved with Class One pattern; water resistant to 10atm.

Dial: matte white lacquer with Class One pattern embossed; 11 diamond hour markers (13 brilliant-cut diamonds, 0.05 carat); applied rhodium-plated Arabic numeral 12 with SuperLumiNova; date window at 6; black-plated hour and minute hands with SuperLumiNova; black-plated seconds hand with round tip filled with SuperLumiNova.
Strap: white vulcanized rubber; polished stainless steel double-folding buckle with safety pushbuttons.
Price: available upon request.

CLASS ONE TITANIUM DEEP BLUE — REF. W1722D-33W

Movement: quartz.
Functions: hours, minutes, seconds; date at 6.
Case: grade 2 blue titanium; Ø 33mm; unidirectional turning bezel with embossed graduation of Arabic numerals and markers; grade 2 blue titanium, fluted, double-security screw-down crown; antireflective curved sapphire crystal; grade 2 blue titanium caseback engraved with Class One pattern; water resistant to 10atm.
Dial: grade 2 blue titanium; 11 diamond hour markers (13 brilliant-cut diamonds, 0.05 carat); applied rhodium-plated Arabic numeral 12 with SuperLumiNova; date window at 6; rhodium-plated hour and minute hands with SuperLumiNova; rhodium-plated seconds hand with round tip filled with SuperLumiNova.
Strap: white vulcanized rubber; stainless steel double-folding buckle with safety pushbuttons and grade 2 blue titanium cover.
Note: additional complimentary blue vulcanized rubber strap.
Price: available upon request.
Also available: lumière (ref. W1722D-33N); black (ref. W1722D-33M); purple (ref. W1722D-33Q); green (ref. W1722D-33S).

CLASS ONE LUMIERE — REF. W17222-33C

Movement: quartz.
Functions: hours, minutes, seconds; date at 6.
Case: polished stainless steel; Ø 33mm; circular fine-brushed unidirectional turning bezel with black lacquered embossed hour markers; polished fluted crown; antireflective curved sapphire crystal; screw-down polished caseback engraved with Class One pattern; water resistant to 10atm.
Dial: marron glacé sunray with Class One pattern embossed; applied rhodium-plated Arabic numeral 12 and hour markers with SuperLumiNova; date window at 6; rhodium-plated hour and minute hands with SuperLumiNova; rhodium-plated seconds hand with round tip filled with SuperLumiNova.
Strap: marron glacé vulcanized rubber; polished stainless steel double-folding buckle with safety pushbuttons.
Price: available upon request.
Also available: Ø 39mm, automatic-winding movement, stainless steel case with brown lacquered unidirectional rotating bezel and brown rubber strap (ref. W17282-38C).

KHESIS CRYSTAL LADY — REF. W19611-34B

Movement: quartz.
Functions: hours, minutes.
Case: polished stainless steel; 14mm (width); polished crown with lumière star crystal cabochon; antireflective curved sapphire crystal; polished caseback; water resistant to 3 atm.
Dial: lumière sunray opaline; 16 brilliant-cut diamond markers (0.06 carat); rhodium-plated hour and minute hands.
Bracelet: polished stainless steel and lumière star crystal; stainless steel double-folding buckle.
Price: available upon request.
Also available: stainless steel and pearl star crystal with white mother-of-pearl dial set with 16 diamonds (ref. W19610-34A); diamond-pavé rhodium-plated 18K white-gold with white natural mother-of-pearl dial set with 16 diamonds (ref. W19612-34A).

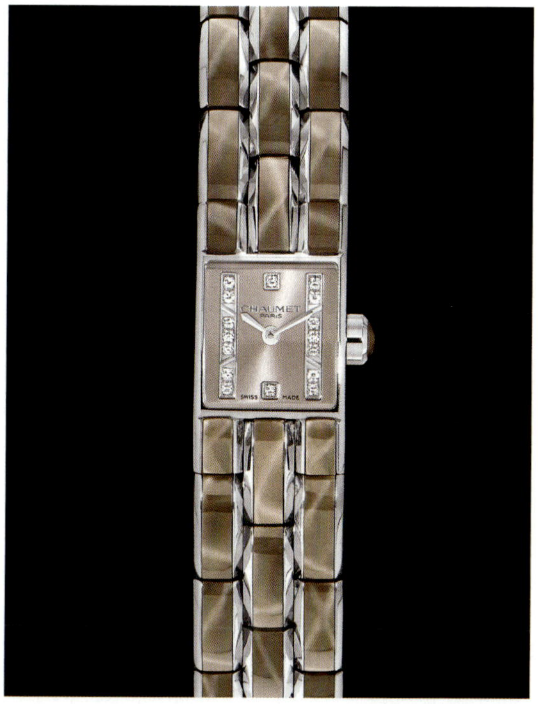

KHESIS CRYSTAL CUFF — REF. W19632-35A

Movement: quartz.
Functions: hours, minutes.
Case: polished stainless steel and blue star crystal; 23mm (width); polished stainless steel crown with blue star crystal cabochon; antireflective curved sapphire crystal; polished caseback; water resistant to 3atm.
Dial: white natural mother-of-pearl; 16 brilliant-cut diamond markers (0.11 carat); rhodium-plated hour and minute hands.
Bracelet: polished stainless steel and blue star crystal; stainless steel double-folding buckle.
Price: available upon request.
Also available: stainless steel and pearl star crystal with white mother-of-pearl dial set with 16 diamonds (ref. W19630-35A); diamond-set stainless steel and lumière star crystal with lumière sunray opaline dial set with 16 diamonds (ref. W19631-35B).

ATTRAPE-MOI… SI TU M'AIMES — REF. W16080-23R

Movement: automatic-winding; 42-hour power reserve; 20 jewels; 28,800 vph.
Functions: hours, minutes.
Case: polished 18K yellow gold; Ø 35mm; bezel and horns set with 102 brilliant-cut diamonds (3.19 carats); 18K yellow-gold hexagonal crown set with a brilliant-cut diamond (0.4 carat); curved sapphire crystal; 18K yellow-gold skeleton caseback; water resistant to 3atm.

Dial: 18K yellow gold; sunray with gold printed honeycomb motif; 18K yellow-gold bees with polished gold wings and each set with one diamond (head) and one citrine (body); 3 honeycomb-shaped diamond markers at 6, 9 and 12 (total of 6 brilliant-cut diamonds, 0.07 carat and 3 citrines, 0.21 carat; 18K yellow-gold leaf-shaped hour and minute hands.
Strap: honey gold lizard; 18K yellow-gold pin buckle set with 63 brilliant-cut diamonds (0.21 carat).
Price: available upon request.
Also available: 18K pink-gold case with 18K pink-gold dial and red lizard strap (ref. W16880-23P); 18K white-gold case with white mother-of-pearl dial and pink lizard strap (ref. W16183-23M).

ATTRAPE-MOI… SI TU M'AIMES — REF. W16187-36K

Movement: automatic-winding; 42-hour power reserve; 20 jewels; 28,800 vph.
Functions: hours, minutes.
Case: polished rhodium-plated 18K white gold; Ø 35mm; bezel and horns set with 102 brilliant-cut diamonds (3.19 carats); 18K white-gold hexagonal crown set with a brilliant-cut diamond (0.056 carat); curved sapphire crystal; rhodium-plated 18K white-gold skeleton caseback; water resistant to 3atm.

Dial: Grand Feu enamel; blue and green rainbow pattern on a 18K white-gold base; 18K white-gold bee with diamond-set wings and opal cabochon body; 4 honeycomb-shaped diamond markers at 3, 6, 9, and 12 (total of 32 brilliant-cut diamonds, 0.19 carat); rhodium-plated 18K white-gold leaf-shaped hour and minute hands.
Strap: dark blue satin with bee embroidery; light green calfskin leather lining; 18K white-gold pin buckle set with 63 brilliant-cut diamonds (0.21 carat).
Note: unique piece.
Price: available upon request.
Also available: in 35 other unique declinations of gold, enamel dials and colors; such as: 18K yellow-gold case with yellow and orange enamel dial and satin strap (ref. W16081-36B); 18K pink-gold case with red, pink and orange enamel dial and dark orange satin strap (ref. W16883-36H).

JOSEPHINE — REF. W13127-23E

Movement: quartz.
Functions: hours, minutes.
Case: polished rhodium-plated 18K white gold; 39x17.5mm; set with 50 brilliant-cut diamonds (0.68 carat) on the case and 38 brilliant-cut diamonds (0.24 carat) on the links; curved sapphire crystal; water resistant to 3atm.
Dial: white mother-of-pearl on an 18K white-gold base; three drop-shaped markers, one set with two diamonds (0.005 carat) at 6; rhodium-plated 18K white-gold hour and minute hands.

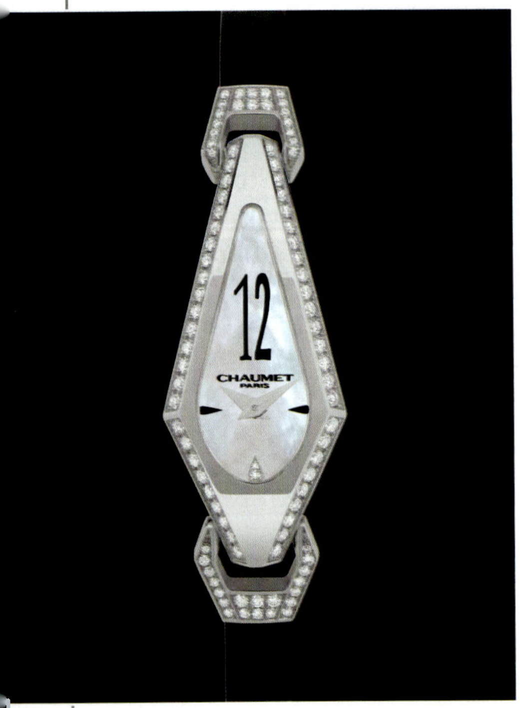

Strap: black satin; polished rhodium-plated 18K white-gold pin buckle set with 32 brilliant-cut diamonds (0.12 carat).
Note: includes rhodium-plated 18K white-gold specific drop-shaped stylus to adjust time.
Price: available upon request.
Also available: 18K pink-gold case with white mother-of-pearl dial and black satin strap (ref. W13820-23F).

BEE MY LOVE — REF. W16002-46A

Movement: quartz.
Functions: hours, minutes.
Case: 18K yellow gold; Ø 19.5mm; case sides engraved with honeycomb pattern; bezel and links set with 4 yellow diamonds (0.92 carat), 2 orange sapphires (0.4 carat) and 32 white diamonds (1.01 carats); sapphire crystal; water resistant to 3atm.
Dial: 18K yellow gold; gold-printed honeycomb motif with 4 honeycomb hour markers set with diamonds (0.03 carat); 18K yellow-gold hour and minute hands.

Strap: black satin; polished 18K yellow-gold pin buckle set with 13 diamonds (0.017 carat).
Total carats: 1.06 carats (49 diamonds) and 1.32 carats (6 yellow and orange sapphires).
Note: includes 18K yellow-gold specific bee motif stylus to adjust time.
Price: available upon request.
Also available: 18K white-gold case set with 59 white diamonds (2.06 carats) or 55 diamonds (1.52 carats), 2 red spinels (0.35 carat) and 2 pink sapphires (0.37 carat) and white natural mother-of-pearl dial (ref. W16101-46A or W16103-46A).

DANDY METRONOMIC — REF. W1118C-25M

Movement: manual-winding CP 12V-VI caliber with Metronomic Seconds; 32-hour power reserve; 17 jewels.
Functions: off-centered hours, minutes; Metronomic small seconds at 6.
Case: polished rhodium-plated 18K white gold; Ø 38mm; 18K white-gold crown set with one onyx cabochon; antireflective curved sapphire crystal; polished rhodium-plated 18K white-gold caseback with a sapphire crystal opening showing the wheel of Metronomic Seconds; water resistant to 3atm.
Dial: black and ivory lacquer; applied hour markers; metronome-shaped opening of small seconds counter showing lyre-shaped openwork wheel; faceted, rhodium-plated hour and minute hands; blue-plated cushion-shaped seconds hand.
Strap: black calfskin patent leather with ivory leather bayadère stripe; black leather lining; polished rhodium-plated 18K white-gold pin buckle.
Note: limited numbered edition of 100 pieces; additional complimentary black alligator skin strap with 18K white-gold pin buckle.
Price: available upon request.

DANDY ARTY OPEN FACE — REF. W18892-40B

Movement: automatic-winding CP12V-V caliber; 42-hour power reserve; 21 jewels.
Functions: off-centered hours, minutes; small seconds at 3.
Case: polished 18K pink gold; Ø 40mm; polished 18K pink-gold crown at 12 set with one onyx cabochon; black metallized antireflective curved sapphire crystal with black metallized vertical bayadère stripes; polished 18K pink-gold sapphire crystal caseback with Dandy pattern metallization; water resistant to 5atm.
Dial: no dial; visible ruthenium dark gray plate of the movement with Côtes de Genève guilloché and black bridges; engraved golden marker and Arabic numeral 12; 18K pink-gold-plated off-centered hour, minute and wheel-shaped seconds hands.
Strap: black calfskin patent leather with charcoal gray satin bayadère stripe and black leather lining; polished 18K pink-gold double-folding buckle with safety pushbuttons.
Note: limited numbered edition of 100 pieces; additional complimentary black alligator leather strap with black leather lining.
Price: available upon request.
Also available: limited numbered edition of 200 stainless steel cases with rhodium-plated movement plate and blue-plated hands, on black calfskin patent leather strap with blue satin bayadère stripe (ref. W18291-40B).

DANDY GRANDE DATE — REF. W11680-47C

Movement: automatic-winding CP 12V-VII caliber; 42-hour power reserve; 21 jewels; 28,800 vph.
Functions: hours, minutes; small seconds at 6; large date at 12.
Case: polished stainless steel; Ø 39mm; polished crown set with one midnight blue lacquered cabochon; antireflective curved sapphire crystal; screw-down polished caseback engraved with Dandy pattern; water resistant to 5atm.
Dial: midnight blue sunray lacquer; engraved vertical bayadère stripes; azuré small seconds counter; applied rhodium-plated hour markers; black printed minute track; rhodium-plated hour and minute hands with SuperLumi-Nova; rhodium-plated small seconds hand; applied rhodium-plated double date window frame.
Bracelet: polished stainless steel; polished double-folding buckle with safety pushbuttons.
Price: available upon request.
Also available: stainless steel case with black dial and black leather strap (ref. W11283-47A); stainless steel case with brown dial and brown leather strap with blue stitching (ref. W11283-47B).

DANDY VINTAGE CHRONOGRAPH XL — REF. W11790-30V

Movement: automatic-winding chronograph; 42-hour power reserve; 33 jewels; 28,800 vph.
Functions: hours, minutes; small seconds at 3; chronograph: 30-minute counter at 9 and central seconds hand.
Case: polished stainless steel; Ø 40mm; polished 18K pink-gold crown and pushbuttons; antireflective curved sapphire crystal; polished stainless steel caseback engraved with Dandy pattern; water resistant to 5atm.
Dial: white silvered sunray opaline; engraved vertical bayadère stripes; applied 18K pink-gold-plated hour markers; black printed minute track with SuperLumiNova markers; azuré counters circled with applied cushion-shaped frames; 18K pink-gold-plated hour and minute hands with SuperLumiNova; 18K pink-gold-plated small seconds counter hand; black chronograph counter minute and central seconds hands.
Strap: vintage charcoal gray semi-matte alligator with light gray double stitching; interchangeable without tool; polished stainless steel double-folding buckle with safety pushbuttons.
Price: available upon request.

CHRISTOPHE CLARET

A CURTAIN FALLS

Driven by the conviction that in watchmaking, everything has already been done, and everything has yet to be invented, Christophe Claret continues to explore uncharted territory.

For years, the manufacture, perched above the town of Le Locle, has established itself as a benchmark in the field of grand complication calibers by providing movements for the world's most prestigious watchmakers. It isn't until recently, however, that the house stepped from behind the curtain and allowed the public to finally discover the industry's most privileged secret.

As part of its Innovation Line, Christophe Claret's limited edition DualTow NightEagle brilliantly upholds the brand's commitment to suggesting original ways of reading the time. Its extremely sophisticated face appears to fade into the background to reveal the extraordinary mechanism below. Two vertical belt-type columns echo the aesthetics of a lunar module and serve to display the hours and minutes, as they slide beneath a subtle aperture in the face.

The avant-garde character of this display is brilliantly contrasted with a three-part central pillar that exhibits the house's evident respect for horological tradition. The very center of the watch features a chronograph wheel, upon which the seconds hand rotates traditionally. Christophe Claret has ingeniously placed, directly above it, a column wheel with adjoining 12-hour and 60-minute counters, and beneath it, a breathtaking tourbillon that brings together the entire design of the watch. Christophe Claret further demonstrates the brand's comprehensive range of skills with a gong that resonates each time the single-pusher planetary-gear chronograph is activated.

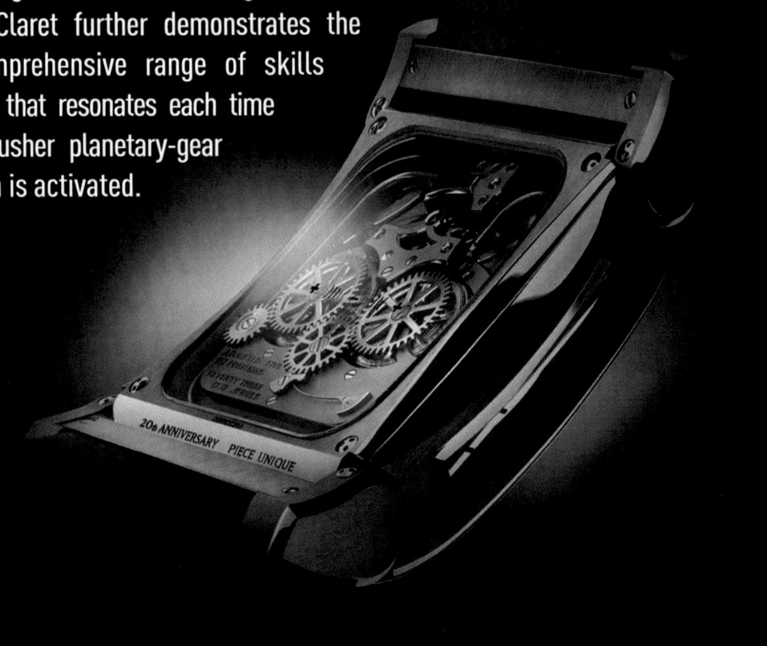

DUALTOW NIGHTEAGLE

This innovative masterpiece draws upon the finest traditions of watchmaking and heavy-machine engineering, as it re-invents the reading of time.

Joining the DualTow NightEagle in Christophe Claret's Innovation Line, the 21 Blackjack applies the mechanical precision of fine Swiss watchmaking to an authentic miniature casino, thus presenting a new interactive paradigm. By adding the sensory effects of blackjack, roulette and dice to a timepiece, Christophe Claret propels the owner of this watch into a new dimension.

The 1.5mm dice, visible through a side window, are housed within a cage at 4 o'clock and offer perfect legibility despite their discreet size. The blackjack feature uses the entirety of the dial as its virtual casino felt. While the upper part of the face contains three windows to show the dealer's cards, the lower half displays the player's own set of apertures. A pusher at 9 o'clock activates a spring that immediately triggers the seven discs on which the cards are printed, before they are randomly stopped by extremely accurate jumper-springs. Adding an audible quality to the interactive authenticity of the game, a hammer, whose mechanism is visible through a side window at 2 o'clock, strikes the cathedral gong each time a shutter is opened. Leaving no space unutilized, the oscillating weight, on the back of the watch, acts as a roulette wheel that is viewed through a glare-proof sapphire crystal.

Christophe Claret's Tradition Line completes a collection that began with ultra-confidential commissioned timepieces for private collectors. Its newest limited edition member, the Adagio, continues this heritage of classical timepieces that pay due respect to the rich history of haute horology. The 455-component SLB88 caliber, entirely developed internally, drives the central hour and minute hands, as well as the small seconds at 9 o'clock, which are presented in two versions—as a subdial or through an aperture. The dial of this distinguished timepiece is completed with a patented large date display at 6 o'clock and secondary time zone at 2 o'clock and is available in three stunning variations that exhibit the brand's masterful level of craftsmanship.

The cathedral gong minute repeater of the Adagio, a renowned specialty of the manufacture, is a nod to Christophe Claret's first creation, conceived more than two decades ago. Armed with a patented device that protects the components from knocking into each other, this mechanism delightfully strikes the hours, quarter-hours, and minutes at the wearer's request.

With three spectacular displays of technique, creativity and commanding character, Christophe Claret takes center stage and lets the public in on a superb secret of haute horology.

21 BLACKJACK

An ingenious use of space and mechanism, the interactive 21 Blackjack turns time into the wearer's own game of chance.

ADAGIO

Available in a series of case, dial, and display variations, the Adagio is a tribute to tradition with a touch of refined modernity.

DUALTOW REF. MTR.CC20A.002

Movement: manual-winding CC20A caliber; 60-hour power reserve; 568 components; 65 jewels; 21,600 vph; eight ball bearings; twin barrels placed in parallel; one-minute tourbillon.
Functions: hours, minutes; single-pusher planetary-gear chronograph with mechanical striking mechanism sounding a cathedral gong for each change of function (start, stop, reset); tourbillon; power reserve display and operating mode indicator of the chronograph.

Case: white gold; rectangular and curved; 42.75x48.2mm, thickness: 15.85mm; crown fitted with locking device; flange features five second indexes for chronograph indications hand-cut from five different stones.
Dial: hour and minute display on belt; chronograph counters: 12 hours, 60 minutes and 60 seconds.
Strap: crocodile leather; triple-blade folding clasp; 10mm wrist extension.
Note: the DualTow model is a limited edition by movement and will feature only 68 unique and personalized configurations in all.
Suggested price: $515,000
Also available: pink gold and black PVD-coated titanium ($515,000); platinum ($567,000); leather strap with a rubber pattern and texture.

DUALTOW - NIGHTEAGLE REF. MTR.CC20A.009

Movement: manual-winding CC20A caliber; 60-hour power reserve; 574 components; 65 jewels; 21,600 vph; eight ball bearings; twin barrels placed in parallel; one-minute tourbillon.
Functions: hours, minutes; small seconds on the tourbillon at 6; single-pusher planetary-gear chronograph with mechanical striking mechanism sounding a cathedral gong for each change of function (start, stop, reset); tourbillon; power reserve display and operating mode indicator of the chronograph. **Case:** black PVD-coated titanium; rectangular and curved; 42.75x48.2mm, thickness: 15.85mm; crown fitted with locking device; flange features five second indexes for chronograph indication in ceramic.

Dial: composed of three tinted sapphire crystals: the first serves as a bridge for the chronograph counters and is engraved with Christophe Claret, the second acts as a central bridge and carries the Swiss Made engraving, the third is the tourbillon bridge which is plated with the small seconds markings; hour and minute display on belt; chronograph counters: 12 hours, 60 minutes and 60 seconds.
Strap: leather with a rubber pattern and texture; triple-blade folding clasp; 10mm wrist extension.
Note: the DualTow model is a limited edition by movement and will feature only 68 unique and personalized configurations in all.
Suggested price: $567,000

ADAGIO REF. MTR.SLB88.107-807

Movement: manual-winding SLB88 caliber; 48-hour power reserve; 455 components; 46 jewels; 18,000 vph.
Functions: hours, minutes; hour, quarter-hour, minute repeater featuring cathedral gongs; large date; GMT with day/night indicator.
Case: rose gold; Ø 44mm; crown fitted with locking device.
Dial: black onyx.

Strap: crocodile leather.
Note: each dial is a limited edition of eight pieces.
Suggested price: $298,500
Also available: white gold ($282,000); platinum ($334,000); dial available in lapis lazuli, ruby, jade, opal, silver and black rhodium-plated gold and hand-guilloché.

ADAGIO REF. MTR.SLB88.119-819

Movement: manual-winding SLB88 caliber; 48-hour power reserve; 455 components; 46 jewels; 18,000 vph.
Functions: hours, minutes; hour, quarter-hour, minute repeater featuring cathedral gongs; large date; GMT with day/night indicator.
Case: white gold; Ø 44mm; crown fitted with locking device.
Dial: silver and black rhodium-plated gold.

Strap: crocodile leather.
Note: each dial is a limited edition of eight pieces.
Suggested price: $298,500
Also available: rose gold ($282,000); platinum ($334,000); dial available in lapis lazuli, ruby, jade, opal, black onyx and hand-guilloché.

21 BLACKJACK — REF. MTR.BLJ08.000-021

Movement: automatic-winding BLJ08 caliber; 72-hour power reserve; 501 components; 40 jewels; 28,800 vph; seven double ceramic ball-bearings; twin barrels.
Functions: hours, minutes; three games: blackjack with striking mechanism, roulette and dice.
Case: white gold and grade-5 black PVD titanium; Ø 45mm; black lacquered bezel indexes; white-gold and grade-5 black PVD titanium crown; two side windows: one revealing the striking hammer and gong and the other two dice; water resistant to 3atm.
Dial: tinted gray sapphire; featuring a plate adorned with playing card motifs; black PVD and ruby hour and minute hands; front: three windows with rhodium-plated frame for the bank, two of which are activated on demand by utilizing a pushbutton at 10 with gong; four windows with rhodium-plated frame for the player, three of which are activated on demand by utilizing pushbutton at 8 with gong; back: 3D roulette rotating in step with the watch movement.
Strap: black crocodile leather; folding buckle with white-gold and grade-5 black PVD titanium clasps with card motifs.
Suggested price: $220,500
Note: limited edition of 21 pieces.
Also available: pink gold and grade-5 black PVD titanium; platinum and grade-5 black PVD titanium; grade-5 black PVD titanium or grade-5 gray titanium; plaque decorated with casino-related motifs (Las Vegas or Joker) or black onyx dial.

21 BLACKJACK — REF. MTR.BLJ08.030-051

Movement: automatic-winding BLJ08 caliber; 72-hour power reserve; 501 components; 40 jewels; 28,800 vph; seven double ceramic ball-bearings; twin barrels.
Functions: hours, minutes; three games: blackjack with striking mechanism, roulette and dice.
Case: 5N rose gold and grade-5 black PVD titanium; Ø 45mm; black lacquered bezel indexes; 5N rose-gold and grade-5 black PVD titanium crown; two side windows: one revealing the striking hammer and gong and the other two dice; water resistant to 3atm.
Dial: tinted gray sapphire; featuring a plate adorned with playing card motifs; yellow spinel and black ceramic hour and minute hands; front: three windows with 4N rose-gold frame for the bank, two of which are activated on demand by utilizing a pushbutton at 10 with gong; four windows with 4N rose-gold frame for the player, three of which are activated on demand by utilizing pushbutton at 8 with gong; back: 3D roulette rotating in step with the watch movement.
Strap: black crocodile leather; folding buckle with 5N rose-gold and grade-5 black PVD titanium clasps with card motifs.
Suggested price: $216,500
Note: limited edition of 21 pieces.
Also available: white gold and grade-5 black PVD titanium; platinum and grade-5 black PVD titanium; grade-5 black PVD titanium or grade-5 gray titanium; plaque decorated with casino-related motifs (Las Vegas or Joker) or black onyx dial.

BACCARA — REF. MTR.BCR09.010-019

Movement: automatic-winding BRC09 caliber; 72-hour power reserve; 501 components; 40 jewels; 28,800 vph; seven double ceramic ball-bearings; twin barrels.
Functions: hours, minutes; three games: Baccara with striking mechanism, roulette and dice game.
Case: white gold and grade-5 black PVD titanium; Ø 45mm; black lacquered bezel indexes; white-gold and grade-5 black PVD titanium crown; two side windows: one revealing the striking hammer and gong and the other two dice; water resistant to 3atm.
Dial: tinted gray sapphire; featuring a plate adorned with dragon; black PVD and ruby hour and minute hands; front: three windows with rhodium-plated frame for the bank, which are activated on demand by utilizing pushbutton at 10 with gong; three windows with rhodium-plated frame for the player, which are activated on demand by utilizing pushbutton at 8 with gong; back: 3D roulette rotating in step with the watch movement.
Strap: black crocodile leather; white gold and grade-5 black PVD titanium folding buckle with card motifs.
Note: limited edition of 9 timepieces.
Suggested price: $220,500
Also available: 5N rose gold and grade-5 black PVD titanium; platinum and grade-5 black PVD titanium; grade-5 black PVD titanium or grade-5 gray titanium.

BACCARA — REF. MTR.BCR09.020-029

Movement: automatic-winding BRC09 caliber; 72-hour power reserve; 501 components; 40 jewels; 28,800 vph; seven double ceramic ball-bearings; twin barrels.
Functions: hours, minutes; three games: Baccara with striking mechanism, roulette and dice game.
Case: 5N rose gold and grade-5 black PVD titanium; Ø 45mm; black lacquered bezel indexes; 5N rose gold and grade-5 black PVD titanium crown; two side windows: one revealing the striking hammer and gong and the other two dice; water resistant to 3atm.
Dial: tinted gray sapphire; featuring a plate adorned with dragon; yellow spinel and black ceramic hour and minute hands; front: three windows with 4N rose-gold frame for the bank, which are activated on demand by utilizing pushbutton at 10 with gong; three windows with 4N rose-gold frame for the player, which are activated on demand by utilizing pushbutton at 8 with gong; back: 3D roulette rotating in step with the watch movement.
Strap: black crocodile leather; 5N rose-gold and grade-5 black PVD titanium folding buckle with card motifs.
Note: limited edition of 9 timepieces.
Suggested price: $216,500
Also available: white gold and grade-5 black PVD titanium; platinum and grade-5 black PVD titanium; grade-5 black PVD titanium or grade-5 gray titanium.

de GRISOGONO
GENEVE

SPIRIT OF INVENTION

Given the unorthodox journey that took de Grisogono's president and founder, Fawaz Gruosi, from a humble childhood in Florence to the status of one of the most sought-after watchmakers of his generation, it's no surprise that his impact in the world of haute horology has been one of daring innovation and relentless rejection of convention.

A hard worker moved by the inherent beauty of nature, Fawaz Gruosi's road to greatness did not begin, as one would expect, with an education in a formal watch-making academy. Having left school at 18, in 1970, to work as a sales assistant for a Florentine jeweler, his obvious talent and brilliant instincts quickly propelled his ascent through the industry, and around the world. Twenty-three years later, trusting the sixth sense that had made him a young star growing the companies of others, the aesthete dove headfirst into his entrepreneurial dream. In 2000, seven years after founding de Grisogono, Fawaz Gruosi presented the Instrumento Numero Uno at BaselWorld, drawing immediate attention to the brand with his incredible degree of inventiveness. Driven by a love of aesthetics and dynamism, this father of two daughters chose to steer the company head-on into a pioneering adventure. Fawaz Gruosi hasn't looked back, and not surprisingly, hasn't slowed his incredible acceleration. Constantly pushing to redefine haute horology, the president and founder, whose passion for beauty never leaves him short of inspiration, once again amazes with astounding feats of creativity and technical excellence.

A testament to the unquenchably innovative spirit of its founder, de Grisogono's Otturatore takes the concept of avant-garde to a dynamic new level.

While the charismatic exuberance of the large rectangular rose- or white-gold case sets the tone for a modern spectacle, this watch's true genius lays in the humility of its character. Conceived with a particular attention to clarity and legibility, the Otturatore is an innovative symbol of Fawaz Gruosi's pursuit of refined simplicity. The patented high-performance sequential display selector of this timepiece allows for an unpretentious dial that is free of distraction, as only one secondary function is visible at any given time. Activated by two stylish gold pushbuttons on the side of the watch, the mobile dial rotates to reveal each of the timepiece's four cleverly hidden complications. The sheer speed of the mechanism maintains the integrity of the charming illusion. At less than two hundredths of a second per 90° rotation, the traveling velocity of the aperture around the three-part Clou de Paris cobbled dial is approximately 15 times faster than the blink of an eye.

This feat of innovation permits an optimal use of space while preserving the serene clarity of the watch. While the dauphine hour and minute hands in 18-karat rose or white gold reign over the opaline dial's center throughout the extraordinary performance, the moonphase, date, power reserve, and seconds—in clockwise order starting from 12 o'clock—appear individually upon the request of the wearer. This ingenious approach by de Grisogono lets each indication shine, while the others patiently await their turn.

Considering the significant inertia, the velocity of motion, and the strict immediacy of the movement's halting the mechanism requires the pinpoint control of extremely powerful counter-forces. Under standard conditions, the brief pressing of a pushbutton would not provide enough force to operate a mechanical process of such precision and sophistication. The Otturatore's patented sequencer, however, can instantly set off several crucial dynamic functions, such as connecting operations and mechanical memory, without compromising power efficiency and friction minimization. By drawing its power from a secondary barrel and mainspring, the sequential selector accomplishes its light-speed task with complete autonomy and impeccable accuracy. This sublime achievement in kinetics is concealed by the very perfection of its result. With its ability to realize immediate maximum speed and an instantaneous stop, de Grisogono's innovative dial leaves its owner no chance to interpret the enigma. Like a magician with undetectable sleight of hand, the Swiss watchmaker's technical mastery hides in the shadows of this sophisticated illusion.

Powered by the self-winding DR 19-89 caliber, this resolutely ultra-modern timepiece boasts a 42-hour power reserve and is produced in five variations including two 55-piece numbered editions with brown or ruthenium dials exclusively available in de Grisogono boutiques. Ironically, given the veiled quality of the dial-side spectacle, the Otturatore's transparent caseback provides a stunning view of the heartbeat of the watch.

The Otturatore is an outstanding symbol of Fawaz Gruosi's rejection of traditional boundaries. With this high-velocity timepiece of deceptive serenity, the serial innovator defies the limits of watchmaking, physics, and creativity.

OTTURATORE

The Otturatore is powered by the DR 19-89 self-winding caliber, which the wearer can admire through the generous caseback window. Thanks to an unprecedented sequential display mechanism, this watch morphs from one personality to another faster than the eye can see.

Winner of the Public Prize at the 2009 Geneva Watchmaking Grand Prix, the Meccanico dG captures the visionary co-existence of tradition and modernity within a timepiece of extraordinary complexity.

While the dial tells a story of remarkable legibility, the incorporation of a secondary time zone that tips its cap to the digital age is the result of exceptional imagination and technical mastery. In radiant contrast to the newly designed case in matte black titanium, the upper half of the dial is home to a bright white circular hour and minute display, through which the owner can enjoy a glimpse of the hand-wound movement's exposed intricacies. On the lower half of the watch face, in equally vivid white, the dual time zone gives the digital interpretation of time its fitting place in haute horology.

Operated by 23 cams, in combination with gears and a triggering/synchronization device, each transition requires the instantaneous rotation of up to 12 individual white mobile micro-segments. As each of the movement's 651 components serve their crucial purpose in this fascinating composition, de Grisogono displays the avant-garde intellectualism that has become synonymous with the brand.

With the release of this limited edition version of the Meccanico dG, the watchmaker not only honors the sleek perfection of deep black intensity, but does so with powerful lines, elegant contrast and a masterful accent of technical ingenuity.

MECCANICO dG BLACK FOREVER LIMITED EDITION

de Grisogono celebrates its iconic black diamond with an exclusive Meccanico dG model in matte black titanium, black vulcanized rubber and a matte black alligator leather strap.

OCCHIO

By enhancing this inventive minute repeater with the brilliance of 154 finely set baguette-cut diamonds, de Grisogono takes the concept of the emotional timepiece to the next level.

Adorning the Occhio with a shower of baguette-cut diamonds, de Grisogono provides the watch that has nothing to hide with an even grander performance stage.

Enhancing the auditory senses with a visual accompaniment, this innovative minute repeater features a 12-blade titanium diaphragm that reveals the watch's dynamic movement during the chiming of its cathedral gongs. As the complication is activated, the camera-like shutter aperture opens to expose the full intricacy of the movement's heartbeat, only to close in time to leave the wearer in anticipation of the next sonorous performance.

Expanding a line celebrated for its ingenious dual-sensory transparency, de Grisogono presents a model that veers away from the collection's understated styling, and toward the luxurious brilliance of a formal tuxedo. This dazzling makeover features 154 finely set baguette-cut diamonds on the bezel, case flanks, and lugs, offering a brilliant contrast to the highly complex mechanical character of the timepiece. With this stunning model, after the three gongs have resonated, the curtain's closing signifies the opening of a new act. When the heartbeat has been admired, and the cathedral has struck its last note, the eye is treated to a spectacle of light and refined intensity.

Maintaining the supreme elegance of the technically sophisticated collection, de Grisogono testifies to the Occhio's conceptual perfection by providing the case with attire appropriate to the occasion.

FUSO QUADRATO N04

A hidden gem beneath a masculine black dial, the second time zone is revealed by the ingenious shutter-like titanium mechanism.

Continuing the theme of inventive wristwatches with multiple personalities, an evident trademark of the manufacture, the Fuso Quadrato N04 brings an extraordinary appeal to the dual time zone principle, with an ingenious mechanism that serves as a window to both the past and the future.

Activated by a sliding lever at 9 o'clock, the clever aperture mechanism, or diaphragm, enables the wearer to reveal the watch's alternative identity as 12 titanium blades act as a futuristic curtain to the secondary time display. Once the opening is revealed, a black pointer, equipped with an open window for optimal legibility, joins the 18-karat white-gold dauphine hands, and offers a clear indication of time in a chosen location. This ingenious creation displays a witty dialogue between classical tradition and a contemporary baroque aesthetic. The primary black dial with large Arabic numerals proclaims a sleek masculine character, and offers a pleasant contrast to the intricate design of the stage that waits beneath it. Decorated with a white-gold Clou de Paris motif and 24-hour display, the watch's lower face is a symbolic revelation of a genuine horological heritage that remains at the heart of innovative Swiss watchmaking.

The square white-gold case is gently rounded and provides an elegant attire for this layered masterpiece. Meanwhile, the DF 21-90 automatic caliber animates the Fuso Quadrato at a frequency of 28,800 vph and provides a 42-hour power reserve.

By harnessing the virtues of multi-leveled architecture, de Grisogono captures the profound essence of the dual time zone concept. As both dials cleverly play off each other, the Fuso Quadrato demonstrates a refined balance of tradition and modernity.

The verve with which Fawaz Gruosi dares to reinvent the story of watchmaking consistently results in timepieces that stop at nothing to astound, yet find a harmonious grace as they do so. This expert instinct and vision is powerfully exhibited in a new chronograph member of the Instrumento Grande collection.

The Grande Chrono N04, whose generous 18-karat white-gold case sets the tone for the uninhibited character of the watch's dial, boasts a design that finds poise in its decisive imbalance. Establishing a circular tone within the rectangular frame, the retrograde date calendar forms a twin arc around the radius of the central hour and minute hands. In doing so, de Grisogono rejects conventional layout principles. While every integer of the dual-ring mechanism is visible at all times, the day's date brightly stands out, outlined by a tinted sapphire window with a white-gold case of its own. In true Fawaz Gruosi flavor, the traditional counters of the watch have undergone a jolt of modernity. The contrasting shapes and colors of the subdials perpetuate the asymmetrical balance of the timepiece. The discreet black running seconds subdial at 12 o'clock is mirrored by a significantly larger 12-hour counter, of identical design and color, at 6 o'clock. Playing off the qualities of the date window on the opposite side of the dial, the 30-minute white square counter sits in the rupture of the retrograde arcs at 9 o'clock. The chronograph, which also includes a black central seconds hand, is activated by pushbuttons on either side of the decorated setting crown. Finally, de Grisogono leaves a creative signature of the manufacture's take on geometry—the time-of-day hour circle boasts two right angles.

With its revealing design, the Grande Chrono offers its owner a brilliant view of the automatic chronograph movement's steady beat through a window on the side of the case at 9 o'clock. In addition, the choreography of the rotor is visible through a transparent sapphire porthole on the watch's caseback.

Worn with an alligator strap, the Grande Chrono is a masterful example of de Grisogono's audacity of design and rejection of convention.

GRANDE CHRONO N04

This timepiece defies conventional chronograph design and expresses the courageous instincts of its creator.

The playfully titled Piccolina collection is a sensual line of feminine wristwatches that work on every level to express the individuality of their owners. Adorned with a multitude of gems and diamonds set in original patterns, the Piccolina wristwatch is a harmonious display of pleasure and glamour. The rigid, curved bracelet, available in three sizes, is carefully shaped for optimal comfort and fit, and is delightfully embellished with a sea of stones, for an haute jewelry impact. Models with a sprinkle of gem setting, or in galuchat leather, provide a gentle contrast that lets the dial stand out as the star of the watch. Along with 20 diamonds acting as hour markers, de Grisogono imprints its habitual touch of visual creativity, with Arabic numerals in 18-karat gold at 4 and 8 o'clock, rising from the watch face as they echo the delicately proportioned hour and minute hands. The bracelet itself does not rest on its abundance of precious ornamentation, as its interior is beautifully engraved with the intricate de Grisogono scroll design.

While the Piccolina is offered in numerous variations, a common theme of lightheartedness and lively sensuality reigns throughout.

PICCOLINA

Eighty-two braun diamonds illuminate the bezel and set an immediate tone of luxurious delight.

With its Instrumentino, de Grisogono presents an easy-to-wear expression of decisive femininity that does not shy away from demonstrating its strong character. Throughout the diminutive (15% smaller than the Instrumento Uno) collection's wide array of splendid multi-colored gem settings, the Instrumentino is an effervescent vision of contemporary timelessness with a dual time zone to boot. The S17 model, for example, captures the profound personality of 405 brown diamonds set on a brown-gold case. Upon the three-level champagne guilloché dial, the 4 and 8 Arabic numerals draw the eye to the ring-like hour circle that indicates the time of day. Finished with a galuchat strap, this model embodies the balance between its organic hues and the modern technical expertise of its 28,800 vph automatic-winding mechanical caliber.

A complete jewelry range filled with a generous spectrum of luxurious colors and designs, the Instrumentino boasts a level of detail true to de Grisogono's spirit of perfectionism. Taking gemstone luxury to a new height of horological refinement, an open sapphire caseback grants the wearer a view of the black-PVD-coated mechanical movement. With the finishing touch of a black-diamond-set crown, this modestly sized collection leaves its feminine wearer wholly entranced by the watchmaking genius of Fawaz Gruosi.

INSTRUMENTINO

The Instrumentino, with its vast range of color codes and brilliant gem settings, is powered by the DF 26-91 automatic mechanical movement, or DF 27-40 quartz caliber, upon the choice of its owner.

DEWITT

ROMANTICALLY HERS

When Jérôme de Witt founded the manufacture that bears his name in 2003, he vowed to honor the audacious DNA of his vision. Dedicated to wooing the world of haute horology with elaborate innovations, the Swiss watchmaker quickly earned a reputation as a daring explorer of the frontiers of mechanical ingenuity.

In keeping with the brand's spirit of artistic curiosity, DeWitt takes a bold step into the realm of poetry with a feminine line that honors the brilliance of 19th-century Victorian romanticism. With the new Golden Afternoon collection, the Genevan house pays tribute to the Pre-Raphaelite movement's avant-garde vision of female sensuality as a powerful beauty, full of character and intensity.

An early innovator in portrait photography, Julia Margaret Cameron emphasized the emotional dimension of her subjects with an array of inventive techniques. By deliberately shooting out of focus, for example, Cameron captured an irresistible melancholy in her portraits, expressing the complex dimension of feminine beauty while rejecting the notion of female passivity.

A graceful touch of fantasy, the Golden Afternoon collection draws from this proud celebration of woman as it offers a timekeeping portal into the elegant heart of sensibility.

The Imperial columns that adorn the 39mm white- or rose-gold case of this automatic timepiece were specially redesigned to echo the feminine finesse of the design, evocative of twelve doors opening onto a beautiful garden.

GOLDEN AFTERNOON MEDIUM DIAMOND SETTING

Twelve specially designed Imperial columns act as subtle doorways into the intricate detail of the dial's poetic bouquet.

The Golden Afternoon dial, in delicate, white, chocolate or black mother-of-pearl, depicts a gentle breeze blowing through a colorful bed of flowers. As the assorted petals pour out from the center, they are poetically dispersed across the mother-of-pearl sky. Subtle puffy clouds offer a delightful backdrop for the dozen water lily diamonds to add a gleaming relief to the enchanting canvas.

The hour and minute hands, finely sculpted into the shape of angel wings, float around the hour markers, which are charmingly spelled out in French across the deep sky. In an added touch of passionate seduction, the thin seconds hand is decorated with an elegant, fiery flame.

As an homage to Julia Margaret Cameron's innovative photographic style, the dial boasts a slightly out-of-focus effect that imbues the watch with a tone of controlled sensuality.

Honoring the range of unique feminine personalities, DeWitt presents three distinct diamond arrangements.

The visual purity of the soft setting, embellished with 146 brilliant-cut diamonds, provides a fresh shade of feminine innocence. The salmon and white mother-of-pearl flowers float through the white or chocolate dial, in a joyful expression of colors.

The partially diamond-set version presents a mature contrast of tonalities. The combination of ruby cabochon, white-gold case, and black mother-of-pearl dial conveys a mysterious atmosphere reminiscent of Dante Gabriel Rosetti's 1880 painting *Day Dream*. The interplay between the dark, profound sky and the radiance of the hands, bezel and crown gracefully speaks to the passionate depth of modern femininity.

Fully pavé, with white mother-of-pearl and 18-karat white gold, the full diamond setting model is a dazzling picture of refined luxury. Enhancing the crown, a blue sapphire cabochon brings together the breathtaking radiance of the dream-like choreography of light, shape, and color in the 2.89-carat timepiece.

Extending the house's creative reach to the realm of poetry, DeWitt's Golden Afternoon collection accomplishes a vision of sensual romanticism. With its abundance of details, intensity of colors and complex composition, this decisively feminine wristwatch mirrors the expressive artistic honesty of a remarkable era.

GOLDEN AFTERNOON FULL DIAMOND SETTING

Set with 412 brilliant-cut diamonds, this full-pavé model with white mother-of-pearl dial dazzles with every shimmering ray of light.

X-WATCH "ONLY WATCH 2011 - CHARITY AUCTION"

Movement: automatic-winding DW8046 caliber; Ø 37.5mm, thickness: 12.45mm; 67-72 hour power reserve; 544 components; 58 jewels; 21,600 vph; variable-inertia (Glucydur) balance; Spiral Straumann Hairspring® with Phillips curve sequenced at 3 Hz; patented Automatic Sequential Winding (A.S.W.) device driven by a peripheral oscillating rotor; manufactured by DeWitt.
Functions: bi-retrograde hours and minutes; small seconds; tourbillon; chronograph; power reserve indicator.
Case: grade 5 titanium and steel "X"-shaped bonnet; reversible, twin-faced case; Ø 49mm, thickness: 21.8mm; DeWitt imperial columns on the bezel; X-shaped bonnet covering the dial and activated by 4 pushbuttons; grade 5 titanium polished crown with blackened titanium ring and the "W" signature; screw-down sapphire crystal caseback; water resistant to 3atm.
Dial: applied center in the shape of an hourglass; background with guilloché pattern; chronograph side: 1mm separation plate in punchy Monaco-red; open-worked hour and minute hands in the shape of two-edged swords; thin seconds hand on the tourbillon; thin power reserve hand; gliding chronograph seconds disk; three-arm chronograph minutes hand.
Strap: semi-matte black calf leather with rubbery aspect; grade 5 titanium and black PVD triple-blade folding clasp, polished, engraved "W" signature.

ACADEMIA CHRONOSTREAM — REF. AC.6005.58.M091

Movement: manual-winding DW6005 (ETA 7753) caliber; Ø 30mm; 48-hour power reserve; 27 jewels; 28,800 vph; three-armed Glucydur balance; flat balance spring.
Functions: hours, minutes; small seconds at 9; chronograph: 30-minute counter at 3 and central seconds hand.
Case: 18K rose gold; Ø 43mm, thickness: 13.35mm; DeWitt's imperial columns on the flanks and bezel; 18K rose-gold polished crown with blackened titanium ring and "W" signature; screw-down sapphire crystal caseback; water resistant to 3atm.
Dial: black sunray; blue-gray tonalities; applied counters with radiator grille in the center; 18K rose-gold-plated center with DeWitt signature; open-worked hour and minute hands in the shape of two-edged swords; thin and elegant chronograph hands.
Strap: matte gray alligator leather; 18K rose-gold triple-blade folding clasp with engraved "W" signature.
Note: limited production of 250 pieces.
Also available: 18K rose gold and white opaline.

ACADEMIA QUANTIEME PERPETUEL SPORT — REF. AC.7888.030A.M095

Movement: automatic-winding DW7004 (ETA 2892) caliber; Ø 30mm; 42-hour power reserve; 29 jewels; 28,800 vph; three-armed Glucydur balance; flat balance spring; bi-retrograde module by Agenhor.
Functions: hours, minutes, seconds; perpetual calendar: date at 3, day at 9 and month and leap year cycle at 12; moonphase.
Case: grade 5 titanium; Ø 44mm, thickness: 12.05mm; black rubber inserts on case and bezel; DeWitt's imperial columns on the flanks and bezel with matte satin-brushed finishing; grade 5 titanium crown with blackened titanium ring and "W" signature; screw-down sapphire crystal caseback; water resistant to 3atm.
Dial: black and red; applied radiator grilles in the center; rhodium-plated open-worked hour and minute hands in the shape of two-edged swords; thin and elegant seconds hand; small red perpetual calendar hands.
Strap: matte black alligator leather with double red stitching; grade 5 titanium triple-blade folding clasp with engraved "W" signature.
Note: limited production of 50 pieces.

ACADEMIA TOURBILLON FORCE CONSTANTE A CHAINE — REF. AC.8050.53.M1030

Movement: manual-winding DW8050 caliber; Ø 30.4mm; 72-hour power reserve; 192 components; 27 jewels; 21,600 vph; flying tourbillon mechanism with constant force; power reserve with chain-driven device, indicated on a worm screw; hand-beveled and decorated with Côtes de Genève; four-armed Glucydur balance; flat balance spring.
Functions: hours, minutes; flying tourbillon; power reserve.
Case: 18K rose gold; Ø 43mm, thickness: 12.95mm; DeWitt's imperial columns; 18K rose-gold polished crown with "W" signature; screw-down sapphire crystal caseback; water resistant to 3atm.
Dial: chocolate brown; decorated with elegant strips; large opening for the tourbillon cage and constant force system; open-worked hour and minute hands in the shape of two-edged swords.
Strap: matte chocolate brown alligator leather; 18K rose-gold triple-blade folding clasp with engraved "W" signature.
Note: limited production of 99 pieces.
Also available: 18K white gold; full titanium (limited edition).

TWENTY-8-EIGHT TOURBILLON — REF. T8.TH.006

Movement: manual-winding DW8028 caliber; Ø 33mm, thickness: 7.45mm; 72-hour power reserve; 185 components; 19 jewels; 18,000 vph; variable-inertia Glucydur balance; spiral with Breguet curve sequenced at 2.5 Hz.
Functions: hours, minutes; tourbillon.
Case: 18K white gold; Ø 43mm, thickness: 10.28mm; DeWitt's imperial columns on the flanks; 18K white-gold polished crown with blackened titanium ring and "W" signature; screw-down sapphire crystal caseback; water resistant to 3atm.
Dial: sunray pattern; central columns; large Roman numerals at 12, 3, 6 and 9; small Arabic numerals at five minute intervals; two applied "children" at 3 and 9; open-worked hour and minute hands in the shape of two-edged swords.
Strap: semi-matte dark gray alligator leather; 18K white-gold triple-blade folding clasp with engraved "W" signature.
Also available: 18K rose gold; various dials.

TWENTY-8-EIGHT REGULATOR A.S.W. HORIZONS — REF. T8.TA.001

Movement: automatic sequential-winding (A.S.W.) device; Ø 37mm, thickness: 6.38mm; 72-hour power reserve; 320 components; 34 jewels; 18,000 vph; driven by a peripheral oscillating rotor; deadbeat second is directly connected to the tourbillon cage; variable-inertia Glucydur balance; Straumann Hairspring® spiral with Phillips curve sequenced at 2.5 Hz.
Functions: hours, minutes; deadbeat seconds; power reserve indicator.
Case: 18K rose gold; Ø 46mm, thickness: 12.88mm; DeWitt's imperial columns pattern on the flanks; 18K rose-gold polished crown with blackened titanium ring and "W" signature; screw-down sapphire crystal caseback; water resistant to 3atm.
Dial: tinted sapphire with chocolate-brown tonalities; applied and printed 5N color numerals; open-worked hour and minute hands in the shape of two-edged swords; thin deadbeat seconds hand; thin power reserve hand with 5N colored tip.
Strap: semi-matte dark brown alligator leather; 18K rose-gold triple-blade folding clasp with engraved "W" signature.
Note: limited edition of 250 pieces.
Also available: titanium and black PVD; titanium and tantalum.

TWENTY-8-EIGHT AUTOMATIC — REF. T8.AU.005

Movement: automatic-winding DWT8AU (ETA 2892) caliber; 42-hour power reserve; 21 jewels; 28,800 vph; three-armed Glucydur balance; flat balance spring.
Functions: hours, minutes, seconds.
Case: 18K white gold; Ø 43mm, thickness: 10.28mm; DeWitt's imperial columns on the flanks; 18K white-gold polished crown with blackened titanium ring and "W" signature; screw-down sapphire crystal caseback; water resistant to 3atm.
Dial: two-zone guilloché: internal flame guilloché and external baguette guilloché; applied circle with columns; large Roman numerals at 12, 3, 6 and 9; small Arabic numerals at five minute intervals; open-worked hour and minute hands in the shape of two-edged swords; thin seconds hand.
Strap: blue alligator leather; 18K white-gold pin buckle engraved with "W" signature.
Also available: 18K rose gold; various dials.

GOLDEN AFTERNOON — REF. GA.AU.002

Movement: automatic-winding ETA 2892; 42-hour power reserve; 21 jewels; 28,800 vph; three-armed Glucydur balance; flat balance spring.
Functions: hours, minutes, seconds.
Case: 18K white gold; Ø 39mm, thickness: 9.28mm; DeWitt's imperial columns on the flanks; polished 18K white-gold crown with blue sapphire cabochon; screw-down sapphire crystal caseback; water resistant to 3atm.
Dial: mother-of-pearl sky with mother-of-pearl flowers; angel wing hour and minute hands; small thin-flame seconds hand.
Strap: blue alligator leather; polished 18K white-gold clasp with engraved "W" signature.
Also available: 18K rose gold; various diamond settings.

DIOR HORLOGERIE

OR THE HERITAGE OF THE ART OF HAUTE COUTURE

Designed in the Avenue Montaigne studios, the Dior Christal, La D de Dior, Chiffre Rouge and Dior VIII timepieces are continually reinvented in the same spirit of creativity, excellence and exceptionalness that has animated the House since 1947.

Time is precious in an Haute Couture House. The closer it gets to the day of the show, the more every second counts, the more ideas fuse together. And the more seamstresses seem to make miracles; cutting, draping, sewing, embroidering the most exceptional dresses imaginable.

In Paris at Christian Dior, all the floors on 30 Avenue Montaigne live in step to the exciting and bustling rhythm of the Design Studio. Time is precious. In the real and in the figurative sense, since this House now creates Haute Horlogerie collections with the same care that is given for the elaboration of Haute Couture dresses.

Dior VIII Diamond Dial

Chiffre Rouge A02

La D de Dior Color

Dior Christal Purple

DIOR IN TIME WITH THE GREAT WATCHMAKERS

Dior VIII
Pink Sapphire Baguette

Dior Haute Horlogerie is in a permanent state of creation. The House's creative teams give free rein to their imagination, making sketches and expressing their desires. Then, they pass the relay on to expert Swiss watchmakers who materialize their ideas. In 2001, Dior set up its own production unit at La Chaux-de-Fonds, legendary cradle of all that is finest in Swiss timekeeping.

Exactly like Avenue Montaigne in Paris, innovation and know-how are put to the service of creation in this watchmaking atelier. This is why it took Dior Horlogerie very little time to propose radically new timepieces. It's a question of style and of a mindset too, derived as much from Haute Couture as from Haute Horlogerie, since both of these domains have more than one thing in common. As the show draws closer, the seamstresses of a Fashion House neither can nor know how to do absolutely everything, so Dior turns towards outside specialized artisans for the feather work or the making of lace and embroidery.

In the same way, when a designer imagines a mechanism, a specific technology, Dior Horlogerie calls upon specialist talents. Time is stimulating and precious in all its forms of creation yet, paradoxically, these are crafts that never count the hours it takes to achieve the sublime. Beautiful workmanship, exquisite embellishment and meticulous festooning or paving are all extremely important details.

Therefore, Dior Horlogerie turned to the Maison Bunter in Geneva, recognized by the entire profession for the precious stone settings of its Haute Horlogerie. For the mechanisms, it called upon another choice partner, the Zenith manufacture, for the making of the Irréductible movement in the Chiffre Rouge limited series, for its manual-winding Elite movement in the 38 and 42 mm La D de Dior timepieces as well as for the automatic version of the Dior Haute Couture timepieces. For the development of its Tourbillon calibre, Dior also teamed up with the designer of the Concepto movement. For the elaboration of its Dior 8 Fuseaux Horaires, Les Ateliers Horlogers Dior worked with Orny & Girardin. And for the recent launch of the Dior VIII, the House sought the expertise of the Soprod manufacture for the development of the "Dior Inversé" caliber. Simultaneously a technical and an aesthetic feat, the oscillating weight that rewinds the movement of this new iconic Dior timekeeper is placed on top of the dial and outlines the swirl of a ball gown. Until now placed at the back of the movement, this oscillating weight recalls the House of Dior's creations that are as refined on the inside as on the outside. Fashioned in gold and diamond-set openwork, this oscillating weight is also decorated with a unique design which requires the recalculation of its inertia as each timepiece is being developed... In brief, a totality of watchmaking challenges and mechanical feats which perfectly illustrate the spirit of Haute Horlogerie, deploying treasures of precision that makes the creative idea possible. This is also the spirit of Haute Couture, a spirit constantly questioning itself, never hesitating to break with habit while tirelessly aiming for perfection.

Dior VIII Grand Bal Dentelle

Dior VIII Grand Bal Organza

Dior VIII Grand Bal Broderie

Dior VIII Grand Bal Plissé

Dior VIII Grand Bal Plumetis

DIOR HAUTE COUTURE

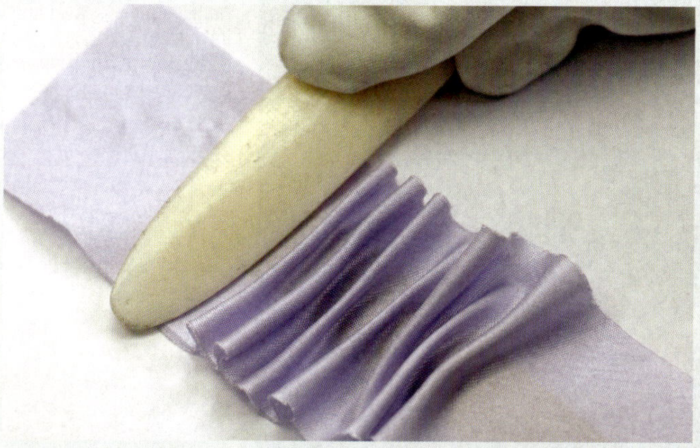

In tribute to Dior Haute Couture, to its palette of colors and its embroidery detailing, linings, plissés, dotted voile, ruffles or rose patterns, the first Haute Couture timepieces, unveiled in 2010, foreshadowed a second collection for 2011, including five new exceptional timekeepers. These one-of-a-kind pieces, in gold and 33mm in diameter, are endowed with a Zenith Elite automatic movement. As Christian Dior used to say, "Elegance is an ensemble where the invisible is as important as the visible." This is why the oscillating weight, the epitome of refinement and visible on the back of the case, is worked like the dial, inserted with mother-of-pearl and embroidered with diamonds and sapphires. Each dial or color combination echoes the subtle details of an Haute Couture silhouette: the bezel and the horns are set with baguette-cut colored stones.

Passage n°1, with its diamond-encrusted mother-of-pearl petal dial, its powdery hues and its rhodolite garnet-set bezel, recalls the intricate embroidery on a ball gown.

The hypnotic spirals of colored mother-of-pearl, encrusted with fancy colored diamonds and sapphires and the intense pink ruby-set bezel make **Passage n°2** look like the counterpart of an intricately ruffled pink cocktail dress.

In complete contrast, rather like a black puff skirt worn under an electric blue Bar jacket, **Passage n°3** teams the blue-black of its diamond-encrusted dial with the icy blue of the aquamarines set on its bezel.

As for **Passage n°4**, it has all the sophistication of an evening dress, whose precise architecture is set off by the softness of satin draping: black Vietnamese mother-of-pearl dial embroidered with diamonds and purple sapphires and amethyst bezel.

Finally, a ballet of diamonds in concentric circles on the jade dial of **Passage n°5** recall the precious hems on an Haute Couture dress, glorified by the chromian tourmalines on the bezel.

DIOR VIII PINK SAPPHIRES BAGUETTE AUTOMATIC — REF. CD1235F2C001

Movement: automatic-winding; 40-hour power reserve; pink lacquered oscillating weight.
Functions: hours, minutes, seconds.
Case: black high-tech ceramic and 18K white gold; Ø 33mm; bezel set with 60 pink baguette sapphires(3.59 carats); crown set with a black ceramic insert; transparent sapphire crystal caseback; water resistant to 5atm.
Dial: black lacquered; set with 32 diamonds (0.10 carat).
Bracelet: black high-tech ceramic; 18K white-gold unfolding clasp.

DIOR VIII GRAND BAL DENTELLE AUTOMATIC — REF. CD124BE0C002

Movement: automatic-winding "Dior Inversé" calibre; 40-hour power reserve; 18K white-gold functional oscillating weight on the dial set with 178 diamonds (0.27 carat).
Functions: hours, minutes.
Case: black high-tech ceramic and stainless steel; Ø 38mm; bezel set with 72 diamonds (0.72 carat) and a ceramic insert; crown set with a black ceramic insert; transparent sapphire crystal caseback; water resistant to 5atm.
Dial: black mother-of-pearl from Vietnam; engraved and set with 28 diamonds.
Bracelet: black high-tech ceramic; stainless steel unfolding clasp.
Note: limited edition of 88 pieces.

DIOR VIII — REF. CD1231E1C001

Movement: quartz.
Functions: hours, minutes, seconds.
Case: black high-tech ceramic and stainless steel; Ø 33mm; turning bezel set with 56 diamonds (0.59 carat) and black ceramic inserts; crown set with a black ceramic insert; water resistant to 5atm.
Dial: black lacquered.
Bracelet: black high-tech ceramic; stainless steel folding clasp.

DIOR VIII — REF. CD1245E0C002

Movement: automatic-winding; 38-hour power reserve; black lacquered oscillating weight.
Functions: hours, minutes, seconds.
Case: black high-tech ceramic and stainless steel; Ø 38mm; turning bezel set with black inserts; crown set with a black ceramic insert; transparent sapphire crystal caseback; water resistant to 5atm.
Dial: black lacquered; set with 34 diamonds (0.17 carat).
Bracelet: black high-tech ceramic; stainless steel folding clasp.

LA MINI D DE DIOR SNOW SET — REF. CD040160A001

Movement: quartz.
Functions: hours, minutes.
Case: 18K white gold; Ø 19mm; bezel set with 40 diamonds (0.32 carat); crown set with 13 diamonds; water resistant to 3atm.
Dial: 18K white gold; set with 145 diamonds (0.46 carat).
Strap: black satin; 18K white-gold ardillon buckle set with 29 diamonds (0.14 carat).

LA D DE DIOR GOLD — REF. CD047170A001

Movement: quartz.
Functions: hours, minutes.
Case: 18K pink gold; Ø 25mm; bezel set with 50 diamonds (0.50 carat); crown set with 13 diamonds; water resistant to 3atm.
Dial: white mother-of-pearl; set with 12 diamonds (0.06 carat).
Strap: black satin; 18K pink-gold ardillon buckle; set with 18 diamonds (0.18 carat).

LA D DE DIOR OPAL — REF. CD043970A002

Movement: manual-winding Elite calibre by Zenith for Dior; 50-hour power reserve.
Functions: hours, minutes.
Case: 18K pink gold; Ø 38mm; bezel set with 72 diamonds (0.72 carat); crown set with 18 diamonds (0.11 carat); water resistant to 3atm.
Dial: white opal from Australia.
Strap: black satin; 18K pink-gold ardillon buckle; set with 62 diamonds (0.45 carat).
Note: limited edition of 10 pieces.

LA D DE DIOR 38MM — REF. CD043113M001

Movement: quartz.
Functions: hours, minutes.
Case: stainless steel; Ø 38mm; bezel set with 72 diamonds (0.72 carat); crown set with 10 diamonds; water resistant to 3atm.
Dial: silver; set with four diamonds (0.03 carat).
Bracelet: stainless steel.

DIOR CHRISTAL DIAMONDS — REF. CD114561M001

Movement: automatic-winding Elite calibre by Zenith for Dior; 50-hour power reserve; oscillating weight with mother-of-pearl insert.
Functions: hours, minutes, seconds.
Case: 18K white gold; Ø 38mm; bezel set with 79 baguette diamonds (3.09 carats); horns set with 12 diamonds (1.10 carats); crown set with a rose-cut diamond (0.20 carat); water resistant to 5atm.
Dial: white mother-of-pearl marquetry; set with 290 diamonds (1.46 carats).
Bracelet: 18K white gold; set with 32 baguette diamonds (5.52 carats).
Note: limited edition of 10 pieces.

DIOR CHRISTAL "8 FUSEAUX HORAIRES" — REF. CD114710M001

Movement: automatic-winding Dior calibre "8 Fuseaux Horaires"; 42-hour power reserve; golden oscillating weight.
Functions: hours, minutes, seconds; eight time zones; day/night indicator.
Case: stainless steel; Ø 38mm; bezel set with 120 diamonds (1.50 carats); transparent sapphire crystal caseback with white mother-of-pearl; water resistant to 5atm.
Dial: golden and white mother-of-pearl; hour indicator on the eight time zone satellite; golden minute and white second hands.
Bracelet: stainless steel; set with three rows of white sapphire crystal inserts.
Note: limited edition of 100 pieces.

DIOR CHRISTAL WHITE — REF. CD112118M003

Movement: quartz.
Functions: hours, minutes, seconds.
Case: stainless steel; Ø 28mm; bezel set with 109 diamonds (0.54 carat) and white sapphire crystal inserts; water resistant to 5atm.
Dial: white mother-of-pearl and silver sun-brushed.
Bracelet: stainless steel; set with three rows of white sapphire crystal inserts.

DIOR CHRISTAL PURPLE — REF. CD11311JM001

Movement: quartz.
Functions: hours, minutes, seconds; date.
Case: stainless steel; Ø 33mm; bezel set with 97 diamonds (0.58 carat) and purple sapphire crystal inserts; water resistant to 5atm.
Dial: purple lacquered.
Bracelet: stainless steel; set with three rows of purple sapphire crystal inserts.

DIOR CHRISTAL MYSTERIEUSE REF. CD116411M001

Movement: electromechanical by Quinting Manufacture for Dior.
Functions: hours, minutes, seconds.
Case: stainless steel; Ø 44mm; bezel set with 52 diamonds (0.91 carat) and black sapphire crystal inserts; central ring set with 28 diamonds (0.42 carat); transparent sapphire crystal caseback; water resistant to 5atm.
Dial: six plates decorated with white and mother-of-pearl from Tahiti; black and golden metallizations.
Bracelet: stainless steel; set with three rows of black sapphire crystal inserts.
Note: limited edition of 100 pieces.

CHIFFRE ROUGE M01 REF. CD084B10M001

Movement: automatic-winding "Dior Inversé" calibre; 42-hour power reserve; 18K white gold functional oscillating weight on the dial.
Functions: hours, minutes, seconds.
Case: stainless steel; Ø 39mm; brushed black ceramic bezel; transparent black sapphire crystal caseback; water resistant to 5atm.
Dial: black lacquered.
Bracelet: stainless steel; comes with black perforated calfskin strap with a stainless steel ardillon buckle.
Note: limited edition of 200 pieces.

CHIFFRE ROUGE A03 REF. CD084510A002

Movement: automatic-winding; 42-hour power reserve.
Functions: hours, minutes, seconds; date.
Case: stainless steel; Ø 36mm; transparent black sapphire crystal caseback; water resistant to 5atm.
Dial: sand sun-brushed.
Strap: slate gray alligator; stainless steel ardillon buckle.
Note: limited edition of 200 pieces.

CHIFFRE ROUGE A05 REF. CD084840R001

Movement: automatic-winding chronograph chronometer; 42-hour power reserve; COSC-certified chronograph.
Functions: hours, minutes, seconds; date; chronograph; tachometer.
Case: stainless steel; Ø 41mm; molded with black rubber; transparent red mineral caseback; water resistant to 5atm.
Dial: black, sun-brushed with tachometer scale.
Bracelet: stainless steel molded with black rubber.

FRANCK MULLER
GENEVE

Master of complications

CONQUERING THE EXTREMES OF EXCELLENCE

The prodigious Swiss manufacture presents two record-setting watches to astonish men and women alike.

In a span of less than twenty years, Franck Muller has grown from an ambitious boutique brand to a manufacture that truly earns its moniker: Master of Complications. Defying the myth that success in watchmaking requires a rich and lengthy tradition, the Genthod-based Swiss house has captured the heart of the horological universe with an audacious conquest of the extreme.

With an astonishing 36 complications, the Aeternitas Mega collection—the world's most complex wristwatch—is one of the several feats of innovation that make Franck Muller not just a player, but a bona fide virtuoso in the watchmaking world.

In keeping with the house's intrepid identity, Franck Muller introduces two watches whose most fundamental difference makes manifest a unified ambition. With its presentation of the Tourbillon Lady Automatic and the Giga Tourbillon, the Master of Complications has achieved the world's smallest and largest tourbillons, respectively.

The Giga Tourbillon is a culmination of the dedication to exactitude of a visionary team of remarkable experts. Due to its world-first 20mm tourbillon, this extraordinary wristwatch requires a challengingly large amount of power. Whereas a traditional tourbillon is powered by one or two barrels, the Giga Tourbillon is driven by four barrels that are paired in series to double the operating reserve, and subsequently assembled parallel to one another to double the power of the movement. This ingenious assembly, as well as the barrels' 16mm diameters (as opposed to the traditional 12mm) provides the almost constant force needed to operate this authoritative timepiece.

Adding to the spectacular nature of this watch, which exposes the splendor of its inner workings, is a reversal of the exceptional movement. Working in conjunction with the placing of the bridges on the dial side, the hour setting and winding section are located at the base, and the hour hand is uniquely positioned atop the minute hand.

Worn on a hand-sewn black alligator strap, the Giga Tourbillon is available in an 18-karat white-gold brushed case, an 18-karat white-gold case fully set with white diamonds or an 18-karat white-gold case with black PVD treatment for a striking monochrome effect.

GIGA TOURBILLON
This largest-ever tourbillon makes a powerful statement as it occupies half of this highly technical skeletonized timepiece.

On the other end of the spectrum, Franck Muller's new Tourbillon Lady Automatic displays, through its dynamic curved case, the smallest tourbillon in the world. With its 11.6mm diameter, the mechanism in the Tourbillon Lady Automatic demonstrates elegance as expressed through diminished volume. With this sublime alliance of technical prowess and the harnessing of the beauty of the form, Franck Muller pays its respects to the women fascinated by the complexities of this mechanical art form.

The curved case and delicately rounded flanks trace a sinuous line that gracefully contours the feminine wrist, while the small tourbillon unveils itself at the 6 o'clock position and offers this feminine timepiece an irresistible grace. Colored Arabic numerals enhance the brilliance of the translucent white dial and complete the exquisite balance of this watch.

The Tourbillon Lady Automatic is powered by the FM2060 T self-winding mechanical movement and comes on a hand-sewn alligator strap.

Perhaps Franck Muller's headquarters' view of the perpetual snows of Mont Blanc have inspired the Swiss manufacture's determination to conquer the limits of haute horology. Whatever the reason, the pioneering extremes achieved with the Giga Tourbillon and Tourbillon Lady Automatic join a growing legacy that captures the technical and visual magnificence of watchmaking excellence.

TOURBILLON LADY AUTOMATIC

With the smallest tourbillon in the world, this watch establishes a new standard for feminine elegance.

TOURBILLON AETERNITAS IV — REF. 8888 T QP S

Movement: automatic-winding FM 3480 QPSE caliber; three-day power reserve; 34.4x41.4mm, thickness: 13.65mm; 1,483 components; 99 jewels; 18,000 vph; world first; Franck Muller exclusive.
Functions: hours, minutes; equation of time; secular calendar accurate for 999 years: day, month, retrograde date display; minute repeater: Westminster carillon on four hammers and four gongs; one-minute tourbillon; flyback chronograph; three time zones with 24-hour indication; moonphase.
Case: white gold; 42x61mm, thickness: 19.15mm; sapphire crystal; sapphire crystal caseback.
Dial: silver; sunray guilloché.
Strap: black alligator.
Price: available upon request.
Also available: platinum.

TOURBILLON 9850 EVOLUTION 3.1 — REF. 9850 T EV 3.1

Movement: manual-winding tri-axial tourbillon caliber; 24-hour power reserve; world first; Franck Muller exclusive.
Functions: hours, minutes; perpetual calendar: day, month, year, retrograde date display; tourbillon on three axes.
Case: white gold; sapphire crystal.
Dial: silver; sunray guilloché.
Strap: black alligator.
Price: available upon request.
Also available: platinum.

TOURBILLON CURVEX POWER RESERVE SQUELETTE — REF. 8888 T PR SQT

Movement: automatic-winding FM 3400 T caliber; eight-day power reserve; 34.4x41.4mm, thickness: 7.55mm; 350 components; 42 jewels; 18,000 vph; tourbillon cage on ball bearings; Franck Muller exclusive.
Functions: hours, minutes; flying tourbillon; power reserve indicator at 12.
Case: white gold; sapphire crystal.
Dial: skeletonized.
Strap: black alligator.
Price: available upon request.
Also available: platinum.

TOURBILLON SQUELETTE — REF. 7008 T SQT

Movement: manual-winding FM 2001R11 caliber; Ø 33.4mm, thickness: 5.3mm; 193 components; 21 jewels; 18,000 vph; Franck Muller exclusive.
Functions: hours, minutes; flying tourbillon.
Case: white gold; Ø 42mm, thickness: 12.4mm; sapphire crystal; water resistant to 3atm.
Dial: skeletonized.
Strap: black alligator.
Price: available upon request.
Also available: platinum.

CINTREE CURVEX — REF. 8880 CC DT CASA BLACK

Movement: automatic-winding caliber; oscillating mass in 950 platinum.
Functions: hours, minutes; date at 6; chronograph to 1/5 of a second: 30-minute counter at 3, 60-second counter at 9 and central second hand.
Case: black-finished steel; sapphire crystal; water resistant to 3atm.
Dial: black; numerals in SuperLumiNova.
Strap: black natural rubber.
Price: available upon request.
Also available: white dial.

CINTREE CURVEX — REF. 8880 SC DT VISANT

Movement: automatic-winding caliber; oscillating mass in 950 platinum.
Functions: hours, minutes, seconds; date at 6.
Case: rose gold; sapphire crystal; water resistant to 3atm.
Dial: sunray guilloché; Arabic numerals.
Strap: brown alligator.
Price: available upon request.
Also available: yellow gold or white gold; numerous color variations on the dial; leather strap.

CHRONOGRAPHE AUTOMATIQUE — REF. 8880 CC AT

Movement: automatic-winding chronograph caliber; oscillating mass in 950 platinum.
Functions: hours, minutes; small seconds at 9; date at 4; chronograph: 12-hour counter at 6, 30-minute counter at 3 and central second hand.
Case: rose gold; sapphire crystal; water resistant to 3atm.
Dial: sunray guilloché.
Strap: brown alligator.
Price: available upon request.
Also available: yellow gold or white gold; numerous color combinations on the dial; leather strap.

CHRONOGRAPHE AUTOMATIQUE MARINER — REF. 8080 CC AT

Movement: automatic-winding chronograph caliber; oscillating mass in 950 platinum.
Functions: hours, minutes; small seconds at 9; date at 6; chronograph to 1/5 of a second: 30-minute counter at 3 and central second hand.
Case: rose gold; Mariner case with pushbuttons and crown protection; sapphire crystal; water resistant to 3atm.
Dial: black; sunray guilloché.
Strap: natural rubber.
Price: available upon request.
Also available: white gold; white dial; leather strap.

CONQUISTADOR GRANDPRIX CHRONOGRAPH — REF. 9900 CC GPG ERG

Movement: automatic-winding FM 7000 caliber; 48-hour power reserve; platinum 950 oscillating mass.
Functions: hours, minutes; small seconds at 3; date at 6; chronograph: 30-minute counter at 3 and 60-second counter at 9.
Case: titanium and ergal; curved shape; sapphire crystal.
Dial: black; flame pattern; Arabic numerals painted in relief.
Strap: black alligator; red stitching.
Price: available upon request.

CONQUISTADOR SC GRANDPRIX — REF. 9900 SC GP 5N

Movement: automatic-winding FM 0800 caliber; oscillating mass in 950 platinum.
Functions: hours, minutes, seconds; date at 6.
Case: titanium and red gold; curved shape; sapphire crystal; water resistant to 3atm.
Dial: black; flame pattern; Arabic numerals painted in relief.
Strap: black alligator.
Price: available upon request.
Also available: red gold; leather strap.

LONG ISLAND — REF. 1300 SC RELIEF

Movement: automatic-winding caliber; oscillating mass in 950 platinum.
Functions: hours, minutes.
Case: 18K rose gold; sapphire crystal; water resistant to 3atm.
Dial: sunray guilloché, applied numerals.
Strap: brown alligator.
Price: available upon request.
Also available: yellow gold, white gold or platinum; numerous color variations for the dial; leather strap.

LONG ISLAND TOURBILLON HEURES SAUTANTES — REF. 1350 T HS

Movement: manual-winding tourbillon caliber.
Functions: jumping hours; minutes; small seconds on tourbillon at 6.
Case: platinum; sapphire crystal; water resistant to 3atm.
Dial: sunray guilloché.
Strap: black alligator.
Price: available upon request.
Also available: yellow gold, rose gold or white gold; numerous color variations for the dial; leather strap.

MASTER SQUARE — REF. 6000 H SC DT

Movement: automatic-winding caliber; oscillating mass in 950 platinum.
Functions: hours, minutes, seconds; date at 6.
Case: platinum; sapphire crystal; water resistant to 3atm.
Dial: sunray guilloché.
Strap: black alligator.
Price: available upon request.
Also available: yellow gold, rose gold or white gold; numerous color variations for the dial; leather strap.

MASTER SQUARE — REF. 6000 K SC DT SERTI

Movement: automatic-winding caliber; oscillating mass in 950 platinum.
Functions: hours, minutes, seconds; date at 6.
Case: rose gold; set with diamonds.
Dial: guilloché; applied Roman numerals.
Strap: white alligator.
Price: available upon request.
Also available: white gold; numerous color variations for the dial; leather strap.

INFINITY REKA SAFARI — REF. 3740 QZ SAF D CD

Movement: quartz.
Functions: hours, minutes.
Case: diamond-pavé red gold; ultra-thin; sapphire crystal; water resistant to 3atm.
Dial: full-set diamond pavé; zebra-print.
Strap: alligator.
Price: available upon request.
Also available: leather strap.

DOUBLE MYSTERY 42 D CD — REF. DBLE MYST. 42 D CD F

Movement: automatic-winding Double Mystery caliber; oscillating mass in 950 platinum; Franck Muller patent; Franck Muller exclusive.
Functions: hours, minutes; mysterious time indication via two rotating discs.
Case: white gold; Ø 42mm; sapphire crystal; water resistant to 3atm.
Dial: two rotating discs; full-set diamond pavé.
Bracelet: white gold; full-set diamond pavé.
Price: available upon request.
Also available: yellow or rose gold; leather strap; yellow-, rose- or white-gold bracelet without diamonds.

FREDERIQUE CONSTANT
GENEVE

FIRE AND WATER

Founded in 1988 as a private family company in Geneva by Peter Stas and his wife Aletta, Frédérique Constant has risen to the esteemed position of a leading Swiss watchmaker whose timepieces are defined by their excellent quality, differentiation, and precision in design and manufacture. Proving its rank in the elite circle of horologers, the house began to develop and produce their hand-assembled movements in-house in 2004.

In 2011, the Frédérique Constant group celebrated the fifth anniversary of its 3,200m^2 state-of-the-art factory in Plan-les-Ouates, Geneva, where its watchmakers undertake every stage, from component production to quality control, in accordance with the highest Genevan standards. This event, which served in large part as a show of gratitude to the never-failing encouragement of the brand's partners and supporters, offered an ideal platform to unveil the 1,888-piece limited edition Manufacture Tourbillon Grand Feu—a splendid combination of technical innovation and rich tradition within a round 18-karat rose-gold case.

To produce the profound gleam of the dial, Frédérique Constant utilized the delicate technique of enameling, one that only a handful of manufacturers dare to endeavor. In this ancient process, finely powdered colored glass is applied to a metal plate that is subsequently fired in an oven heated to over 900° Celsius. Since the slightest mote of dust or imperfection in the powder or metal plate is sure to ruin the dial, few of the applied plates even survive the process.

The piece's innovative tourbillon caliber with silicon escapement wheel boasts an incredibly precise Smart Weight Balancing feature. While achieving a perfectly equal distribution of weight is generally impossible, the patented Smart Screw system allows, through an eight-hour process, a highly skilled watchmaker to balance the weight inside the 80-component tourbillon cage, by adding or exchanging tiny metal rings under the two screws on the main cage wheel.

In addition, the use of silicon in the escapement wheel and lever provides a level of durability and energy efficiency through lubricant-free running, low inertia and reduced friction.

Featuring a rose-gold and blue steel day/night indicator and one-minute tourbillon, this genuinely enameled watch is worn with a hand-stitched alligator leather strap and does just what a horological masterpiece should—unite the splendor of the past with the technical mastery of modern innovation.

MANUFACTURE TOURBILLON GRAND FEU
The decoration of the bridges with Côtes de Genève and perlage is just one of the many features of this self-winding timepiece that reminds the wearer of Frédérique Constant's devotion to magnificent craftsmanship.

In keeping with the fine heritage of Old World glory, Frédérique Constant presents its automatic Runabout Moonphase and Date models in conjunction with the Lake Tahoe Concours d'Elegance Wooden Boat Show.

The event, a compilation of the best vintage boats in North America competing in specialized classes, is the perfect setting to reveal this tribute timepiece to the Runabout yachts of the Roaring Twenties. Available in stainless steel or rose-gold-plated versions, this limited edition 43mm timepiece exudes the tidy elegance of the boats that inspired it. Its finely embellished silver dial features a delicate guilloché decoration at the center that gives the watch a captivating texture, along with hand-applied Arabic numerals and methodically positioned day-date and moonphase indicators. The sapphire caseback acts as a porthole through which the adorned automatic movement can be admired. As a reminder of this graceful timepiece's muse, each Runabout Moonphase comes in a luxurious handmade wooden case that also houses a miniature reproduction of a classic Runabout boat.

As the official sponsor of this 39-year-old event honoring the art of classical restoration and maritime enthusiasm, Frédérique Constant has fittingly chosen to house this watch in a box that echoes the passionate artistry of the brand and the yachts that inspired the timepiece.

The Runabout Moonphase and Manufacture Tourbillon Grand Feu are testaments to Frédérique Constant's refined ability to marry the past to the present. With watches that honor the heritage of dedicated craftsmanship, the Genevan house celebrates its triumph with a dashing balance of performance and style.

RUNABOUT MOONPHASE

Honoring the legendary motorboats of the 1920s, this watch with guilloché embellishment empowers its wearer with the liberating thrill of the nautical spirit.

MANUFACTURE TOURBILLON GRAND FEU — REF. FC-980EGF4H9

Movement: automatic-winding FC-980 caliber; Ø 30.5mm; 13¼ lines; 48-hour power reserve; 188 components; 33 jewels; 28,800 vph; Incabloc antishock system; Glucydur balance; Nivarox No. 1 balance spring; bridges decorated with Côtes de Genève and perlage with anglage and rhodiage finishing; silicium escapement; individually numbered.
Functions: hours, minutes, seconds; tourbillon; day/night indicator.
Case: 18K rose gold; three-piece case; Ø 42mm, thickness: 11mm; convex antireflective sapphire crystal; antireflective sapphire crystal caseback secured with six screws; each individually numbered; water resistant to 3atm.
Dial: genuine enameled; black Roman numerals; black steel hands; rose-gold and blued steel day/night indicator hand.
Strap: genuine hand-stitched alligator leather with water resistant lining; additional folding buckle included.
Note: limited edition of 188 pieces.
Suggested price: $48,500

HEART BEAT MANUFACTURE GMT AUTOMATIC — REF. FC-938MC4H6

Movement: automatic-winding Heart Beat Manufacture FC-938 caliber; Ø 30.5mm; 13¼ lines; 42-hour power reserve; 27 jewels; 28,800 vph; balance cock on dial side; KIF antishock system; Glucydur balance; Nivarox No. 1 balance spring; bridges decorated with Côtes de Genève and perlage with anglage and rhodiage finishing.
Functions: hours, minutes; second time zone; day/night indicator at 12.
Case: polished stainless steel; Ø 42mm; convex sapphire crystal; transparent caseback secured with six screws; water resistant to 5atm.
Dial: silver; black decorated Roman numerals; Clous de Paris guilloché in the center; Heart Beat aperture at 6; black nickel hands.
Strap: brown alligator with white stitching; folding buckle.
Note: limited edition of 1888 pieces.
Suggested price: $4,995
Also available: 18K rose gold (limited edition of 188 pieces); two other dial versions.

MAXIME MANUFACTURE AUTOMATIC SILICIUM — REF. FC-700SMG5M6

Movement: automatic-winding Maxime Manufacture FC-700 caliber; 42-hour power reserve; 26 jewels; 28,800 vph; perlage and sunray Côtes de Genève decoration; silicium escapement; individually numbered.
Functions: hours, minutes; date at 6.
Case: polished and fine-brushed stainless steel; Ø 42mm; convex sapphire crystal; transparent caseback secured with four screws; water resistant to 5atm.
Dial: black; central guilloché decoration; hand-polished and -applied hour markers; hand-polished hands with white SuperLumiNova.
Strap: black alligator with water resistant lining; stainless steel deployment buckle.
Note: limited edition of 888 pieces.
Suggested price: $2,950

VINTAGE RALLY — REF. FC-396S6B6

Movement: automatic-winding FC-396 caliber; 42-hour power reserve; 25 jewels; 28,800 vph; original Peking to Paris decoration on the rotor.
Functions: hours, minutes; small seconds at 9; chronograph; 12-hour counter at 6, 30-minute counter at 3 and central seconds hand.
Case: stainless steel; Ø 43mm; convex sapphire crystal; transparent caseback secured with six screws; water resistant to 10atm.
Dial: silver; polished and hand-applied stainless steel hour markers; hand-polished hands with white SuperLumiNova.
Strap: black crocodile calf skin with water resistant lining; folding clasp.
Note: limited edition of 1888 pieces; delivered in a special gift box with a Peking to Paris Rally plate, describing the route of the Rally.
Suggested price: $2,995
Also available: two other dial versions.

RUNABOUT MOONPHASE & DATE — REF. FC-360RM6B4

Movement: automatic-winding FC-360 caliber; 42-hour power reserve; 21 jewels; 28,800 vph.
Functions: hours, minutes, seconds; day at 9; date at 3; moonphase at 6.
Case: polished rose-gold plated; Ø 43mm; convex sapphire crystal; transparent caseback secured with six screws; water resistant to 10atm.
Dial: silvered; central Pavé de Paris guilloché; applied hand polished rose-gold-plated Arabic markers; hand polished rose-gold-plated hands with white Super-LumiNova.
Strap: dark brown crocodile calf skin with water-resistant lining; rose-gold plated buckle.
Note: limited edition of 1888 pieces; delivered in a special gift box with a Runabout boat miniature.
Suggested price: $2,750
Also available: stainless steel.

LADY AUTOMATIC AMOUR HEART BEAT — REF. FC-310SQ2PD6

Movement: automatic-winding FC-310 caliber; 42-hour power reserve; 25 jewels; 28,800 vph; balance bridge opening decorated with perlage finishing.
Functions: hours, minutes, seconds.
Case: stainless steel; Ø 34mm; bezel set with 48 diamonds; crown set with a blue cabochon; convex sapphire crystal; screw-down transparent caseback; water resistant to 6atm.
Dial: white opaline; mother-of-pearl outer ring; hearts guilloché in the center; Amour aperture at 12, set with diamonds.
Strap: white alligator with water resistant lining.
Note: designed by Shu Qi (Taiwanese actress and brand Ambassador of the Brand for Greater China); limited edition of 888 pieces.
Suggested price: $4,350
Also available: rose-gold plated case with vanilla or chocolate color dials.

SLIM LINE AUTOMATIC GENTS — REF. FC-306V4STZ9

Movement: automatic-winding FC-306 caliber; 42-hour power reserve; 25 jewels; 28,800 vph.
Functions: hours, minutes; date at 3.
Case: titanium; Ø 40mm, thickness: 8.79mm; 18K rose-gold bezel; convex sapphire crystal; transparent caseback secured with four screws; water resistant to 3atm.
Dial: silver sunray; hand-polished and hand-applied hour markers; hand-polished curved hour and minute hands to follow the shape of the case.
Strap: brown crocodile calf with folding buckle.
Suggested price: $2,995
Also available: stainless steel; yellow-gold plated and 18K rose gold; black dial with metal bracelet.

JUNIOR LADY — REF. FC-200WHD1ER6B

Movement: quartz FC-200 caliber.
Functions: hours, minutes.
Case: stainless steel; Ø 26mm; crown set with a blue cabochon; convex sapphire crystal; caseback secured with four screws; water resistant to 3atm.
Dial: white; mother-of-pearl outer ring set with 10 full-cut H color, VS clarity diamonds (0.1 carat); guilloché hearts in the center; polished and hand-applied stainless steel Roman numeral markers.
Bracelet: stainless steel.
Note: caseback can be engraved for a personal message.
Suggested price: $850
Also available: satin strap.

GP

GIRARD-PERREGAUX

BEAUTY THROUGH PERFORMANCE

Girard-Perregaux again looks to the past to invent the future of time.

TOURBILLON WITH THREE GOLD BRIDGES

The self-winding GP9600C movement powers this tourbillon timepiece and furthers the pride of the collection's enduring history.

It was while conducting research in the field of tourbillon escapement, in 1860, that Constant Girard created a timepiece that won a first-class prize from the Neuchâtel Observatory. By patenting his discovery and work in horological engineering, Girard-Perregaux established a new concept in watch-making. A century and a half later, the manufacture that carries his name and legacy continues to amaze watch lovers around the world.

The pocket watch in question featured three parallel bridges under which the barrel, center wheel, and tourbillon were aligned. No longer was the movement simply to be a functional component—it had become a design element in its own right. In 1889, Girard-Perregaux's Tourbillon with three gold bridges received the ultimate accolade in the form of a gold medal at the Paris Universal Exhibition.

Today, more than three decades since the Swiss house resumed production of this icon of haute horology, it rejuvenates its legacy with the adoption of a round 41mm case and a rare shape for the bridges themselves. The latter have been reinterpreted while keeping to the spirit and principles that earned Girard-Perregaux accolades from the Neuchâtel Observatory in 1860. Dedicated and scrupulous craftsmanship results in bridges that are hollowed and finely polished for a result that imbues the watch with a sense of contemporary purity.

Along with bridges that require a full seven days of careful finishing, this timepiece is armed with a delicate tourbillon worthy of the history inherent in the watch's name. Girard-Perregaux engineers display their incredible dexterity with the assembly of 72 components within a diameter of just 1cm. The tourbillon weighs 0.3g, about the same as a swan's feather. A small-diameter platinum oscillating weight fitted below and around the barrel accompanies the manufacture's own self-winding system, preserving the movement's dimensions and architecture.

Girard-Perregaux is equally proud to present its newest expression of the exquisite marriage of feminine curves and precious mechanisms. Since its creation in 2004, the Cat's Eye collection has been a poetic manifestation of the Swiss watchmaker's renowned expertise. While always a seductive display, this collection has also exemplified the merits of haute horology's finest self-winding mechanisms.

The new Cat's Eye small seconds full paved case model adds a new facet to the collection. The feminine watch complements the sensual curves and oval form of the gold case with an elegant and beautifully balanced small seconds feature at 9 o'clock that is enhanced by a delicately traced radiating motif. Each sparkling hour index is a precious stone, while numerals at 6, 9, and 12 o'clock are sculpted in gold wire that is cut and hand-polished before being riveted to the mother-of-pearl dial.

Remaining true to the brand's philosophy and its quest for excellence in every detail, Girard-Perregaux has equipped this model with the self-winding GP3300 movement, whose refined character can be appreciated through the sapphire crystal caseback.

Whether it is honoring the birth of the acclaimed manufacture, or dreaming up a modern expression of a woman's watch that marries beauty and performance, Girard-Perregaux furthers and rejuvenates a legacy of innovation and excellence with every detail of these two dazzling new releases .

CAT'S EYE SMALL SECONDS FULL PAVED

Do not be fooled by the sensual exterior of this woman's watch, as it makes no concessions in terms of technical performance.

TOURBILLON BI-AXIAL REF. 99810-53-000-BA6A

Movement: manual-winding GPE0201; caliber 15⅓ lines; 72-hour power reserve; 28 jewels; 21,600 vph.
Functions: hours, minutes; bi-axial tourbillon at 6.
Case: 18K white gold; Ø 45mm, thickness: 18.5mm; sapphire crystal caseback secured by six screws; water resistant to 3atm.
Strap: black large-scale alligator leather, hand-stitched; 18K white-gold folding buckle.
Note: limited and numbered edition of 33 pieces.
Also available: 18K 5N pink gold.

GIRARD-PERREGAUX 1966 TOURBILLON WITH GOLD BRIDGE 220TH ANNIVERSARY REF. 99535-52-111-BK6A

Movement: automatic-winding GP9600-0014; caliber Ø 28.6mm; 46-hour power reserve; 26 jewels; 21,600 vph.
Functions: hours, minutes; small seconds on the tourbillon at 6.
Case: 18K 5N pink gold; Ø 40mm, thickness: 10.9mm; caseback secured by six screws; water resistant to 3atm.
Dial: silver opaline; eleven black transferred Arabic numerals.
Strap: black large-scale alligator leather, hand-stitched; 18K pink-gold pin buckle.
Note: limited and numbered edition of 50 pieces.

GIRARD-PERREGAUX 1966 PERPETUAL CALENDAR REF. 90535D52A1A1-BK6A

Movement: automatic-winding GP033Q0; caliber Ø 26.2mm; 46-hour power reserve; 26 jewels; 28,800 vph.
Functions: hours, minutes; perpetual calendar: month counter at 12, day of the week counter at 9 and date counter at 3; moonphase at 6.
Case: 18K 5N pink gold; Ø 40mm, thickness: 10.74mm; set with 60 diamonds (1.5 carats); press-in sapphire crystal caseback; water resistant to 3atm.
Dial: silvered opaline; four applied 18K 5N pink-gold hour markers and eight diamond hour markers; leaf-shaped hour and minute hands.
Strap: black large-scale alligator leather; 18K 5N pink-gold pin buckle.
Also available: 18K white gold.

GIRARD-PERREGAUX 1966 ANNUAL CALENDAR AND EQUATION OF TIME REF. 49538-52-131-BK6A

Movement: automatic-winding GP3300-0010; caliber 11½ lines; 46-hour power reserve; 44 jewels; 28,800 vph.
Functions: hours, minutes; small seconds at 9; date at 1:30; month at 7; equation of time at 4:30.
Case: 5N 18K pink gold; Ø 40mm, thickness: 10.72mm; press-in sapphire crystal caseback; water resistant to 3atm.
Dial: silvered opaline; applied hour markers; leaf-shaped hour and minute hands.
Strap: black large-scale alligator leather; 18K pink-gold pin buckle.
Also available: 18K white gold.

WW.TC CHRONOGRAPH — REF. 49815-52-151-BACA

Movement: automatic-winding GP033CO; caliber 13 lines; 46-hour power reserve; 63 jewels; 28,800 vph.
Functions: hours, minutes; small seconds at 3; date between 1 and 2; chronograph: 12-hour counter at 6, 30-minute counter at 9 and central chronograph hand; world time with day/night indicator.
Case: 18K 5N pink gold; Ø 43mm, thickness: 13.4mm; sapphire crystal caseback secured by six screws; water resistant to 5atm.
Dial: silver; applied Arabic numeral 12; eight round luminescent hour markers.
Strap: brown large-scale alligator leather; 18K pink-gold folding buckle.
Also available: 18K white-gold case with black leather strap.

WW.TC LADY — REF. 49860D52P761-KK7A

Movement: automatic-winding GP033G0; caliber 11½ lines; 46-hour power reserve; 27 jewels; 28,800 vph.
Functions: hours, minutes; small seconds; power reserve indicator; world time with day/night indicator.
Case: 18K 5N pink gold; Ø 41mm, thickness: 11mm; set with 274 white round diamonds (4.12 carats); crown set with two diamonds (0.4 carat); sapphire crystal caseback secured by six screws; water resistant to 5atm.
Dial: white mother-of-pearl; nine white diamond hour markers.
Strap: white satin; 18K pink-gold folding buckle set with 18 diamonds (0.2 carat).

VINTAGE 1945 XXL — REF. 25880-52-721-BB6A

Movement: automatic-winding GP3300; caliber 11½ lines; 46-hour power reserve; 32 jewels; 28,800 vph.
Functions: hours, minutes; small seconds at 6.
Case: 18K 5N pink gold; 36.2x35.25mm, thickness: 10.83mm; sapphire crystal secured by four screws; water resistant to 3atm.
Dial: silvered opaline; painted Arabic numerals.
Strap: black large-scale alligator leather, hand-stitched, 18K 5N pink-gold folding buckle.
Also available: stainless steel.

CAT'S EYE ANNUAL AND ZODIAC CALENDARS — REF. 80483D52A761-KK7A

Movement: automatic-winding GP030M0; caliber 11½ lines; 46-hour power reserve; 42 jewels; 28,800 vph.
Functions: hours, minutes; small seconds at 9; date at 1:30; zodiac calendar between 4 and 8; moonphase.
Case: 18K 5N pink gold; 35.25x30.25mm, thickness: 10.95mm; set with 68 diamonds (0.68 carats); press-in sapphire crystal; water resistant to 3atm.
Dial: white mother-of-pearl.
Strap: white satin; 18K pink-gold folding buckle.
Also available: 18K white gold.

Glashütte ORIGINAL

SAVE THE DATE

As Glashütte Original brilliantly demonstrates with the Senator Diary, it is a duty of the time-keeping innovator to extend its expert heritage to the service of the resolutely contemporary.

Creating an unprecedented function that permits the setting of an alarm up to 30 days in advance, the German manufacture addresses the needs of the modern businessman, whose schedule grants him little time to keep track of his most essential priorities. The new white-gold version of the Senator Diary sets an elegant perimeter for a dial as tastefully understated as it is expressive. Endowed with Incabloc shock protection, the 42mm case initiates the refined design balance of the timepiece. A crown and pushbutton combination on either side of the frame is met by its reversed counterpart on the opposite side, as if each element were extended through the watch, piercing it through its exact center. Standing out from the black watch face, the intricate lines of the ruthenium subdial at 9 o'clock are contrasted by a rotating red hand that indicates the chosen date for the special appointment. Pressing the pushbutton at 8 o'clock until the letter "d" appears in the window, the owner is then able to rotate the winding stem at 10 o'clock to position the pointer on the appropriate Arabic numeral date. Once this has been done, an additional touch of the pusher indicates the letter "h" in the opening. A turn of the 10 o'clock crown now allows the selection of the alarm's desired triggering time, in quarter-hour intervals, on the panoramic 24-hour display aperture at 6 o'clock. One final push of the button and winding of the crown, and the sonorous reminder is set. Stopping the alarm—during its resonance or at any time before—is as easy as a single push of the 8 o'clock activator to drive a black line through the window's revealed bell.

Through an ingenious interlocking system, the 600-component Glashütte Original 100-13 automatic caliber, with fine swan-neck adjustment, allows the setting of the alarm beyond the end of the calendar month. A pragmatic addition, any manual correction of the date is transmitted to the appointment mechanism, removing the owner's need to reset the reminder. Completing the innovative excellence of the Senator Diary's unique complication, a third spring barrel is built into the module so that the alarm remains wound, even if the watch runs down past its 55-hour power reserve.

On the caseback, an antireflective sapphire crystal reveals the exquisite finish of the Glashütte Original divided three-quarter plate, skeletonized rotor and 21-karat gold oscillating weight.

Extending the reach of the timepiece to the digital playground, Glashütte Original presents a free Senator Diary iPhone application, complete with an interactive catalogue and tour of the manufacture's facility, instructive games, and of course, a functioning Diary to help manage the special dates in the owner's life.

Oscillating at a frequency of 28,800 vph, and worn on a finely worked Louisiana alligator leather strap, the Senator Diary is a decisively contemporary and relevant timepiece that elegantly exhibits the innovative vision and technical expertise of the German watchmaker.

SENATOR DIARY

Available in stainless steel, or in rose gold with blue alarm pointers, as well as white gold, the Senator Diary is more than a resonating appointment reminder; it is a trusted horological companion in a fast-moving world.

Glashütte
ORIGINAL
3
31
29
27
25
23
21
19
17
15
13
11
9
GLASHÜT

SENATOR DIARY WHITE GOLD — REF. 100-13-04-04-04

Movement: automatic-winding 100-13 caliber; Ø 34mm, thickness: 8.4mm; 55-hour power reserve; 86 jewels; 28,800 vph; screw balance with 18 gold weighted screws; Nivarox flat balance spring; Incabloc shock protection; beveled edges; Glashütte three-quarter plate with stripe finish; centralized positioned and skeletonized rotor with Glashütte stripe finish; rotor with 21K gold oscillating weight; swan-neck fine adjustment.

Functions: hours, minutes, seconds; panorama date; appointment mode, day and hour; reminder function with sound signal (approx. 8-seconds); reset function.
Case: white gold; Ø 42mm, thickness: 14.4mm; two crowns; two pushbuttons; antireflective sapphire crystal on both sides; water resistant to 5atm.
Dial: galvanized ruthenium.
Strap: gray nubuck Louisiana alligator leather.
Suggested price: $38,200

SENATOR PERPETUAL CALENDAR RED GOLD — REF. 100-02-25-05-05

Movement: automatic-winding 100-02 caliber; Ø 31.15mm, thickness: 7.1mm; 55-hour power reserve; 59 jewels; 28,800 vph; screw balance with 18K gold weighted screws; Nivarox flat balance spring; Incabloc shock protection; polished steel parts; beveled edges; Glashütte three-quarter plate with stripe finish; skeletonized rotor with Glashütte stripe finish; rotor with 21K gold oscillating weight; swan-neck fine adjustment.

Functions: hours, minutes, seconds; panorama date; perpetual calendar: day of the week, month and leap year cycle; moonphase.
Case: red gold; Ø 42mm, thickness: 13.6mm; antireflective sapphire crystal; sapphire crystal caseback; water resistant to 5atm.
Dial: matte black; white Roman numerals; red-gold hands.
Strap: black Louisiana alligator leather.
Suggested price: $35,300
Also available: black rubber strap (ref. 100-02-25-05-04).

PANOINVERSE XL — REF. 66-04-04-02-05

Movement: manual-winding 66 caliber; 40-hour power reserve; Glashütte three-quarter plate with stripe finish; swan-neck fine adjustment; Incabloc shock protection; hand-engraved balance cock; screw-mounted gold chatons.
Functions: off-centered hours, minutes; small seconds; power reserve indicator.
Case: stainless steel; Ø 42mm, thickness: 11.2mm; antireflective sapphire crystal on both sides; water resistant to 3atm.

Dial: ruthenium; mounted numerals; hour and minute hands with luminescent coating.
Strap: gray Louisiana nubuck alligator leather; stainless steel folding clasp.
Suggested price: $12,600

PANOMATICLUNAR XL — REF. 90-02-36-12-05

Movement: automatic-winding 90 caliber; Glashütte three-quarter plate with stripe finish; blued screws; swan-neck fine adjustment; hand-engraved balance cock; skeletonized rotor with 21K gold oscillating weight.
Functions: off-centered hours, minutes; small seconds; panorama date; moonphase.
Case: stainless steel; Ø 42mm, thickness: 12.5mm; crown with double G; antireflective sapphire crystal on both sides; water resistant to 3atm.

Dial: ruthenium; white-gold hour and minute hands with luminescent coating; white-gold hour markers with luminescent coating; applied white-gold Arabic numeral at 12; finely milled and galvanized hour, minute and small seconds counters; polished and satin-finished.
Strap: gray Louisiana nubuck alligator leather; stainless steel folding clasp.
Suggested price: $11,600

SENATOR CHRONOMETER — REF. 58-01-01-01-04

Movement: manual-winding 58-01 caliber; 45-hour power reserve; Glashütte three-quarter plate with stripe finish; hand-engraved balance cock; screw-mounted gold chatons.
Functions: hours, minutes; small seconds at 6; power reserve indicator; day/night indicator; stop seconds/reset mechanism with minute detent; panorama date at 3.
Case: 18K rose gold; Ø 42mm, thickness 12.3mm; antireflective sapphire crystal on both sides; water resistant to 5atm.
Dial: silver with l'argenture grainée (frosted silver plating); milled railroad chapter ring; milled Roman numerals; blued hands; manually polished arbor.
Strap: black Louisiana alligator leather with integrated lugs; 18K rose-gold folding clasp.
Suggested price: $28,100
Also available: 18K white gold.

SEVENTIES PANORAMA DATE — REF. 39-47-13-12-14

Movement: automatic-winding 39-47 caliber; Ø 30.95mm, thickness: 5.9mm; 40-hour power reserve; 39 jewels; 28,800 vph; Nivarox flat balance spring; Incabloc shock protection; polished steel parts; beveled edges; Glashütte three-quarter plate with stripe finish; skeletonized rotor with Glashütte stripe finish; rotor with 21K gold oscillating weight; swan-neck fine adjustment.
Functions: hours, minutes, seconds; panorama date at 6.
Case: stainless steel; 40x40mm, thickness: 11.5mm; antireflective sapphire crystal on both sides; water resistant to 10atm.
Dial: blue; hour markers and hands with luminescent coating.
Bracelet: brushed and polished stainless steel; push-button fold over clasp.
Suggested price: $11,100
Also available: galvanized ruthenium dial (ref. 39-47-12-12-14); galvanized silver dial (ref. 39-47-11-12-14).

SIXTIES PANORAMA DATE — REF. 39-47-02-01-04

Movement: automatic-winding 39-47 caliber; Ø 30.95mm, thickness: 5.9mm; 40-hour power reserve; 39 jewels; 28,800 vph; German silver balance; Nivarox flat balance spring; Incabloc shock protection; polished steel parts; beveled edges; Glashütte three-quarter plate with stripe finish; skeletonized rotor with Glashütte stripe finish; rotor with 21K gold oscillating weight; swan-neck fine adjustment.
Functions: hours, minutes, seconds; panorama date at 6.
Case: rose gold; Ø 42mm, thickness: 12.4mm; antireflective sapphire crystal on both sides; water resistant to 3atm.
Dial: galvanized black; rose-gold hands and hour markers with luminescent coating.
Strap: black Louisiana alligator leather.
Suggested price: $16,800

PANOMATICLUNA — REF. 90-12-01-12-04

Movement: automatic-winding 90-12 caliber; Ø 32.6mm, thickness: 7mm; 40-hour power reserve; 47 jewels; 28,800 vph; screw balance with 18K gold weighted screws; Nivarox flat balance spring; Incabloc shock protection; polished steel parts; beveled edges; Glashütte three-quarter plate with stripe finish; skeletonized rotor with Glashütte stripe finish; rotor with 21K gold oscillating weight; duplex swan-neck fine adjustment.
Functions: off-centered hours and minutes; small seconds; panorama date; moonphase; stop seconds.
Case: stainless steel; Ø 39.4mm, thickness: 12mm; antireflective sapphire crystal on both sides; water resistant to 3atm.
Dial: light-colored mother-of-pearl; set with 18 diamonds (0.042 carat).
Strap: white rubber.
Suggested price: $18,500
Also available: Louisiana alligator leather strap (ref. 90-12-01-12-02).

GRAHAM
LONDON

THE ELEGANCE OF SPEED

Wearing the thrill of adventure with uncompromising elegance, Graham-London unveils three chronographs that blur the line between adrenaline and modern refinement.

To put it into context, the Silverstone Tourbillograph Full Black belongs in the driver's seat of a speed-demon sports car, letting the engine roar while wearing a sharp black tuxedo. Turning the ordinarily fragile tourbillon into an affair of military resistance, the shockproof double-bridge construction of the cage is systematically designed to experience reduced magnetic sensitivity. As it performs its one-minute revolution within a blackened aperture with black PVD-coated upper bridge, the timepiece's lightweight tourbillon welcomes admiration via the smooth transparent design of its skeleton cage. Leaving behind none of the manufacture's valiant DNA, the sophisticated cintré construction integrates the tourbillon into the high-performance column-wheel

CHRONOFIGHTER OVERSIZE GMT BLACK STEEL

This combination of column-wheel chronograph and sophisticated tourbillon is a sleek mirage of blackened perfection.

Armed with the clarity of a peripheral secondary time zone, the Chronofighter Oversize GMT Black Steel puts its owner's finger on time's own fast-action trigger. As the highly shock-resistant automatic bi-compax chronograph's G1733 caliber powers the watch's 4Hz frequency and 48-hour power reserve, the design of the 47mm timepiece tells a consistent story of extreme performance. The steel and sapphire bezel initiates the assertive tone as the eye is drawn to the highly visible black dial upon which the red chronograph hands stand out without ambiguity. Echoing the luminosity of the Arabic numerals, as well as central and small seconds hands, the skeleton GMT indicator uses white SuperLumiNova for optimal nighttime visibility, while its red contour clearly differentiates one time zone from the other. Completing, and for that matter initiating, the powerful aesthetic of the timepiece, the black PVD, left-hand fast-action start/stop trigger ensures a precise level of control befitting this high-speed GMT chronograph.

Piston-like pushbuttons with high-grip Clous de Paris finishing quickly declare the identity of the limited edition Silverstone Stowe GMT Blue & Yellow. If the message needed more clarification, an integrated tire-tread rubber strap with yellow inset confirms the timepiece's unquestionable connection to the high-speed world of motor racing. On the black carbon-fiber checkered-flag dial, numerous time-keeping layers demonstrate the Anglo-Swiss watch-maker's mastery of clarity. Along with its display of the hours and seconds with yellow SuperLumiNova hands and yellow lacquered numerals, this colorful flyback chronograph exhibits its GMT function with ingenious discretion. Seemingly disappearing against its race-inspired backdrop, the black GMT stem leaves only the illusion of an orbiting red-contoured white triangle, hovering as it points to the appropriate hour on the 24-hour blue ring of the carbon bezel. With the addition of a subtle tachometer scale on the outside of the dial, the Silverstone Stowe GMT Blue & Yellow vividly gives its owner comprehensive control of all things fast, faster and fastest.

Ranging from the James Bond of wristwatches to a timepiece that resounds with the screeching of tires, Graham-London's new chronographs share a common passion and a decisive implication: the measure of speed is to be worn with pride, power, and style.

SILVERSTONE STOWE GMT BLUE & YELLOW

A double-disc date at 6 o'clock sits discreetly within a vibrant presentation of precise time measurements.

CHRONOFIGHTER OVERSIZE GMT BLACK STEEL — REF. 20VGS.B39A

Movements: automatic-winding G1733 caliber; 48-hour power reserve; 28 jewels; 28,800 vph; bi-compax chronograph; Incabloc shock absorber.
Functions: hours, minutes; small seconds at 3; large date with double disc at 12; chronograph: 30-minute counter at 9 and central seconds hand; GMT/second time zone.
Case: steel; Ø 47mm; steel and sapphire bezel; black and silver GMT ring; steel with black PVD-coating left-hand fast-action start/stop trigger and reset pushbuttons; antireflective domed sapphire crystal; smoked sapphire caseback; water resistant to 10atm.
Dial: black; silver counters; white hour, minute and seconds hands with SuperLumiNova; white numerals with SuperLumiNova; white skeleton GMT hand with white SuperLumiNova tip and red contour; red chronograph and minute hands.
Strap: integrated black crocodile.
Also available: steel and gold or gold; integrated black rubber or calf strap.
Suggested price: $11,950

CHRONOFIGHTER OVERSIZE DIVER — REF. 20VEB.B40A

Movements: automatic-winding G1734 caliber; 48-hour power reserve; 27 jewels; 28,800 vph; bi-compax chronograph; Incabloc shock absorber.
Functions: hours, minutes; small seconds at 3; date at 7; chronograph: 30-minute counter at 9 and central seconds hand; helium escape valve.
Case: steel with black PVD-coating; Ø 47mm; steel and black PVD bezel rotating rim to measure decompression time; steel with black PVD left-hand fast-action start/stop trigger and reset pushbuttons with Clous de Paris high grip pattern; antireflective domed sapphire crystal; steel with black PVD caseback with Royal Marine crown symbol; water resistant to 33atm.
Dial: black; black counters; black nickel hour and minute hands with black SuperLumiNova; black nickel hour markers with black SuperLumiNova; black chronograph and minutes hands with orange tip.
Strap: integrated black rubber; ceramic pin buckle.
Suggested price: $12,235

SILVERSTONE STOWE GMT BLUE & YELLOW — REF. 2BLCH.B06A

Movement: automatic-winding G1721 caliber; 48-hour power reserve; 28 jewels; 28,800 vph; bi-compax chronograph; Incabloc shock absorber.
Functions: hours, minutes; small seconds at 9; large date with double disc at 6; chronograph: 30-minute counter at 3 and central seconds hand; flyback; GMT/second time zone.
Case: steel with black PVD-coating; Ø 48mm; black carbon bezel; blue GMT ring; steel right-hand control pushbuttons with Clous de Paris high grip pattern; antireflective domed sapphire crystal; transparent sapphire caseback with limited edition serial number engraved; water resistant to 10atm.
Dial: black carbon; black snailed minutes counter with blue ring; black tachometer scale on outer ring; yellow hour and minute hands with SuperLumiNova; yellow-lacquered numerals; black GMT hand with white SuperLumiNova tip and red contour.
Strap: integrated black-tire tread rubber with yellow inset.
Note: limited edition of 250 pieces.
Suggested price: $11,550

SILVERSTONE STOWE CLASSIC GOLD — REF. 2BLDZ.B12A

Movement: automatic-winding G1742 caliber; 48-hour power reserve; 27 jewels; 28,800 vph; bi-compax column-wheel chronograph; Incabloc shock absorber.
Functions: hours, minutes; small seconds at 9; date at 7; column-wheel chronograph: 30-minutes counter at 3 and central seconds hand.
Case: steel with black PVD-coating; Ø 48mm; black ceramic bezel; 18K red-gold internal ring with tachometer scale; 18K red-gold right-hand control pushbuttons with Clous de Paris high grip pattern; antireflective domed sapphire crystal; transparent sapphire caseback; water resistant to 10atm.
Dial: black carbon; black carbon seconds counter; black snailed minutes counter with gold ring; white hour and minute hands with SuperLumiNova and gold counter; white numerals and hour markers with SuperLumiNova and gold counter.
Strap: integrated black-tire tread rubber with yellow inset.
Suggested price: $13,810
Also available: classic steel and racing yellow.

CHRONOFIGHTER FORTRESS — REF. 2CRBS.B10A

Movement: automatic-winding G1742 caliber; 48-hour power reserve; 28 jewels; 28,800 vph; column-wheel bi-compax chronograph; Incabloc shock absorber.
Functions: hours, minutes; small seconds at 3; date at 4:30; column-wheel chronograph: 30-minute counter at 9 and central seconds hand.
Case: steel; Ø 43mm; steel bezel; left-hand fast-action start/stop trigger and reset pushbuttons; antireflective domed sapphire crystal; transparent sapphire caseback; water resistant to 10atm.
Dial: black; black snailed minutes and seconds counters; beige hour and minute hands with SuperLumiNova; beige numerals and hour markers with SuperLumiNova.
Strap: light brown bomber jacket calf.
Suggested price: $9,265

SWORDFISH BOOSTER BLACK BLUE HANDS — REF. 2SWBB.U36L

Movement: automatic-winding G1710 caliber; 48-hour power reserve; 34 jewels; 28,800 vph; bi-compax chronograph; Incabloc shock absorber.
Functions: hours, minutes, small seconds; chronograph: 12-hour counter at 3, 30-minute counter at 9 and central seconds hand.
Case: steel with black PVD-coating; Ø 48mm; steel with black PVD bezel; two steel with black PVD portholes at 3 and 9; steel left-hand control pushbuttons with Clous de Paris high grip pattern; antireflective flat sapphire crystal; smoked screw-down transparent sapphire caseback; water resistant to 10atm.
Dial: black; black snailed hour and minute counters; skeleton hour and minute hands with black SuperLumiNova; blue chronograph hour, minutes and central seconds hand; hour markers with black SuperLumiNova.
Strap: integrated black rubber.
Suggested price: $11,535
Also available: gray and yellow with red hands.

SILVERSTONE TOURBILLOGRAPH FULL BLACK — REF. 2TSAB.B02A

Movement: automatic-winding G1780 caliber; 48-hour power reserve; 34 jewels; 28,800 vph; bi-compax column-wheel chronograph-tourbillon; Incabloc shock absorber; ruthenium blackened movement with Haute Horlogerie finishing; perlages, sandblasted, manually chamfered and polished bridges and bottom plate; column-wheel with polished segments and black low-friction coating; ruthenium oscillating weight with skeletonized rotor and 925 sterling silver segment; blackened tourbillon cage: 48 components, 0.485g; off-centered construction at 11; complete transparent tourbillon; two patents; double bridge construction with black PVD-coated upper bridge; black-gold balance.
Functions: hours, minutes; small seconds; tourbillon; column-wheel chronograph: 12-hour counter at 6, 30-minute counter at 3 and central seconds hand.
Case: steel with black PVD-coating; Ø 48mm; steel bezel with black PVD; steel with black PVD right-hand start/stop and reset pushbuttons with Clous de Paris high grip pattern; antireflective domed sapphire crystal; transparent sapphire caseback; water resistant to 50atm.
Dial: black; tachometer scale on the external ring; rhodium hands and numerals.
Strap: black crocodile; black ceramic folding buckle.
Suggested price: $55,760

SILVERSTONE TOURBILLOGRAPH GOLD — REF. 2TSAR.W01A

Movement: automatic-winding G1780 caliber; 48-hour power reserve; 34 jewels; 28,800 vph; bi-compax column-wheel chronograph-tourbillon; Incabloc shock absorber; black-gold movement with Haute Horlogerie finishing; perlages, sandblasted, manually chamfered and polished bridges and bottom plate; column-wheel with polished segments and black low-friction coating; black-gold oscillating weight with skeletonized rotor and 18K red-gold segment; rhodium tourbillon cage: 48 components, 0.485g; off-centered construction at 11; complete transparent tourbillon; two patents; double bridge construction with 18K red-gold coated upper bridge; golden balance.
Functions: hours, minutes; small seconds; tourbillon; column-wheel chronograph: 12-hour counter at 6, 30-minute counter at 3 and central seconds hand.
Case: 18K red gold; Ø 48mm; 18K red-gold bezel; 18K red-gold right-hand start/stop and reset pushbuttons with Clous de Paris high grip pattern; antireflective domed sapphire crystal; transparent sapphire caseback; water resistant to 50atm.
Dial: white; tachometer scale on the external ring, golden minute scale rim; golden hands and numerals.
Strap: black crocodile; 18K red-gold pin buckle.
Suggested price: $73,550
Also available: black dial.

GREUBEL FORSEY

INVENTEURS HORLOGERS

AS THE WORLD TURNS

Immune to convention, Robert Greubel and Stephen Forsey prove once again that true genius requires the courage to stand by one's visionary spirit.

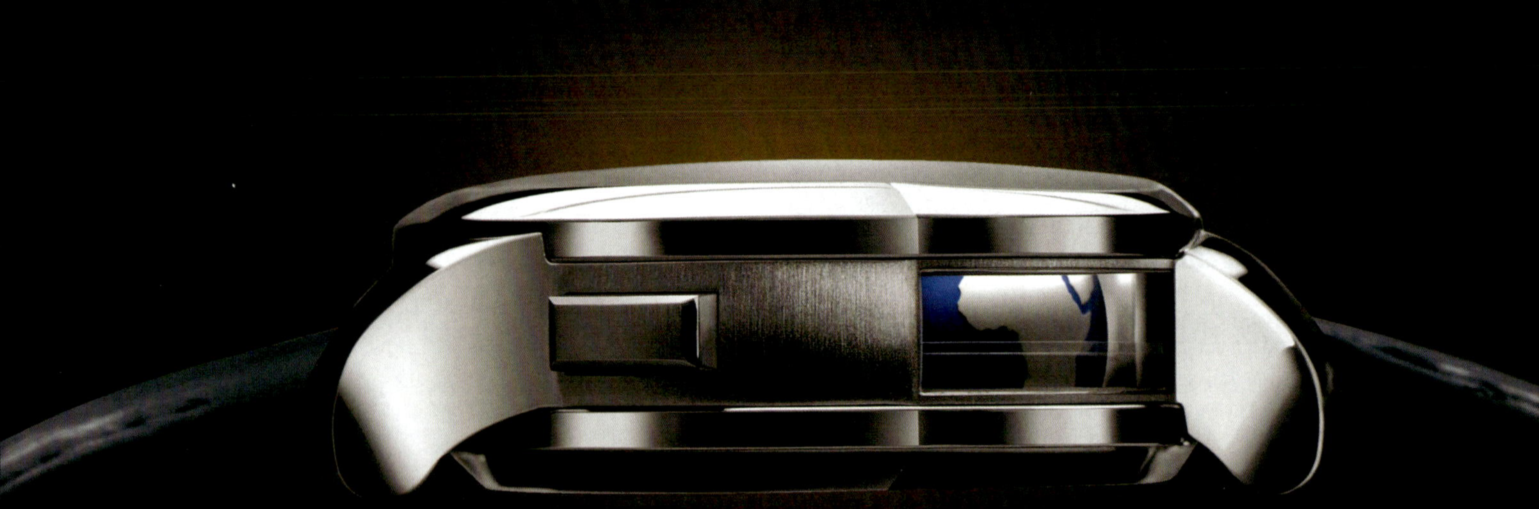

After a decade devoted to exploring, inventing and developing brilliant new mechanisms in the world of the tourbillon, the virtuoso team turn their imaginative intelligence to the indication of a secondary time zone.

With the new GMT wristwatch, Greubel Forsey presents the indication of time as a marvelous three-dimensional tableau. Prominently placed at 8 o'clock, a terrestrial globe offers a jaw-dropping view of time all over the world. Following the earth's natural rotational direction, the flying globe completes one counterclockwise revolution every 24 hours. Secured only at the South Pole, the titanium sphere allows for an optimal view of its intricate surface while the continents are easily cross-referenced with the 24-hour day/night indicator on the equatorial chapter ring. A blackened half of the ring around the globe indicates the nighttime hemisphere while a whitened section underscores the daytime hemisphere. As a touch of poetry in motion, a window on the side of the case cleverly lets in light and further symbolizes the brightness of day on the appropriate half of the globe.

One quick glance, and the wearer is immediately connected to sunrise in New York, lunch hour in Florence, or sunset on the Indian coast. With a single glimpse of the delightfully detailed globe, the entire world is united by the notion of time.

A second time zone at 10 o'clock complements the intuitive globe with a precise indication of time in a designated location and is easily adjusted with a dual-function pushbutton on the caseband.

The small seconds indicator at 2 o'clock rests gracefully on the ring of the principal hour and minute dial and creates a gentle border for the 72-hour power reserve at 3 o'clock. Finally, this Greubel Forsey masterpiece would not be complete without its superb 25° inclined Tourbillon 24 Secondes cage. Proposing a strong architectural dimension, this patented Greubel Forsey invention enhances the daring asymmetry of the GMT with its placement at 5 o'clock. As each component of this timepiece finds its careful place on the dial, the game of shape, color and depth creates a graceful tension that keeps the eyes marveling at the peaceful complexity of the watch.

The caseback of the GMT reveals a finely crafted world-time disc upon which 24 cities represent each of the planet's time zones. This interactive module, with which the owner aligns the appropriate city with its local hour, may be used to set the dial-side globe to the correct position. A shining sun adjacent to the disc acts as a coordinated reference to midday, as it illuminates the movement of this masterful work of timekeeping architecture.

As they have done so successfully over the last decade, Robert Greubel and Stephen Forsey demonstrate once more that their ingenuity knows only the bounds of their masterful exuberance. An ingenious combination of the finest technical expertise and an audacious play on three-dimensional geometry, Greubel Forsey's GMT sets a new definition of the world-time concept, offering a visual interpretation that adorns the wrist with a planet of its own.

GMT

Housed within a 43.5mm white-gold case, the 436-component movement powers a dazzling orchestra of timekeeping complications.

TOURBILLON 24 SECONDES — REF. 9000 1151

Movement: manual-winding GF01 caliber; Ø 36.4mm, thickness: 9.35mm; 72-hour power reserve; 280 components; 36 jewels; 21,600 vph; rapid rotating twin barrels (1 turn in 3.2 hours) one of which is equipped with a slipping spring to avoid excess tension; free sprung variable-inertia balance wheel with gold mean-time screws (Ø 10mm); Phillips terminal curve with Geneva-style stud; nickel silver main plates, spotted and snailed with polished beveling and nickel-palladium finish; nickel silver bridges, frosted and spotted with polished beveling with nickel-palladium finish; three engraved gold plates (Greubel Forsey, individual number and name of the invention); steel barrel polished tourbillon bridge; black PVD-coated titanium platform under the tourbillon and polished backdrop; Involute circle profile Tangential inclined gear with profiled teeth on fixed wheel and escape wheel pinion.

Functions: hours, minutes; small seconds; power reserve indicator; 24-second tourbillon at 8.
Case: 5N 18K red gold; Ø 43.5mm, thickness: 16.11mm; polished bezel and center band with hand-finished straight graining; convex sapphire crystal; transparent sapphire crystal caseback; raised polished "Tourbillon 24 Secondes Incliné" engraving on a hand-punched background; gold security screws; hand-engraved individual number; water resistant to 3atm.
Dial: silvered; gold hour markers; gold display sectors; polished gold hour, minute, small seconds and power reserve hands; black anodized aluminum double-tipped 24-second hand; applied gold Greubel Forsey logo.
Strap: hand-sewn black alligator; 5N 18K rose-gold folding clasp, hand-engraved with the Greubel Forsey logo.
Price: available upon request.

TOURBILLON 24 SECONDES — REF. 9000 1154

Movement: manual-winding GF01 caliber; Ø 36.4mm, thickness: 9.35mm; 72-hour power reserve; 282 components; 36 jewels; 21,600 vph; rapid rotating twin barrels (1 turn in 3.2 hours) one of which is equipped with a slipping spring to avoid excess tension; free sprung variable-inertia balance wheel with gold mean-time screws (Ø 10mm); Phillips terminal curve with Geneva-style stud; nickel silver main plates, spotted and snailed with polished beveling and nickel-palladium finish; nickel silver bridges, frosted and spotted with polished beveling with nickel-palladium finish; three engraved gold plates (Greubel Forsey, individual number and name of the invention); steel barrel polished tourbillon bridge; black PVD-coated titanium platform under the tourbillon and polished backdrop; Involute circle profile Tangential inclined gear with profiled teeth, on fixed wheel and escape wheel pinion.

Functions: hours, minutes; small seconds; power reserve indicator; 24-second tourbillon at 8.
Case: 950 platinum; Ø 43.5mm, thickness: 16.11mm; polished bezel and center band with hand-finished straight graining; platinum crown with engraved and black lacquered GF logo; convex sapphire crystal; transparent sapphire crystal caseback; raised polished "Tourbillon 24 Secondes Incliné" engraving on a hand-punched background; gold security screws; hand-engraved individual number; water resistant to 3atm.
Dial: 18K gold with anthracite finish; gold hour markers; gold display sectors; relief-engraved zone of text; applied gold GF logo; gold hour and minute hands with SuperLumiNova; polished gold small seconds and power reserve hands; black anodised aluminum 24-second double-tipped hand.
Strap: hand-sewn black alligator; 950 platinum folding clasp, hand-engraved with the Greubel Forsey logo.
Price: available upon request.

DOUBLE TOURBILLON 30° TECHNIQUE — REF. 9000 2394

Movement: manual-winding GF02s caliber; Ø 38.4mm, thickness: 12.15mm; 120-hour power reserve; 385 components; 43 jewels; 21,600 vph; gold nickel-palladium finished barrels covered with relief engraving, four coaxial series-coupled fast-rotating barrels (1 turn in 3.2 hours) one of which is equipped with a slipping spring to avoid excess tension; free sprung variable-inertia balance wheel with white-gold mean-time screws (Ø 10.7mm); Phillips terminal curve balance spring with Geneva-style stud; nickel silver mainplates frosted with polished beveling, ruthenium finish; nickel silver bridges, frosted, spotted with polished beveling, nickel-palladium finish and gold nameplate bearing the individual number; involute circle profile gearing, conical gearing with corrected profile; inner tourbillon: inclined at a 30° angle with one rotation per minute; outer tourbillon: one rotation in 4 minutes, hand-beveled and openworked cage pillars with gold counterweight.

Functions: hours, minutes; small seconds; power reserve indicator; 4-minute out tourbillon rotation indicator.
Case: 18K white gold; Ø 47.5mm, thickness: 16.84mm; white-gold crown engraved and black lacquered with GF logo; three-dimensional, variable geometrically-shaped lugs secured with screws; convex sapphire crystal; transparent sapphire crystal caseback; raised and polished with "Double Tourbillon 30° Technique" engraving on a hand-punched background; gold security screws; two white-gold engraved and hand-finished plates bearing text screwed to the caseband; hand-engraved individual numbers; water resistant to 3atm.
Dial: sapphire crystal hour ring; gold small seconds and power reserve indicator; polished gold hour and minute hands with SuperLumiNova; small seconds and power reserve indicator red triangle hands; sapphire crystal 4-minute tourbillon engraved indicator.
Strap: hand-sewn black alligator; 18K white-gold folding clasp hand-engraved with Greubel Forsey logo.
Price: available upon request.

DOUBLE TOURBILLON 30° TECHNIQUE — REF. 9000 2395

Movement: manual-winding GF02s caliber; Ø 38.4mm, thickness: 12.15mm; 120-hour power reserve; 385 components; 43 jewels; 21,600 vph; gold nickel-palladium finished barrels covered with relief engraving, four coaxial series-coupled fast-rotating barrels (1 turn in 3.2 hours) one of which is equipped with a slipping spring to avoid excess tension; free sprung variable-inertia balance wheel with white-gold mean-time screws (Ø 10.7mm); Phillips terminal curve balance spring with Geneva-style stud; nickel silver mainplates frosted with polished beveling, ruthenium finish; nickel silver bridges, frosted, spotted with polished beveling, nickel-palladium finish and gold nameplate bearing the individual number; involute circle profile gearing, conical gearing with corrected profile; inner tourbillon: inclined at a 30° angle with one rotation per minute; outer tourbillon: one rotation in 4 minutes, hand-beveled and openworked cage pillars with gold counterweight.

Functions: hours, minutes; small seconds; power reserve indicator; 4-minute out tourbillon rotation indicator.
Case: 5N red gold; Ø 47.5mm, thickness: 16.84mm; 5N red-gold crown with engraved and black lacquered GF logo; three-dimensional, variable geometrically-shaped lugs secured with screws; convex sapphire crystal; transparent sapphire crystal caseback; raised and polished with "Double Tourbillon 30° Technique" engraving on a hand-punched background; gold security screws; two 5N red-gold engraved and hand-finished plates bearing text screwed to the caseband; hand-engraved individual numbers; water resistant to 3atm.
Dial: sapphire crystal hour ring; gold small seconds and power reserve indicator; polished gold hour and minute hands with SuperLumiNova; small seconds and power reserve indicator red triangle hands; sapphire crystal 4-minute tourbillon engraved indicator.
Strap: hand-sewn black alligator; 5N red-gold folding clasp hand-engraved with Greubel Forsey logo.
Price: available upon request.

DOUBLE TOURBILLON 30° TECHNIQUE — REF. 9000 2181

Movement: manual-winding GF02s caliber; Ø 38.4mm, thickness: 12.15mm; 120-hour power reserve; 385 components; 43 jewels; 21,600 vph; gold nickel-palladium finished barrels covered with relief engraving, four coaxial series-coupled fast-rotating barrels (1 turn in 3.2 hours) one of which is equipped with a slipping spring to avoid excess tension; free sprung variable-inertia balance wheel with white-gold mean-time screws (Ø 10.7mm); Phillips terminal curve balance spring with Geneva-style stud; nickel silver mainplates frosted with polished beveling, ruthenium finish; nickel silver bridges, frosted, spotted with polished beveling, nickel-palladium finish and gold nameplate bearing the individual number; involute circle profile gearing, conical gearing with corrected profile; inner tourbillon: inclined at a 30° angle with one rotation per minute; outer tourbillon: one rotation in 4 minutes, hand-beveled and openworked cage pillars with gold counterweight.

Functions: hours, minutes; small seconds; power reserve indicator; 4-minute out tourbillon rotation indicator.

Case: 950 platinum; Ø 47.5mm, thickness: 16.84mm; 950 platinum crown with engraved and black lacquered GF logo; three-dimensional, variable geometrically-shaped lugs secured with screws; convex sapphire crystal; transparent sapphire crystal caseback; raised and polished with "Double Tourbillon 30° Technique" engraving on a hand-punched background; gold security screws; two 950 platinum engraved and hand-finished plates bearing text screwed to the caseband; hand-engraved individual numbers; water resistant to 3atm.

Dial: sapphire crystal hour ring; gold small seconds and power reserve indicator; polished blued steel hour and minute hands; small seconds and power reserve indicator red triangle hands; sapphire crystal 4-minute tourbillon engraved indicator.

Strap: hand-sewn black alligator; 950 platinum folding clasp hand-engraved with Greubel Forsey logo.

Price: available upon request.

QUADRUPLE TOURBILLON — REF. 9000 2703

Movement: manual-winding GF03 caliber; Ø 36.4mm, thickness: 9.7mm; 50-hour power reserve; 531 components; 63 jewels; 21,600 vph; rapid rotating twin barrels (1 turn in 3.2 hours) one of which is equipped with a slipping spring to avoid excess tension; free sprung variable-inertia balance wheel with white-gold mean-time screws (Ø 10.7mm); Phillips terminal curve balance spring with Geneva-style stud; nickel silver main plates, spotted with polished beveling, straight-grained flanks, polished counter-sinks, nickel-palladium finish; nickel silver bridges, frosted, spotted with polished beveling, nickel-palladium finish; gold nameplate bearing the individual number of the timepiece; two steel tourbillon bridges (movement side): hand-beveled, flat black polished with polished counter-sinks; two sapphire crystal tourbillon bridges (dial side); Involute circle profile with conical gearing with corrected profiles.

Functions: hours, minutes; small seconds; power reserve indicator; 4-minute outer-tourbillon rotation indicator at 8.

Case: 950 platinum; Ø 43.5mm, thickness: 16.11mm; polished bezel and center band with hand-finished straight graining; three-dimensional, variable geometrically-shaped lugs; gold security screws; raised polished "Quadruple Tourbillon" engraving on a hand-punched background; convex sapphire crystal; transparent sapphire crystal caseback; hand-engraved individual number; water resistant to 3atm.

Dial: silvered; gold hour markers and display sectors; polished gold hour, minute, small seconds and power reserve hand; applied gold logo.

Strap: hand-sewn black alligator; 950 platinum clasp hand-engraved with Greubel Forsey logo.

Price: available upon request.

QUADRUPLE TOURBILLON — REF. 9000 2705

Movement: manual-winding GF03 caliber; Ø 36.4mm, thickness: 9.7mm; 50-hour power reserve; 531 components; 63 jewels; 21,600 vph; rapid rotating twin barrels (1 turn in 3.2 hours) one of which is equipped with a slipping spring to avoid excess tension; free sprung variable-inertia balance wheel with white-gold mean-time screws (Ø 10.7mm); Phillips terminal curve balance spring with Geneva-style stud; nickel silver main plates, spotted with polished beveling, straight-grained flanks, polished counter-sinks, nickel-palladium finish; nickel silver bridges, frosted, spotted with polished beveling, nickel-palladium finish; gold nameplate bearing the individual number of the timepiece; two steel tourbillon bridges (movement side): hand-beveled, flat black polished with polished counter-sinks; two sapphire crystal tourbillon bridges (dial side); Involute circle profile with conical gearing with corrected profiles.

Functions: hours, minutes; small seconds; power reserve indicator; 4-minute outer-tourbillon rotation indicator at 8.

Case: 5N 18K red gold; Ø 43.5mm, thickness: 16.11mm; polished bezel and center band with hand-finished straight graining; three-dimensional, variable geometry-shaped lugs; gold security screws; raised polished "Quadruple Tourbillon" engraving on a hand-punched background; convex sapphire crystal; transparent sapphire crystal caseback; hand-engraved individual number; water resistant to 3atm.

Dial: black; gold hour markers and display sectors; polished gold hour, minute, small seconds and power reserve hand; applied gold logo.

Strap: hand-sewn black alligator; 5N 18K red-gold clasp hand-engraved with Greubel Forsey logo.

Price: available upon request.

INVENTION PIECE 2 — REF. 9000 2982

Movement: manual-winding GF03n caliber; Ø 37mm, thickness: 11.87mm; 56-hour power reserve; 594 components; 43 jewels; 21,600 vph; rapid rotating triple barrels (1 turn in 3.2 hours) equipped with a slipping spring to avoid excess tension; free sprung variable-inertia balance wheel with white-gold mean-time screws (Ø 10.7mm); Phillips terminal curve balance spring with Geneva-style stud; nickel silver main plates, spotted, hand beveled, straight grained flanks, polished counter-sinks with part of black-ruthenium finish; nickel silver bridges, frosted, spotted with polished beveling, nickel-palladium finish; gold nameplate bearing the individual number of the timepiece; four steel Double Tourbillon bridges hand-beveled, flat black polished with polished counter-sinks; Involute circle profile conical gearing with corrected profiles.

Functions: hours, minutes; small seconds; power reserve indicator; 4-minute outer tourbillon rotation indicator at 1.

Case: 5N 18K red gold; Ø 43.5mm, thickness: 16.28mm; 5N 18K red-gold crown with engraved and black lacquered GF logo; convex sapphire crystal; transparent sapphire crystal caseback; polished bezel and center band with hand-finished straight graining; gold security screws; raised "Invention Piece 2" engraving on a hand-punched background; hand-engraved individual numbers; water resistant to 3atm.

Dial: black; 22K hour indicator; 22K Greubel Forsey logo; red triangle hour hand; rotating disc with fixed blue triangle minute indicator; polished blued steel small seconds hand; polished white gold power reserve indicator hand; sapphire crystal 4-minute indicator.

Strap: hand-sewn black alligator; 5N 18K red-gold folding clasp hand-engraved with Greubel Forsey logo.

Note: limited to 11 pieces.

Price: available upon request.

GUY ELLIA

AN AVANT-GARDE ADVENTURE

Widely considered to be as exceptional a brand in haute horology as in haute jewelry, watchmaker Guy Ellia offers a vision that can be found nowhere else. Every Guy Ellia watch is a quest for perfection: design requirements drive the development of innovative and aesthetically daring solutions.

The brand launched its first—already highly original—line of timepieces in 1999. Its unique style, based on a strong visionary design, immediately propelled Guy Ellia to the highest end of luxury watchmakers. This dynamic vision continues, using radical and technical innovations to found incredible advances and imbue the watches with a distinctive spirit. For example, Guy Ellia was a pioneer in removing the watch's dial, making the highly unusual—at the time—choice to create the Time Space without the key component in 2006. The design reveals the watch's top-quality movement and lends a distinctive, futuristic style to the design.

TOURBILLON MAGISTERE II OR
A masterful Christophe Claret tourbillon rotates visibly within the sturdy red-gold case.

TOURBILLON ZEPHYR

Placing a circle within a square on the blue platinum dial, this piece adds the aesthetic appeal of a visible movement.

REPETITION MINUTE ZEPHYR

A Christophe Claret movement powers this piece's five time zones and minute repeater.

Another breakthrough came in 2007, when the Tourbillon Zephyr elevated the art of watchmaking to a new level. Lightness and transparency are its chief qualities: the manually wound Christophe Claret caliber is sheathed in a sapphire crystal case with a winding ring set with 36 baguette-cut diamonds. Decorated with two platinum carriages, the tourbillon hovers in transparent space.

The Répétition Minutes Zephyr made its debut at BaselWorld 2008, winning accolades as a marvel of form and function. Housed in a sapphire crystal case that is enhanced with white gold, red gold or titanium, the minute repeater complication chimes a cathedral tone upon request for the hours, quarter-hours and minutes, while the multiple time zones complication allows the wearer to view the local time and that of four other time zones by means of rollers.

Because of the level of complication, Guy Ellia watches can take five or six years to develop, but it is worth expending the immense effort involved in making stunning pieces. "The brand Guy Ellia is one of the best in the business for getting ideas and finding the techniques to make its complicated designs happen," says Carla Chalouhi, owner of Arije, the famous haute jewelry and haute horology boutiques in Paris, Cannes and London.

In an era when watches are no longer necessities, the timepiece a person chooses to wear tells much more about that person than ever before. Men and women who favor Guy Ellia are hip, yet refined, savvy and individualistic—more likely to start their own trends than to join in on someone else's. With its latest designs, Guy Ellia offers watches that transcend time.

CONVEX MIROIR

Diamond-pavé numerals that edge off the dial add glamour to this chic rose-gold model.

CIRCLE

Diamond hour markers and a diamond-pavé case make this a favorite among jewelry lovers.

REPETITION MINUTE ZEPHYR

Movement: manual-winding Christophe Claret GEC 88 caliber; 41.2x38.2mm, thickness: 9.41mm; 48-hour power reserve; 720 components; 72 jewels; 18,000 vph; flat balance-spring; gear wheels with different platings; five-position adjustment.
Functions: hours, minutes; power reserve indicator; minute repeater; five time zones with day/night indicators.
Case: sapphire crystal block; 53.6x43.7mm, thickness: 14.8mm; sapphire and 18K gold crown set with a diamond (Ø 2.2mm); water resistant to 3atm.
Strap: black rubber; 18K solid white-gold folding buckle (17.27g).
Note: limited edition of 20 numbered pieces.
Also available: pink gold and titanium; alligator strap.

TOURBILLON ZEPHYR

Movement: manual-winding Christophe Claret GES 97 caliber; 37x37mm, thickness: 6.21mm; 110-hour power reserve; 233 components; 17 jewels; 21,600 vph; flat balance-spring; winding ring set with 36 baguette-cut diamonds (1.04 carats) or guilloché; entirely hand-chamfered cage; bottom plate and bridges in blue sapphire; five-position adjustment.
Functions: hours, minutes; tourbillon.
Case: 950 platinum sides (54.9g); 54x45.3mm, thickness: 15.4mm; crown set with one diamond (Ø 1mm); sapphire crystal with thermal counter-shock marking; transparent caseback with hearth engraving; water resistant to 3atm.
Strap: black alligator; 18K solid gold folding buckle (15.64g).
Note: limited edition of 12 numbered pieces.
Also available: pink gold; bottom plate and bridges in crystal, blue or smoky sapphire.

TOURBILLON MAGISTERE TITANIUM

Movement: manual-winding Christophe Claret TGE 97 caliber; 37.4x29.9mm, thickness: 5.4mm; 110-hour power reserve; 20 jewels; 21,600 vph; flat balance-spring; mysterious winding; skeletonized barrel and ratchet-wheel; entirely hand-chamfered cage; titanium bottom plate and bridges.
Functions: hours, minutes; tourbillon.
Case: titanium (18.2g); 43.5x36mm, thickness: 10.9mm; sapphire crystal with thermal counter-shock marking; water resistant to 3atm.
Strap: black alligator; solid 18K white-gold folding buckle (9.65g) and titanium hood.

TOURBILLON MAGISTERE II

Movement: manual-winding Christophe Claret MGE-97 caliber; 38.4x30.9mm, thickness: 5.71mm; 90-hour power reserve; 266 components; 33 jewels; 21,600 vph; flat balance-spring; mysterious winding; skeleton ratchet and wheels with curved arms and wolf-teeth; entirely hand-chamfered cage; barrel bridges and tourbillon in 18K gold.
Functions: hours, minutes; tourbillon.
Case: 5N 18K red gold (97.54g); 44.2x36.7mm, thickness: 15mm; sapphire crystal with antireflective treatment; transparent caseback; water resistant to 3atm.
Strap: brown alligator; 5N 18K red-gold folding buckle (14.61g).
Note: limited edition of 12 numbered pieces.
Also available: white gold.

JUMBO CHRONO

Movement: automatic-winding Frédéric Piguet PGE 1185 caliber; Ø 26.2mm, thickness: 5.5mm; 45-hour power reserve; 41 jewels; 21,600 vph; five-position adjustment; Côtes de Genève-finished bridges with rhodium plating; GUY ELLIA logo engraved on rotor with rhodium plating.
Functions: hours, minutes at 12; small seconds at 6; date at 2; column-wheel chronograph: 12-hour counter at 8, 30-minute counter at 4 and central sweep seconds hand.
Case: 18K pink gold (85.75g); Ø 50mm, thickness: 11.5mm; sapphire crystal with thermal counter-shock marking; water resistant to 3atm.
Strap: brown alligator; 18K pink-gold folding buckle (11.9g).
Also available: pink-gold bezel set, full-set pink gold; black gold, black-gold bezel set, full-set black gold; white gold, white-gold bezel set, full-set white gold.

TIME SPACE QUANTIEME PERPETUEL

Movement: manual-winding Frédéric Piguet PGE 5615 D caliber; Ø 35.64mm, thickness: 4.7mm; 43-hour power reserve; 20 jewels; 21,600 vph; five-position adjustment; Côtes de Genève-finished bridges with black PVD treatment; GUY ELLIA logo engraved on stippled plate with black PVD treatment; watch box with an integrated specific automatic winder.
Functions: hours, minutes; perpetual calendar: day, date, month, leap-year cycle; moonphase.
Case: 18K black gold (32.87g); Ø 46.8mm, thickness: 7.75mm; sapphire middle ring; sapphire crystal; water resistant to 3atm.
Strap: black alligator; 18K black-gold pin buckle (4.73g).
Also available: black-gold bezel set, full-set black gold; white gold, white-gold bezel set, full-set white gold; pink gold, pink-gold bezel set, full-set pink gold.

TIME SPACE

Movement: manual-winding Frédéric Piguet PGE 15 caliber; Ø 35.64mm, thickness: 1.9mm; 43-hour power reserve; 20 jewels; 21,600 vph; five-position adjustment; Côtes de Genève-finished bridges with black PVD treatment; GUY ELLIA logo engraved on stippled plate with black PVD treatment.
Functions: hours, minutes.
Case: 18K pink gold (33.5g); Ø 46.8mm, thickness: 4.9mm; sapphire crystal with thermal counter-shock marking; water resistant to 3atm.
Strap: brown alligator; 18K solid pink-gold pin buckle (4.73g).
Also available: pink-gold bezel set, full-set pink gold; black gold, black-gold bezel set, full-set black gold; white gold, white-gold bezel set, full-set white gold.

CONVEX MIROIR

Movement: quartz; Frédéric Piguet caliber PGE 820; Ø 18.8mm, thickness: 1.95mm.
Functions: hours, minutes.
Case: 18K pink gold (56.61g); 41x41mm, thickness: 7.1mm; bezel set with 100 diamonds (Ø 1.5mm); crown set with one diamond (Ø 2.3mm); sapphire crystal with thermal counter-shock marking; mirror-polished caseback set with one diamond (Ø 0.95mm) on the "I" of ELLIA; water resistant to 3atm.
Dial: solid 18K pink gold (27.15g); four Arabic numerals set with 204 diamonds (0.79 carat); 18K pink-gold hands.
Bracelet: solid 18K pink gold; pin buckle set with 40 diamonds (0.49 carat), pin set with one diamond (Ø 0.9mm).
Also available: white gold; yellow gold; solid 18K gold dial (25.35g) full-set with 558 diamonds (2.28 carats) and four gold Arabic numerals; mother-of-pearl dial with four gold Arabic numerals or four outlined Arabic numerals.
Note: limited edition.

H. Moser & Cie.

FOR YOUR EYES ONLY

Crafting discreet timepieces that enclose stunning technological innovations, H. Moser & Cie. dazzles by not dazzling.

Five years ago, H. Moser & Cie. demonstrated significant courage in its development of the world's first perpetual calendar that could be easily adjusted in both directions, entirely via the double-pull crown. Perhaps as daring was the brand's decision to effectively conceal its pioneering exploit.

In celebration of the Moser Perpetual 1's anniversary, the Swiss manufacture presents the exclusive Perpetual Golden Edition. While at first sight, only the large date indicates the presence of a calendar, let alone an unprecedented perpetual calendar mechanism, a closer inspection of the solid-gold dial reveals a small third gold central hand. A clever employment of numerical symmetry, H. Moser & Cie. indicates the months on the same solid-gold appliqué markers used by the hour and minute hands. Equipped with a gravity-defying double hairspring escapement, the Moser Perpetual Golden Edition embodies the supreme watchmaking excellence of the house. Decisively understated yet remarkably precious and sophisticated, this timepiece reigns with the quiet elegance of a well-kept secret.

MOSER PERPETUAL GOLDEN EDITION

Limited to 100 pieces, this precious triumph chooses optimal clarity over the ostentatious declaration of its unprecedented mechanical achievements.

MOSER PERPETUAL DOUBLE HAIRSPRING

The manufacture's innovative double hairspring escapement stabilizes the movement's center of gravity, preemptively eliminating the errors that most choose to correct.

Rejecting the common horological practice of error correction, H. Moser & Cie. instead tackles the gravitational challenge head on. The manufacture's escapement, the shining star of the Moser Perpetual Double Hairspring timepiece, uses the self-compensating alloys of Straumann hairsprings, in combination with a Glucydur balance, to eliminate irregularities in accuracy caused by the watch's ever-changing position. Arranged one above the other, the hairsprings ingeniously vibrate in opposing directions, keeping the center of gravity... exactly central. In addition, the watch's adjustment in all six possible positions further minimizes the discrepancies caused by the positional inconsistencies of wristwatch wearing. Once again, H. Moser & Cie.'s admirable quest for optimal accuracy and mechanical stability remains a secret among true connoisseurs. While the earth's virtually constant gravitational pull has puzzled watchmaking since its beginning, H. Moser & Cie. establishes its status in the elite with its innovative mastery of the uncontrollable force.

Equipped with the world's first interchangeable escapement module, and featuring the patented hardened solid-gold execution of the pallet fork and escape wheel, the Monard Marrone models fascinate with their pure and understated elegance. H. Moser & Cie. achieves optimal efficiency through its utilization of true bevel wheels and the Moser tooth system, as the hand-wound HMC343.505 caliber's dual spring barrel provides a seven-day power reserve. Presented in a three-part designer case in white or rose gold, with a rich dark brown dial, the Monard Marrone is a picture of distinguished clarity. Discreet, yet unmistakable once perceived, the central minute and seconds hands extend to the edge of the face's periphery, making the most of the watch's fiery finish.

While the Swiss watchmaker's energetic drive to ameliorate and innovate makes H. Moser & Cie. an embodiment of horological courage, the house's commitment to understated elegance through design humility may be the bravest emblem of its excellence.

MONARD MARRONE

With a seven-day power reserve visible through the sapphire caseback, this timepiece radiates the quiet elegance of time told by three exquisite central hands.

MONARD MARRONE — REF. 343.505-018

Movement: manual-winding HMC343.505 caliber; 7-day power reserve; bevel wheels; dual barrel; Straumann hairspring with stabilized Breguet overcoil; pallet fork and escapement wheel made of hardened gold; interchangeable Moser escapement module.
Functions: hours, minutes; seconds with stop function; power reserve display on the movement side.
Case: 18K rose gold; Ø 40.8mm, thickness: 10.85mm; sapphire crystal caseback.
Dial: light brown with sun-pattern ground finish.
Strap: brown alligator leather; solid rose-gold clasp.
Suggested price: $21,200

MONARD MARRONE — REF. 343.505-019

Movement: manual-winding HMC343.505 caliber; 7-day power reserve; bevel wheels; dual barrel; Straumann hairspring with stabilized Breguet overcoil; pallet fork and escapement wheel made of hardened gold; interchangeable Moser escapement module.
Functions: hours, minutes; seconds with stop function; power reserve display on the movement side.
Case: 18K white gold; Ø 40.8mm, thickness: 10.85mm; sapphire crystal caseback.
Dial: dark brown with sun-pattern ground finish.
Strap: brown alligator leather; solid white-gold clasp.
Suggested price: $21,200

MONARD — REF. 343.505-017

Movement: manual-winding HMC343.505 caliber; 7-day power reserve; bevel wheels; dual barrel; Straumann hairspring with stabilized Breguet overcoil; pallet fork and escapement wheel made of hardened gold; interchangeable Moser escapement module.
Functions: hours, minutes; seconds with stop function; power reserve display on the movement side.
Case: 18K rose gold; Ø 40.8mm, thickness: 10.85mm; sapphire crystal caseback.
Dial: black with sun-pattern ground finish.
Strap: black alligator leather; solid rose-gold clasp.
Suggested price: $21,200

MONARD FUME — REF. 343.506-016

Movement: manual-winding HMC343.505 caliber; 7-day power reserve; bevel wheels; dual barrel; Straumann double hairspring; pallet fork and escapement wheel made of white gold; interchangeable Moser escapement module.
Functions: hours, minutes; seconds with stop function; power reserve display on the movement side.
Case: palladium; Ø 40.8mm, thickness: 10.85mm; sapphire crystal caseback.
Dial: fumé with sun-pattern ground finish.
Strap: black alligator leather; solid palladium clasp.
Suggested price: $27,000

MOSER PERPETUAL 1 DOUBLE HAIRSPRING — REF. 341.101-009

Movement: manual-winding HMC341.101 caliber; 7-day power reserve; bevel wheels; dual barrel; Straumann double hairspring; pallet fork and escapement wheel made of white gold; interchangeable Moser escapement module.
Functions: hours, minutes; small seconds with stop function at 6; big date; perpetual calendar anytime adjustable forwards and backwards via crown independently of movement; double pull crown mechanism; power reserve display on dial.
Case: palladium; Ø 40.8mm, thickness: 11.05mm; sapphire crystal caseback.
Dial: fumé with sun-pattern ground finish.
Strap: black alligator leather; solid palladium folding clasp.
Suggested price: $58,400

MONARD DATE — REF. 342.502-003

Movement: manual-winding HMC342.502 caliber; 7-day power reserve; bevel wheels; dual barrel; Straumann hairspring with stabilized Breguet overcoil; pallet fork and escapement wheel made of hardened gold; interchangeable Moser escapement module.
Functions: hours, minutes; seconds with stop function; big date; calendar anytime adjustable forwards and backwards via crown independently of movement; double pull crown mechanism; power reserve display on the movement side.
Case: 18K rose gold; Ø 40.8mm, thickness: 10.85mm; sapphire crystal caseback.
Dial: silvered with sun-pattern ground finish.
Strap: brown alligator leather; solid rose-gold clasp.
Suggested price: $27,800

MOSER PERPETUAL 1 — REF. 341.501-004

Movement: manual-winding HMC341.501 caliber; 7-day power reserve; bevel wheels; dual barrel; Straumann hairspring with stabilized Breguet overcoil; pallet fork and escapement wheel made of hardened gold; interchangeable Moser escapement module.
Functions: hours, minutes; small seconds with stop function at 6; big date; perpetual calendar anytime adjustable forwards and backwards via crown independently of movement; double pull crown mechanism; power reserve display on dial.
Case: 18K rose gold; Ø 40.8mm, thickness: 11.05mm; sapphire crystal caseback.
Dial: silvered with sun-pattern ground finish.
Strap: brown alligator leather; solid rose-gold folding clasp.
Suggested price: $47,800

PERPETUAL MOON — REF. 348.901-015

Movement: manual-winding HMC348.901 caliber; 7-day power reserve; bevel wheels; dual barrel; Straumann hairspring with stabilized Breguet overcoil; pallet fork and escapement wheel made of hardened gold; interchangeable Moser escapement module.
Functions: hours, minutes; seconds with stop function; perpetual moonphase with one day of discrepancy after 1027 years; anytime adjustable forwards and backwards via crown independently of movement; power reserve display on the movement side.
Case: platinum; Ø 40.8mm, thickness: 11.05mm; sapphire crystal caseback.
Dial: blue fumé with sun-pattern ground finish.
Strap: black alligator leather; solid platinum folding clasp.
Suggested price: $48,400

HAMILTON

THE AMERICAN BRAND SINCE 1892

KHAKI FLIGHT TIMER

The new Hamilton Khaki Flight Timer is a "cockpit for the skies" with logbook capabilities of up to 99 flights.

HAMILTON'S AMERICAN HERITAGE: 120 YEARS OF DESIGN AND INNOVATION

Hamilton's genuine American heritage is deeply rooted in the US Armed Forces, aviation and Hollywood filmmaking. As the brand celebrates its 120th anniversary, we reflect on a century of design and innovation.

Hamilton's relationship with the American spirit began in 1892 when the watch company was founded in Lancaster, Penn. It was at that foundational time that Hamilton's first series of pocket watches earned the title of "the watch of railroad accuracy." In 1914, as World War I raged, Hamilton earned the prestigious position of supplier to the US Armed Forces. Trusted by early 20th-century aviation pioneers, the watchmaker's exceptional mechanical precision made it the timekeeper of the skies, regulating the timing of the first American airmail service.

Elvis Presley wearing the Ventura in *Blue Hawaii*.

As the end of World War II established relative global peace, Hamilton's involvement with the military transitioned from the real world to the cinema. In 1951, Hamilton made its first on-screen appearance in the Oscar-nominated film *The Frogmen*. Throughout this contextual evolution of the brand, the American watchmaker never ceased to innovate. Developed in 1957, the Ventura, worn by Elvis Presley in his 1961 film *Blue Hawaii*, became the first battery-powered watch in the world. With each decade, Hamilton created a new watchmaking first. Inspired by its own futuristic clock used in the classic film *2001: A Space Odyssey*, the brand introduced, in 1970, the Pulsar, the world's first digital electronic watch.

VENTURA
This modern day version of the Ventura was developed in honor of Elvis' birthday.

Enjoying a reputation for horological excellence and cultural pertinence, Hamilton's relationship with Hollywood continues to grow to this day, as evidenced by its timepieces' roles in over 400 motion pictures, including *Men in Black*, *Fight Club* and *Lethal Weapon 4*. It is thus no surprise that on its 120th birthday, the manufacturer affirmed its presence in American cinematography by hosting the fifth annual Behind the Camera Awards. Produced in conjunction with *Los Angeles Confidential* magazine, the awards honored the off-screen heroes of cinema and television.

Today, Hamilton remains focused on bringing stylish, high-functioning watches to its customers. The launch of the Khaki Flight Timer reinforces Hamilton's commitment to both innovation and aviation. It also marks the beginning of an official partnership between Hamilton and Air Zermatt, a helicopter rescue and transportation organization. Swiss watchmakers and Air Zermatt pilots collaborated on the design of the Khaki Flight Timer to ensure the integration of relevant aviation functions. The rugged yet sophisticated Flight Timer also incorporates a pilot's logbook to record details of up to 20 flights and for each flight, 99 landings.

Hamilton's journey can best be traced through its relationships with aviation, Hollywood and the armed forces, as well as its unwavering dedication to style and innovation. Whether Hamilton's watches appear on the big screen, in the cockpit of an airplane or on the watch of a consumer, they are always identified by their style and unmistakable passion for the American spirit.

Legendary actor Harrison Ford honored his long-time friend and stunt double Vic Armstrong, with the Hamilton Behind the Camera Lifetime Achievement Award for Stunt Choreography, November 6, 2011 in Los Angeles.

Isaiah Mustafa, Melanie Griffith, Hamilton International CEO Sylvain Dolla and Antonio Banderas smile for the camera at this year's Hamilton Behind the Camera Awards.

VENTURA REF. H24411732

Movement: ETA quartz 955.412 caliber; 7 jewels.
Functions: hours, minutes; seconds.
Case: stainless steel; water resistant to 5atm.
Dial: black.
Strap: black leather.

JAZZMASTER SQUARE LADY REF. H32291114

Movement: quartz 901.001 caliber; 3 jewels.
Functions: hours, minutes.
Case: steel; 29x29mm; bezel set with six diamonds; sapphire crystal.
Dial: white mother-of-pearl; water resistant to 10atm.
Bracelet: stainless steel; SuperLumiNova hour and minute hands.

JAZZMASTER SLIM REF. H38655515

Movement: ETA Auto 2895-2 caliber; 27 jewels.
Functions: hours, minutes; small seconds; date.
Case: steel; Ø 43mm; sapphire crystal.
Dial: white; SuperLumiNova hour and minute hands.
Strap: brown leather.

JAZZMASTER MAESTRO REF. H32576515

Movement: ETA Auto H21 caliber; 60-hour power reserve; 25 jewels.
Functions: hours, minutes, seconds; day; date; chronograph: 12-hour counter at 6 and 30-minute counter at 12.
Case: steel; Ø 41mm; sapphire crystal; transparent caseback.
Dial: white; SuperLumiNova hour and minute hands.
Strap: brown leather.

KHAKI FLIGHT TIMER — REF. H64554131

Movement: ETA quartz Analog Digital E20-373 caliber; 9 jewels.
Functions: hours, minutes, seconds; date; log book up to 20 flights; alarm; temperature indicator; second time zone; countdown; Isa T°; UTC time; SWAP.
Case: steel; Ø 40mm; sapphire crystal; water resistant to 10atm.
Dial: black; SuperLumiNova hour and minute hands.
Bracelet: stainless steel.

KHAKI PILOT — REF. H64785835

Movement: ETA Auto 2836-2 caliber; 25 jewels.
Functions: hours, minutes, seconds; day; date.
Case: steel black PVD; Ø 46mm; sapphire crystal; transparent caseback; water resistant to 20atm.
Dial: black; SuperLumiNova hour and minute hands.
Strap: black leather.

KHAKI FIELD — REF. H71566553

Movement: ETA Auto H21 caliber; 60-hour power reserve; 25 jewels.
Functions: hours, minutes; day; date; chronograph: 12-hour counter at 6 and 30-minute counter at 12.
Case: steel; Ø 42mm; sapphire crystal; transparent caseback; water resistant to 10atm.
Dial: silver; SuperLumiNova hour and minute hands.
Strap: brown leather.

KHAKI OFFICER 44MM SMALL SECOND — REF. H70655733

Movement: ETA Auto 2895-2 caliber; 27 jewels.
Functions: hours, minutes; small seconds at 6; date at 3.
Case: stainless steel; Ø 44mm; sapphire crystal; transparent caseback; water resistant to 10atm.
Dial: black; SuperLumiNova hour and minute hands.
Strap: beige nubuck leather.

HARRY WINSTON

CAPTURING THE ELUSIVE NOTION OF TIME

Driven by a passion for conquering the boundaries of the unimaginable, Harry Winston continues to astonish the horological community with timepieces of unparalleled energy and distinguished character.

Joining forces with the engineering virtuosity of Denis Giguet, Harry Winston presents a timepiece that treads the line between genius and insanity. At the top of each hour, the 566-component mechanism lets chaos reign briefly before taking complete control of the spectacular anarchy, by presenting the hour as an evident digit in the center of the dial. Capitalizing on the most modern technologies, the Opus Eleven eschews the hour hand, replacing it with 24 placards that revolve and rotate on a complicated system of gears mounted on an epicycloidal gear train. Through vertical transmission, ultra-precise micro-components, and sophisticated calculations, the Opus Eleven creates a mind-boggling hourly demonstration of time's disintegration and reconfiguration.

As the curtain rises on the 11th Opus rendition, this union of passionate masterminds reveals time as a feat of determined sportsmanship. By posing and solving an intricate puzzle, Harry Winston and Denis Giguet honor the fine tradition of haute horology by brilliantly reinventing the very notion of timekeeping.

OPUS ELEVEN

The 566 components of this highly sophisticated mechanism are synchronized with microscopic exactitude to orchestrate the controlled detonation at the top of the hour.

HARRY WINSTON MIDNIGHT TOURBILLON GMT
The combination of a GMT complication with clever city aperture and tourbillon offers profound insight into Harry Winston's creative personality.

Traversing the principal subdial's chapter ring, the Harry Winston Midnight Tourbillon GMT's exposed regulator with small seconds, at 6 o'clock, delicately exhibits the exceptional precision of the watch. Smaller in diameter, but just as prominent as its primary counterpart, the GMT dial at 9 o'clock is complete with a day/night indicator, while a gentle aperture at 11 o'clock clearly identifies the city whose time zone is being represented. This decisively contemporary vision of time turns the intricate white or black dial into a fascinating horological canvas. The timepiece's exhibition caseback is superbly finished and reveals the decorated 22-karat rose-gold oscillating weight.

With the Avenue C Large, the American watchmaker uses the gleam of 456 baguette-cut and 13 brilliant-cut diamonds to emulate the mirror effects of New York's skyscrapers in an ode to the city that never sleeps.

While the 18-karat white-gold case, set with 53 diamonds, is itself a brilliantly reflective beauty, the sunray dial, composed of 156 baguette-cut diamonds, captures the swarming romanticism of the city's soaring architecture and endless corridors of light. Worn on a stunning bracelet with 260 baguette-cut diamonds, the Avenue C Large is a timepiece of unrivaled luxurious elegance.

With three timepieces that capture the ineffable and find brilliance in their distinctive personalities, Harry Winston brings forth a new standard of synergy between watchmaking excellence and fearless imagination.

AVENUE C LARGE
A total of 34.8 total carats adorns this luminous New York-inspired timepiece.

OCEAN TRIPLE RETROGRADE CHRONOGRAPH BLACK ZALIUM REF. 400/MCRA44ZKL.S

Movement: automatic-winding; 42-hour power reserve; ruthenium-treated movement decorated with Côtes de Genève.
Functions: off-centered hours and minutes; triple retrograde chronograph: 12-hour counter at 9, 30-minutes counter at 3 and 60-seconds counter at 6.
Case: Zalium® with DLC coating; Ø 44mm; satin finish; sapphire crystal; open sapphire crystal caseback displaying an 18K rose-gold rotor with ruthenium treatment; water resistant to 10atm.
Dial: open sapphire; engraved Harry Winston logo; transferred subdials with sanded circles; black hands with SuperLumiNova.
Strap: black rubber; Zalium® folding clasp with DLC coating.

PROJECT Z6 BLACK EDITION REF. 400/MMAC44ZKC.K2

Movement: manual-winding; 72-hour power reserve.
Functions: off-centered hours and minutes; small seconds (shuriken); alarm; double day and night indicators (time and alarm).
Case: Zalium® with DLC coating; Ø 44mm; sapphire crystal; water resistant to 10atm.
Dial: black; open dial with view of the hammer of the alarm clock.
Strap: black rubber; Zalium® folding clasp with DLC coating.
Note: limited to 300 pieces.

OCEAN MOON PHASE REF. 400/UQMP36RL.MD02/D3.1

Movement: quartz.
Functions: hours, minutes; date; moonphase.
Case: 18K rose gold; Ø 36mm; set with 57 brilliant-cut-diamonds (2.1 carats); sapphire crystal; water resistant to 10atm.
Dial: white mother-of-pearl; set with 76 brilliant cut diamonds (0.3 carat).
Strap: white rubber; 18K rose-gold folding clasp set with 33 brilliant-cut diamonds (0.3 carat).

OCEAN SPORT™ CHRONOGRAPH REF. 411/MCA44ZC.K

Movement: automatic-winding; skeletonized chronograph; 42-hour power reserve.
Functions: hours, minutes; small seconds at 3; date at 12; chronograph: 12-hour counter at 6, 30-minute counter at 9 and central seconds hand.
Case: Zalium®; Ø 44mm; unidirectional rotating bezel comprised of 2 parts: satin-finished Zalium® with DLC-coated hour markers and SuperLumiNova at 12; sapphire crystal; water resistant to 21atm.
Dial: smoked sapphire; black subdials; satin-brushed flange; black ruthenium-colored and skeletonized date disc; hands with SuperLumiNova.
Strap: black rubber; Zalium® folding clasp.

HARRY WINSTON MIDNIGHT AUTOMATIC REF. 450/MA42WL.W

Movement: automatic-winding; 45-hour power reserve.
Functions: hours, minutes; date at 12.
Case: 18K white gold; Ø 42mm; sapphire crystal; water resistant to 4atm.
Dial: silver; sunray satin-brushed finish.
Strap: black alligator leather; 18K white-gold folding clasp.

HARRY WINSTON MIDNIGHT AUTOMATIC BIG DATE REF. 450/MABD42RL.W

Movement: automatic-winding; 70-hour power reserve.
Functions: off-centered hours and minutes; big date at 6.
Case: 18K rose gold; Ø 42mm; sapphire crystal; water resistant to 4atm.
Dial: silver broad snailed-finish base; sunray satin-brushed slate-gray chapter ring at 12; silver fine snailed-finish chapter center ring; set with 1 brilliant-cut diamond at 6.
Strap: brown alligator leather; 18K rose-gold folding clasp.

HARRY WINSTON MIDNIGHT TOURBILLON GMT REF. 450/MATTZ45WL.K

Movement: automatic-winding.
Functions: off-centered hours and minutes; small seconds on the tourbillon at 6; second time zone at 9 with day/night indicator; city names display at 11.
Case: 18K white gold; Ø 45mm; sapphire crystal; open sapphire crystal caseback; water resistant to 4atm.
Dial: black broad snailed main dial; hours and minutes dial with satin finishing and fine-snailed finishing in the center.
Strap: black alligator leather; 18K white-gold folding clasp.

HARRY WINSTON MIDNIGHT 39MM REF. 450/UQ39RL.W1/D3.1

Movement: quartz.
Functions: hours, minutes.
Case: 18K rose gold; Ø 39mm, thickness: 7mm; bezel set with 103 brilliant-cut diamonds (0.94 carat); sapphire crystal; water resistant to 4atm.
Dial: rose champagne toned; sunray satin-brushed finish 12, 3, 6 and 9 hour markers set with 3 brilliant-cut diamonds.
Strap: brown satin; 18K rose-gold folding clasp.

HERMÈS
PARIS

TIME TO DREAM

Hermès's imagination brilliantly shatters the regularity of time.

ARCEAU LE TEMPS SUSPENDU

With a world-first triple retrograde function, this watch suspends time and vanishes the date at one's command without interrupting the precise running of its patented movement.

Hermès's presentation of its Time to Dream collection is a demonstration of seamless synergy between horological mastery and sharp-witted imagination. The release of Arceau Le Temps Suspendu and Cape Cod Grandes Heures is a revelation of true wonderment. The two watches, both with 42-hour power reserve, are not merely exhibitions of mechanical proficiency, but rather the culminating results of a graceful dance between technical finesse and intelligent creativity.

The Arceau Le Temps Suspendu provides its owner with a concrete materialization of his most abstract reveries. As its name indicates, this triple retrograde self-winding timepiece allows its wearer to suspend time for as long as he wishes. With the simple push of a button situated at 9 o'clock, the hour and minute hands halt and hover around noon, and the date hand simply disappears. All the while, standard time continues its path through the intricate workings of the mechanism. Push the button again and the hour and minute hands reposition themselves at the actual time, the date slyly reappearing.

This whimsical articulation is made possible by Hermès's newly developed Time Suspended module. The innovative complication fits right in with the manufacture's philosophy that "Hermès time is dream time." While the world of horology is one of ultimate precision, the Arceau Le Temps Suspendu allows its user to control the passage of time like never before. The 174-piece limited edition rose-gold model of this flagship of Hermès's season comes in a 43mm case that is home to an opaline-silvered dial with herringbone motif. A steel variation additionally offers the option of a black dial with the same herringbone pattern. All models come with the "Hermès Paris" logo in the center left of the face and "Le temps suspendu" in cursive lettering between 4 and 6 o'clock in the retrograde date display. Meanwhile, the Time Suspended zone at 12 o'clock is a constant reminder of the magical possibilities of this playful yet refined timepiece, which is available with a choice of matte Havana or black alligator strap.

CAPE COD GRANDES HEURES

Three available dials and a variable speed hour hand allow for a more personal approach to timekeeping than ever before.

A further exploration of the Parisian house's ingenious theme bears fruit as a watch that lets its owner define the rhythm of time. With the Cape Cod Grandes Heures on one's wrist, time is truly made to measure. The self-winding piece's sophisticated mechanism drives an hour hand of variable speed that allows a seemingly chaotic choreography. Such is accomplished with a toothed oval wheel system that uses the shape of the gears to change the speed of its motion while the minutes and seconds move at a constant pace. Three different dials to choose from offer different spacing of the hours, hence a different tempo to one's time. The stylized arched numerals on a silver or anthracite dial, both with a beautiful guilloché setting, create a contrast to the curved rectangular case, providing a fittingly unconventional form of elegance.

With its Time to Dream collection, Hermès intelligently marries the open-minded curiosity of a child with the refinement of a distinguished mind, by creating a magical blend of imagination and innovative engineering.

CAPE COD GRANDES HEURES REF. 036314 WW00

Movement: automatic-winding Grand Hours module; Ø 27mm, thickness: 5.6mm; 42-hour power reserve; 133 components; 21 jewels; 28,800 vph; circular-grained and snailed bridges; oscillating weight decorated with Côtes de Genéve.
Functions: hours (variable speed), minutes, seconds.
Case: 316L stainless steel; 36.5x35.4mm; antireflective sapphire crystal; water resistant to 5atm.
Dial: silvered; variable-speed hour hand.
Strap: matte Havana; stainless steel folding safety clasp.
Price: available upon request.
Also available: stainless steel case and anthracite dial; graphite alligator strap; available in three different displays.

ARCEAU LE TEMPS SUSPENDU REF. 03875 WW00

Movement: automatic-winding Time Suspended module; Ø 34mm, thickness: 6.15mm; 42-hour power reserve; 254 components; 45 jewels; 28,800 vph; circular-grained and snailed bridges; oscillating weight decorated with Côtes de Genéve.
Functions: hours, minutes; date on an arch between 3:30 and 6:30; retrograde; Time Suspended zone at 12.
Case: 750 18K rose gold (79 grams); Ø 43mm; antireflective sapphire crystal; water resistant to 3atm.
Dial: opaline silvered with herringbone motif.
Strap: matte Havana alligator; 750 18K rose-gold folding safety clasp.
Price: available upon request.
Also available: 316L stainless steel case with opaline silvered or black dial and black alligator leather strap.
Note: limited numbered edition of 174 in rose gold.

ARCEAU CHRONO COLORS REF. 036249 WW00

Movement: automatic-winding; 42-hour power reserve.
Functions: hours, minutes; small seconds; date between 4 and 5; chronograph: 60-second counter at 3, 30-minute counter at 9 and 12-hour counter at 6.
Case: stainless steel; Ø 43mm; antireflective sapphire crystal; water resistant to 5atm.
Dial: white; varnished; dark gray transfer; rhodium-plated hour and minute hands; large orange seconds and counter hands.
Strap: white Epsom calf.
Price: available upon request.
Also available: other straps.

ARCEAU GRANDE LUNE REF. 036756 WW00

Movement: automatic-winding Dubois-Dépraz 9313 caliber; large moonphase; 42-hour power reserve.
Functions: hours, minutes, seconds; date and large moonphase at 6; day display at 11; month display at 1.
Case: stainless steel; Ø 43mm; antireflective sapphire crystal; water resistant to 3atm.
Dial: opaline silver; stamped herringbone motif; rhodium-plated hour and minute hands; large blue seconds hand.
Strap: matte Havana alligator.
Price: available upon request.
Also available: other straps.

CLIPPER CHRONO MECANIQUE PLONGEE — REF. 035437 WW00

Movement: automatic-winding chronograph; 46-hour power reserve; 28,800 vph.
Functions: hours, minutes; small seconds at 9; date at 3; chronograph: central seconds counter, 12-hour counter at 6 and 30-minute counter at 12.
Case: titanium; Ø 44mm; antireflective sapphire crystal; titanium caseback; water resistant to 20atm.
Dial: dark gray.
Strap: orange rubber.
Price: available upon request.
Also available: other straps.

CAPE COD SIMPLE CALENDAR — REF. 036308 WW00

Movement: automatic-winding in both directions; 42-hour power reserve; circular-grained and snailed bridges; oscillating weight adorned with Côtes de Genève motif.
Functions: hours, minutes, seconds; date at 3.
Case: stainless steel; 36.5x35.4mm; antireflective sapphire crystal; water resistant to 5atm.
Dial: opaline silver; rhodium-plated hour, minute and seconds hands.
Strap: matte Havana alligator.
Price: available upon request.
Also available: other straps.

CAPE COD TONNEAU — REF. 035236 WW00

Movement: quartz.
Functions: hours, minutes.
Case: 750 18K rose gold; set with 52 brilliant-cut diamonds; 26.5x28mm; antireflective sapphire crystal; water resistant to 3atm.
Dial: natural white mother-of-pearl.
Strap: smooth Etruscan alligator leather; 750 18K rose-gold pin buckle.
Price: available upon request.
Also available: other straps.

H HOUR TGM — REF. 036850 WW00

Movement: quartz
Functions: hours, minutes, seconds.
Case: stainless steel; 30.5x30.5mm; set with 64 full-cut round brilliant diamonds (2.25 carats); antireflective sapphire crystal; water resistant to 3atm.
Dial: white natural mother-of-pearl; dark gray transfer; set with eleven full-cut round brilliant diamonds (0.18 carat).
Strap: smooth ember alligator.
Price: available upon request.
Also available: other straps and sizes.

HUBLOT
GENEVE

CHALLENGE ACCEPTED

When Hublot's Chairman of the Board, Jean-Claude Biver inspired his new Complications Department to push the envelope of time, he propelled the Swiss manufacture on a quest for new frontiers.

The opening of two new boutiques, one in Beverly Hills, and the other on Madison Avenue in New York, further underscores the brand's maturation into a leading player in the world of luxury and innovative design. In addition, the Beverly Hills store is the only one to offer the King Power Beverly Hills, a limited edition of 50 pieces.

These new frontiers extend beyond the addition of extraordinary boutiques, or the bridging of the gap between fantasy and innovative horology, into a complete vision of the "art of fusion" as a mantra deeply imbedded in the brand's philosophy.

Hublot's presentation of the Cathedral Minute Repeater Tourbillon and Column Wheel Chronograph is a perfect illustration of fusion between the tradition of haute horology and the spirit of modernity. The watch's carbon fiber case houses a tourbillon and column-wheel chronograph, with carbon fiber bridges, under an anti-reflective sapphire crystal. The highlight of this timepiece, however, is the minute repeater, activated by a lever between 8 and 10 o'clock, featuring two "cathedral" type gongs, one for hours and the other for minutes.

While these three complications are traditionally prized by connoisseurs, it is their visibility from the dial side that fascinates and intrigues. The flying tourbillon with suspended cage is situated at 6 o'clock and boasts an unusual structure of the highest quality. Meanwhile, the chronograph control is subtly integrated into the watch's crown and the minute repeater bolt finds an ingenious home in the King Power case middle.

The overall consolidated design results in a surprisingly uncomplicated visual effect for a piece of this advanced level of mechanical mastery.

Beverly Hills boutique

Jean-Claude Biver and Dr. Mathilde Krim

Usain Bolt celebrating the opening of the Hublot boutique in Beverly Hills, racing with Hublot for the KEF Foundation (Children).

CATHEDRAL MINUTE REPEATER TOURBILLON AND COLUMN WHEEL CHRONOGRAPH

It is a World Premiere with the case and its two bridges 100% made in carbon fiber.

MP-02 KEY OF TIME
With a user-controlled three-position speed of time indicator, Hublot's new creation makes the jump from timepiece to time machine.

With the presentation of its newest masterpiece, the MP-02 Key of Time—of which only 50 numbered pieces will be produced—the innovative Genevan watchmaker conquers the notion of time and transforms it into the wearer's playground.

Through cutting-edge engineering and extraordinary imagination, the MP-02 Key of Time enables its owner to control the speed at which time passes, capturing the abstraction of "the moment": our time's truest luxury. The watch's three-position crown permits the modulation of the pace of motion of the hands through three positional settings:

1. In which time is slowed by four, thereby representing one hour as a quarter thereof on the MP-02 display.
2. In "Real time," where each segment of time is displayed conventionally, equating one hour on the Key of Time to one standard hour.
3. In which an accelerated hand multiplies time by four, representing a quarter of an hour as a full hour on the MP-02 Key of Time display.

While the complex mechanism can be kept indefinitely in the altered modes, a simple return to the second position lets the wearer watch the hands readjust to a conventional time display. A veritable third dimension is added with seconds being displayed via the vertical flying tourbillon cage. Completing this technical and imaginative concept is the grade 5 micro-blasted titanium case with black DLC coating, whose futuristic allusions offer the subtle semblance of a time traveling device.

Continuing the list of daring new releases is a watch that exemplifies the audacious "practice what you preach" attitude of the manufacture's Chairman of the Board. In fact, the 3 Million USD BB, a secret project of the house, was conceived as a "light-hearted confidential challenge" between Biver and Hublot's master gemsetters. No less than twelve months later, this astonishing timepiece was finally brought to life.

This dazzling fusion of jewelry and horology, made up of 637 baguette diamonds and a rose-cut diamond on the crown, features a Vendôme tourbillon, named in tribute to the recent opening of the Hublot boutique at 10, Place Vendôme, in Paris. Harvested from a mine in the Russian Far East, the diamonds used in this watch are of remarkable quality, color-graded as Top Wesselton with A VVS clarity. In the nine months required by the master gemstone setters, the diamonds were meticulously selected, individually cut to the technical designs of the piece, and patiently set in a Clou de Paris motif. Two small columns on the dial side frame the tourbillon cage, and are replicas of the ones recently illuminated by Hublot, while the flying tourbillon movement, HUB6003, was entirely developed within the manufacture.

More than 140 carats of baguette diamonds make up the 3 Million USD BB, nearly 103 of which can be found in the brilliant white-gold bracelet with deployant buckle.

This one-off piece is a breathtaking celebration of the fusion of the creativity, skill, fearless confidence—and most of all, ingenious madness—required to create a masterpiece of such magnitude.

3 MILLION USD BB
Once a closely guarded secret, this watch has found a fitting home against a luxurious Monaco backdrop.

KING POWER DWYANE WADE

In collaboration with the perennial All-Star, Hublot makes a charitable leap into the world of basketball.

Hublot's spectacular quest for noble frontiers made its next stop in Beijing, in the heart of the Forbidden City. It is in this magnificent setting that NBA superstar and Hublot ambassador Dwyane Wade met the One Million RMB Basketball Chinese Charity Challenge.

Wade, a pioneering fund-raiser for children's charities, and brand ambassador since February 2011, took on the challenge to score a maximum number of baskets, each corresponding to an extensive sum of money. The collected benefits were then donated to leading non-profit organization One Foundation, on behalf of Hublot and Wade's World Foundation. While his accomplishments in the NBA are as legendary as they are awe-inspiring, his leadership of the Olympic Gold medal-winning US basketball team in Beijing 2008 makes this event all the more special.

On the occasion of this joint effort to support children's aid in China, the collaborative union proudly revealed the new King Power Dwyane Wade. This sports icon, who never shies away from an opportunity to effect positive change, explains, "I'm excited to debut the King Power during the charity challenge, which not only raises money for a worthy cause but also provides the perfect setting to showcase such a unique, yet distinctive timepiece."

Inspired by his career and the world of basketball, this 500-piece limited edition watch prominently features Wade's jersey number at 3 o'clock. Enhancing the reference, the micro-blasted black ceramic case's face evokes the surface texture of a basketball, and the strap's stitching unmistakably suggests the aesthetics of a basketball net. Hublot's own fusion-driven DNA raises its voice with the use of titanium, ceramic, tungsten, rhodium plating and composite elements such as the bezel's red resin, part of a color theme representative of the Miami Heat and its leader.

Finally, Hublot continues its fun and sophisticated Tutti Frutti collection. Four new models with gold cases are sure to capture the lighter side of the haute horology enthusiast. With colored matte dials that match the alligator straps, these four pieces bring even more color to an already animated line of automatic timepieces. All four watches—available in dark blue, dark green, brown, or camel—feature gold-plated hands and 37 adorning jewels, and are powered by an automatic chronograph movement with a 42-hour power reserve.

Inspired by the vision of its daring Chairman of the Board, Hublot makes a giant leap toward the adventurous and bold frontiers of the watchmaking industry... and takes the time to give something back to the next generation in need.

TUTTI FRUTTI

Hublot's addition of these Tutti Frutti Gold models expands upon and adds more depth to this colorful collection.

FORMULA 1™ KING POWER CERAMIC REF. 703.CI.1123.NR.FMO10

Movement: automatic-winding HUB4100 caliber; 42-hour power reserve; 252 components; 27 jewels; microblasted, beveled and polished bridges; black PVD-coated oscillating weight with tungsten carbide heavy segment; rhodium-plated and circular-grained mainplate; reinforced spring barrel; Glucydur hairspring escapement.
Functions: hours, minutes, seconds; date at 4:30; chronograph.
Case: King Power; microblasted black ceramic; Ø 48mm; carbon and black ceramic bezel with six H-shaped black PVD-coated titanium screws; bezel lugs with black composite resin; black PVD-coated titanium crown with black rubber inserts; lateral inserts with black composite resin; start pushbutton at 2 with red rubber inserts and black text; reset pushbutton at 4 with black rubber and red text; antireflective sapphire crystal; microblasted black ceramic caseback; water resistant to 10atm.
Dial: multi-piece matte black; black nickel hour markers with red Super-LumiNova; satin-finished black nickel hour and minute hands with red SuperLumiNova; Formula 1™ logo at 12.
Strap: black rubber and Nomex with Formula 1™ logo and red stitching; King Power microblasted black PVD-coated titanium deployant buckle; cap in microblasted black PVD-coated titanium; microblasted black ceramic decorative plate.
Note: limited to 500 pieces numbered from 01/500 to 500/500.
Suggested price: $23,900

KING POWER RED DEVIL REF. 716.CI.1129.RX.MAN11

Movement: automatic-winding HUB4245 caliber; 42-hour power reserve; microblasted and beveled bridges with black galvanic treatment; microblasted mainplate with black galvanic treatment; reinforced spring barrel; Swiss lever escapement; monobloc oscillating weight in heavy metal with ceramic ball bearings.
Functions: hours, minutes, seconds; date at 4; chronograph: central 45-minute counter and central seconds hand.
Case: King Power; microblasted black ceramic; Ø 48mm; microblasted black ceramic bezel with black rubber molding and six H-shaped black PVD-coated titanium screws; bezel lugs with black composite resin; black PVD-coated steel crown with black rubber inserts; black PVD-coated steel pushbuttons with black and red rubber molding; lateral inserts with black composite resin at 3; antireflective sapphire crystal; microblasted black ceramic caseback; water resistant to 10atm.
Dial: sapphire; hour markers made of grass from the hallowed turf of Manchester United's Old Trafford stadium; satin-finished black nickel hour and minute hands with red luminescent coating; Red Devil logo at 3.
Strap: black rubber; black PVD-coated titanium deployant buckle; microblasted black ceramic decorative.
Note: limited to 500 pieces numbered from 01/500 to 500/500.
Suggested price: $24,900

KING POWER UNICO ALL BLACK REF. 701.CI.0110.RX-SD-HR-W

Movement: automatic-winding HUB1240 UNICO caliber; 72-hour power reserve; microblasted and beveled bridges with black galvanic treatment; microblasted mainplate with black galvanic treatment; reinforced spring barrel; Swiss pallet escapement with silicium pallet fork and escapement wheel.
Functions: hours, minutes, seconds; date at 4:30; flyback chronograph.
Case: King Power; microblasted black ceramic; Ø 48mm; micro-blasted black ceramic bezel with black rubber molding and six H-shaped titanium screws; bezel lugs with black composite resin; black ceramic crown and pushbuttons with black rubber inserts; lateral inserts with black composite resin; antireflective sapphire crystal; microblasted black ceramic caseback; water resistant to 10atm.
Dial: multi-piece with carbon base; microblasted matte black counters and flange; applied hour markers with black nickel treatment and black Super-LumiNova; satin-finished black nickel hour and minute hands with luminescent coating.
Strap: black rubber; microblasted black ceramic and black PVD steel deployant buckle.
Note: limited to 500 pieces numbered from 01/500 to 500/500.
Suggested price: $19,900

HUBLOT CALIBER HUB1240

Movement: automatic-winding ceramic ball bearing; Pellaton type 2-way winding; Ø 30.4mm, thickness: 8.05mm; 70-hour power reserve; 330 components; 36 jewels; column-wheel chronograph mechanism integrated on the dial side; bi-compax; two pushbuttons; double horizontal clutch; no jumper in the chronograph mechanism; removable platform escapement.
Functions: hours, minutes, seconds; date; flyback chronograph.

BIG BANG ALL BLACK CARBON — REF. 301.QX.1740.GR

Movement: automatic-winding HUB4100 caliber; 42-hour power reserve; 252 components; 28 jewels; satin-finished, beveled and polished bridges; oscillating weight tungsten carbide with black ruthenium-coated dimpled surface; black ruthenium-coating mainplate; reinforced spring barrel; escapement Glucydur hairspring.
Functions: hours, minutes, seconds; date at 4:30; chronograph.
Case: Big Bang; black carbon fiber; Ø 44.5mm; black carbon fiber bezel with six H-shaped black PVD-coated titanium screws, countersunk, polished and locked; bezel lugs with black composite resin; black PVD-coated steel crown with black rubber inserts; black PVD-coated steel pushbuttons with black rubber inserts; lateral inserts with black composite resin; antireflective sapphire crystal; carbon fiber sapphire crystal caseback; water resistant to 10atm.
Dial: matte black carbon fiber; applied black hour markers; faceted matte black hour and minute hands; brilliant black logo transfer.
Strap: black alligator gummy, stitched onto black natural rubber; black PVD-coated steel clasp.
Suggested price: $19,900

BIG BANG BLACK CAVIAR — REF. 346.CX.1800.RX

Movement: automatic-winding HUB1112 caliber; 42-hour power reserve; 63 components; 25 jewels; satin-finished, beveled and polished bridges; oscillating weight tungsten carbide with black ruthenium-coated dimpled surface; reinforced spring barrel; escapement Glucydur hairspring.
Functions: hours, minutes, seconds; date at 3.
Case: Big Bang; polished black ceramic; Ø 41mm; polished black ceramic bezel with six titanium H-shaped screws countersunk, polished and locked; bezel lugs with black composite resin; polished black ceramic crown; lateral inserts with black composite resin; antireflective sapphire crystal; antireflective polished black ceramic sapphire crystal caseback; water resistant to 10atm.
Dial: polished black ceramic; faceted, diamond-polished, rhodium-plated, skeleton hour and minute hands; Hublot logo transfer at 12.
Strap: black rubber with the Hublot logo; black PVD-coated stainless steel deployant buckle.
Suggested price: $9,500

BIG BANG LEOPARD — REF. 341.PX.7610.NR.1976

Movement: automatic-winding HUB4300 caliber.
Functions: hours, minutes, seconds; date at 4:30; chronograph.
Case: Big Bang; 5N 18K red gold; Ø 41mm; satin-finished 5N 18K red-gold bezel set with 48 baguette-cut andalusites, smoked quartz and citrines with six H-shaped black PVD-coated titanium screws, countersunk and polished; bezel lugs with black composite resin; 5N 18K red-gold crown and pushbuttons with black rubber inserts; lateral inserts with black composite resin; antireflective sapphire crystal; 5N 18K red-gold caseback; water resistant to 10atm.
Dial: leopard print; eight yellow diamond hour markers; faceted and polished 5N 18K red-gold hour and minute hands.
Strap: leopard-print denim, stitched into black rubber; 5N 18K red-gold deployant buckle.
Suggested price: $39,900

CLASSIC FUSION CHRONOGRAPH — REF. 521.OX.1180.LR

Movement: automatic-winding HUB1143 caliber; 42-hour power reserve; 280 components; 59 jewels; satin-finished, beveled and polished bridges; tungsten carbide oscillating weight with black ruthenium-coated dimpled surface; reinforced spring barrel; escapement Glucydur hairspring.
Functions: hours, minutes, seconds; date at 6; chronograph.
Case: Classic Fusion; 18K King Gold; Ø 45mm; satin-finished end-pieces; satin-finished 18K King Gold bezel with six H-shaped screws, countersunk, polished and locked; satin-finished 18K King Gold crown with Hublot logo; antireflective sapphire crystal; satin-finished antireflective 18K King Gold sapphire crystal caseback; water resistant to 5atm.
Dial: matte black; applied 18K King-Gold; faceted, diamond-polished, skeleton, 18K King-Gold hour and minute hands.
Strap: black alligator and rubber; 18K King Gold deployant buckle.
Suggested price: $27,500

IWC

INTERNATIONAL WATCH CO. SCHAFFHAUSEN
SWITZERLAND, SINCE 1868

TAKING THE TIME

La dolce vita of Portofino ticks on with an elegant collection and splendid photographs.

The Italian fishing village of Portofino—a destination of choice for the most distinguished and successful over the last fifty years—serves not only as a muse for IWC's horological tribute to the Mediterranean lifestyle, but also as inspiration and backdrop for an enchanting photo essay by renowned photographer Peter Lindbergh.

The Portofino Hand-Wound Eight Days, the new flagship of the 27-year-old Portofino collection, carries on IWC's tradition of elegance and precision mechanics. The newly developed manual-winding 59210 caliber ticks away inside the ample yet tasteful 45mm case. Although it is capable of storing enough energy for a full nine days, IWC designers strategically inserted a gear that stops the movement after precisely 192 hours, or eight days. In doing so, IWC eliminates the effect of reduced torque in the mainspring as it winds down, ensuring the same level of accuracy the whole time the watch is running. Such a detail, in addition to the 28,800 beats per hour and the Breguet spring bent into shape in accordance with ancient watchmaking tradition, makes this watch as precise as it is elegant.

Available in 18-karat red gold with ardoise-colored dial, and stainless steel with black or silver-plated dials, all mounted on alligator leather straps by Santoni, the Hand-Wound Eight Days features small seconds at 6 o'clock, date at 3 o'clock, and a power reserve between 8 and 9 o'clock, finely balanced for an exquisite layout.

To wind this watch once a week is a delicious reminder of the relaxed pace of Portofino itself: that there is no pleasure like the pleasure of taking the time.

PORTOFINO HAND-WOUND EIGHT DAYS

The elegant power reserve display lets the owner look forward to the pleasure of winding this flagship piece of the Portofino collection.

The case of the Portofino Chronograph evokes the steering wheels of the yachts anchored in Portofino's harbor. Its striking pushbuttons are reminiscent of the dynamic elegance of a 1960s Italian sports car—exciting yet understated. While the top figures of the 30-minute counter at 12 o'clock and the 12-hour counter at 6 o'clock stand out in red, the small seconds at 9 o'clock is decidedly low key and offers a graceful counterbalance to the day and date display on the opposite side of the dial. This energetic automatic-winding chronograph with cumulative stopwatch displays is equipped with a 44-hour power reserve and is available on an alligator leather strap or Milanese mesh bracelet.

PORTOFINO CHRONOGRAPH
Intelligent integration of its chronometric components lends this piece an understated dynamism reminiscent of a 1960s Italian sports car.

Schaffhausen completes the newest generation of the Portofino collection with the unassuming star of the family. The Portofino Automatic achieves a perfection of simplicity with three hands and a discreet date—it needs nothing more. The evenly rounded sides of the 40mm case make it appear even slimmer. Also available in stainless steel on a Milanese mesh bracelet or alligator leather strap, the 18-karat red-gold model features a caseback decorated with an engraved view of the harbor of Portofino.

This year of Portofino also marks the unveiling of Peter Lindbergh's fabulous new exhibition. "A Night in Portofino" is nothing short of a brilliant work of transcendence. IWC Schaffhausen's collaboration with the legendary photographer and talented friends of the brand bends the boundaries of time, space, and reality. More than just a virtuoso reflection on nostalgia, the photographic work of genius reveals the very touch of the dolce vita of 1960s Portofino. As Lindbergh states, "Time moves on. Only in Portofino does it stand still."

PORTOFINO AUTOMATIC
The new Portofino Automatic remains classical and proudly simple as it unveils a new perfectly round 40mm case.

IWC AQUATIMER DEEP TWO — REF. IW354703

Movement: automatic-winding 30110 caliber; 42-hour power reserve; 21 jewels.
Functions: hours, minutes; stop seconds; date at 3; depth gauge with split indicator showing maximum depth to 50m from 6 to 12.
Case: stainless steel; Ø 46mm, thickness: 15.5mm; external rotating bezel; screw-down crown; sapphire crystal, antireflective coating on both sides; water resistant to 12atm.
Dial: black; hands, dial and external rotating bezel with white SuperLumiNova.
Bracelet: stainless steel.
Suggested price: $15,900-$16,900
Also available: black rubber strap.

IWC AQUATIMER AUTOMATIC 2000 — REF. IW356810

Movement: automatic-winding 30110 caliber; 42-hour power reserve; 21 jewels.
Functions: hours, minutes; stop seconds; date at 3.
Case: stainless steel; Ø 44mm, thickness: 14mm; external rotating bezel; screw-down crown; sapphire crystal, antireflective coating on both sides; water resistant to 200atm.
Dial: black; hands, dial and external rotating bezel with white SuperLumiNova.
Strap: black rubber.
Suggested price: $4,600-$5,600
Also available: stainless steel bracelet; white dial on black rubber strap or stainless steel bracelet.

IWC DA VINCI PERPETUAL CALENDAR DIGITAL DATE-MONTH — REF. IW376107

Movement: automatic-winding 89800 caliber; 68-hour power reserve; 52 jewels.
Functions: hours, minutes; small stop seconds and leap year at 6; large date at 9; month at 3; flyback chronograph: combined 12-hour and 30-minute counters at 12 and central seconds hand; perpetual calendar.
Case: 18K rose gold; 44x52.8mm, thickness: 16.3mm; screw-down crown; sapphire crystal, antireflective coating on both sides; exhibition caseback; water resistant to 3atm.
Dial: silver-plated.
Strap: dark brown alligator leather.
Suggested price: $44,300-$70,000
Also available: platinum on black alligator strap (limited to 500 pieces).

IWC INGENIEUR AUTOMATIC MISSION EARTH — REF. IW323601

Movement: automatic-winding 80110 caliber; 44-hour power reserve; 28 jewels; integrated shock-absorption system.
Functions: hours, minutes; stop seconds; date at 3.
Case: stainless steel; Ø 46mm, thickness: 15mm; screw-down crown; soft iron for protection against magnetic fields up to 80,000 A/m; sapphire crystal, antireflective coating on both sides; water resistant to 12atm.
Dial: black.
Strap: black rubber.
Suggested price: $7,300-$8,300
Also available: stainless steel bracelet.

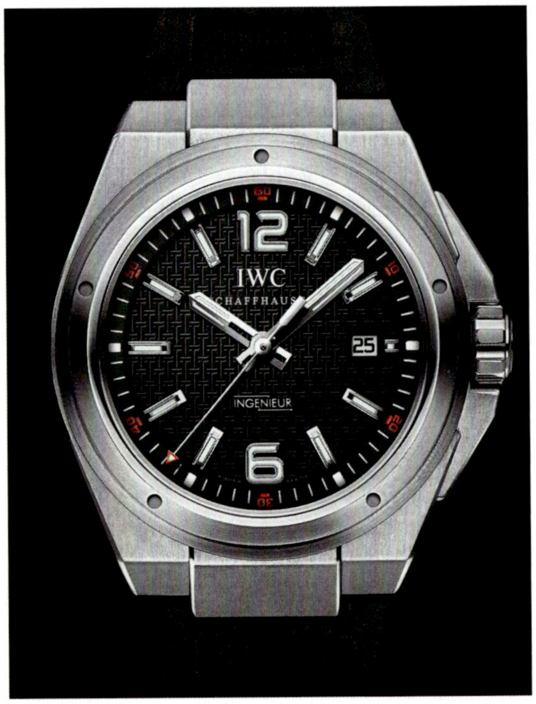

IWC INGENIEUR AUTOMATIC, VINTAGE COLLECTION — REF. IW323301

Movement: Pellaton automatic-winding 80111 caliber; 44-hour power reserve; 28 jewels.
Functions: hours, minutes; stop seconds; date at 3.
Case: stainless steel; Ø 42.5mm, thickness: 14.5mm; screw-down crown; sapphire crystal, antireflective coating on both sides; exibition caseback; water resistant to 12atm.
Dial: black.
Strap: black alligator leather.
Suggested price: $7,300-$38,000
Also available: platinum (limited to 500 pieces); rose gold; white gold.

IWC PILOT'S WATCH CHRONO-AUTOMATIC — REF. IW371701

Movement: automatic-winding 79320 caliber; 44-hour power reserve; 25 jewels.
Functions: hours, minutes; small stop seconds at 9; day and date at 3; chronograph: 12-hour counter at 6, 30-minute counter at 12 and central seconds hand.
Case: stainless steel; Ø 42mm, thickness: 14.7mm; screw-down crown; soft iron for protection against magnetic fields; sapphire crystal, antireflective coating on both sides and secured against displacement by drop in air pressure; water resistant to 6atm.
Dial: black.
Strap: black alligator leather.
Suggested price: $5,100-$15,900
Also available: stainless steel bracelet; 18K red-gold case on a brown alligator strap.

IWC BIG PILOT'S WATCH — REF. IW500401

Movement: Pellaton automatic-winding 51111 caliber; 7-day power reserve; 42 jewels; Glucydur® beryllium alloy balance with high-precision adjustment cam on balance arms; Breguet spring.
Functions: hours, minutes; stop seconds; date at 6; power reserve indicator at 3.
Case: stainless steel; Ø 46.2mm, thickness: 15.8mm; screw-down crown; soft iron for protection against magnetic fields; sapphire crystal, antireflective coating on both sides and secured against displacement by drop in air pressure; water resistant to 6atm.
Dial: black.
Strap: black alligator leather.
Suggested price: $14,300-$28,100
Also available: white gold.

IWC PORTUGUESE AUTOMATIC — REF. IW500106

Movement: Pellaton automatic-winding 51010 caliber; 7-day power reserve; 42 jewels; Glucydur® beryllium alloy balance with high-precision adjustment cam on balance arms; Breguet spring; 18K gold medallion rotor.
Functions: hours, minutes; small stop seconds at 9; date at 6; power reserve indicator at 3.
Case: 18K white gold; Ø 42.3mm, thickness: 14mm; sapphire crystal, antireflective coating on both sides; exhibition caseback; water resistant to 3atm.
Dial: ardoise.
Strap: dark brown alligator leather.
Suggested price: $12,400-$23,700
Also available: stainless steel; rose gold.

IWC PILOT'S WATCH DOUBLE CHRONOGRAPH EDITION TOP GUN — REF. IW379901

Movement: automatic-winding 79230 caliber; 44-hour power reserve; 29 jewels.
Functions: hours, minutes; small stop seconds at 9; day and date at 3; chronograph: 12-hour counter at 6, 30-minute counter at 12 and split-seconds central hands.
Case: ceramic and titanium; Ø 46mm, thickness: 17.8mm; screw-down crown; soft iron for protection against magnetic fields; sapphire crystal, antireflective coating on both sides and secured against displacement by drop in air pressure; titanium caseback with Top Gun logo; water resistant to 6atm.
Dial: black.
Strap: black.
Suggested price: $11,900

IWC PILOT'S WATCH MARK XVI — REF. IW325501

Movement: automatic-winding 30110 caliber; 42-hour power reserve; 21 jewels.
Functions: hours, minutes; stop seconds; date at 3.
Case: stainless steel; Ø 39mm, thickness: 11.5mm; screw-down crown; soft iron for protection against magnetic fields; sapphire crystal, antireflective coating on both sides and secured against displacement by drop in air pressure; water resistant to 6atm.
Dial: black.
Strap: black alligator leather.
Suggested price: $4,100-$5,500
Also available: stainless steel bracelet.

IWC PORTUGUESE HAND-WOUND, VINTAGE COLLECTION — REF. IW544501

Movement: manual-winding 98295 caliber; 46-hour power reserve; 18 jewels; Glucydur® beryllium alloy balance with high-precision adjustment cam on balance arms; Breguet spring; three-quarter bridge.
Functions: hours, minutes; small stop seconds at 6.
Case: stainless steel; Ø 44mm, thickness: 10mm; sapphire crystal, antireflective coating on both sides; exhibition caseback; water resistant to 3atm.
Dial: black.
Strap: black alligator leather.
Suggested price: $9,900-$41,500
Also available: platinum (limited to 500 pieces); rose gold; white gold.

IWC PORTUGUESE GRANDE COMPLICATION — REF. IW377402

Movement: automatic-winding 79091 caliber; 44-hour power reserve; 75 jewels.
Functions: hours, minutes; small stop seconds at 9; chronograph: 12-hour counter at 6, 30-minute counter at 12 and central seconds hand; moonphase; perpetual calendar; minute repeater: hours, quarter-hours and minutes.
Case: 18K red gold; Ø 45mm, thickness: 16.5mm; sapphire crystal, antireflective coating on both sides; special caseback engraving; water resistant to 3atm.
Dial: silver-plated.
Strap: dark brown alligator leather.
Note: limited edition of 50 pieces per year.
Suggested price: $233,000-$260,000
Also available: platinum.

IWC PORTUGUESE TOURBILLON MYSTERE RETROGRADE REF. IW504402

Movement: Pellaton automatic-winding 51900 caliber; 7-day power reserve; 44 jewels; Glucydur® beryllium alloy balance with high-precision adjustment cam on balance arms; Breguet spring; 18K gold medallion rotor.
Functions: hours, minutes; retrograde date on an arc between 6 and 9; power reserve indicator between 2 and 3; flying tourbillon at 12.
Case: 18K red gold; Ø 44.2mm, thickness: 15.5mm; sapphire crystal, antireflective coating on both sides; exhibition sapphire crystal caseback; water resistant to 3atm.
Dial: silver-plated.
Strap: dark brown alligator leather.
Note: limited edition of 500.
Suggested price: $114,000-$136,000
Also available: platinum (limited edition of 250).

IWC PORTUGUESE TOURBILLON HAND-WOUND REF. IW544705

Movement: manual-winding 98900 caliber; 54-hour power reserve; 21 jewels; three-quarter bridge.
Functions: hours, minutes; small seconds at 6; flying tourbillon at 9.
Case: 18K red gold; Ø 43.1mm, thickness: 11mm; sapphire crystal, antireflective coating on both sides; exhibition sapphire crystal caseback; water resistant to 3atm.
Dial: black.
Strap: black alligator leather.
Note: limited edition of 500 pieces.
Suggested price: $61,100

IWC PORTUGUESE MINUTE REPEATER REF. IW544906

Movement: manual-winding 98950 caliber; 46-hour power reserve; 52 jewels; Glucydur® beryllium alloy balance with high-precision adjustment cam on balance arms; Breguet spring; three-quarter bridge.
Functions: hours, minutes; small stop seconds at 6; minute repeater: hours, quarter-hours and minutes.
Case: platinum; Ø 44mm, thickness: 14mm; sapphire crystal, antireflective coating on both sides; exhibition sapphire crystal caseback.
Dial: silver-plated.
Strap: black alligator leather.
Note: limited edition of 500 pieces.
Suggested price: $93,200-$116,000
Also available: 18K red gold (limited to 500 pieces).

IWC PORTUGUESE PERPETUAL CALENDAR REF. IW503203

Movement: Pellaton automatic-winding 51614 caliber; 7-day power reserve; 62 jewels; Glucydur® beryllium alloy balance with high-precision adjustment cam on balance arms; Breguet spring; 18K gold medallion rotor.
Functions: hours, minutes; small stop seconds at 9; power reserve indicator at 3; perpetual moonphase for the northern and southern hemispheres at 12; perpetual calendar: date, day, month and year.
Case: 18K white gold; Ø 44.2mm, thickness: 15.5mm; sapphire crystal, antireflective coating on both sides; exhibition sapphire crystal caseback; water resistant to 3atm.
Dial: midnight blue.
Strap: black alligator leather.
Suggested price: $37,900-$41,900
Also available: red gold.

IWC PORTUGUESE PERPETUAL CALENDAR REF. IW502307

Movement: Pellaton automatic-winding 51613 caliber; 7-day power reserve; 62 jewels; Glucydur® beryllium alloy balance with high-precision adjustment cam on balance arms; Breguet spring; 18K gold medallion rotor.
Functions: hours, minutes; small stop seconds at 9; power reserve indicator at 3; perpetual moonphase at 12; perpetual calendar: date, day, month and year.
Case: 18K white gold; Ø 44.2mm, thickness: 15.5mm; sapphire crystal, antireflective coating on both sides; exhibition sapphire crystal caseback; water resistant to 3atm.
Dial: ardoise.
Strap: dark brown alligator leather.
Suggested price: $37,100-$41,100
Also available: red gold.

IWC PORTUGUESE YACHT CLUB CHRONOGRAPH REF. IW390211

Movement: automatic-winding 89360 caliber; 68-hour power reserve; 40 jewels.
Functions: hours, minutes; small stop seconds at 6; date at 3; flyback chronograph: 12-hour and 60-second counters at 12 and central seconds hand.
Case: stainless steel; Ø 45.4mm, thickness: 14.5mm; screw-down crown; sapphire crystal, antireflective coating on both sides; exhibition sapphire crystal caseback; water resistant to 6atm.
Dial: silver-plated.
Strap: black rubber.
Suggested price: $14,000-$26,400
Also available: red gold on black rubber strap; stainless steel with black dial on black rubber strap.

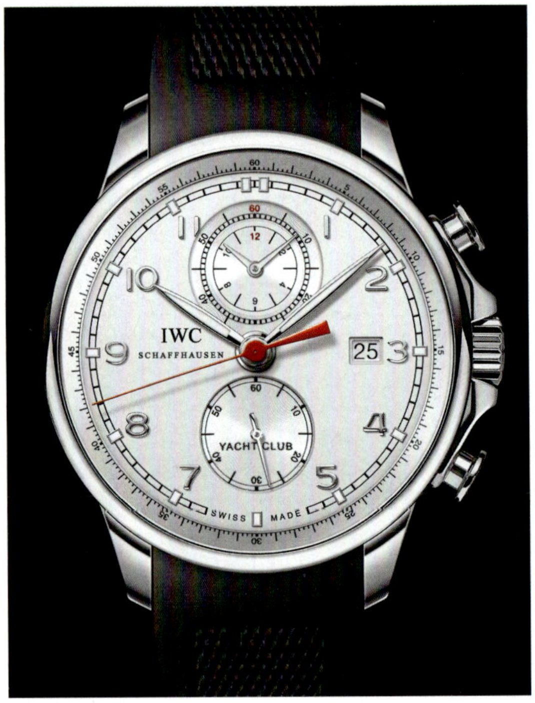

IWC PORTUGUESE CHRONOGRAPH REF. IW371482

Movement: automatic-winding 79350 caliber; 44-hour power reserve; 31 jewels.
Functions: hours, minutes; small stop seconds at 6; chronograph: 30-minute counter at 12 and central seconds hand.
Case: 18K red gold; Ø 40.9mm, thickness: 12.3mm; sapphire crystal, antireflective coating on both sides; water resistant to 3atm.
Dial: ardoise.
Strap: dark black alligator leather.
Suggested price: $7,400-$16,400
Also available: stainless steel.

IWC DA VINCI CHRONOGRAPH CERAMIC REF. IW376601

Movement: automatic-winding 89360 caliber; 68-hour power reserve; 40 jewels.
Functions: hours, minutes; small stop seconds and date at 6; chronograph: 12-hour and 30-minute counters at 12 and central seconds hand; flyback.
Case: ceramic and grade 5 titanium; 44x52.8mm, thickness: 15.1mm; screw-down crown; sapphire crystal, antireflective coating on both sides; water resistant to 3atm.
Dial: black.
Strap: black calfskin.
Suggested price: $17,200

IWC PORTOFINO AUTOMATIC — REF. IW356504

Movement: automatic-winding 35110 caliber; 42-hour power reserve; 25 jewels.
Functions: hours, minutes; stop seconds; date at 3.
Case: 18K red gold; Ø 40mm, thickness: 9.5mm; sapphire crystal, antireflective coating on both sides; special caseback engraving; water resistant to 3atm.
Dial: silver-plated.
Strap: dark brown alligator leather.
Suggested price: $4,500-$11,700
Also available: stainless steel.

IWC PORTOFINO CHRONOGRAPH — REF. IW391001

Movement: automatic-winding 79320 caliber; 44-hour power reserve; 25 jewels.
Functions: hours, minutes; small stop seconds at 9; day and date at 3; chronograph: 12-hour counter at 6, 30-minute counter at 12 and central seconds hand.
Case: stainless steel; Ø 42mm, thickness: 13.5mm; sapphire crystal, antireflective coating on both sides; water resistant to 3atm.
Dial: silver-plated.
Strap: dark brown alligator leather.
Suggested price: $5,900-$6,900
Also available: stainless steel.

IWC PORTOFINO HAND-WOUND EIGHT DAYS — REF. IW510104

Movement: manual-winding 59210 caliber; 8-day power reserve; 30 jewels; Breguet spring.
Functions: hours, minutes; small stop seconds at 6; date at 3; power reserve indicator at 9.
Case: 18K red gold; Ø 45mm, thickness: 12mm; sapphire crystal, antireflective coating on both sides; water resistant to 3atm.
Dial: ardoise.
Strap: Santoni dark brown alligator leather.
Suggested price: $10,800-$20,200
Also available: stainless steel.

IWC INGENIEUR DOUBLE CHRONOGRAPH TITANIUM — REF. IW376501

Movement: automatic-winding; 44-hour power reserve; 29 jewels.
Functions: hours, minutes; small stop seconds at 9; day and date at 3; chronograph: 12-hour counter at 6, 30-minute counter at 12 and central split-seconds hands.
Case: titanium; Ø 45mm, thickness: 16mm; screw-down crown; sapphire crystal, antireflective coating on both sides; water resistant to 12atm.
Dial: black.
Strap: black rubber.
Suggested price: $12,700

JACOB & CO

PENTACULAR SPECTACULAR

Jacob & Co. presents two series of watches that defy location and make time an international matter.

GLOBAL 1

Five individually powered dials express a truly global vision of time.

With its new G5 series, Jacob & Co. injects the spirit of its renowned Five Time Zone collection into a daring new shape that highlights the bold, cosmopolitan essence of the brand.

The New York jeweler introduces a series of watches that feature a striking new pentagonal case to best express its vision of the modern jetsetter.

The newly presented Global collection takes advantage of the rarely utilized pentagon to feature local time with the same dimensions as the other four time zones, making the powerful visual statement that its wearer is a genuine citizen of the world.

Although the collection is comprised of several models that embrace a variety of materials, designs, and decorative techniques, the concept that its owner's time never sleeps pervades the collection. Individually powered by high-precision Swiss ETA quartz movements that provide hour-and-minute control for each time zone, the five dedicated crowns form a synergic emblem of global modernity. All models display local time and four additional dials inscribed with the names of cultural and economic powerhouses: Tokyo, New York, Paris and Los Angeles.

The Global 1 model brings together a case in gleaming black PVD, bezels in brilliant red anodized aluminum, and a black alligator strap with red accents. Global 2's steel case offers a more luminous style and contrasts with bezels in rose gold. The rose-gold bezels in Global 3 and 4 rest atop steel cases in black PVD, though Global 4 adds carbon fiber for distinctive contrast. Of course, Jacob & Co. imbues this collection with the brand's spirit on the Global 5, whose stainless steel case sports diamonds on the bezels and

The Grand collection, also introduced at BaselWorld, is a contemporary take on the glamour and luxury of the Jet Age. Like the Global collection, Grand consists of five equally sized, individually powered, dials within a pentagonal case. However, an additional design touch evokes the adventurous spirit of the 1960s jetsetter. As an emphasis within the already bold contour, Jacob & Co. has added a central turbine accent that anchors the whole composition. The wearer of this watch is sure to be reminded of the power of jet engines with this reference to the aeronautical world. The five dials, one local and four inscribed with the names of New York, LA, Tokyo, and Paris, united by the central turbine, bring together the on-the-go world of international business and the design of the early jet travel era. Continuing the pentacular theme, the brand offers five models, each with a particular combination: Grand 1, 4, and 5 in steel cases in black PVD, Grand 2 in an 18-karat rose-gold case and Grand 3 in a stainless steel case. Grand 1 through 3 feature combinations of colored dial surroundings in stainless steel, black PVD, and rose gold. Jacob & Co. completes the collection with Grand 4's bright red theme and Grand 5's particularly striking full black PVD treatment. All five models come on a natural black rubber strap with folding clasp.

Jacob & Co.'s new Grand and Global collections express the international vision of their wearers by bringing global hubs together on equal footing and taking to the air to remind their owners of their adventurous spirit.

GRAND 2

An engine turbine accent in the center of the pentagonal case symbolizes the 1960s jetsetter spirit that lives on to this day.

EPIC TOURBILLON REF. ET2

Movement: manual-winding; 120-hour power reserve; 27 jewels; 21,600 vph.
Functions: hours, minutes; tourbillon at 6; 12- and 24-hour time zones.
Case: black PVD; Ø 47mm; 18K rose-gold bezel and caseback.
Dial: six-layer multi-tiered; signature Jacob & Co. geometric subdials and hands.
Strap: black rubber.
Suggested price: $220,000

EPIC TOURBILLON REF. ET3

Movement: manual-winding; 120-hour power reserve; 27 jewels; 21,600 vph.
Functions: hours, minutes; tourbillon at 6; 12- and 24-hour time zones.
Case: black PVD; Ø 47mm; rubber bezel.
Dial: six-layer multi-tiered; signature Jacob & Co. geometric subdials and hands.
Strap: black rubber.
Suggested price: $200,000
Also available: 18K rose gold; stainless steel.

EPIC II REF. E3RGR

Movement: automatic-winding Jacob & Co. 2121 caliber; 48-hour power reserve; 27 jewels; 28,800 vph; Incabloc shock-absorption system.
Functions: hours, minutes; small seconds at 9; date at 1; chronograph: 12-hour counter at 6, 30-minute counter at 3 and central seconds hand.
Case: 18K rose gold; Ø 47mm; black rubber bezel.
Dial: six-layer multi-tiered; signature Jacob & Co. geometric subdials and hands.
Strap: black rubber.
Suggested price: $27,000
Also available: black PVD; stainless steel.

EPIC II REF. E15

Movement: automatic-winding Jacob & Co. 2121 caliber; 48-hour power reserve; 27 jewels; 28,800 vph; Incabloc shock-absorption system.
Functions: hours, minutes; small seconds at 9; date at 1; chronograph: 12-hour counter at 6, 30-minute counter at 3 and central seconds hand.
Case: black PVD; Ø 47mm; ceramic bezel.
Dial: six-layer multi-tiered; signature Jacob & Co. red geometric subdials and hands.
Strap: black alligator with red stitching.
Suggested price: $16,800
Also available: yellow and blue.

EPIC I V.2 — REF. V.2Q2B

Movement: automatic-winding Jacob & Co. 2121 caliber; 48-hour power reserve; 27 jewels; 28,000 vph; Incabloc shock-absorption system.
Functions: hours, minutes, seconds; date at 12:30; chronograph: 12-hour counter at 6 and 30-minute counter at 3.
Case: black PVD; 47.5x41mm, thickness: 17mm.
Dial: six-layer multi-tiered; signature Jacob & Co. geometric subdials and hands.
Strap: black rubber.
Suggested price: $12,000
Also available: 18K rose gold; stainless steel.

EPIC I V.2 — REF. V.2QB

Movement: automatic-winding Jacob & Co. 2121 caliber; 27 jewels; 28,000 vph; Incabloc shock-absorption system.
Functions: hours, minutes, seconds; date at 12:30; chronograph: 12-hour counter at 6 and 30-minute counter at 3.
Case: 18K rose gold and titanium; 47.5x41mm, thickness: 17mm.
Dial: six-layer multi-tiered; signature Jacob & Co. geometric subdials and hands.
Strap: black rubber.
Suggested price: $25,000
Also available: black PVD; stainless steel.

QUENTTIN TOURBILLON — REF. QUENRG

Movement: vertical Jacob & Co.; 31-day power reserve; winding escapement with Swiss anchor mounted in tourbillon cage; cage suspended without roller bearings and positioned vertically; winding via integrated key, external hand key or motorized in the box.
Functions: hours, minutes; power reserve made by vertical discs assembled coaxially; tourbillon.
Case: 18K rose gold; 56x47mm, thickness: 21.5mm; carbon fiber applications on case sides.
Dial: transparent vertical mechanical movement with winding escapement in tourbillon cage.
Strap: black rubber.
Suggested price: $440,000
Also available: 18K white gold or magnesium with carbon fiber applications on case sides.

GMT — REF. GMT-7RG

Movement: automatic-winding Jacob & Co. ETA A07.111; 46-hour power reserve; 24 jewels; 28,800 vph.
Functions: hours, minutes; sweep seconds; date at 3; five time zones.
Case: 18K rose gold; Ø 47.5mm; sapphire crystal caseback.
Dial: 18K rose gold; painted and embossed with special guilloché; black accents; 18K rose-gold subdials; steel leaf-shaped hands; Roman numerals on main dial.
Strap: black alligator.
Suggested price: $59,000
Also available: yellow gold; stainless steel and white gold.

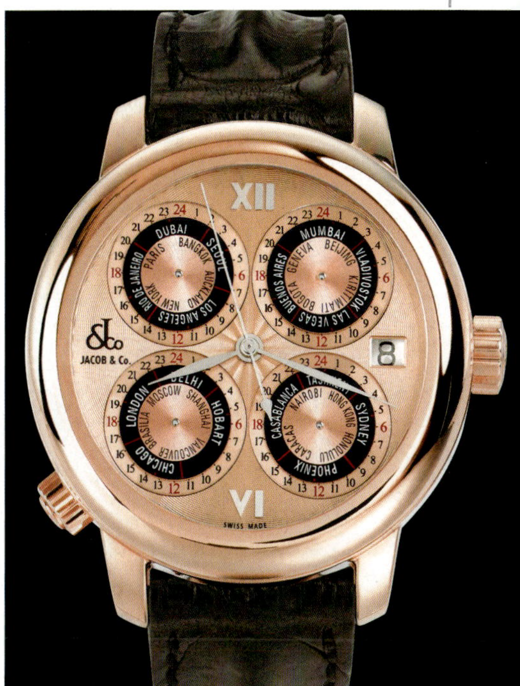

H24 — REF. H24CRFG

Movement: automatic-winding Jacob & Co. caliber ETA A07.11.
Functions: hours, minutes; sweep seconds; date at 3; five time zones.
Case: 18K rose gold; Ø 47.5mm, thickness: 15.95mm.
Dial: black carbon fiber; ivory-colored subdials and date indicator; 18K rose-gold leaf-shaped hands; Roman numerals on the main dial.
Strap: black alligator.
Suggested price: $58,000
Also available: stainless steel and black PVD.

NAPOLEON QUADRA TOURBILLON — REF. QUADRG

Movement: manual-winding Jacob & Co. 8082 caliber; 652 components; 78 jewels; sapphire bridges.
Functions: hours, minutes; four 60-second tourbillons; four time zones.
Case: 18K rose gold; Ø 55.5mm, thickness: 10.05mm; exhibition caseback.
Dial: transparent sapphire disc revealing four skeletonized tourbillon escapements and four time zone apertures.
Strap: alligator.
Suggested price: $680,000
Also available: black PVD; 18K white gold.

RAINBOW TOURBILLON — REF. RUBY1

Movement: manual-winding; 120-hour power reserve; 24 jewels; 21,600 vph.
Functions: hours, minutes; 24-hour time zones; tourbillon at 6; GMT.
Case: 18K white gold; Ø 47.5mm, thickness: 14.95mm; set with 294 baguette rubies (33.54 total carats including the buckle).
Dial: 18K white gold; set with 204 baguette rubies (5.98 carats) white-gold subdials; leaf-shaped hands with gunmetal treatment.
Strap: white alligator; buckle set with baguette-cut rubies.
Suggested price: $1,500,000

RAINBOW TOURBILLON — REF. R15WG

Movement: manual-winding; 120-hour power reserve; 24 jewels; 21,600 vph.
Functions: hours, minutes; 24-hour time zones; tourbillon at 6; GMT.
Case: 18K white gold; Ø 47.5mm, thickness: 14.95mm; set with black baguette diamonds (25.53 carats).
Dial: black carbon fiber; set with black baguette diamonds (5.46 carats); white-gold subdials; leaf-shaped hands with gunmetal treatment.
Strap: black alligator; buckle set with black baguette diamonds (2.22 carats).
Suggested price: $1,100,000

RAINBOW TOURBILLON REF. R1WGDC

Movement: manual-winding; 120-hour power reserve; 24 jewels; 21,600 vph.
Functions: hours, minutes; 12- and 24-hour time zones; tourbillon at 6.
Case: 18K white gold; Ø 47.5mm; set with white diamonds (13.12 carats); exhibition caseback with multi-row Rainbow Tourbillon movement.
Dial: multi-colored; timers painted and embossed with a special guilloché; steel leaf-shaped hands with gunmetal treatment.
Strap: blue alligator.
Suggested price: $300,000
Also available: 18K rose gold and yellow gold.

PANGEA TOURBILLON REF. PANGWG

Movement: Jacob & Co. 2901 caliber; 50-hour power reserve; 18 jewels; 28,800 vph.
Functions: hours, minutes; tourbillon at 6.
Case: 18K white gold; Ø 46mm.
Dial: Côtes de Genève; tourbillon cage featuring Jacob & Co. logo.
Strap: black alligator.
Suggested price: $180,000

FIVE TIME ZONE REF. JC-SKULL 10

Movement: Swiss quartz ETA 956.102, 280.002; 27 jewels.
Functions: hours, minutes, seconds; date at 6; five time zones.
Case: stainless steel and black PVD-coating; Ø 47mm; bezel set diamonds (3.25 carats).
Dial: skull set with diamonds and black enamel.
Strap: black alligator; stainless steel and black PVD buckle.
Suggested price: $28,150

FIVE TIME ZONE REF. JC58DA

Movement: Swiss quartz ETA 956.112, 280.002; 27 jewels.
Functions: hours, minutes, seconds; date at 6; five time zones.
Case: stainless steel; Ø 47mm; case and bezel set with 51 diamonds (3.25 carats).
Dial: dark gray guilloché; primary color subdials set with pavé diamonds (0.56 carats).
Strap: gray alligator.
Suggested price: $19,900

MOSCOW — REF. MANMDC2

Movement: Swiss quartz ETA 01001; 5 jewels.
Functions: hours, minutes.
Case: stainless steel; 37x37mm; set with 498 pavé diamonds (6.7 carats).
Dial: multi-dimensional mother-of-pearl; Roman numerals set with pavé diamonds (0.25 carat); colored buildings.
Strap: alligator.
Suggested price: $48,400

MANHATTAN — REF. MANWGBB

Movement: Swiss quartz ETA E01-701; 5 jewels.
Functions: hours, minutes.
Case: 18K white gold; 37x37mm; unique square case with no crown; set with 364 baguette-cut diamonds (17.5 carats).
Dial: multi-dimensional; set with 403 round diamonds (1.81 carats) and 20 baguette-cut diamonds in the center (0.9 carat).
Strap: black alligator; buckle set with baguette-cut diamonds (0.62 carat).
Suggested price: $660,000

CRYSTAL — REF. CR47SRWRRG-F

Movement: Swiss quartz ETA 956.102; 7 jewels.
Functions: hours, minutes, seconds.
Case: 18K rose gold; Ø 44mm; case and crown set with 485 pavé diamonds (6.75 carats).
Dial: mother-of-pearl; world map design set with pavé diamonds (1.19 carats).
Strap: brown alligator; 18K rose-gold buckle set with 60 diamonds (0.55 carat).
Suggested price: $59,500

CRYSTAL — REF. CR47SR-F

Movement: Swiss quartz ETA 956.102; 7 jewels.
Functions: hours, minutes, seconds.
Case: stainless steel; Ø 44mm; case and crown set with 485 pavé diamonds (6.75 carats).
Dial: red enamel; world map set with pavé diamonds (1.2 carats).
Strap: red alligator; stainless steel buckle set with 60 diamonds (0.55 carat).
Suggested price: $36,000

CRYSTAL — REF. CR9RG-F

Movement: Swiss quartz ETA 956.102; 7 jewels.
Functions: hours, minutes, seconds.
Case: 18K rose gold; Ø 44mm; case and crown set with pavé diamonds (7.3 carats).
Dial: 18K rose gold; set with pavé diamonds (2.9 carats).
Strap: brown alligator; 18K rose-gold buckle set with diamonds.
Suggested price: $61,000

ROYAL — REF. ROYAL 1 RG

Movement: automatic-winding ETA 2004-1; 20 jewels.
Functions: hours, minutes, seconds.
Case: 18K rose gold; Ø 42mm, thickness: 10.54mm; set with 342 baguette diamonds (21.26 carats).
Strap: brown alligator; 18K rose-gold buckle set with baguette-cut diamonds (1.15 carats).
Suggested price: $380,000

CRYSTAL TOURBILLON — REF. CRY20

Movement: manual-winding Jacob & Co. 7 caliber; sapphire bridges; Ø 32.6mm, thickness: 5.2mm; set with baguette diamonds (1.6 carats); crafted, assembled, and decorated by hand to the highest of Jacob & Co. quality standards; skeleton movement.
Functions: hours, minutes; tourbillon.
Case: 18K white gold; Ø 47mm, thickness: 14mm; case and crown set with 264 baguette-cut rubies; sapphire crystal caseback.
Dial: transparent; skeleton tourbillon movement.
Strap: green alligator; 18K white-gold clasp set with 30 baguette-cut rubies.
Suggested price: $1,200,000

CRYSTAL TOURBILLON — REF. CRYSTAL TOUR

Movement: manual-winding Jacob & Co. 7 caliber; sapphire bridges; Ø 32.6mm, thickness: 5.2mm; set with baguette diamonds (1.6 carats); crafted, assembled, and decorated by hand to the highest of Jacob & Co. quality standards; skeleton movement.
Functions: hours, minutes; tourbillon.
Case: 18K white gold; Ø 47mm, thickness: 14mm; case and crown set with baguette-cut diamonds (17.48 carats); sapphire crystal caseback.
Dial: transparent; skeleton tourbillon movement.
Strap: black alligator; 18K white-gold clasp set with baguette-cut diamonds (2.22 carats).
Note: limited edition of 18 pieces.
Suggested price: $900,000

Jaeger-LeCoultre

TWO SIDES TO TELL A STORY

Celebrating the iconic Reverso and its legendary swivel case, Jaeger-LeCoultre takes the magic of its reversible case to extraordinary new dimensions.

With the Reverso Répétition Minutes à Rideau, the Swiss watchmaker adds an additional touch of poetic mystery to a design whose duality has fascinated the world of haute horology for eight decades. By pushing the spring-loaded Venetian blind that acts as an operatic curtain to the openwork front dial, the owner becomes the conductor of an orchestrated minute repeater melody. As the curtain is lifted, the wearer is additionally treated to the visual intricacies of the complication's sophisticated mechanism. Within the classical design of its 18-karat white-gold case, the dual-side wristwatch illustrates the timelessness of the manufacture's flagship innovation.

Playing off the inspired secrecy of the curtain, Jaeger-LeCoultre presents two dials that reveal the complete luster of the manufacture's hand-assembled and hand-decorated 340-component 944 caliber. Worn front-side-up, with the artful metal blind on display, or by highlighting the bridges on the back dial, the Reverso Répétition Minutes à Rideau affords its owner spectacular creative liberty in illustrating the precise keeping of time. Disconnected from the winding mechanism, the 75-piece limited edition's curtain joins the swiveling case in providing the wearer the freedom to change his wrist adornments with his mood.

REVERSO RÉPÉTITION MINUTES À RIDEAU

Hand-wound, with a Venetian blind and a melody that serenades the ear of its owner, this timepiece bridges the gap between man and his timekeeping companion.

GRANDE REVERSO ULTRA-THIN TRIBUTE TO 1931

Imagining the gracious aging of a legendary 1931 timepiece, this ultra-thin homage lets the wisdom of the past find a new voice.

Originally developed in 1931 for polo players, the Reverso's flipping dial provided needed shock protection while offering the fine craftsmanship of a personalized engraved caseback. As an homage to Jaeger-LeCoultre's legendary innovation, the house presents its Grande Reverso Ultra-Thin Tribute to 1931, exclusively sold in the United States. Emulating the refined aging of the 1931 original, the Swiss manufacture's ultra-thin timepiece is fitted with hands and markers made of beige luminescent material, which celebrate the passing years of its vintage classic, and stand out gracefully from the glistening black dial. With a Reverso logo on the dial that replicates that of its 1931 muse, and a cordovan leather strap made by Argentinian polo boot-maker Eduardo Fagliano, the Grande Reverso Ultra-Thin Tribute to 1931 shines with the subtlety of its design and the authenticity of its sporty heritage.

Taking the Reverso concept to the full height of timekeeping duality, the Grande Reverso Duo in 18-karat pink-gold bestows upon two selected time zones, the precise oscillation frequency of its Jaeger-LeCoultre 986 caliber. On the white dial, which emerges from the radiant case with its vertical guilloché and Clous de Paris motif, the traveler's local time is demonstrated in a subtle multi-leveled approach, through central hour and minute hands, rectangular small seconds, and bi-directional date in a panoramic aperture at 12 o'clock. On the black dial, Jaeger-LeCoultre brilliantly meets the challenge of a single mechanism powering independently adjustable hands that rotate in opposite directions. Upon a stage decorated with Clous de Paris, horizontal guilloché, and the vibrant texture of satin-brushed surfaces, the home time zone is complemented by a 24-hour sub-dial with unequivocal day/night indication. With two definitive personalities and an oscillation frequency of 28,800 vph, the Grande Reverso Duo ingeniously doubles the sophisticated elegance and timekeeping excellence of an 80-year-old legend of haute horology.

As the Reverso celebrates its 1931 birth, Jaeger-LeCoultre proves that although time is irreversible, the keeping thereof plays by its own set of rules.

GRANDE REVERSO DUO

The Grande Reverso Duo Pink Gold expresses the duality of time with spectacular craftsmanship on two dials with a shared mechanical movement.

GRANDE REVERSO ULTRA THIN — REF. 278.85.20

Movement: manual-winding 822 caliber; 45-hour power reserve; 134 components; 21 jewels; 21,600 vph; one barrel.
Functions: hours, minutes.
Case: stainless steel; 46x27mm, thickness: 7.23mm; water resistant to 3atm.
Dial: silvered; vertical guilloché; transferred numerals; baton-shaped hour and minute hands.
Strap: matte black alligator leather; stainless steel pin buckle.
Price: available upon request.

GRANDE REVERSO ULTRA-THIN 1931 — REF. 278.85.70

Movement: manual-winding 822 caliber; 45-hour power reserve; 134 components; 21 jewels; 21,600 vph; one barrel.
Functions: hours, minutes.
Case: stainless steel; 46x27mm, thickness: 7.23mm; water resistant to 30atm.
Dial: black; numerals and hour markers with luminescent coating; baton-shaped hour and minute hands.
Strap: black matte alligator leather; stainless steel pin buckle.
Price: available upon request.

GRANDE REVERSO EMAIL — REF. 373.25.23

Movement: manual-winding 822 caliber; 45-hour power reserve; 134 components; 21 jewels; 21,600 vph; one barrel.
Functions: hours, minutes; small seconds; date.
Case: 18K pink gold; 48.5x30mm, thickness: 9.7mm; water resistant to 3atm.
Dial: enamel; baton-shaped hour and minute hands.
Strap: chocolate brown alligator leather; 18K pink-gold pin buckle.
Note: limited to 200 pieces.
Price: available upon request.

GRANDE REVERSO LADY ULTRA THIN — REF. 320.24.21

Movement: manual-winding 846/1 caliber; 40-hour power reserve; 93 components; 18 jewels; 21,600 vph; one barrel.
Functions: hours, minutes.
Case: 18K pink gold; 40x24mm, thickness: 7.2mm; case set with 31 F-G, VVS diamonds (0.45 carat); water resistant to 3atm.
Dial: silvered sun-brushed guilloché; baton-shaped hour and minute hands.
Strap: black alligator leather; 18K pink-gold double-folding buckle.
Price: available upon request.

GRANDE REVERSO LADY ULTRA THIN — REF. 320.81.20

Movement: quartz 657 caliber; 4 jewels.
Functions: hours, minutes.
Case: stainless steel; 40x24mm, thickness: 7.2mm; case set with 31 F-G, VVS diamonds (0.45 carat); water resistant to 3atm.
Dial: silvered sun-brushed guilloché; baton-shaped hour and minute hands.
Bracelet: stainless steel.
Price: available upon request.

MASTER ULTRA-THIN MOON PHASE — REF. 136.25.20

Movement: automatic-winding 925 caliber; 43-hour power reserve; 246 components; 30 jewels; 28,800 vph; one barrel; 22K pink-gold oscillating weight.
Functions: hours, minutes, seconds; date counter; moonphase.
Case: 18K pink gold; Ø 39mm, thickness: 9.9mm; sapphire crystal caseback; water resistant to 5atm.
Dial: beige sunray brushed; rhodium-plated numerals and hour markers; alpha hour and minute hands.
Strap: chocolate brown alligator leather; 18K pink-gold pin buckle.
Price: available upon request.

MASTER GEOGRAPHIC — REF. 142.84.21

Movement: automatic-winding 939A caliber; 43-hour power reserve; 310 components; 34 jewels; 28,800 vph; one barrel; 22K pink-gold oscillating weight.
Functions: hours, minutes, seconds; date counter; 24-hour display; 24 time zones; power reserve indicator.
Case: stainless steel; Ø 39mm, thickness: 11.77mm; sapphire crystal caseback; water resistant to 5atm.
Dial: silvered sunray brushed; numerals and hour markers with luminescent coating; alpha hour and minute hands.
Strap: matte black alligator leather; stainless steel double-folding buckle.
Price: available upon request.

MASTER EIGHT DAYS PERPETUAL — REF. 161.24.20

Movement: manual-winding 876-440B caliber; 8-day power reserve; 262 components; 37 jewels; 28,800 vph; two barrels.
Functions: hours, minutes; perpetual calendar: date, day, month and year; day/night indicator; power reserve indicator; moonphase.
Case: 18K pink gold; Ø 40mm, thickness: 12.84mm; sapphire crystal caseback; water resistant to 5atm.
Dial: matte beige; gilt numerals and hour markers; dauphine-shaped hour and minute hands.
Strap: matte chocolate brown alligator leather; 18K pink-gold double folding buckle.
Price: available upon request.

DUOMETRE A QUANTIEME LUNAIRE REF. 604.35.70

Movement: manual-winding 381 caliber; 50-hour power reserve; 369 components; 40 jewels; 21,600 vph; two barrels.
Functions: hours, minutes; jumping seconds; date counter; moonphase; twin power reserve.
Case: 18K white gold; Ø 42mm, thickness: 13.5mm; water resistant to 5atm.
Dial: black; applied numerals; feuille-shaped hour and minute hands.
Strap: black alligator leather; 18K white-gold pin buckle.
Note: limited to 100 pieces.
Price: available upon request.

MASTER GRANDE TRADITION TOURBILLON REF. 166.25.10

Movement: automatic-winding 978 caliber; 48-hour power reserve; 302 components; 33 jewels; 28,800 vph; one barrel.
Functions: hours, minutes, seconds; date; tourbillon; second time zone; 24 hour display.
Case: 18K pink gold; Ø 43mm, thickness: 12.95mm; sapphire crystal caseback; water resistant to 5atm.
Dial: matte beige; gilt numerals and hour markers; dauphine-shaped hour and minute hands.
Strap: chocolate brown alligator leather; 18K pink gold pink buckle.
Price: available upon request.

MEMOVOX TRIBUTE TO DEEP SEA USA REF. 202.84.40

Movement: automatic-winding 956 caliber; 45-hour power reserve; 268 components; 23 jewels; 28,800 vph; one barrel.
Functions: hours, minutes, seconds; alarm.
Case: stainless steel; Ø 40.5mm, thickness: 13.8mm; water resistant to 10atm.
Dial: black; numerals and hour markers with luminescent coating; triangle alarm indication with luminescent coating; baguette-style seconds hand.
Strap: black calfskin leather; stainless steel pin buckle.
Note: limited to 359 pieces.
Price: available upon request.

MASTER COMPRESSOR CHRONOGRAPH REF. 204.C4.70

Movement: automatic-winding 751F caliber; 65-hour power reserve; 277 components; 39 jewels; 28,800 vph; two barrels.
Functions: hours, minutes; small seconds; date; chronograph: 12-hour counter, 30-minute counter and central seconds hand.
Case: ceramic; Ø 44mm, thickness: 13.27mm; water resistant to 10atm.
Dial: black; trapezoid hour and minute hands; hour markers and numerals with luminescent coating.
Strap: black alligator leather; stainless steel pin buckle.
Note: limited to 500 pieces.
Price: available upon request.

MASTER GRANDE TRADITION MINUTE REPEATER — REF. 501.T4.50

Movement: manual-winding 947 caliber; 15-day power reserve; 413 components; 43 jewels; 21,600 vph; two barrels.
Functions: hours, minutes; power reserve indicator; minute repeater; barrel torque indicator.
Case: titanium; Ø 44mm, thickness: 15.6mm; sapphire crystal caseback; water resistant to 5atm.
Dial: dauphine-shaped hour and minute hands.
Strap: matte black alligator leather; stainless steel double-folding buckle.
Price: available upon request.
Note: limited to 100 pieces.

MASTER LADY NIGHT AND DAY — REF. 346.32.01

Movement: automatic-winding 967A caliber; 42-hour power reserve; 214 components; 28 jewels; 28,800 vph; one barrel.
Functions: hours, minutes, seconds; day/night indicator.
Case: 18K white gold; Ø 29mm, thickness: 12.4mm; bezel set with 209 F-G, VVS diamonds (1.05 carats); sapphire crystal caseback; water resistant to 3atm.
Dial: mother-of-pearl; florale hour and minute hands.
Bracelet: 18K white gold.
Price: available upon request.

MASTER LADY NIGHT AND DAY — REF. 346.34.01

Movement: automatic-winding 967A caliber; 42-hour power reserve; 214 components; 28 jewels; 28,800 vph; one barrel.
Functions: hours, minutes, seconds; day/night indicator.
Case: 18K white gold; Ø 29mm, thickness: 12.4mm; bezel set with 177 F-G, VVS diamonds (0.82 carats); sapphire crystal caseback; water resistant to 3atm.
Dial: mother-of-pearl; florale hour and minute hands.
Strap: matte black alligator leather; 18K white-gold double-folding buckle.
Price: available upon request.

MASTER TOURBILLON 39 — REF. 341.34.03

Movement: automatic-winding 978 caliber; 48-hour power reserve; 302 components; 33 jewels; 28,800 vph; one barrel.
Functions: hours, minutes; small seconds; tourbillon.
Case: white gold; Ø 39mm, thickness: 12.4mm; bezel set with 254 F-G, VVS diamonds (3 carats); sapphire crystal caseback; water resistant to 5atm.
Dial: mother-of-pearl; florale hour and minute hands.
Strap: black alligator leather; 18K white-gold double folding buckle.
Price: available upon request.

JAQUET DROZ

A FIGURE OF EXCELLENCE

Faithful to a strict aesthetic code of design and technical craftsmanship, Jaquet Droz perpetuates a bold tradition of noble refinement.

From Pierre Jaquet Droz's founding of the house in 1738, to the inauguration of its new Parisian boutique at 8, rue de la Paix, the figure eight has been an eternal source of evolving inspiration and influence on the brand's design.

To understand the manufacture's commitment to its aesthetic codes, one need look no further than the creation of its Parisian boutique. The numeral 8, a numerological obsession of Jaquet Droz that has shaped the architecture of its dials since the beginning, appears on the storefront window. The interior draws inspiration from the brand's characteristic clean lines, black, ivory, or gray shades, and alternation of matte and glossy finishings—as well as the figure eight.

Through three new watches that extend the tradition of the horologer's legacy, Jaquet Droz proudly displays its prodigious history within the innovative frame of its designs.

The Tourbillon strikes a balance between cutting-edge technical performance and the simplicity of the house's most emblematic model. Liberating the watch from the deregulating effects of gravity, the tourbillon is enclosed in a white-gold case with Côtes de Genève dial. Jaquet Droz reveals a tourbillon carriage crafted from sapphire crystal, the same exceptional material used for the figure eight-shaped ring applied to the dial.

The classical beauty of the hours and minutes subdial at 6 o'clock amplifies the virtuoso effect of the placement of the tourbillon at the heart of the seconds subdial, off-centered at 12 o'clock. Jaquet Droz's self-winding 25JD movement powers this watch, whose tapered Roman numerals and finely proportioned hands offer a quiet elegance to this marriage of venerable tradition and inventive intelligence.

TOURBILLON

A transparent caseback reveals both the inner workings and oscillating weight of this timepiece, which possesses a seven-day power reserve.

GRANDE SECONDE SW

This flagship model of the house celebrates the figure eight design within an ultra-modern framework that imbues the brand's third century with sleek elegance.

The addition of two Grande Seconde SW models—one in steel and ceramic, one in red gold and titanium—offers an ultra-modern take on the favored figure eight dial design.

While every groove of the SW Steel – Ceramic represents an exploit of technical mastery, the combination of the dial's inky brilliance and fastidiously worked steel highlights the watch's architectural purity. The dial boasts indicators and touches of hand-painted blue while the glowing SuperLumiNova offers nocturnal radiance to this timepiece of tasteful modernity.

The SW Red Gold – Titanium plays on the interaction between matte and polished surfaces. The great lightness and strength of titanium and radiance of fine-brushed red gold form the cohesive contrast necessary to highlight the figure eight. The geometric motif of the dial, made of woven carbon fibers, offers ever-changing reflective tendencies as the wearer moves his wrist.

With the Grande Seconde Quantième, Jaquet Droz presents a steel timepiece that suggests the strength, simplicity and nobility of the material. The model exhibits the modern ambitions of the La Chaux-de-Fonds manufacture in its third century.

True to its avant-garde spirit, Jaquet Droz has utilized, for the first time in watchmaking, a process in which each dial component is crafted from solid metal and dipped into a chemical bath to obtain a perfect black coating. The result of this innovative operation is a unique interplay of light and texture that brings out the beauty of the fine-brushed or black indicators. Another model displays the pure aesthetic of a silvery-white dial that features the manufacture's traditional expertise. All models possess a date hand cleverly positioned within the seconds subdial at 6 o'clock.

The Grande Seconde Quantième creates a stunning dialogue between the gleam of metal and the chromatic uniformity of the dial—a conversation worthy of the eavesdrop of the most enthusiastic connoisseur.

These three newly presented revitalizations of the watchmaker's aesthetic and technical identity are proud interpretations of Jaquet Droz's heritage, and express the brand's crusading spirit of modernity within the realm of classical elegance.

GRANDE SECONDE QUANTIÈME

The coexistence of Roman and Arabic numerals is one of several well-proportioned contrasts that give this timepiece a constantly evolving appeal.

TOURBILLON REF. J013034240

Movement: automatic-winding Jaquet Droz 25JD caliber; 7-day power reserve; 31 jewels; 21,600 vph; single barrel; 18K white-gold oscillating weight with black onyx.
Functions: off-centered hours and minutes at 6; tourbillon and small seconds at 12.
Case: 18K white gold; Ø 43mm; individual serial number engraved on the caseback; water resistant to 3atm.

Dial: matte black with Côtes de Genève; sapphire double ring; 18K white-gold hour and minute hands; blued steel seconds hand.
Strap: rolled-edge handmade black alligator leather; 18K white-gold folding clasp.
Price: available upon request.

THE ECLIPSE REF. J012633202

Movement: automatic-winding Jaquet Droz 6553L caliber; 68-hour power reserve; 28 jewels; 28,800 vph; double barrel; 22K white-gold oscillating weight; date with a hand.
Functions: hours, minutes; central date hand; day and month at 12; moonphase at 6.
Case: 18K red gold; Ø 43mm; individual serial number engraved on the caseback; water resistant to 3atm.

Dial: black Grand Feu enamel, hand crafted; eight 18K red-gold stars; applied 18K red-gold moon with black varnished sapphire moonphase; 18K red-gold hour, minute and date hands.
Strap: rolled-edge handmade black alligator leather; 18K red-gold ardillon buckle.
Price: available upon request.

GRANDE SECONDE SW RED GOLD - TITANIUM REF. J029037440

Movement: automatic-winding Jaquet Droz 2663A-S caliber; 68-hour power reserve; 30 jewels; 28,800 vph; double barrel; 18K white-gold oscillating weight.
Functions: off-centered hours and minutes at 12; small seconds at 6.
Case: titanium; Ø 45mm; titanium bezel; titanium crown with black rubber cast; 18K red-gold claws and horns; individual serial number engraved on the caseback; water resistant to 5atm.

Dial: raw carbon; hour markers and numerals 5, 6 and 7 with white SuperLumiNova; applied ring with red-gold treatment; plates with rhodium treatment; hour, minute and seconds hands with red-gold treatment and white SuperLumiNova tips.
Strap: natural black rubber; titanium folding clasp with 18K red-gold security clasp.
Price: available upon request.

GRANDE SECONDE SW STEEL – CERAMIC REF. J029030440

Movement: automatic-winding Jaquet Droz 2663A-S caliber; 68-hour power reserve; 30 jewels; 28,800 vph; double barrel; 18K white-gold oscillating weight.
Functions: off-centered hours and minutes at 12; small seconds at 6.
Case: stainless steel; Ø 45mm; ; ceramic bezel; stainless steel crown with black rubber cast; individual serial number engraved on the caseback; water resistant to 5atm.

Dial: shiny black varnish; hour markers and numerals 5, 6 and 7 with blue SuperLumiNova; applied ring and plates with rhodium treatment; hour, minute and seconds hands with rhodium treatment and blue SuperLumiNova tips.
Strap: natural black rubber; stainless steel folding clasp.
Price: available upon request.

GRANDE SECONDE QUANTIEME — REF. J007030241

Movement: automatic-winding Jaquet Droz 2660Q2 caliber; 68-hour power reserve; 30 jewels; 28,800 vph; double barrel; heavy metal oscillating weight.
Functions: off-centered hours and minutes at 12; small seconds and date at 6.
Case: stainless steel; Ø 43mm; individual serial number engraved on the caseback; water resistant to 3atm.
Dial: black; fine-brushed finished hour markers and numerals; hour, minute and seconds hands with rhodium treatment; date hand with rhodium treatment and red varnished tip.
Strap: rolled-edge handmade black alligator leather; stainless steel folding clasp.
Price: available upon request.

GRANDE HEURE MINUTE ONYX — REF. J017030201

Movement: automatic-winding Jaquet Droz 1169 caliber; 68-hour power reserve; 31 jewels; 28,800 vph; double barrel; heavy metal oscillating weight.
Functions: hours, minutes; small seconds at 9.
Case: stainless steel; Ø 43mm; individual serial number engraved on the caseback; water resistant to 3atm.
Dial: onyx; applied ring with rhodium treatment; hour, minute and small seconds hands with rhodium treatment.
Strap: rolled-edge handmade black alligator leather; stainless steel ardillon buckle.
Price: available upon request.

PETITE HEURE MINUTE ART DECO — REF. J005014571

Movement: automatic-winding Jaquet Droz 2653 caliber; 68-hour power reserve; 28 jewels; 28,800 vph; double barrel; 22K white-gold oscillating weight.
Functions: off-centered hours and minutes at 12.
Case: 18K white gold; Ø 39mm; set with 248 diamonds (1.84 carats); individual serial number engraved on the caseback; water resistant to 3atm.
Dial: white mother-of-pearl Ramolayée; white mother-of-pearl center; applied 18K white-gold ring; blued steel hour and minute hands.
Strap: rolled-edge handmade black satin; 18K white-gold ardillon buckle set with 24 diamonds (0.15 carat).
Price: available upon request.

GRANDE SECONDE CIRCLED LADY — REF. J014013227

Movement: automatic-winding Jaquet Droz 2663 caliber; 68-hour power reserve; 30 jewels; 28,800 vph; double barrel; 22K white-gold oscillating weight.
Functions: off-centered hours and minutes at 12; small seconds at 6.
Case: 18K red gold; Ø 39mm; set with 248 diamonds (1.84 carats); individual serial number engraved on the caseback; water resistant to 3atm.
Dial: white mother-of-pearl; 18K red-gold ring set with 88 diamonds (0.14 carat); blued steel hour, minute and seconds hands.
Strap: rolled-edge handmade white satin; 18K red-gold ardillon buckle set with 24 diamonds (0.15 carat).
Price: available upon request.

LONGINES®

THE LONGINES SAINT-IMIER COLLECTION

Saint-Imier, land of watchmaking.
47°9'10.03"N 7°0'0.07"E

Longines has been located in Saint-Imier since 1832. With The Longines Saint-Imier Collection, the brand is launching a series of exceptional timepieces exclusively fitted with mechanical movements. These models have sprung from the fertile area that constitutes the watchmaking heritage of Longines's home territory.

Located in Saint-Imier since 1832, Longines has established close links with the village that has seen the foundation and development of the firm. As the only watchmaking company that was founded and still remains in Saint-Imier, Longines has stayed true to its historical values: tradition, elegance and sport. Today at the occasion of its 180th anniversary, the brand is launching, with The Longines Saint-Imier Collection, a series of exceptional timepieces fitted with mechanical movements that has sprung from the fertile area that constitutes the watchmaking heritage of its home territory.

The Longines Saint-Imier Collection has been inspired by the foundations of the watchmaking tradition on which the brand, known by its winged hourglass trademark, has been built. Longines was set up in 1832 in what was then a small village nestling in a valley deep in the Swiss Jura mountains: Saint-Imier. Right from the firm's early days, Longines Watch Co. Francillon Ltd. has played a central role in life in Saint-Imier, which has since become a watchmaking hub. The fate of Longines and the village of Saint-Imier has thus been closely interwoven. This long relationship has now been sealed by a collection of exceptional timepieces all fitted with mechanical movements: The Longines Saint-Imier Collection.

The shape of the case—inspired by a model dating from 1945—is a common theme throughout the collection. The sleek lines and distinctive lugs provide these new models with a subtle balance between classical and contemporary design.

The versions that show the hours, minutes and seconds with a date aperture at 3 o'clock are available in steel or in rose gold and certain versions are in steel and rose gold. With a choice of four case sizes (26mm, 30mm, 38.50mm and 41mm), including some set with diamonds, all our customers will find a version that fits snugly on their wrist. The choice of dials includes black, silvered or white mother-of-pearl with diamonds index and, thanks to the SuperLumiNova coating on the hands, reading the time is never a problem. The watches in this collection are fitted on a black or brown alligator strap, or a steel or steel and rose-gold bracelet, with a folding safety clasp, to match the dial.

The chronographs are fitted with an L688.2 column-wheel movement specially developed and produced by ETA exclusively for Longines. The case is made of steel, steel and rose gold or, for certain models, rose gold alone, and is available in two diameter sizes: 39mm and 41mm. The silvered or black dial shows the hours and minutes and has small seconds at 9 o'clock and a date aperture as well as the chronograph functions: a center sweep seconds, a 30-minute counter at 3 o'clock and a 12-hour counter at 6 o'clock. These chronographs are fitted on a black or brown alligator strap or on a steel or steel and rose-gold bracelet, all having a folding safety clasp.

Finally, a prestige model embodies the quintessence of Longines' watchmaking know-how. This timepiece, with a diameter of 44mm, houses calibre L707, specially developed and produced by ETA exclusively for Longines. There is a choice of a black or silvered dial featuring 12 Arabic numerals and showing four retrograde functions (day of the week at 12 o'clock, date on the right-hand side of the dial, second time zone with a 24-hour scale on the left-hand side of the dial and a small seconds at 6 o'clock) as well as day/night and the phases of the moon. These exclusive models are mounted on a black or brown alligator strap, or a steel bracelet to match the rest of the design, all with a folding safety clasp.

THE LONGINES SAINT-IMIER COLLECTION

With The Longines Saint-Imier Collection, the brand is launching a series of exceptional timepieces exclusively fitted with mechanical movements.

Saint-Imier: the origins of Longines watchmaking know-how

In 1832, Auguste Agassiz entered the world of watchmaking by establishing a partnership with a watchmaking establishment in Saint-Imier. Before long, he quickly took control of the enterprise and renamed it "Agassiz & Compagnie." At the time, the company assembled watches according to the "établissage" method, with people working at home, and developed trade links that enabled the company to sell its timepieces around the world, particularly in North America.

In the 1850s, Ernest Francillon, a nephew of Agassiz, took over the management of the reputed company and looked for ways to improve the traditional manufacturing methods used in local watchmaking. His idea was to group the different operations involved in the finalisation of timepieces together in one factory, where he would use mechanical production methods to assemble and finish complete watches.

To bring this project to fruition, he purchased two adjoining plots of land on the right bank of the river Suze in the Saint-Imier valley in 1866. This area of land was called "Les Longines." To help him develop the machines he needed to perfect the watchmaking processes, Ernest Francillon employed a young relative, an engineer named Jacques David.

In the 1870s, the industrial approach that Francillon had chosen proved highly successful and the factory continued to grow until the first third of the 20th century.

By 1911, the Longines factory employed more than 1,100 people and its watches were being distributed around the world.

LONGINES®

LONGINES DOLCEVITA — REF. L5.155.5.19.7

Movement: quartz caliber L178.2.
Functions: hours, minutes; small seconds at 6.
Case: stainless steel and rose gold; 19.8x24.5mm; set with 32 Top Wesselton VVS diamonds (0.269 carat); sapphire crystal; water resistant to 3atm.
Dial: white; ten hour markers and one rose-gold Arabic numeral; rose-gold hands.
Bracelet: stainless steel and rose gold with folding safety clasp and pushpieces.

LONGINES PRIMALUNA — REF. L8 .110.5.79.6

Movement: quartz caliber L250.2.
Functions: hours, minutes, seconds; date at 3.
Case: stainless steel and rose gold; Ø 26.5mm; set with 44 Top Wesselton VVS diamonds (0.299 carat); antireflective sapphire crystal; water resistant to 3 atm.
Dial: silvered with flinqué decoration; 11 blue Roman numerals; blued-steel hands.
Bracelet: stainless steel and rose gold with folding safety clasp and pushpieces.

LA GRANDE CLASSIQUE DE LONGINES — REF. L4.241.0.11.6

Movement: quartz caliber L209.
Functions: hours, minutes.
Case: stainless steel; Ø 24mm; thickness: 4.4mm; set with 48 Top Wesselton VVS diamonds (0.403 carat); sapphire crystal; water resistant to 3 atm.
Dial: white; 12 black Roman numerals; blackened steel hands.
Bracelet: stainless steel with triple-folding safety clasp and pushpieces.

LA GRANDE CLASSIQUE DE LONGINES "TONNEAU" — REF. L4.205.4.11.6

Movement: quartz caliber L209.
Functions: hours, minutes.
Case: stainless steel; ultra-thin; 22.2x24.5mm; sapphire crystal; water resistant to 3atm.
Dial: white; black Roman numerals; blackened steel hands.
Bracelet: stainless steel with triple-folding safety clasp and pushpieces.

THE LONGINES MASTER COLLECTION REF. L2.673.4.78.3

Movement: automatic-winding L678 caliber; 13¼ lines; 48-hour power reserve; 25 jewels; 28,800 vph.
Functions: hours, minutes; small seconds and 24-hour indicator at 9; date; day and month at 12; chronograph: 12-hour counter at 6, 30-minute counter at 12 and central seconds hand; moonphase at 6.
Case: stainless steel; Ø 40mm; antireflective sapphire crystal; sapphire crystal caseback; water resistant to 3atm.
Dial: silver-finished stamped "barleycorn"; nine Arabic numerals; blued-steel hands; black painted minute track, 31-day calendar.
Strap: dark brown alligator; triple-folding safety clasp.

THE LONGINES MASTER COLLECTION REF. L2.717.4.71.3

Movement: automatic-winding L698 caliber; 16½ lines; 46-hour power reserve; 25 jewels; 28,800 vph.
Functions: hours, minutes; four retrograde functions: day, date, seconds and second time zone on a 24-hour scale.
Case: stainless steel; Ø 44mm; antireflective sapphire crystal; transparent sapphire crystal caseback; water resistant to 3atm.
Dial: silver-finished stamped "barleycorn"; 11 Roman numerals; six blued-steel hands; black painted minute track.
Strap: dark brown alligator; triple-folding safety clasp.

LONGINES EVIDENZA REF. L2.643.4.73.4

Movement: automatic-winding L650 caliber; 12½ lines; 42-hour power reserve; 37 jewels; 28,800 vph.
Functions: hours, minutes; small seconds at 3; date at 6; chronograph: 12-hour counter at 6, 30-minute counter at 9 and central seconds hand.
Case: stainless steel; 34.9x40mm; antireflective sapphire crystal; water resistant to 3atm.
Dial: silvered "flinqué"; ten blue-painted Arabic numerals; blued-steel hands.
Strap: dark brown alligator; triple-folding safety clasp.

THE LONGINES COLUMN-WHEEL CHRONOGRAPH REF. L2.733.4.72.2

Movement: automatic-winding L688.2 caliber; 13¼ lines; 54-hour power reserve; 27 jewels; 28,800 vph.
Functions: hours, minutes; small seconds at 9; date at 4:30; column-wheel chronograph: 12-hour counter at 6, 30-minute counter at 3 and central sweep seconds.
Case: stainless steel; Ø 39mm; antireflective sapphire crystal; sapphire crystal caseback; water resistant to 3atm.
Dial: silvered; thirteen applied rhodium-plated hour markers with SuperLumiNova; rhodium-plated dauphine-style hands with SuperLumiNova.
Strap: dark brown alligator with buckle.

THE LONGINES SAINT-IMIER COLLECTION REF. L2.563.5.87.7

Movement: automatic-winding L595 caliber; 8¾ lines; 40-hour power reserve; 20 jewels; 28,800 vph.
Functions: hours, minutes, seconds; date at 3.
Case: steel and rose gold; Ø 30mm; set with 72 Top Wesselton VVS diamonds (0.208 carat); antireflective sapphire crystal; sapphire crystal caseback; water resistant to 3atm.
Dial: white mother-of-pearl; 12 diamond hour markers; rose-gold hours and minutes hands with SuperLumiNova.
Bracelet: steel and rose gold with folding safety clasp.

THE LONGINES SAINT-IMIER COLLECTION CHRONOGRAPH REF. L2.753.5.72.7

Movement: automatic-winding L688 caliber; 13¼ lines; 54-hour power reserve; 27 jewels; 28,800 vph.
Functions: hours, minutes; small seconds at 9; date at 4:30; column-wheel chronograph: dragging 12-hour counter at 6, dragging 30-minute counter at 3 and central sweep seconds hand.
Case: steel and rose gold; Ø 39mm; antireflective sapphire crystal; sapphire crystal caseback; water resistant to 3atm.
Dial: silvered; eight applied hour markers and "12" Arabic numeral; rose-gold hour and minute hands with SuperLumiNova.
Bracelet: steel and rose gold with folding safety clasp.

CONQUEST REF. L2.744.4.56.7

Movement: automatic-winding L688.2 caliber; 13¼ lines; 54-hour power reserve; 27 jewels; 28,800 vph.
Functions: hours, minutes; small seconds at 9; date at 4:30; column-wheel chronograph: dragging 12-hour counter at 6, dragging 30-minute counter at 3 and central sweep seconds hand.
Case: stainless steel; Ø 41mm; black ceramic bezel and crown; bezel with tachometer; antireflective sapphire crystal; screw-down sapphire crystal caseback; water resistant to 5atm.
Dial: black; silvered "12" Arabic numeral and 11 applied rhodium-plated hour markers with SuperLumiNova; rhodium-plated and polished hands with SuperLumiNova.
Bracelet: stainless steel with central links in black ceramic.

LONGINES ADMIRAL REF. L3.667.4.56.7

Movement: automatic-winding L705 caliber; 16½ lines; 46-hour power reserve; 27 jewels; 28,800 vph.
Functions: hours, minutes; small seconds at 9; date at 6; chronograph: 30-minute counter at 3 and central seconds hand.
Case: stainless steel; Ø 42mm; black ceramic bezel with tachometer; screw-down ceramic crown and ceramic pushpieces with protective shoulder; screw-down caseback; water resistant to 10atm.
Dial: black; large "12" Arabic numeral with SuperLumiNova; eight applied polished rhodium-plated hour markers with SuperLumiNova; polished rhodium-plated hands with SuperLumiNova.
Bracelet: stainless steel with central links in black ceramic; triple-folding safety clasp.
Also available: gray version.

FLAGSHIP HERITAGE REF. L4.795.4.78.2

Movement: automatic-winding L615.2 caliber; 11½ lines; 42-hour power reserve; 27 jewels; 28,800 vph.
Functions: hours, minutes; small seconds and date at 6.
Case: stainless steel; Ø 38.5mm; antireflective sapphire crystal; water resistant to 3atm.
Dial: stainless steel; 11 golden hour markers; golden dauphine-style hands with SuperLumiNova.
Strap: brown alligator with buckle.

THE LONGINES LEGEND DIVER WATCH REF. L3.674.4.50.0

Movement: automatic-winding L633 caliber; 11½ lines; 38-hour power reserve; 25 jewels; 28,800 vph.
Functions: hours, minutes, seconds; date at 3.
Case: stainless steel; Ø 42mm; internal turning diving bezel; two screw-down crowns; antireflective sapphire crystal; screw-down caseback with embossed diver symbol; water resistant to 30atm.
Dial: black lacquered with SuperLumiNova; rhodium-plated hands with SuperLumiNova.
Strap: black synthetic fabric with buckle.

THE LONGINES WEEMS SECOND-SETTING WATCH REF. L2.713.8.11.0

Movement: automatic-winding L699 caliber; 16½ lines; 46-hour power reserve; 24 jewels; 28,800 vph.
Functions: hours, minutes, seconds; rotating central dial for synchronization to the second with a radio time signal.
Case: polished 18K rose gold; Ø 47.5mm; engraved and numbered (not limited edition) caseback with opening to reveal antireflective sapphire crystal; water resistant to 3atm.
Dial: white lacquer; black-painted external railway track minute ring; 12 black painted Roman numerals; opaline silvered rotating center dial; black painted railway track minute ring; blued-steel Breguet hands.
Strap: brown alligator; "Charleston" clasp and extension.

LONGINES LINDBERGH'S ATLANTIC VOYAGE WATCH REF. L2.730.4.18.0

Movement: automatic-winding L705 caliber; 16½ lines; 46-hour power reserve; 27 jewels; 28,800 vph.
Functions: hours, minutes, seconds; date at 6; chronograph: 30-minute counter at 3 and 60-minute counter at 9.
Case: stainless steel; Ø 47.5mm; engraved and numbered (not limited edition) caseback with opening to reveal antireflective sapphire crystal; water resistant to 3atm.
Dial: silvered; nine black Arabic numerals; black tachometer, 500-600 kph; blued-steel Breguet hour and minute hands; blued-steel counter-weight line pear flyback hand; blued-steel arrow 30-minute counter hand; blued-steel counter-weight stick pear small seconds hand.
Strap: brown alligator; triple-folding safety clasp.

LOUIS VUITTON

TAMBOUR RÉPÉTITION MINUTES

This 44mm rose-gold model with 100-hour power reserve puts a twist on dual time, with a repeater that chimes the secondary time zone.

HOME IS WHERE THE HEART CHIMES

Ringing in the expansion of its manufacturing infrastructure through a major strategic acquisition, Louis Vuitton celebrates the traveling spirit of the brand with an ingenious and spectacular timepiece. With the release of its Tambour Répétition Minutes, the Parisian house further raises the benchmark of creativity and detailed excellence for which it is renowned.

It is in the Louis Vuitton watchmaking workshops, in Switzerland, that the manufacture's engineers have, since 2002, been reinventing this spirit of travel that is so precious to the brand. The Tambour, the house's first watch, opened a new chapter in Louis Vuitton's rich tradition of innovative and luxurious design. Combining timeless personality with the highest technical standards, this blend of tradition and modernity has become an iconic symbol of the house's identity.

Always aiming to surprise its audience with the development of original ways to tell time, Louis Vuitton made a leap in July 2011 with its acquisition of La Fabrique du Temps, a Geneva-based enterprise that masters the conception and manufacturing of movements and complications of the highest order, such as tourbillons and minute repeaters. It is this expansion of the brand's intellectual and technical resources that allowed Louis Vuitton to extend a daring challenge to its best craftsmen and engineers—to create a superb timepiece that would express the house's passion for travel, sublime craftsmanship, and high-end mechanisms.

With the Tambour Répétition Minutes, consider the mission accomplished. This manually wound timepiece adds a sentimental element to the dual time concept. While the current time is read conventionally on the outer ring, a second time zone—"home time"—shows up in a small dial, accompanied by a day/night indicator, at the center of the watch. Regardless of the traveler's location, a minute repeater that chimes the home time, or any time that he holds dear, reminds him of the loved ones from whom he is separated. The skeletonized dial housed within the iconic gold Tambour case of this timepiece, however, never lets him forget his other love: the magnificent perfectionism of haute horology.

With its LV caliber made of 178 components, as well as its back entirely engraved with Côtes de Genève and polished by hand, the Tambour Répétition Minutes represents the values of excellence and attention to detail that are synonymous with the Louis Vuitton brand, and captures the House's everlasting spirit of wanderlust.

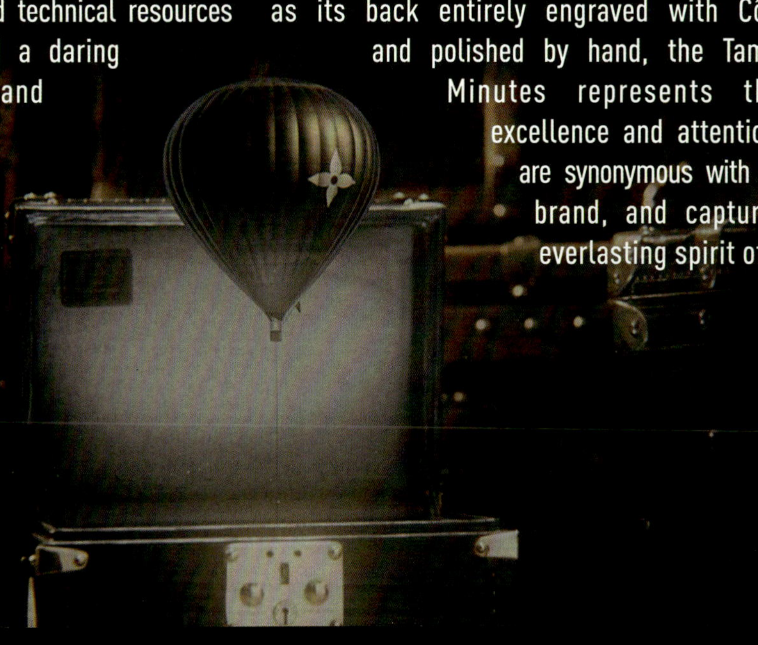

TAMBOUR RÉPÉTITION MINUTES

Movement: manual-winding LV178 caliber; 100-hour power reserve.
Functions: hours, minutes, seconds; minute repeater; home time; night/day indicator; power reserve indicator.
Case: 18K rose gold; Ø 44mm; transparent caseback; water resistant to 3atm.
Dial: skeletonized.
Strap: brown alligator; 18K rose-gold buckle.
Note: personalized upon request.

TAMBOUR TOURBILLON MONOGRAM

Movement: manual-winding LV103 caliber; 90-hour power reserve.
Functions: hours, minutes, seconds; tourbillon.
Case: 18K white gold; Ø 40.45mm; transparent caseback; water resistant to 10atm.
Dial: skeletonized.
Strap: black alligator; 18K white-gold buckle.
Note: personalized upon request.

TAMBOUR SPIN TIME AUTOMATIC GMT

Movement: automatic-winding LV119 caliber; 40-hour power reserve.
Functions: hours, minutes; date; GMT; spin time function: hours appear on rotating cubes.
Case: 18K white gold; Ø 44mm; transparent caseback; water resistant to 10atm.
Dial: black.
Strap: black alligator; 18K white-gold buckle.

TAMBOUR SPIN TIME DIAMONDS

Movement: automatic-winding LV96 caliber; 40-hour power reserve.
Functions: hours, minutes; spin time function: hours appear on rotating cylinders.
Case: 18K white gold; Ø 39.5mm; horns set with diamonds; transparent caseback; water resistant to 10atm.
Dial: black and white diamond-pavé.
Strap: white alligator; 18K white-gold buckle.

TAMBOUR LV277 AUTOMATIC CHRONOGRAPH

Movement: automatic-winding LV277 caliber; 50-hour power reserve; COSC-certified chronograph.
Functions: hours, minutes, seconds; date; chronograph.
Case: steel; Ø 41.5mm; transparent caseback; water resistant to 10atm.
Dial: brown and black.
Strap: brown alligator.

TAMBOUR LV277 FOREVER AUTOMATIC CHRONOGRAPH

Movement: automatic-winding LV277 caliber; 50-hour power reserve; COSC-certified chronograph.
Functions: hours, minutes, seconds; date; chronograph.
Case: 18K white gold; Ø 41.5mm; case, horns and crown set with diamond-pavé; transparent caseback; water resistant to 10atm.
Dial: diamond-pavé.
Strap: black alligator.

TAMBOUR AUTOMATIC CHRONOGRAPH

Movement: automatic-winding ETA 2894.2; 42-hour power reserve.
Functions: hours, minutes, seconds; date; chronograph.
Case: steel; Ø 41.5mm; water resistant to 10atm.
Dial: brown.
Strap: brown alligator.

TAMBOUR ORIENTATION AUTOMATIC

Movement: automatic-winding LV122 caliber; 42-hour power reserve.
Functions: hours, minutes, seconds; date; indication of the North direction in both hemispheres.
Case: steel; Ø 44mm; transparent caseback; water resistant to 10atm.
Dial: brown and black; Tahitian mother-of-pearl counters.
Strap: brown alligator.

TAMBOUR IN BLACK POWER RESERVE

Movement: automatic-winding LV91 caliber; 42-hour power reserve.
Functions: hours, minutes, seconds; large date; power reserve indicator.
Case: steel; Ø 44mm; water resistant to 10atm.
Dial: black.
Strap: steel and rubber.

TAMBOUR DIVING II GREY

Movement: automatic-winding ETA 2895.2; 42-hour power reserve.
Functions: hours, minutes; small seconds; date; diving function: unidirectional turning bezel to measure diving time.
Case: steel; Ø 44mm; water resistant to 30atm.
Dial: grey; sunray effect.
Strap: black rubber.

TAMBOUR IN BLACK LV277 AUTOMATIC CHRONOGRAPH

Movement: automatic-winding LV277 caliber; 50-hour power reserve; COSC-certified chronograph.
Functions: hours, minutes, seconds; date; chronograph.
Case: Black Force steel and pink gold; Ø 44mm; transparent caseback; water resistant to 10atm.
Dial: black.
Strap: black Damier rubber.

TAMBOUR AMERICA'S CUP AUTOMATIC

Movement: automatic-winding LV171 caliber.
Functions: hours, minutes, seconds; date; chronograph; 5-minute countdown.
Case: steel overmolded with rubber; Ø 44mm; water resistant to 10atm.
Dial: black.
Strap: black rubber.

TAMBOUR LOVELY CUP

Movement: quartz ETA 251.471.
Functions: hours, minutes; small seconds; date; chronograph.
Case: steel; Ø 34mm; water resistant to 10atm.
Dial: white mother-of-pearl.
Strap: white Monogram rubber.

TAMBOUR LOVELY CUP DIAMONDS

Movement: quartz ETA 251.272.
Functions: hours, minutes; small seconds; date; chronograph.
Case: steel; Ø 39.5mm; diamond-pavé horns; water resistant to 10atm.
Dial: black; diamond-pavé hour markers.
Strap: black Monogram rubber.

TAMBOUR HOLOGRAM MONOGRAM

Movement: quartz ETA 256.461.
Functions: hours, minutes, seconds; date.
Case: steel; Ø 28mm; water resistant to 10atm.
Dial: silver; Hologram Monogram pattern.
Bracelet: steel.

TAMBOUR DISC DIAMONDS

Movement: quartz ETA 955.432.
Functions: hours, minutes.
Case: steel; Ø 39.5mm; diamond-pavé horns; water resistant to 10atm.
Dial: grey; diamond-pavé dial and hour markers; Monogram pattern silver.
Strap: grey Monogram vernis leather.

MASTERING THE INTERVALS

Long intertwined with the spirit of the age, Montblanc melds modernist values and modern techniques in the quest to measure what cannot be captured: time.

With the Nicolas Rieussec Chronograph Open Hometime, Montblanc digs to the bottom of its inventive profundity to honor the man whose invention forever redefined the notion of timekeeping. A master of the measurement of time intervals, Rieussec revolutionized the horological world with the public presentation of the Time Writer, with revolving disc and ink-writing mechanism, in 1821. Nearly two centuries after the French watchmaker's pioneering invention of the chronograph, Montblanc brilliantly revisits Rieussec's decisive technical novelty—a rotating dial that indicates the elapsed seconds.

Decisively rebellious in its design, the Nicolas Rieussec Chronograph Open Hometime possesses a single pushbutton at 8 o'clock—perfectly positioned for right-hand manipulation as well as to avoid inadvertent contact with its owner's surroundings. The timepiece's rotating counter discs at 4 and 8 o'clock deliver unmistakable personality that rejects the conventional chronographic design, while paying a powerful tribute to the father of the complication. Held in place by a red-gold-plated bridge with ruby bearings, the discs reveal the measure of a time interval—seconds at 8 o'clock and up to 30 minutes across the dial—by comparing their position with the immobile indexes above them. In true Montblanc form, the mechanical excellence does not conclude with this declaration. Powered by the in-house MB R210 caliber, this vibrant chronograph displays a second time zone via an ingenious skeletonized rotating disc, visible through apertures in the dial. On the upper half of the pierced anthracite-colored watch face, whose indicators are adorned with magnificent grain d'orge guilloché, an off-centered subdial presents running time with a twist. While ordinary time is shown with traditional convention, "home time," as labeled by a red triangular pointing index, demonstrates the hour in the owner's home time zone, and is executed in similar technical fashion to the chronograph's counters. While a window at 3 o'clock indicates the date in the local time zone, the comet-shaped opening at 9 o'clock presents a day/night indicator that is synchronized to the owner's home time. In addition, the space between the chronograph discs features a dazzling view of the low-wear vertical coupling, spiral-coil hairspring of the screw balance, and escape wheel's precisely shaped teeth.

The exhibition continues through the transparent sapphire crystal on the watch's caseback, where Montblanc lets connoisseurs enjoy the watch's splendid inner workings. Within a case made of 95g of 18-karat red gold, the Nicolas Rieussec Chronograph Open Hometime is as much an homage to a revolutionary figure, as an innovative integration of the dial into the fundamentals of the movement.

NICOLAS RIEUSSEC CHRONOGRAPH OPEN HOMETIME

A modern tribute to the inventor of the chronograph, this precious gold timepiece is a masterful fusion of outstanding tradition and contemporary innovation.

CHRONOGRAPH
NICOLAS RIEUSSEC
MONTBLANC
HOME TIME
SWISS MADE

Remaining on the trail of historical acknowledgment, Montblanc's Vintage TachyDate, part of the Collection Villeret 1858, recaptures the vital functionality of World War I chronographs. The first two decades of the 20th century, characterized by the devastating effects of combat and a growing fascination with speed in the spheres of art and science, hold particular significance in the heart of the renowned brand. Minerva, now known as Montblanc Manufacture Villeret, was a significant player in the domain of strategic time measurement. Minerva's chronographs with tachometers (also known as tachymeters) allowed soldiers to precisely, and instantly, measure the speed of an oncoming enemy, while telemeter scales facilitated, through the differing velocities of light and sound, the determining of one's distance from hostile artillery. Driven by the MB M16.32 manufacture caliber, the limited edition Vintage TachyDate features a hand-guided date subdial at 6 o'clock that visually anchors the design's highly technical allure. While the small running seconds at 9 o'clock and 30-minute chronograph counter at 3 o'clock complete the gold dial's delicate three-dimensional interior, a peripheral double tachometer scale, calibrated from 1,000 to 30, provides the prominent aesthetic of a high-precision time-keeping instrument. In reference to Minerva's founding year, this expressive timepiece is produced in two limited series of 58 units—18-karat white gold with silvery-white grained finish and 18-karat 5N red gold with ivory-colored lacquer—each with an exhibition caseback.

The Vintage TachyDate's elegant design and crown-integrated single-push chronograph evoke the early 1900s and its heady emphasis on movement at top speeds. Meanwhile, a commemorative double tachometer scale honors an era in Montblanc's inherited past, which brought watchmaking to the forefront of a battlefield that forever marked the landscape of modern history.

VINTAGE TACHYDATE

With a dial that evokes the finest high-precision instruments, this is the first member of Montblanc's Collection Villeret 1858 to possess a date display.

Extending Montblanc's expertise to the realm of the modern, the TimeWalker TwinFly Chronograph GreyTech makes a counter-cultural statement with its defiant absence of color. Seeking the serenity of the monochrome principle, this 888-piece limited edition timepiece's gray titanium case proclaims a sophisticated nostalgia for the black-and-white epoch. Through intelligent shading of the various tones of gray, as well as generous apertures, the dial finds a captivating depth of structure that sets the stage for its elaborate components. In an innovative and exclusive statement of design, Montblanc's self-winding MB LL100 caliber expresses both of its chronographic intervals on one central axis. While a long hand with light gray tip illustrates the elapsed seconds on the outmost periphery of the dial, a shorter hand with a dark anthracite tip, directly below, reads elapsed minutes on a prominently placed 60-minute scale in the center of the watch. Upon the activation of the integrated flyback function, both hands race back to their shared starting position and immediately recommence the precise measurement of a new time interval. As the small seconds at 6 o'clock, and 24-hour second time zone with raised relief interior at 12 o'clock, contribute a pulsating aesthetic dimension to the dial, the rotating date component circulates theatrically beneath the watch face. Through a clearly identified white frame at 9 o'clock, Montblanc singles out the current date from the underlying sea of Arabic numerals.

A declaration of Montblanc's inventive merging of a bygone era with the innovative drive of the present, the TimeWalker TwinFly Chronograph GreyTech is a fascinating monochrome timepiece that shines through mechanical excellence and highly sophisticated tranquility.

With three stunning timepieces that capture the chronograph concept's historical intervals, Montblanc ingeniously traces the finest points of chronographic chronology. Through the development of distinguished mechanical movements, and a unique aesthetic sensibility, the manufacture marks a remarkable moment of its own in the continued pursuit of elapsed time.

TIMEWALKER
TWINFLY CHRONOGRAPH GREYTECH

Innovatively equipped with two centrally mounted chronograph hands, this multi-complication timepiece offers exceptional measuring legibility of elapsed time intervals.

MONTBLANC NICOLAS RIEUSSEC CHRONOGRAPH OPEN HOMETIME REF. 107067

Movement: automatic-winding MB R210 caliber; 72-hour power reserve; 295 components; 40 jewels; 28,800 vph; monopusher chronograph with column-wheel control and vertical disc coupling; double barrel; screw balance; flat hairspring; rhodium-plated and circular-grained plate; rhodium-plated, Côtes de Genève bridges; gear train with special toothing for more efficient power transmission.

Functions: off-centered hour and minute hands; date on rotating disc; second time zone on rotating disc; day/night display for second time zone; chronograph: rotating discs for 60-second and 30-minute counters beneath fixed hands; travel function with rapid reset, either forward or backward, for the hour hand and date display.

Case: 18K red gold; Ø 43mm, thickness: 15mm; 5N 18K red-gold crown with mother-of-pearl and Montblanc logo; monopusher pushbutton at 8; cambered antireflective sapphire crystal; screw-down sapphire crystal caseback; water resistant to 3atm.

Dial: anthracite-colored; white Arabic numerals; barleycorn guilloché (grain d'orges); feuille-shaped hour and minute hands with luminescent coating.

Strap: black alligator skin; 18K red-gold double-folding clasp.

Suggested price: $36,400

TIMEWRITER II: CHRONOGRAPHE BI-FREQUENCE 1.000 REF. 107343

Movement: manual-winding MB TW02 caliber; Ø 38.4mm; 18,000 vph; balance wheel for the chronograph; balance spring with Phillips curve; rhodium-plated German silver plate, circular-grained on both sides with hand-chamfered edges; rhodium-plated German silver bridges with Côtes de Genève, circular-grained on both sides, hand-chamfered edges; going train: gold-plated wheels, circular-grained, chamfered, diamond hubs on both sides and pinions with polished faces and toothing, burnished pivots.

Functions: hours, minutes; small seconds at 9; column-wheel monopusher chronograph: 50-minute and seconds counter at 6; central 1/100th seconds, 1/100th seconds dashboard indicator at 12; power reserve indicator at 3.

Case: 18K white gold; Ø 47mm; crown with mother-of-pearl Montblanc emblem; cambered sapphire crystal; sapphire crystal caseback; water resistant to 3atm.

Dial: open anthracite revealing two balance wheels.

Strap: black hand-stitched alligator skin with red double stitching; 18K white-gold pin bucklc.

Note: limited to 36 pieces.

Suggested price: $269,800

MONTBLANC TIMEWALKER CHRONOGRAPH TWINFLY GREYTECH REF. 107338

Movement: automatic-winding MB LL100 caliber; 72-hour power reserve; 36 jewels; 28,800 vph; double barrel; screw-down balance; flat hairspring; wheels with special toothing for more efficient power transmission.

Functions: hours, minutes; small seconds at 6; date at 9; flyback column-wheel chronograph: central chronograph seconds and central 60-minute counter; 24-hour dial at 12.

Case: satin-finished and bead-blasted titanium; Ø 43mm; cambered scratch-resistant antireflective sapphire crystal; bead-blasted titanium sapphire crystal caseback; water resistant to 3atm.

Dial: gray; rhodium-plated numerals and black pierced luminescent hands.

Strap: anthracite alligator leather with tone-in-tone gray stitching; bead-blasted titanium pronged buckle.

Suggested price: $14,800

MONTBLANC COLLECTION VILLERET 1858 – VINTAGE TACHYDATE REF. 107342

Movement: manual-winding MB M16.32 caliber; Ø 38.3mm, thickness: 7mm; 50-hour power reserve; 268 components; 22 jewels; 18,000 vph; monopusher chronograph with column-wheel control and horizontal disc coupling; screw balance; Phillips terminal curve spring; rhodium-plated nickel silver plate with circular graining on both surfaces; rhodium-plated nickel silver bridges with Côtes de Genève; faceted arms going-train hubs with diamond-polished surfaces.

Functions: hours, minutes; small seconds at 9; date; chronograph: 30-minute counter at 3 and central seconds hand; tachometer with an outer circle calibrated from 1,000 to 60 and an inner scale marked from 60 to 30.

Case: 18K red gold; Ø 43.5mm, thickness: 13mm; domed sapphire crystal; screw-down sapphire crystal caseback; water resistant to 3atm.

Dial: solid gold with ivory-colored lacquer; blued stainless steel hands.

Strap: hand-sewn alligator skin; 18K red-gold buckle.

Suggested price: $58,000

Note: limited to 58 pieces (red gold) and 58 pieces (white gold).

Also available: white gold with silvery white-grained finish.

STAR CLASSIC AUTOMATIC — REF. 107075

Movement: automatic-winding MB 4810/408 caliber; approx. 42-hour power reserve; 27 jewels; 28,800 vph.
Functions: hours, minutes; small seconds at 6.
Case: 18K red gold (40.2g); Ø 39mm, thickness: 8.9mm; fixed bezel; non-screw crown; one 18K red-gold O-ring with mother-of-pearl Montblanc emblem; domed sapphire crystal with double-sided antireflective coating; sapphire crystal caseback; water resistant to 3atm.
Dial: anthracite; red-gold-plated numerals and hour markers; red-gold-plated feuillle-shaped hands.
Strap: brown alligator; 18K red-gold pin buckle.
Suggested price: $10,100

STAR CLASSIC AUTOMATIC — REF. 107076

Movement: automatic-winding MB 4810/408 caliber; approx. 42-hour power reserve; 27 jewels; 28,800 vph.
Functions: hours, minutes; small seconds at 6.
Case: 18K red gold (40.2g); Ø 39mm, thickness: 8.9mm; fixed bezel; non-screw crown; one 18K red-gold O-ring with mother-of-pearl Montblanc emblem; domed sapphire crystal with double-sided antireflective coating; sapphire crystal caseback; water resistant to 3atm.
Dial: silver-colored; red-gold-plated numerals and hour markers; red-gold-plated feuillle-shaped hands.
Strap: brown alligator; 18K red-gold pin buckle.
Suggested price: $10,100

PRINCESSE GRACE DE MONACO COLLECTION — REF. 106499

Movement: quartz MB 4810/160 caliber; 4 jewels.
Functions: hours, minutes; small seconds at 6.
Case: stainless steel; Ø 34mm, thickness: 9.7mm; fixed bezel; non-screw crown; one O-ring with mother-of-pearl Montblanc emblem; domed sapphire crystal with double antireflective coating; stainless steel caseback engraved with Princess Grace monogram; water resistant to 3atm.
Dial: white; red-gold-plated numerals; 6 Top Wesselton diamonds (0.0204 carat); drop-cut pink sapphire (0.02 carat) at 6; flange set with 130 Top Wesselton diamonds (0.39 carat); red-gold-plated hour and minute hands.
Strap: white alligator skin with pin buckle.
Suggested price: $6,600

PRINCESSE GRACE DE MONACO COLLECTION — REF. 106884

Movement: quartz MB 106884 caliber; 4 jewels.
Functions: hours, minutes; small seconds at 6.
Case: stainless steel; Ø 34mm, thickness: 9.7mm; fixed bezel; non-screw crown; one O-ring with mother-of-pearl Montblanc emblem; domed sapphire crystal with double antireflective coating; stainless steel caseback engraved with Princess Grace monogram; water resistant to 3atm.
Dial: white; silver-colored numerals; 6 Top Wesselton diamonds (0.0204 carat); drop-cut pink sapphire (0.02 carat) at 6; flange set with 130 Top Wesselton diamonds (0.39 carat); rhodium-plated feuille-shaped hour and minute hands.
Strap: black alligator skin with pin buckle.
Suggested price: $6,600

PANERAI

A BATTLE-TESTED HERITAGE

Founded more than one and a half centuries ago in the geographic heart of the Renaissance, Panerai's blend of Italian aesthetic sensibilities and the excellence of fine Swiss watchmaking make the brand as unique as its illustrious heritage. Giovanni Panerai's 1860 creation of Florence's first workshop marked the beginning of a history filled with a spirit of innovation in the service of high-performance functionality.

In 1900, having taken over his grandfather's business and expanded its reach with a newfound dynamism, Guido Panerai moved the Orologeria Svizzera to the Piazza San Giovanni, where it is found to this day. Injected with a new vitality, the manufacture began its historical relationship with the Royal Italian Navy, conducting its first deliveries of precision instruments to the Ministry of Defense. In 1916, with the registration of the first of numerous patents, Panerai leapt into a new innovative tradition, creating a radium-based powder named Radiomir, which it used as a source of luminosity in dials and sighting instruments.

With World War II knocking on the door, Panerai's developments for the Royal Italian Navy took on a role of strategic proportions. Created for the underwater exploits of the Command of the First Submarine Corps, the prototype of the Radiomir watch, designed to withstand truly extreme conditions, possesses many features that still distinguish it today. In the 1940s, in an effort to improve its performance, the Radiomir watch underwent a series of innovations that culminated in the watch becoming the first underwater model resistant to 200 meters in the history of horology. The invention of a unique lever bridge device, along with the increased luminosity and legibility of a new sandwich dial, and the more resistant case-integrated strap attachments, were among the advancements responsible for this watch of unprecedented strength and water tightness. In 1949, Panerai patented Luminor, an isotope of tritium-based hydrogen, with which it replaced the radioactive Radiomir powder, exemplifying the watchmaker's quest for perfection.

Throughout the 20th century, Panerai's devotion to creating high-performance, function-driven timekeeping instruments solidified the brand's pivotal relationship with the region's Navies. In 1956, the manufacture used a marked rotating bezel, ideal for calculating immersion times, in the Egiziano, an exceptionally solid and sizeable underwater Radiomir watch with eight-day power reserve designed for the Navy of Egypt. Never resting in its innovative determination, the Tuscan house was soon thereafter granted a patent for a bridge device that fastens the crown's position and ensures the watch's impermeability.

Only in 1998, one year after being acquired by the Richemont group, then Vendôme, would Panerai launch its collections in the international market. In 2002, Panerai opened its manufacturing facility in Neuchâtel, Swiss watchmaking's epicenter. In doing so, the Florentine house opened a new chapter in its illustrious heritage. Thus, after 100 years devoted to the high-performance world of military timekeeping, Panerai entered the 21st century with a new impetus for innovation in the field of in-house-developed mechanical movements.

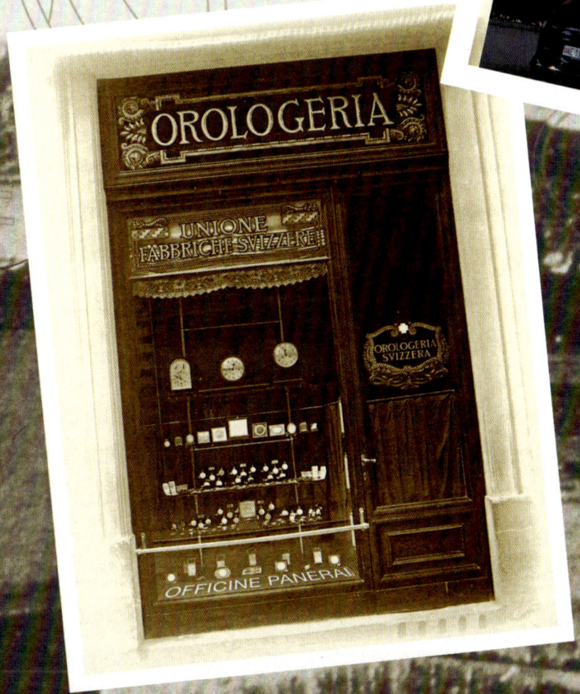

OROLOGERIA SVIZZERIA

Initially located on the Ponte alle Grazie, Panerai's Orologeria Svizzeria was Florence's first watchmaking school.

The P.2000 family of manufacture calibers provides a range of functions within hand-wound and automatic movements. However, several elements unite the six calibers, which oscillate at a frequency of 28,800 vph. First, the sandwich structure of the mechanisms, with the bottom and top plates being connected by a set of small pillars, provides a significantly firmer construction than the traditional cantilevered bridges. Featuring exceptionally thin and long springs, the three barrels, connected in series, deliver not only a longer lasting power reserve, but also a crucial consistency of amplitude to ensure optimal accuracy throughout the balance wheel's operation.

The P.2002, P2003, P.2004, P2005, P.2005G, and P.2006 manufacture calibers each possess a range of capabilities that testifies to Panerai's significant wealth of expertise. With power reserves as long as 10 days, a 12/24-hour GMT function, the rapid adjustment of local time, a unique seconds reset function for perfect synchronization, a single-button chronograph, split-seconds chronograph, tourbillon, equation of time, representation of the night sky, summer/winter time corrections, date and month, and time of sunrise and sunset, all equipped with the KIF Parechoc anti-shock device, the P.2000 family of movements is a statement of constant forward-thinking inventiveness by Panerai.

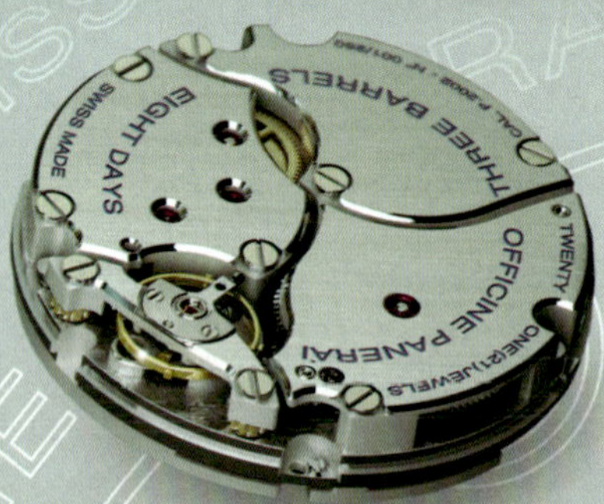

P.2002 CALIBER

Like the P.2000 family, the P.9000 automatic movement boasts a frequency of oscillation of 28,800 vph, and an ingenious rapid adjustment system, which uses a small spring clutch to enable the local time's hour hand to move in clicks of one hour at a time without interfering with the minute hand or the overall running of the watch. Unique to this series, however, are the variable inertia balance wheel with radially arranged adjusting screws, as the single base balance cock, the two-barrel driven three-day power reserve, and the date at 3 o'clock with small seconds at 9 o'clock. Variants of the P.9000, the P.9001 and P.9002 possess the same structural characteristics and 7.9mm thickness as the former, with the addition of a second time zone, a seconds reset function, and a power reserve indication. Unlike on the P.9001, where the remaining energy is shown on the back of the watch, the P.9002 displays the indication as a hand moving through an arc-shaped sector on the dial.

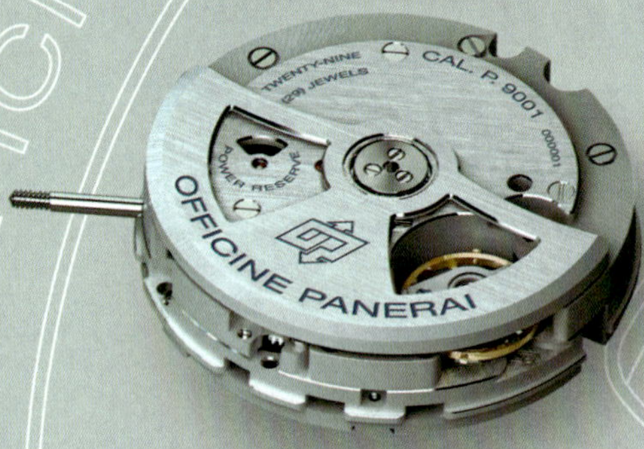

P.9001 AUTOMATIC CALIBER

Designed to fit perfectly within the elegant disposition of the Radiomir watch's 42mm case, the 154-component, 19-jewel, P.999 hand-wound movement is, at 3mm thick, the thinnest caliber of the house. The single-spring barrel with fixed bridle provides a power reserve of 60 hours, while the annular balance wheel offers a frequency of 21,600 vph. Executed by a sophisticated swan-neck regulator, the flat balance spring's active length adjustment is set with micrometric precision. Given the caliber's extremely complex execution requirements, the P.999 is developed as a 500-unit limited edition.

P.999 HAND-WOUND CALIBER

Finally, the substantially sized P. 3000 hand-wound family of movements has been developed with inspiration from the movements that have powered historic Panerai timepieces. Designed in accordance with the house's values of performance, accuracy, long power reserve, and robust strength, this in-house produced caliber features a remarkably rigid structure of two bridges, fixed to the bottom plate by a series of thick screws. Two barrels, in series, ensure a consistent delivery of force over the length of the three-day power reserve. Armed with a variable inertia balance wheel that oscillates at 21,600 vph, the P.3000 boasts brush-finished bridges, smoothed and polished angles, hours, minutes, small seconds, and the same spring-clutch rapid adjustment system as the house's other caliber series.

P.3000 HAND-WOUND CALIBER

It is fitting that Panerai would pay tribute, in its own language of haute horology, to the celestial genius of Galileo Galilei. Having spent a major portion of his childhood just a short walk away from the doorstep where, nearly three centuries later, Giovanni Panerai would open his initial workshop, Galileo's connection to the world of timekeeping ran deep. His application of a counter device that used the constancy of pendulum swings to measure longitude may not have offered the desired results, but the system can be seen as the ancestor of modern watchmaking, as can the man's relentlessly inventive disposition.

With L'Astronomo, the Luminor 1950 Equation of Time Tourbillon Titanio, Panerai honors the celebrated astronomer, with the most technically sophisticated wristwatch ever produced by the legendary watchmaker. Upon its unmistakable Panerai sandwich dial, the timepiece, powered by the P.2005G caliber, demonstrates a wealth of complications fit for the father of modern science. The indications of date, month, and small seconds are gracefully complemented by two cursors displaying sunrise and sunset time along circular sectors at 4 and 8 o'clock, and, most impressively, the equation of time beneath the central hour and minute hands. While universal time is conventionally read on the luminescent face of the watch, the equation of time takes into account the Earth's eccentric orbit and axial inclination, indicating the discrepancy, up to about 15 minutes faster or slower, between the time that we accept, and real, or solar time. This revered complication is joined on the watch's caseback by a visible 30-second tourbillon regulator, a 4-day hand-indicated power reserve display, and a fascinating map of the sky that rotates to update the night's celestial coordinates based on the chosen city of the watch's owner.

LUMINOR 1950 EQUATION OF TIME TOURBILLON TITANIO

This tribute to the great Galileo Galilei fittingly boasts a number of celestial measurements, making it the most technically complex in the history of Panerai.

While the Luminor 1950 Equation of Time Tourbillon Titanio with 50mm titanium case stays true to the notable heritage of the Officine Panerai design codes, the celebratory incorporation of sophisticated astronomical complications attests to the manufacture's never-ending quest for the exceptionally functional.

Seemingly recovered as a sunken treasure from the depths of the ocean, the Luminor Submersible 1950 3 Days Automatic Bronzo is a high-precision renaissance of underwater antiquity. Beneath the alluring 47mm brushed-bronze case, the P.9000 caliber provides this 300m water resistant timepiece with an oscillation frequency of 28,800 vph. The CuSn8 bronze chosen by Panerai is an alloy of copper and pure tin that is particularly resistant to seawater corrosion and atmospheric agents. As the heavy-duty material ages, a patina, acquired in reaction to external influences, enhances the profundity of its appearance. On the side of the case, a trademark brushed-bronze device protects the crown and completes the unique appearance of this inspiring tribute to the timeless infinity of the sea.

Having established its pedigree on the testing battlegrounds of the Royal Italian Navy, Panerai has expanded its rich expertise with the confidence to honor its distinguished heritage. Filled with innovations and in-house developments, the house's newest chapter extends a story that prides itself on the values of tradition and the elegance of excellent performance.

LUMINOR SUBMERSIBLE 1950 3 DAYS AUTOMATIC BRONZO

Equipped with a unidirectional rotating bezel with graduated scale, this bronze underwater titan delivers an optimal measurement of immersion time.

LUMINOR 1950 3 DAYS — REF. PAM00372

Movement: manual-winding Panerai P.3000 caliber; 16½ lines; thickness 5.3mm; 3-day power reserve; 160 components; 21 jewels; 21,600 vph; Glucydur® balance; Incabloc® antishock device; two barrels.
Functions: hours, minutes.
Case: polished steel; Ø 47mm; polished steel bezel; brushed steel trademark crown-protection device; sapphire Plexiglas® crystal; transparent sapphire crystal caseback; water resistant to 10atm.
Dial: black; Arabic numerals and hour markers with luminescent coating.
Strap: brown PANERAI-personalized leather; large-size brushed steel buckle.
Note: supplied with a second interchangeable strap and a steel screwdriver.
Suggested price: $10,400

RADIOMIR 3 DAYS PLATINO — REF. PAM00373

Movement: manual-winding Panerai P.3000 caliber; 16½ lines; thickness: 5.3mm; 3-day power reserve; 160 components; 21 jewels; 21,600 vph; Glucydur® balance; Incabloc® antishock device; two barrels.
Functions: hours, minutes.
Case: platinum; Ø 47mm; platinum bezel; OP-personalized winding crown; patented with removable wire loop strap attachments; sapphire Plexiglas® crystal; transparent sapphire crystal caseback; water resistant to 10atm.
Dial: brown; hour markers with luminescent coating.
Strap: brown PANERAI-personalized alligator leather; large-size white-gold buckle.
Suggested price: $44,800
Also available: white gold with brown dial and PANERAI-personalised brown alligator strap (PAM00376, $29,900); 18K pink gold with brown dial and PANERAI-personalized brown alligator strap (PAM00379, $26,700).

LUMINOR COMPOSITE 1950 3 DAYS — REF. PAM00375

Movement: manual-winding Panerai P.3000/1 caliber; 16½ lines; thickness: 5.3mm; 3-day power reserve; 160 components; 21 jewels; 21,600 vph; Glucydur® balance; Incabloc® antishock device; two barrels.
Functions: hours, minutes; small seconds at 9.
Case: brown Panerai composite; Ø 47mm; brown Panerai composite bezel integrated into the case; brown trademark crown-protection device; antireflective sapphire corundum crystal; transparent burnished sapphire crystal caseback; water resistant to 10atm.
Dial: brown; Arabic numerals and hour markers with luminescent coating.
Strap: brown PANERAI-personalized leather; large-size Panerai composite buckle.
Note: supplied with a second interchangeable strap and a steel screwdriver.
Suggested price: $14,100

RADIOMIR — REF. PAM00337

Movement: manual-winding Panerai P.999/1 caliber; 12 lines; thickness: 3mm; 60-hour power reserve; 144 components; 19 jewels; 21,600 vph; Incabloc® antishock device; one barrel.
Functions: hours, minutes; small seconds.
Case: AISI 316L steel; Ø 42mm; OP-personalized screw-down crown; patented with removable wire loop strap attachments; antireflective sapphire corundum crystal; transparent sapphire crystal caseback; water resistant to 10atm.
Dial: black; Arabic numerals and hour markers and luminescent coating.
Strap: brown PANERAI-personalized alligator leather; polished steel buckle.
Suggested price: $7,700
Also available: titanium with black sandwich dial and PANERAI-personalised black alligator strap (PAM00338, $8,700); 18K pink gold with black sandwich dial and PANERAI-personalized black alligator strap (PAM00378, $19,100).

RADIOMIR ORO ROSA — REF. PAM00378

Movement: manual-winding Panerai P.999 caliber; 12 lines; thickness: 3.4mm; 60-hour power reserve; 154 components; 19 jewels; 21,600 vph; Glucydur® balance; Incabloc® antishock device; swan's neck regulator; one barrel.
Functions: hours, minutes; small seconds at 9.
Case: polished 18K pink gold; Ø 42mm; OP-personalized screw-down crown; patented with removable wire loop strap attachments; antireflective sapphire corundum crystal; transparent sapphire crystal caseback; water resistant to 10atm.
Dial: black; Arabic numerals and hour markers with luminescent coating.
Strap: black PANERAI-personalized alligator leather; polished 18K pink-gold buckle.
Suggested price: $19,100
Also available: polished 316L steel with black sandwich dial and PANERAI-personalized brown alligator strap (PAM00337, $7,700); titanium with black sandwich dial and PANERAI-personalised black alligator strap (PAM00338, $8,700).

RADIOMIR 8 DAYS TITANIO — REF. PAM00346

Movement: manual-winding Panerai P.2002/9 caliber; 13¾ lines; thickness: 6.6mm; 8-day power reserve; 246 components; 21 jewels; 28,800 vph; Glucydur® balance; KIF Parechoc® antishock device; three barrels.
Functions: hours, minutes; small seconds at 9; date at 3; power reserve indicator on the back; seconds reset.
Case: brushed titanium; Ø 45mm; polished titanium bezel; OP-personalized screw-down winding crown; patented with removable wire loop strap attachments; antireflective sapphire corundum crystal; transparent sapphire crystal caseback; water resistant to 10atm.
Dial: brown; Arabic numerals and hour markers with luminescent coating.
Strap: brown PANERAI-personalized alligator; large-size titanium buckle.
Suggested price: $14,700
Also available: polished 316L steel with black sandwich dial and PANERAI-personalised black alligator strap (PAM00268, $13,100); black ceramic with black sandwich dial and PANERAI-personalised black leather strap (PAM00384, $15,500).

RADIOMIR 8 DAYS CERAMICA — REF. PAM00384

Movement: manual-winding Panerai P.2002/3 caliber; 13¾ lines; thickness: 6.6mm; 8-day power reserve; 225 components; 21 jewels; 28,800 vph; monometallic Glucydur® balance; KIF Parechoc® antishock device; three barrels.
Functions: hours, minutes; small seconds at 9; date at 3; linear power reserve indicator at 6.
Case: black ceramic; Ø 45mm; black ceramic bezel; OP-personalized screw-down winding crown; patented with removable wire loop strap attachments; antireflective sapphire corundum crystal; transparent smoked sapphire crystal caseback; water resistant to 10atm.
Dial: black; Arabic numerals and hour markers with luminescent coating.
Strap: black PANERAI-personalized leather; large-size titanium buckle with special hard black coating.
Suggested price: $15,500
Also available: brushed titanium with brown sandwich dial and PANERAI-personalised brown alligator strap (PAM00346, $14,700); polished 316L steel with black sandwich dial and PANERAI-personalised black alligator strap (PAM00268, $13,100).

PANERAI LUMINOR 1950 8 DAYS GMT — REF. PAM00233

Movement: manual-winding Panerai P.2002 caliber; 13¾ lines; thickness: 6.6mm; 8-day power reserve; 247 components; 21 jewels; 28,800 vph; Glucydur® balance; KIF Parechoc® antishock device.
Functions: hours, minutes, seconds; date at 3; 12-hour second time zone and day/night indication at 9; linear power reserve indicator at 6.
Case: brushed steel; Ø 44mm; polished steel bezel; brushed steel trademark crown-protection device; antireflective sapphire crystal; transparent sapphire crystal screw-down caseback; water resistant to 10atm.
Dial: black; Arabic numerals and hour markers with luminescent coating.
Strap: black PANERAI-personalized alligator; large-size steel buckle.
Note: supplied with a second interchangeable strap and a steel screwdriver.
Suggested price: $15,500
Also available: brushed and polished 18K pink gold and PANERAI-personalized brown alligator strap (PAM00289, $32,200).

LUMINOR 1950 8 DAYS GMT ORO ROSA — REF. PAM00289

Movement: manual-winding Panerai P.2002 caliber; 13¾ lines; thickness: 6.6mm; 8-day power reserve; 247 components; 21 jewels; 28,800 vph; Glucydur® balance; KIF Parechoc® antishock device.
Functions: hours, minutes; small seconds; date; second time zone; 24-hour indicator; linear power reserve indicator; second reset.
Case: brushed 18K pink gold; Ø 44mm; polished 18K pink gold bezel; brushed 18K pink gold OP-personalized crown; antireflective sapphire corundum crystal; transparent sapphire crystal caseback; water resistant to 10atm.
Dial: brown; Arabic numerals and hour markers with luminescent coating.
Strap: brown PANERAI-personalized alligator; 18K pink-gold buckle.
Suggested price: $32,200
Also available: brushed steel with black dial and PANERAI-personalized black calf strap (PAM00233, $15,500).

LUMINOR 1950 TOURBILLON GMT — REF. PAM00306

Movement: manual-winding Panerai P.2005 caliber; 16¼ lines; thickness: 9.1mm; 6-day power reserve; 239 components; 31 jewels; 28,800 vph; Glucydur® balance; KIF Parechoc® antishock device; three barrels.
Functions: hours, minutes; small seconds in the tourbillon at 9; second time zone; 24-hour indicator at 3; power reserve indicator on the back.
Case: brushed titanium; Ø 47mm; polished titanium bezel; brushed titanium OP-personalized crown; antireflective sapphire corundum crystal; transparent sapphire crystal caseback; water resistant to 10atm.
Dial: brown; Arabic numerals and hour markers with luminescent coating.
Strap: brown PANERAI-personalized alligator; large-size brushed titanium buckle.
Note: supplied with a second interchangeable strap and a steel screwdriver.
Suggested price: $127,200

LUMINOR 1950 CHRONO MONOPULSANTE 8 DAYS GMT TITANIO — REF. PAM00311

Movement: manual-winding Panerai P. 2004 caliber; 13¾ lines; 8-day power reserve; 321 components; 29 jewels; 28,800 vph; Glucydor® balance, KIF Parechoc® antishock device; three barrels.
Functions: hours, minutes; small seconds; second time zone; 24-hour indicator; linear power reserve indicator; seconds reset; chronograph.
Case: brushed titanium; Ø 44mm; polished titanium bezel; brushed titanium trademark crown-protection device; antireflective sapphire corundum crystal; transparent sapphire crystal caseback; water resistant to 10atm.
Dial: brown; Arabic numerals and hour markers with luminescent coating.
Strap: brown PANERAI-personalized alligator large-size brushed titanium buckle.
Note: supplied with a second interchangeable strap and a steel screwdriver.
Suggested price: $22,400
Also available: brushed 316L steel with black sandwich dial with PANERAI-personalised black alligator strap (PAM00275, $20,000); black ceramic with black sandwich dial and PANERAI-personalised black leather strap (PAM00317, $26,700).

LUMINOR MARINA 1950 3 DAYS AUTOMATIC — REF. PAM00312

Movement: automatic-winding Panerai P.9000 caliber; 13¾ lines; thickness: 7.9mm; 3-day power reserve; 197 components; 28 jewels; 28,800 vph; Glucydur® balance; Incabloc® antishock device; two barrels.
Functions: hours, minutes; small seconds at 9; date at 3.
Case: AISI 316L brushed steel; Ø 44mm; polished steel bezel; brushed steel trademark crown-protection device; antireflective sapphire corundum crystal; transparent sapphire crystal caseback; water resistant to 30atm.
Dial: black; Arabic numerals and hour markers with luminescent coating.
Strap: black PANERAI-personalized alligator leather; large-size brushed steel buckle.
Note: supplied with a second interchangeable strap and a steel screwdriver.
Suggested price: $8,300
Also available: brushed 316L steel with PANERAI-personalised steel bracelet (PAM00328, $9,400.00); polished 316L steel with PANERAI-personalised black leather strap (PAM00359, $8,300); titanio with brown dial and PANERAI-personalised brown alligator strap (PAM00351, $8,900); titanio with brown dial and PANERAI-personalised titanium bracelet (PAM00352, $10,100); Panerai Composite® on PANERAI-personalised brown leather strap (PAM00386, $ 10,400).

LUMINOR MARINA 1950 3 DAYS AUTOMATIC — REF. PAM00328

Movement: automatic-winding Panerai P.9000 caliber; 13¾ lines; thickness: 7.9mm; 3-day power reserve; 197 components; 28 jewels; 28,800 vph; Glucydur® balance; Incabloc® antishock device; two barrels.
Functions: hours, minutes; small seconds at 9; date at 3.
Case: AISI 316L brushed steel; Ø 44mm; polished steel bezel; brushed steel trademark crown-protection device; antireflective sapphire corundum crystal; transparent sapphire crystal caseback; water resistant to 30atm.
Dial: black; Arabic numerals and hour markers with luminescent coating.
Bracelet: steel PANERAI-personalized with vertical brushed finishing and polished surfaces between the links; large-size buckle.
Note: supplied with a steel screwdriver and tool to change the bracelet.
Suggested price: $9,400
Also available: titanium on PANERAI-personalised titanium bracelet (PAM00352, $10,100); brushed 316L steel on PANERAI-personalised black alligator strap (PAM00312, $8,300); titanium with brown dial on PANERAI-personalised brown alligator strap (PAM00351, $8,900).

LUMINOR MARINA 1950 3 DAYS AUTOMATIC — REF. PAM00359

Movement: automatic-winding Panerai P.9000 caliber; 13¾ lines; thickness: 7.9mm; 3-day power reserve; 197 components; 28 jewels; 28,800 vph; Glucydur® balance; Incabloc® antishock device; two barrels.
Functions: hours, minutes; small seconds at 9; date at 3.
Case: AISI 316L polished steel; Ø 44mm; polished steel bezel; brushed steel trademark crown-protection device; antireflective sapphire corundum crystal; transparent sapphire crystal caseback; water resistant to 30atm.
Dial: black; Arabic numerals and hour markers with luminescent coating.
Strap: black PANERAI-personalized leather; large-size brushed steel buckle.
Note: supplied with a second interchangeable strap and a steel screwdriver.
Suggested price: $8,300
Also available: brushed 316L steel on PANERAI-personalised black alligator strap (PAM00312, $8,300); titanium with brown dial and PANERAI-personalised brown alligator strap (PAM00351, $8,900); titanium with brown dial and PANERAI-personalised titanium bracelet (PAM00352, $10,100); Panerai Composite® and PANERAI-personalised brown leather strap (PAM00386, $ 10,400).

LUMINOR MARINA 1950 3 DAYS AUTOMATIC TITANIO — REF. PAM00351

Movement: automatic-winding Panerai P.9000 caliber; 13¾ lines; thickness: 7.9mm; 3-day power reserve; 197 components; 28 jewels; 28,800 vph; Glucydur® balance; Incabloc® antishock device; two barrels.
Functions: hours, minutes; small seconds at 9; date at 3.
Case: brushed titanium; Ø 44mm; polished titanium bezel; brushed titanium trademark crown-protection device; antireflective sapphire corundum crystal; transparent sapphire crystal caseback; water resistant to 30atm.
Dial: brown; Arabic numerals and hour markers with luminescent coating.
Strap: brown PANERAI-personalized leather; large-size brushed titanium buckle.
Note: supplied with a second interchangeable strap and a steel screwdriver.
Suggested price: $8,900
Also available: brushed 316L steel on PANERAI-personalised steel bracelet (PAM00328, $9,400); polished 316L steel with black dial on PANERAI-personalised black calf strap (PAM00359, $8,300); brown dial on PANERAI-personalised brown alligator strap (PAM00351, $8,900).

LUMINOR MARINA 1950 3 DAYS AUTOMATIC TITANIO — REF. PAM00352

Movement: automatic-winding Panerai P.9000 caliber; 13¾ lines; thickness: 7.9mm; 3-day power reserve; 197 components; 28 jewels; 28,800 vph; Glucydur® balance; Incabloc® antishock device; two barrels.
Functions: hours, minutes; small seconds at 9; date at 3.
Case: polished titanium; Ø 44mm; polished titanium bezel; brushed titanium trademark crown-protection device; antireflective sapphire corundum crystal; transparent sapphire crystal caseback; water resistant to 30atm.
Dial: brown; Arabic numerals and hour markers with luminescent coating.
Bracelet: titanium PANERAI-personalized with vertical brushed finishing and polished surfaces between the links; large-size brushed titanium buckle.
Note: supplied with a steel screwdriver and tool to change the bracelet.
Suggested price: $10,100
Also available: brushed 316L steel on PANERAI-personalised steel bracelet (PAM00328, $9,400); brushed 316L steel on PANERAI-personalised black alligator strap (PAM00312, $8,300); Panerai Composite® on PANERAI-personalised brown leather strap (PAM00386, $10,400); polished 316L steel with black dial and PANERAI-personalised black leather strap (PAM00359, $8,300).

LUMINOR COMPOSITE MARINA 1950 3 DAYS AUTOMATIC REF. PAM00386

Movement: automatic-winding Panerai P.9000 caliber; 13¾ lines; thickness: 7.9mm; 3-day power reserve; 197 components; 28 jewels; 28,800 vph; Glucydur® balance; Incabloc® antishock device; two barrels.
Functions: hours, minutes; small seconds at 9; date at 3.
Case: brown Panerai composite; Ø 44mm; brown Panerai composite bezel integrated into the case; brown trademark crown-protection device; antireflective sapphire corundum crystal; transparent burnished sapphire crystal caseback; water resistant to 30atm.

Dial: brown; Arabic numerals and hour markers with luminescent coating.
Strap: brown PANERAI-personalized leather; large-size Panerai composite buckle.
Note: supplied with a second interchangeable strap and a steel screwdriver.
Suggested price: $10,400
Also available: brushed 316L steel on PANERAI-personalised steel bracelet (PAM00328, $9,400); polished 316L steel with black dial on PANERAI-personalised black calf strap (PAM00359, $8,300); titanium with brown dial on PANERAI-personalised brown alligator strap (PAM00351, $8,900); titanium with brown dial on PANERAI-personalised titanium bracelet (PAM00352, $10,100).

LUMINOR SUBMERSIBLE 1950 3 DAYS AUTOMATIC TITANIO REF. PAM00305

Movement: automatic-winding Panerai P.9000 caliber; 13¾ lines; thickness: 7.9mm; 3-day power reserve; 197 components; 28 jewels; 28,800 vph; Glucydur® balance; Incabloc® antishock device; two barrels.
Functions: hours, minutes; small seconds at 9; date at 3; calculation of immersion time.
Case: brushed titanium; Ø 47mm; brushed titanium unidirectional bezel with polished edges and graduated scale for calculating the time of immersion and ratchet click at minute intervals; brushed titanium trademark crown-protection device; antireflective sapphire corundum crystal; transparent sapphire crystal caseback; water resistant to 30atm.

Dial: black; hour markers with luminescent coating.
Strap: black PANERAI-personalized rubber; large-size brushed titanium buckle.
Note: supplied with a second interchangeable strap and a steel screwdriver.
Suggested price: $10,300

LUMINOR 1950 3 DAYS GMT AUTOMATIC REF. PAM00329

Movement: automatic-winding Panerai P.9001 caliber; 13¾ lines; thickness: 7.9mm; 3-day power reserve; 229 components; 29 jewels; 28,800 vph; Glucydur® balance; Incabloc® antishock device; two barrels.
Functions: hours, minutes; small seconds at 9; date at 3; second time zone; power reserve indicator on the back; seconds reset.
Case: AISI 316L brushed steel; Ø 44mm; polished steel bezel; brushed steel trademark crown-protection device; antireflective sapphire corundum crystal; transparent sapphire crystal caseback; water resistant to 30atm.

Dial: black; Arabic numerals and hour markers with luminescent coating.
Bracelet: steel PANERAI-personalized with vertical brushed finishing and polished surfaces between the links.
Note: supplied with a steel screwdriver and tool to change the bracelet.
Suggested price: $10,800
Also available: brushed 316L steel on PANERAI-personalised brown alligator strap (PAM00320, $9,900).

LUMINOR 1950 3 DAYS GMT POWER RESERVE AUTOMATIC REF. PAM00321

Movement: automatic-winding Panerai P.9002 caliber; 13¾ lines; thickness: 7.9mm; 3-day power reserve; 237 components; 29 jewels; 28,800 vph; Glucydur® balance; Incabloc® antishock device; two barrels.
Functions: hours, minutes; small seconds at 9; date at 3; second time zone; power reserve indicator at 5; seconds reset.
Case: AISI 316L brushed steel; Ø 44mm; polished steel bezel; brushed steel trademark crown-protection device; antireflective sapphire corundum crystal; transparent sapphire crystal caseback; water resistant to 30atm.

Dial: black; Arabic numerals and hour markers with luminescent coating.
Strap: black PANERAI-personalized alligator large-size brushed steel buckle.
Note: supplied with a second interchangeable strap and a steel screwdriver.
Suggested price: $10,100
Also available: brushed 316L steel on PANERAI-personalised steel bracelet (PAM00347, $11,000).

LUMINOR 1950 3 DAYS GMT POWER RESERVE AUTOMATIC REF. PAM00347

Movement: automatic-winding Panerai P.9002 caliber; 13¾ lines; thickness: 7.9mm; 3-day power reserve; 237 components; 29 jewels; 28,800 vph; Glucydur® balance; Incabloc® antishock device; two barrels.
Functions: hours, minutes; small seconds at 9; date at 3; second time zone; power reserve indicator at 5; seconds reset.
Case: AISI 316L brushed steel; Ø 44mm; polished steel bezel; brushed steel trademark crown-protection device; antireflective sapphire corundum crystal; transparent sapphire crystal caseback; water resistant to 30atm.
Dial: black; Arabic numerals and hour markers with luminescent coating.
Bracelet: metal PANERAI-personalized with vertical brushed finishing and polished surfaces between the links.
Note: supplied with a steel screwdriver and tool to change the bracelet.
Suggested price: $11,000
Also available: brushed 316L steel on black PANERAI-personalized alligator strap (PAM00321, $10,100).

LUMINOR 1950 10 DAYS GMT CERAMICA REF. PAM00335

Movement: automatic-winding Panerai P.2003 caliber; 13¾ lines; thickness: 8mm; 10-day power reserve; 296 components; 25 jewels; 28,800 vph; Glucydur® balance; KIF Parechoc® antishock device; three barrels.
Functions: hours, minutes, seconds; date at 3; second time zone; 24-hour indicator at 9; linear power reserve indicator at 6; second reset.
Case: black ceramic; Ø 44mm; black ceramic bezel; black ceramic OP-personalized crown; antireflective sapphire corundum crystal; transparent smoked sapphire crystal caseback; water resistant to 10atm.
Dial: black; Arabic numerals and hour markers with luminescent coating.
Strap: black PANERAI-personalized leather; large-size titanium buckle with special hard black coating.
Note: supplied with a second interchangeable strap and a steel screwdriver.
Suggested price: $20,900
Also available: steel with black dial and PANERAI-personalised brown alligator strap (PAM00270, $17,900).

RADIOMIR CHRONOGRAPH REF. PAM00369

Movement: automatic-winding Panerai OP XXIII caliber; 12½ lines; thickness: 8mm; 42-hour power reserve; 37 jewels; 28,800 vph; monometallic Glucydur® balance; Incabloc® antishock device; Côtes de Genève on the bridges; COSC-certified chronograph.
Functions: hours, minutes; small seconds at 3; chronograph: 30-minute counter at 9 and central seconds hand.
Case: AISI 316L polished steel; Ø 42mm; polished steel bezel; OP-personalized winding crown; polished steel chronograph pushbuttons; antireflective sapphire corundum crystal; water resistant to 10atm.
Dial: black; Arabic numerals and hour markers with luminescent coating.
Strap: black PANERAI-personalized leather; polished steel buckle.
Suggested price: $7,600

RADIOMIR BLACK SEAL LOGO REF. PAM00380

Movement: manual-winding Panerai OP II caliber; 16½ lines; 56-hour power reserve; 17 jewels; 21,600 vph; monometallic Glucydur® balance; Incabloc® antishock device; COSC-certified chronograph.
Functions: hours, minutes; small seconds at 9.
Case: AISI 316L polished steel; Ø 45mm; polished steel bezel; patented with removable wire loop strap attachments; antireflective sapphire corundum crystal; screw-down steel caseback; water resistant to 10atm.
Dial: black; Arabic numerals and hour markers with luminescent coating.
Strap: black PANERAI-personalized leather; large-size polished steel buckle.
Suggested price: $4,600

PATEK PHILIPPE
GENEVE

LET HARMONY SING

Patek Philippe introduces two masterpieces of micro-mechanical genius that prove that the domain of the extraordinary is, for this leader of fine Swiss watchmaking, an everyday reality.

Patek's Philippe's Ref. 7000 Ladies First Minute Repeater is a proud testimony of the brand's passionate devotion to innovation and its absolute refusal to compromise. Though the Swiss manufacturer first presented repeaters for women more than a hundred years ago, in the form of necklaces, this timepiece with its delicate silhouette marks Patek Philippe's introduction of the queen of horological complications for the feminine wrist.

The Genevan house breaks from convention and rejects the idea that minute repeaters only belong in large wristwatches. Thanks to the self-winding R 27 PS caliber, with its off-centered 22K gold minirotor fully recessed in the plate, the Ladies First Minute Repeater boasts a diminutive height of 5.05mm. This technical finesse permits an aesthetic commitment to feminine elegance, turning time into a game of audible seduction.

The warm rose-gold case with convex bezel and cream-colored dial offers an exquisite playground for the tantalizing complication. The activating slide of the minute repeater finds a home at 9 o'clock, juxtaposed with the fluted crown on the right-hand side for perfect equilibrium. Nine applied Breguet numerals in rose gold and rose-gold pearls mark the periphery of a dial upon which the Poire Stuart hour and minute hands in 18K rose gold can conduct their symphony—and what a symphony it is.

While the resonant sound of the Patek Philippe repeater is a work of art in itself, the refined comprehension of the high degree of technical complexity of this ladies' timepiece is the wearer's ultimate delight.

LADIES FIRST MINUTE REPEATER REF. 7000
This ultra-thin exhibit of the queen of complications is an irresistible feminine interpretation of horological sophistication.

Another first in Patek Philippe's illustrious history is the presentation of the brand's Triple Complication Ref. 5208P. A triumph that underscores the Genevan manufacture's leadership in haute horology, this self-winding grand complication wristwatch features the supreme combination of minute repeater, monopusher chronograph, and instantaneous perpetual calendar with aperture displays, as well as moonphase. Though a self-winding movement with minute repeater mechanism does not allow the chronograph's arbors to extend through the strike train from the back, the calendar discs must lie directly beneath the dial to assure optimal legibility of the aperture displays. This monumental challenge of engineering required the manufacture's entire repository of expertise. The culmination is an intelligent arrangement of the 701 individual parts that permits all functions to harmonize flawlessly. The seeming simplicity of this watch, whose aesthetic humility is second only to its technical brilliance, is an exploit in itself.

The sapphire crystal caseback reveals the remarkable sight of the escapement and balance spring made of Silinivar®, a silicon derivative whose special properties make it ideal to power the masterful R CH 27 PS QI caliber. This hard, lightweight, anti-magnetic, corrosion-resistant, nearly friction-free material, in conjunction with Patek Philippe's innovative and patented geometry, produces the energy gain required to power the chronograph function.

In order to sustain the manufacture's hallmark of understated elegance, the arrangement of the 12 indications on the charcoal-colored solid-gold sunburst dial is impressively fit within a diameter of less than 40mm. Its calm yet assertive platinum case gives this fusion masterpiece a charisma that reflects the mechanical ingenuity of its elaborate construction.

This Triple Complication by Patek Philippe may fool an onlooker with its graceful design. The wearer of this feat of ingenious engineering, however, is sure to be regularly reminded of the countless innovations that went into producing a wristwatch of such understated complexity.

Patek Philippe's presentation of these two grand complication wristwatches, fit for a modern king and queen, is a resounding testament to the Genevan house's devotion to integrate its technical genius into a canvas of glorious elegance.

TRIPLE COMPLICATION REF. 5208P

If the wearer of this highly complex *coup d'élégance* is patient, a veritable ballet awaits him at the year's change, when the elements of the perpetual calendar present their own harmonious extravaganza.

GRAND COMPLICATION — REF. 5073P

Movement: automatic-winding R 27 Q caliber; Ø 28mm, thickness: 6.9mm; 48-hour power reserve; 467 components; 39 jewels; 21,600 vph; Gyromax® balance; flat balance spring; adjustable balance spring stud; Patek Philippe hallmark.
Functions: hours, minutes; date at 6; minute repeater with cathedral gongs; perpetual calendar: day of week, 24-hour display, month and leap-year cycle; moonphase.
Case: 950 platinum; Ø 42mm, thickness: 11.11mm; bezel and lugs set with 103 baguette diamonds (4.33 carats); two-position crown (pulled out: to set the time and pushed in: to wind the watch); diamond set lugs at 6 (approx. 0.02 carat); slide on the left side of the case to actuate the minute repeater; solid platinum interchangeable caseback with sapphire crystal window.

Dial: black; thirteen baguette diamond (0.25 carat) hour markers; 18K white gold leaf-shaped hour, minute, date, day and month hands; baton-style 18K white-gold and white-lacquered hands for 24-hour display and leap-year cycle; railway track minute scale on dial periphery.
Strap: hand-stitched large-scale shiny black alligator leather; platinum fold-over clasp set with 42 baguette diamonds (0.69 carats).
Price: available upon request.
Note: complimentary correction stylus in ebony and 18K white gold.

CALIBER R 27 Q

Movement: automatic-winding R 27 Q caliber; Ø 28mm, thickness: 6.9mm; 48-hour power reserve; 467 components; 39 jewels; 21,600 vph; Gyromax® balance; flat balance spring; adjustable balance spring stud; Patek Philippe hallmark.
Functions: hours, date at 6, minutes; minute repeater with cathedral gongs; perpetual calendar: day of week, 24-hour display, month, and leap-year cycle; moonphase.

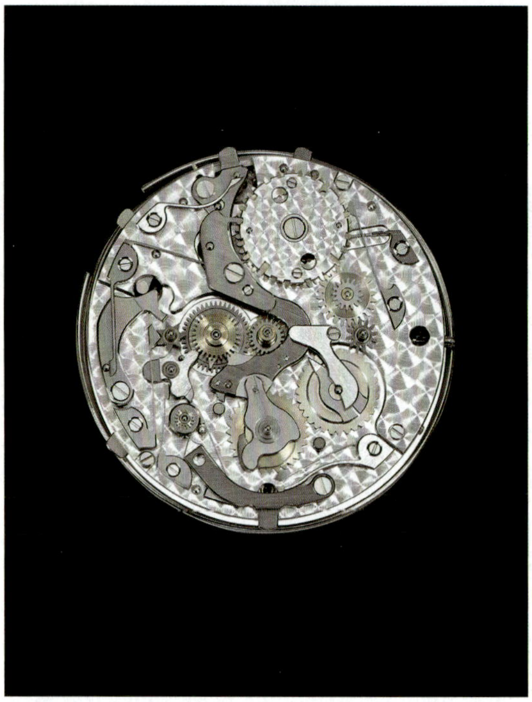

TRIPLE COMPLICATION — REF. 5208P

Movement: automatic-winding R CH 27 PS QI caliber; Ø 32mm, thickness: 10.35mm; 48-hour power reserve; 701 components; 58 jewels; 21,600 vph; Gyromax® balance; Spiromax® balance spring; Pulsomax® (lever and escape wheel in Silinvar®) escapement; adjustable balance spring stud; Patek Philippe hallmark.
Functions: hours, minutes; small seconds at 6; chronograph: 12-hour counter at 9, 60-minute counter at 3 and central sweep seconds hand; instantaneous perpetual calendar: day, date, month, and leap-year cycle; day/night indicator; minute repeater; moonphase.

Case: 950 platinum; Ø 44mm, thickness: 15.7mm; two-position crown at 3 (pulled out: to set the time and pushed in: to wind the watch); three-phase chronograph monopusher at 2 to start, stop, reset; diamond lugs at 6 (approx. 0.02 carat); 950 platinum slide on the left side of the case to activate the minute repeater; platinum interchangeable caseback with sapphire crystal window.
Dial: 18K white gold; sunburst charcoal finish; eleven applied obus 18K white-gold hour markers; 18K white-gold dauphine-style hour and minute hands; baton-style counterbalanced 18K white-gold and white lacquered chronograph hands; baton-style 18K white-gold and white lacquered 12-hour, 60-minute and small seconds hands; railway track scale on dial periphery; 18K white-gold hammered and diamond-polished date, day and month disc.
Strap: hand-stitched large-scale alligator leather; matte black, platinum fold-over clasp.
Price: available upon request.
Note: complimentary correction stylus in ebony and 18K white gold.

CALIBER R CH 27 PS QI

Movement: automatic-winding R CH 27 PS QI caliber; Ø 32mm, thickness: 10.35mm; 48-hour power reserve; 701 components; 58 jewels; 21,600 vph; Gyromax® balance; Spiromax® balance spring; Pulsomax® (lever and escape wheel in Silinvar®) escapement; adjustable balance spring stud; Patek Philippe hallmark.
Functions: hours, minutes; small seconds at 6; chronograph: 12-hour counter at 9, 60-minute counter at 3 and central sweep seconds hand; instantaneous perpetual calendar: day, date, month, and leap-year cycle; day/night indicator; minute repeater; moonphase.

GRAND COMPLICATION REF. 5216R

Movement: manual-winding R TO 27 PS QR LU caliber; Ø 28mm, thickness: 8.6mm; 48-hour power reserve; 506 components; 28 jewels; 21,600 vph; Gyromax® balance; Breguet balance spring; adjustable balance spring stud; Patek Philippe hallmark.
Functions: hours, minutes; small seconds at 6; retrograde date on an arc from 8 to 4; minute repeater; tourbillon; perpetual calendar: day of week, month and leap-year cycle; moonphase.
Case: 5N 18K rose gold; Ø 39.5mm, thickness: 12.23mm; two-position crown (pulled out: to set the time and pushed in: to wind the watch); slide on the left side of the case to actuate the minute repeater; solid 18K rose-gold interchangeable caseback with sapphire crystal window.
Dial: silvery opalescent; thirteen applied obus 18K rose-gold hour markers; dauphine-style 18K rose-gold hour and minute hands; date scale with black Arabic numerals from 1 to 31 and a red-tipped arrow hand; 18K rose-gold pearl minute markers on the dial periphery.
Strap: hand-stitched large-scale shiny chocolate brown alligator leather; 18K rose-gold fold-over clasp.
Price: available upon request.
Note: complimentary correction stylus in ebony and 18K rose gold.

CALIBER R 27 PS QR

Movement: manual-winding R TO 27 PS QR LU caliber; Ø 28mm, thickness: 8.6mm; 48-hour power reserve; 506 components; 28 jewels; 21,600 vph; Gyromax® balance; Breguet balance spring; adjustable balance spring stud; Patek Philippe hallmark.
Functions: hours, minutes; small seconds at 6; retrograde date on an arc from 8 to 4; minute repeater; tourbillon; perpetual calendar: day of week, month, and leap-year cycle; moonphase.

PERPETUAL CALENDAR CHRONOGRAPH REF. 5270G

Movement: manual-winding CH 29-535 PS Q caliber; Ø 32mm, thickness: 7mm; 65-hour power reserve; 456 components; 33 jewels; 28,800 vph; Gyromax® balance; Breguet balance spring; Patek Philippe hallmark.
Functions: hours, minutes; small seconds at 9; date at 6; column-wheel chronograph: instantaneous 30-minute counter at 3 and central seconds hand; perpetual calendar: day, month, leap-year cycle and day/night indication; moonphase.
Case: 18K white gold; Ø 41mm, thickness: 12.4mm; two-position crown (pulled out: to set the time and pushed in: to wind the watch); chronograph pushers (start/stop at 2 and reset at 4); slide on the left side of the case to actuate the minute repeater; sapphire crystal; screwed sapphire crystal caseback with window; water resistant to 3atm.
Dial: silvery opalescent; twelve applied black-oxidized gold hour markers; leaf-shaped black-oxidized gold hour and minute hands; counter-balanced chronograph hand from the center; counters with circular guilloché pattern; leaf-shaped black-oxidized gold hands for 30-minute, small seconds and date.
Strap: hand-stitched large-scale alligator matte black leather; 18K white-gold fold-over clasp.
Price: available upon request.
Note: complimentary correction stylus in ebony and 18K white gold.

CALIBER CH 29-535 PS Q

Movement: manual-winding CH 29-535 PS Q caliber; Ø 32mm, thickness: 7mm; 65-hour power reserve; 456 components; 33 jewels; 28,800 vph; Gyromax® balance; Breguet balance spring; Patek Philippe hallmark.
Functions: hours, minutes; small seconds at 9; date at 6; column-wheel chronograph: 30-minute counter at 3 and central seconds hand; perpetual calendar: day, month, leap-year cycle and day/night indication; moonphase.

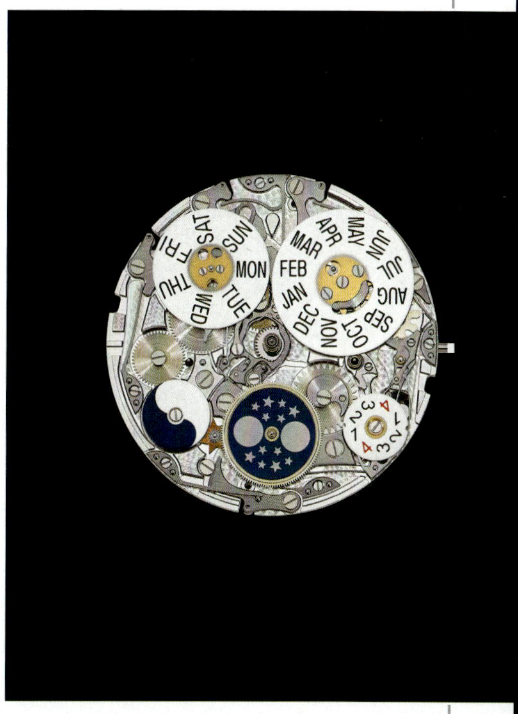

ANNUAL CALENDAR CHRONOGRAPH REF. 5960P

Movement: automatic-winding CH 28-520 IRM QA 24H caliber; Ø 33mm, thickness: 7.68mm; 55-hour power reserve; 456 components; 40 jewels; 28,800 vph; four-arm Gyromax balance, four poising weights; Breguet balance spring.
Functions: hours, minutes; date at 12; power reserve indicator at 12; column-wheel chronograph: combined monocounter 60-minute counter (counts the elapsed minutes on two concentric scales from 0 to 30 in blue and from 30 to 60 in black) and 12-hour counter at 6 and central sweep seconds hand; annual calendar: day of week between 10 and 11; month between 1 and 2; day/night indicator at 6.
Case: 950 platinum; Ø 40.5mm, thickness: 13.55mm; cambered sapphire crystal; sapphire crystal caseback; water resistant to 3atm.
Dial: matte blue sunburst and silvered; eight 18K white-gold hour markers; eleven SuperLumiNova luminescent dots; 18K white-gold leaf-shaped hour and minute hands with SuperLumiNova; rhodium-plated steel baton-style chronograph hand with counterweight; rhodium-plated 18K white-gold power reserve indicator with baton-style hand; subdial with circular guilloché pattern and a matte blue center and silvery periphery; white-lacquered brass baton-style hour-counter hand with counterweight; red-lacquered brass baton-style minute counter hand with counterweight.
Strap: hand-stitched large-scaled blue alligator; platinum fold-over clasp.
Price: available upon request.

ANNUAL CALENDAR REGULATOR REF. 5235G

Movement: automatic-winding 31-260 REG QA caliber; ultra-thin; Ø 33mm (basic caliber 31.74mm, annual calendar 33mm), thickness: 5.08mm (basic caliber 2.6mm, annual calendar 2.48mm); 60-hour power reserve; components 320 (basic caliber 181, annual calendar 139); 29 jewels; 23,040 vph; 22K gold unidirectionally mini winding rotor; Gyromax® balance; Spiromax® balance spring; Pulsomax® escapement (lever and escape wheel in Silinvar®); adjustable balance spring stud; Patek Philippe hallmark.
Functions: sweep minute hand; small seconds at 6; 12-hour counter at 12; date at 6; annual calendar: day of week at 10 and month at 2.
Case: 18K white gold; Ø 40.5mm, thickness: 10.65mm; two-position crown (pulled out: to set the time and pushed in: to wind the watch); sapphire crystal caseback; water resistant to 3atm.
Dial: silvery gray, vertical satin finish; blue transfer printed regulator displays; blued steel hour, minute, and seconds hands; railway track minute scale on periphery, blue transfer printed; PATEK PHILIPPE GENEVE engraving at 3.
Strap: hand-stitched large-scale matte night-blue alligator leather; 18K white-gold 16mm prong buckle with Patek Philippe engraving.
Price: available upon request.
Note: complimentary correction stylus in ebony and 18K white gold.

CHRONOGRAPH REF. 5170J

Movement: manual-winding CH 29-535 PS caliber; Ø 29.6mm, thickness: 5.35mm; 65-hour power reserve; 269 components; 33 jewels; 28,800 vph; four-arm Gyromax balance, four poising weights; Breguet balance spring.
Functions: hours, minutes; small seconds at 9; column-wheel chronograph: instantaneous 30-minute counter between 3 and 4 and central sweep seconds; chronograph start and stop at 2; chronograph reset at 4.
Case: 18K yellow gold; Ø 39mm, thickness: 10.9mm; two-position crown (push: to wind the watch; pull: to set the time and stop seconds); sapphire crystal, screw-down sapphire crystal caseback; water resistant to 3atm.
Dial: silvery opaline; Pulsimeter scale calibrated to 15 beats and railway-track minute scale, transfer-printed in black along the periphery; six applied baton-style 18K yellow-gold hour markers; two applied 18K yellow-gold Roman numerals at 12 and 6; 18K yellow-gold baton-style hour and minute hands; black oxidized counterbalanced arrow-style chronograph hand; white subdials with circular guilloché patterns; 18K yellow-gold baton-style hands; 18K yellow-gold black nickel-plated baton-style hands.
Strap: hand-stitched large-scale matte brown alligator skin; 18K yellow-gold fold-over clasp.
Price: available upon request.

ADVANCED RESEARCH PERPETUAL CALENDAR REF. 5550P

Movement: automatic-winding 240 Q Si caliber; ultra-thin; Ø 27.5mm, thickness: 3.88mm; 70-hour power reserve; 281 components; 25 jewels; 21,600 vph; 22K gold unidirectional Mini winding rotor; Oscillomax® balance; GyromaxSi® (in Silinvar® and 24K gold); Spiromax® balance spring (in Silinvar®); Pulsomax® escapement (lever and escape wheel in Silinvar®); Patek Philippe hallmark.
Functions: hours, minutes; date at 6; perpetual calendar: day of the week, month, and leap-year cycle; moonphase; 24-hour display.
Case: 950 platinum; Ø 37.2mm, thickness: 8.8mm; lugs at 12 set with one diamond (0.02 carat); two-position crown (pulled out: to set the time and pushed in: to wind the watch); snap-on sapphire crystal caseback with integrated loupe; water resistant to 3atm.
Dial: silvery gray, vertical satin finish; Advanced Research inscription; twelve obus 18K rose-gold hour markers with luminous coating; 18K rose-gold leaf-shaped hour and minute hands with luminous coating; 18K rose-gold leaf-shaped hands for 24-hour display, leap-year cycle, date, day of week, and month.
Strap: hand-stitched large-scale shiny chocolate brown alligator leather; platinum fold-over clasp.
Price: available upon request.
Note: complimentary correction stylus in ebony and 18K white gold.

SPLIT-SECONDS MONOPUSHER CHRONOGRAPH WITH PERPETUAL CALENDAR REF. 5951P

Movement: manual-winding CHR 27-525 PS Q caliber; Ø 27.3mm, thickness: 7.3mm; 48-hour power reserve; 400 components; 27 jewels; 21,600 vph; two-arm Gyromax balance, eight poising weights; Breguet balance spring.
Functions: hours, minute; small seconds at 9; split-seconds monopusher chronograph with column-wheel: 60-minute counter at 3, date at 6 and central rattrapante seconds hand; perpetual calendar: day, month, leap-year cycle and day/night indication; moonphase.
Case: 950 platinum; Ø 37mm, thickness: 12.35mm; interchangeable solid platinum and sapphire crystal caseback; satin-finished frame with fold-filled engravings in the corners; water resistant to 3atm.
Dial: black; transfer-printed railway track minute scale; twelve applied 18K white-gold baton-style hour markers; 18K white-gold leaf-shaped hour and minute hands; red painted arrow-style counterbalanced sweep chronograph and rattrapante hands; rhodium-plated subdials with circular guilloché patterns; 18K white-gold and painted black leaf-shaped seconds hand; 18K white-gold and painted red leaf-shaped minute-counter hand; rhodium-plated date subdial with black center and 18K white-gold and painted white leaf-shaped hand.
Strap: hand-stitched large-scale matte black alligator with red stitching; platinum prong buckle.
Price: available upon request.

SPLIT-SECONDS MONOPUSHER CHRONOGRAPH REF. 5950A

Movement: manual-winding CHR 27-525 PS caliber; Ø 27.3mm, thickness: 5.25mm; 48-hour power reserve; 252 components; 27 jewels; 21,600 vph; two-arm Gyromax balance, eight poising weights; Breguet balance spring.
Functions: hours, minutes; small seconds at 9; split-seconds monopusher chronograph with column-wheel: 60-minute counter at 3 and central rattrapante seconds hand.
Case: stainless steel; Ø 37mm, thickness: 10.15mm; cambered sapphire crystal caseback; interchangeable solid stainless steel and sapphire crystal snap caseback; satin-finished frame with fold-filled engravings in the corners; water resistant to 3atm.
Dial: silvery opaline; black lacquered corner engravings; transfer-printed railway-track minute scale along the periphery; ten applied 18K white-gold and black oxidized Breguet numerals; 18K yellow-gold and black oxidized leaf-shaped hour and minute markers; black oxidized counterbalanced chronograph and rattrapante arrow-style hands; subdials with circular guilloché patterns; 18K yellow-gold and black oxidized leaf-shaped hands; 18K yellow-gold and black oxidized leaf-shaped hand.
Strap: hand-stitched large-scale shiny brown alligator skin; 18K white-gold prong buckle with black-lacquered engraving.
Price: available upon request.

LADIES FIRST MINUTE REPEATER REF. 7000R

Movement: automatic-winding R 27 PS caliber; Ø 28mm, thickness: 5.05mm; 48-hour power reserve; 342 components; 39 jewels; 21,600 vph; 22K gold unidirectional mini winding rotor; Gyromax® balance; flat balance spring; adjustable balance spring stud; Patek Philippe hallmark.
Functions: hours, minutes; small seconds at 6; minute repeater.
Case: 4N 18K rose gold; Ø 33.7mm, thickness: 9.5mm; two-position crown (pulled out: to set the time and pushed in: to wind the watch); slide on the left side of the case to activate the minute repeater; sapphire crystal; solid 18K rose-gold interchangeable caseback with sapphire-crystal window.
Dial: cream-colored; transfer-printed in antique rose gold; nine applied 18K rose-gold Breguet numerals; Poire Stuart 18K rose-gold hour and minute hands; 18K rose-gold small seconds hand.
Strap: hand-stitched large-scale matte mother-of-pearl hue alligator leather; 18K rose-gold prong buckle.
Price: available upon request.

LADIES FIRST SPLIT-SECONDS CHRONOGRAPH REF. 7059R

Movement: manual-winding CHR 27-525 PS caliber; ultra thin; Ø 27.3mm, thickness: 5.25mm; 48-hour power reserve; 252 components; 27 jewels; 21,600 vph; 2-arm Gyromax balance with eight poising weights; Breguet balance spring.
Functions: hours, minutes; small seconds at 9; chronograph: 60-minute counter at 3 and central split-seconds hands.
Case: 4N 18K rose gold; Ø 33.2mm, thickness: 8.6mm; bezel set with 153 flawless Top Wesselton diamonds (0.72 carat); cambered sapphire crystal; two-position crown (pulled out: to set the time and pushed in: to wind the watch); screwed sapphire crystal caseback set with 76 flawless Top Wesselton diamonds (0.40 carat); water resistant to 3atm.
Dial: matte opalescent; powder rose imprint; ten applied 18K rose-gold Breguet numerals; Poire Stuart 18K rose-gold hour and minute hands; counter balanced 18K rose-gold chronograph and split-seconds hands; 18K rose-gold hands for small seconds and 60-minute.
Strap: hand-stitched large-scale matte mother-of-pearl hue alligator leather; 18K rose-gold prong buckle set with 26 diamonds (0.18 carat).
Price: available upon request.

PIAGET

ELEGANT EXPOSURE

For more than a half a century, Piaget has written some of the finest chapters in the history of ultra-thin movements.

Drawing upon its exceptional wealth of expertise, the Swiss watchmaker proudly presents two record-setting watches of elegant exhibitionism. With its newly unveiled Piaget Altiplano Skeleton Ultra-Thin, the manufacture expresses its devotion to the purity of the essential. Powering the world's thinnest self-winding skeleton model (5.34mm) with the world's thinnest self-winding skeleton movement (2.4mm), Piaget takes a daring leap forward in the art of the openwork concept.

Derived from the 1200P caliber, the finely tuned 1200S caliber boasts an hour-wheel bridge—slimmed down to a mere 0.11mm—that ensures the extreme thinness of this unprecedented movement. While the exceptional size of this mechanism is a revelation of Piaget's unique expertise in the field of the ultra-thin, the stunning quality of the artwork is a testament to the skills of the house's artisan engravers. The creation of this thinnest-ever openwork movement was a challenge appropriately reserved for the finest craftsmen in the world. New calculations and innovative design conceptions, such as the long curves that extend across the mainplate and bridges, were vital in order to engrave and hollow this masterpiece without influencing its rigidity, and consequently its performance. It is this coordinated rapport between engineering and artistry that allows Piaget to continuously conquer new ground in the fields of skeletonization and of the infinitesimally small.

The acme of more than three years of research and development, Piaget's 1200S caliber features a micro-rotor in 950 platinum, further enhancing the exclusivity of this exceptional movement, and is housed within a specifically designed 38mm white-gold case. This harmonious interaction between the heart of a timepiece and the body in which it resides is a display of synchronized mastery that pervades this decisively modern timepiece.

In its pursuit of micro-excellence, Piaget never neglects the house's prestigious tradition of refined aesthetics. The use of contrast between sunray-brushed or sandblasted matte surfaces, polished angles, and the rhodium or black colors, gives this timepiece the sophisticated visuals that allow the wearer to fully experience its uninhibited intricacies.

The Piaget Altiplano Skeleton Ultra-Thin is a truly exceptional display of masterful precision and intelligent harmonization of the manufacture's full range of competencies. By integrating a commitment to beauty into the process of mechanical conception, Piaget brilliantly shrugs off the traditional limits of haute horology.

PIAGET ALTIPLANO SKELETON ULTRA-THIN

This openwork record-setter exposes the entirety of its finely decorated ultra-thin movement, rewarding the curiosity of its owner.

Joining this twice record-setting timepiece that captures the purity of essentialism, is a wristwatch that honors the codes of Piaget's collections with an exceptional world-first stance of its own.

The Emperador Coussin Tourbillon Automatic Ultra-Thin boasts a movement derived from the house's 600P caliber, the world's thinnest shaped hand-wound tourbillon movement, and 1208P caliber, the world's thinnest self-winding movement equipped with a micro-rotor. The culmination, Piaget's 1270P caliber, is a 5.5mm-thick, cushion-shaped, self-winding tourbillon movement featuring components as small as 0.12mm. This exceptional result of a three-year development process is the epitome of authentic Swiss watchmaking, using a tradition of excellence to push the limits of the ultra-thin concept.

This newest member of the Piaget Emperador collection, however, does not rest on its laurels of micro-mechanical innovation. Its powerful design and decidedly avant-garde character make it a timepiece of stunning contemporary elegance. The laser-engraved sapphire crystal, through which the wearer can admire the offset gold micro-rotor and imposing tourbillon carriage, acts as a window into the fascinating world of haute horology's most intricate components. This confident overturning of the established aesthetics of fine watchmaking forms a symbolic figure eight, a tribute to the Swiss manufacture's lucky number. The decision to present a transparent view of the intricate mechanism is a demonstration of Piaget's commitment to placing technical mastery at the service of design.

Continuing the architectural theme of the watch, the tapered hour markers point to the off-centered hour and minute hands at 5 o'clock in a daring rejection of the conventional center. The cushion-shaped Emperador case, in 18-karat pink or white gold, mirrors the geometry of the extremely complex 269-part mechanism that allows this watch to measure a record-setting 10.4mm in thickness.

The aesthetic codes inherent to Piaget's Black Tie collection are interpreted in elegant, contemporary fashion, as can be admired through the delicate laser-guilloché work on the dial and the beautifully highlighted gold-rimmed oscillating weight and tourbillon displays. Fitted with a brown or black alligator strap with 18-karat gold folding clasp, this daring timepiece features a 40-hour power reserve, displayed through an opening in the delicately engraved caseback.

The contrast of resolute modernity and traditional haute horology adds a timeless element to the Emperador Coussin Tourbillon Automatic Ultra-Thin and highlights the constant innovation that defines Piaget's proud heritage. A picture of technical ingenuity, the brilliant craftsmanship of this timepiece truly honors the elegant beauty of mechanical excellence.

With the launch of these two record-setting masterpieces, Piaget continues a prestigious lineage that is founded on the pioneering mastery of the ultra-thin. Utilizing its vast range of skills, the manufacture presents a pair of stunning wristwatches that let their virtues spread from the very core.

EMPERADOR COUSSIN TOURBILLON AUTOMATIC ULTRA-THIN

The dial-side view of this timepiece's superb inner workings is a testament to Piaget's passion for the beauty of mechanical excellence.

1270P MOVEMENT

Piaget's first ultra-thin self-winding tourbillon movement powers the Emperador Coussin Tourbillon Automatic Ultra-Thin.

PIAGET EMPERADOR — REF. GOA33069

Movement: automatic-winding Piaget 551P caliber; Ø 20.5mm, thickness: 4.9mm; approx. 40-hour power reserve; 27 jewels; 21,600 vph; circular Côtes de Genève; circular grained plate; beveled bridges, blued screws on bridges.
Functions: hours, minutes; small seconds at 10; power reserve indicator at 6.
Case: 18K white gold.
Dial: silvered sunburst guilloché; applied 18K white-gold hour markers; Piaget coat of arms.
Strap: black alligator leather; 18K white-gold pin buckle.

PIAGT EMPERADOR SKELETON — REF. GOA30037

Movement: manual-winding Piaget 600D caliber; ultra-thin; 28.6x22.4mm, thickness: 3.5mm; approx. 40-hour power reserve; 23 jewels; 21,600 vph; diamond-set skeleton tourbillon; diamond-set gold plate (160 diamonds, 0.4 carat and 7 cabochon sapphires, 0.2 carat); guilloché bridges; hand-circular-grained plate and bridges; hand-bevelled and hand-drawn bridges and carriage.
Functions: hours, minutes, seconds; flying tourbillon at 12.
Case: 18K white gold; set with 151 diamonds (approx. 2.4 carats); sapphire crystal caseback.
Strap: black alligator leather; 18K white-gold folding clasp set with 26 diamonds (approx. 0.4 carat).

PIAGET EMPERADOR COUSSIN PERPETUAL CALENDAR — REF. GOA33019

Movement: automatic-winding Piaget 855P caliber; ultra-thin; Ø 28.4mm, thickness: 5.6mm; approx. 72-hour power reserve; 38 jewels; 21,600 vph; circular Côtes de Genève; circular-grained mainplate; bevelled bridges, blued screws on bridges; oscillating weight engraved with the Piaget coat of arms.
Functions: hours, minutes; small seconds at 4; perpetual calendar: retrograde date at 3; second time zone at 8; day/night indicator; retrograde day at 9; month and leap year cycle at 12.
Case: 18K pink gold; Ø 46.5mm; sapphire crystal caseback.
Dial: blue; three satin-finished counters; applied 18K pink-gold hour markers.
Strap: brown alligator leather; 18K pink-gold folding clasp.

PIAGET EMPERADOR COUSSIN MOON PHASE — REF. GOA34022

Movement: automatic-winding Piaget 860P caliber; Ø 28.4mm, thickness: 6.1mm; approx. 72-hour power reserve; 25 jewels; 21,600 vph; circular Côtes de Genève; circular-grained mainplate; bevelled bridges; oscillating weight engraved with the Piaget coat of arms.
Functions: hours, minutes; moonphase.
Case: 18K pink gold; Ø 46.5mm; sapphire crystal caseback.
Dial: blue; silvered center; applied 18K pink-gold hour markers; large 18K white-gold moon at 6.
Strap: brown alligator leather; 18K pink-gold folding clasp.

PIAGET EMPERADOR COUSSIN REF. G0A36016

Movement: automatic-winding Piaget 850P caliber; Ø 26.8mm, thickness: 4mm; approx. 72-hour power reserve; 30 jewels; 21,600 vph; circular Côtes de Genève; circular-grained plate; bevelled bridges, blued screws on bridges.
Functions: hours, minutes; small seconds at 4; date at 12; second time zone at 8; day/night indicator.
Case: 18K white gold; Ø 42mm; sapphire crystal caseback.
Dial: slate-gray; sunburst guilloché; polished 18K white-gold counters; applied 18K white-gold hour markers.
Strap: slate-gray alligator leather; 18K white-gold folding clasp.

PIAGET EMPERADOR COUSSIN XL TOURBILLON REF. G0A36041

Movement: automatic-winding Piaget 1270P caliber; ultra-thin; Ø 34.9mm, thickness: 5.5mm; approx. 40-hour power reserve; 35 jewels; 21,600 vph; circular Côtes de Genève; circular-grained plate and bridges; hand-bevelled and hand-drawn plate; hand circular-grained; hand-drawn and sunburst, satin-brushed bridges, blued screws on bridges; circular satin-brushed wheels and sunburst satin-brushed barrel cover.
Functions: hours, minutes, seconds; flying tourbillon power reserve indicator on the back.
Case: 18K pink gold; Ø 46.5mm; small sapphire crystal caseback.
Dial: laser engraved sapphire crystal.
Strap: brown alligator leather; 18K pink-gold folding clasp.

PIAGET ALTIPLANO REF. G0A29112

Movement: manual-winding Piaget 430P caliber; ultra-thin; Ø 20.5mm, thickness: 2.1mm; 18 jewels; 21,600 vph; circular Côtes de Genève; circular-grained plate and bridges; beveled bridges, blued screws on bridges.
Functions: hours, minutes.
Case: 18K white gold; Ø 38mm.
Dial: white; black baton hour markers.
Strap: black alligator leather; 18K white-gold pin buckle.

PIAGET ALTIPLANO REF. G0A35131

Movement: automatic-winding Piaget 1208P caliber; ultra-thin; Ø 29.9mm, thickness: 2.35mm; approx. 40-hour power reserve; 27 jewels; 21,600 vph; circular Côtes de Genève; circular-grained plate; sunburst-brushed wheels; "P" fixed to the regulator-assembly as Piaget signature; bevelled bridges, blued screws on bridges; pink-gold oscillating weight engraved with the Piaget coat of arms.
Functions: hours, minutes; small seconds at 5.
Case: 18K pink gold; Ø 43mm; sapphire crystal caseback.
Dial: silvered; black baton hour markers.
Strap: brown alligator leather; 18K pink-gold pin buckle.

PIAGET ALTIPLANO REF. G0A33115

Movement: manual-winding Piaget 838S caliber; ultra-thin; skeleton; Ø 26.8mm, thickness: 2.7mm; approx. 60-hour power reserve; 19 jewels; 21,600 vph; sunburst guilloché motif; hand-circular-grained plate and bridges; hand-bevelled and hand-drawn plate and bridges; blued screws on bridges.
Functions: hours, minutes; small seconds at 10.
Case: 18K white gold; Ø 40mm; sapphire crystal caseback.
Dial: silvered flange.
Strap: black alligator leather; 18K white-gold pin buckle.

PIAGET ALTIPLANO REF. G0A34113

Movement: manual-winding Piaget 838P caliber; ultra-thin; Ø 26.8mm, thickness: 2.5mm; approx. 60-hour power reserve; 19 jewels; 21,600 vph; circular Côtes de Genève; circular-grained plate; bevelled bridges, blued screws on bridges; engraved with the Piaget coat of arms.
Functions: hours, minutes; small seconds at 10.
Case: 18K pink gold; Ø 40mm; sapphire crystal caseback.
Dial: silvered; black baton hour markers.
Strap: brown alligator leather; 18K pink-gold ardillon buckle.

PIAGET ALTIPLANO REF. G0A36129

Movement: manual-winding Piaget 430P caliber; ultra-thin; Ø 20.5mm, thickness: 2.1mm; approx. 40-hour power reserve; 18 jewels; 21,600 vph; circular Côtes de Genève; circular grained plate and bridges; bevelled bridges; blued screws on bridges.
Functions: hours, minutes.
Case: 18K white gold; Ø 38mm; set with 78 diamonds (approx. 0.7 carat).
Dial: 18K white gold; set with 735 diamonds (approx. 2.1 carat); applied 18K white-gold hour markers.
Strap: black alligator leather; 18K white-gold ardillon buckle set with 23 diamonds (approx. 0.05 carat).

PIAGET ALTIPLANO REF. G0A36107

Movement: manual-winding Piaget 450P caliber; ultra-thin; Ø 20.5mm, thickness: 2.1mm; approx. 40-hour power reserve; 18 jewels; 21,600 vph; circular Côtes de Genève; circular-grained plate and bridges; bevelled bridges, blued screws on bridges.
Functions: hours, minutes; small seconds at 10.
Case: 18K pink gold; Ø 34mm; set with 72 diamonds (approx. 0.5 carat).
Dial: white; 18K pink-gold small seconds subdial set with 28 diamonds (approx. 0.1 carat); gilded Roman numerals.
Strap: white alligator leather; 18K pink-gold ardillon buckle.

PIAGET POLO FORTYFIVE CHRONOGRAPH REF. GOA34002

Movement: automatic-winding Piaget 880P caliber; ultra-thin; Ø 27mm, thickness: 5.6mm; approx. 50-hour power reserve; 35 jewels; 28,800 vph; circular Côtes de Genève; circular-grained mainplate; bevelled bridges, blued screws on bridges; black PVD-treated oscillating weight engraved with the Piaget coat of arms.
Functions: hours, minutes; small seconds at 6; date at 12; second 24-hour time zone at 9; flyback chronograph: 30-minute counter at 3.
Case: titanium; Ø 45mm; titanium bezel with alternating satin-brushed surfaces and polished steel gadroons; titanium and rubber screw-down crown and push-buttons; sapphire crystal caseback; water resistant to 10atm.
Dial: black; applied hour markers with luminescent coating.
Strap: black rubber with steel inserts; steel triple-folding safety clasp with summer/winter positions.

PIAGET POLO REF. GOA31149

Movement: automatic-winding Piaget 800P caliber; Ø 26.8mm, thickness: 4mm; approx. 72-hour power reserve; 25 jewels; 21,600 vph; circular Côtes de Genève; circular-grained plate; beveled bridges, blued screws on bridges; oscillating weight engraved with the Piaget coat of arms.
Functions: hours, minutes, seconds; date at 6.
Case: 18K pink gold; Ø 43mm; sapphire crystal caseback.
Dial: silvered; applied 18K pink-gold Arabic numerals and hour markers.
Strap: brown alligator leather; 18K pink-gold folding clasp.

PIAGET POLO FORTYFIVE LADY REF. GOA35013

Movement: quartz; Piaget 15P caliber.
Functions: hours, minutes, seconds; date at 6.
Case: 18K pink gold; Ø 38mm; bezel set with 50 brilliant-cut diamonds (approx 0.7 carat); polished gadroons; water resistant to 5atm.
Dial: white; set with 8 brilliant-cut diamonds (approx. 0.05 carat); applied hour markers and Arabic numerals with luminescent coating.
Strap: white rubber with 18K pink-gold inserts; 18K pink-gold pin buckle.

PIAGET POLO TOURBILLON RELATIF REF.GOA35123

Movement: manual-winding Piaget 608P caliber; Ø 25.6mm, thickness: 9.1mm; approx. 72-hour power reserve; 21,600 vph; circular Côtes de Genève; hand-circular-grained plate and bridges; hand-bevelled and hand-drawn bridges and carriage; engraved coat of arms; blued screws on bridges.
Functions: hours, minutes; seconds; flying tourbillon.
Case: 18K white gold; Ø 45mm; black PVD treated bezel.
Dial: black; applied white-gold Arabic numeral and hour markers.
Strap: black alligator leather, rubber touch; 18K white-gold folding clasp.

LIMELIGHT MAGIC HOUR — REF. GOA35099

Movement: quartz; Piaget 56P caliber.
Functions: hours, minutes.
Case: 18K pink gold; set with 302 brilliant-cut diamonds (approx. 4.9 carats).
Dial: white flinqué; applied pink-gold diamond-set Arabic numeral; copper-colored hour markers.
Strap: brown satin; 18K pink-gold set ardillon buckle.

Note: an invisible mechanism developed in-house endows this timepiece with the unique power to be three watches in one: when positioned horizontally, the ellipse provides a generous dial opening with timeless style; with a gentle touch, the oval swivels to take an impish slant; with another 45° turn, diamond-set golden numerals are revealed.

PIAGET LIMELIGHT TWICE — REF. GOA34137

ONE WATCH, TWO DIALS: two quartz 56P calibers; total of 332 brilliant-cut diamonds (approx. 6 carats); black satin strap with reversible integrated clasp.
FIRST DIAL:
Case: 18K white gold; 52 brilliant-cut diamonds (approx. 1.2 carats).
Dial: silver colored; black Roman numerals.
Clasp: 18K white gold.

SECOND DIAL:
Case: 18K white gold; sunburst motif; set with 226 brilliant-cut diamonds (approx. 4.6 carats).
Dial: black.
Clasp: 18K white gold; set with 54 brilliant-cut diamonds (approx. 0.2 carat).

LIMELIGHT DANCING LIGHT — REF. GOA36157

Movement: quartz; Piaget 56P caliber.
Functions: hours, minutes.
Case: 18K pink gold; set with 68 brilliant-cut diamonds (approx. 1.7 carats).
Dial: silvered; 18K pink-gold rotating circle set with 98 brilliant-cut diamonds (approx. 0.2 carat); applied and polished 18K pink-gold Roman numerals and hour markers.
Strap: brown satin; 18K pink-gold ardillon buckle set with 15 brilliant-cut diamonds (approx. 0.1 carat).

LIMELIGHT DANCING LIGHT — REF. GOA36158

Movement: quartz; Piaget 56P caliber.
Functions: hours, minutes.
Case: 18K white gold; set with 52 brilliant-cut diamonds (approx. 1.6 carats).
Dial: 18K white gold; diamond-paved set with 335 brilliant-cut diamonds (approx. 2.3 carats); applied and polished 18K white-gold Roman numerals and hour markers.
Bracelet: 18K white gold; set with 522 brilliant-cut diamonds (approx. 16.3 carats) with an integrated folding clasp.

PIAGET TRADITION REF. G0A10800

Movement: manual-winding Piaget 430P caliber; Ø 20.5mm, thickness: 2.15mm; 40-hour power reserve; 18 jewels; 21,600 vph; circular Côtes de Genève; circular-grained plate; bevelled hand-drawn bridges; blued screws.
Functions: hours, minutes.
Case: 18K white gold; set with 50 brilliant-cut diamonds (approx. 0.8 carat).
Dial: silvered; 12 brilliant-cut diamond indexes (approx. 0.1 carat).
Bracelet: 18K white-gold; integrated clasp.

DANCER REF. G0A34055

Movement: manual-winding Piaget 430P caliber; ultra-thin; Ø 20.5mm, thickness: 2.15mm; 40-hour power reserve; 18 jewels; 21,600 vph; circular Côtes de Genève; circular grained plate; bevelled and drawn bridges; blued screws.
Functions: hours, minutes.
Case: 18K pink gold.
Dial: silvered; applied 18K pink-gold and black hour markers.
Bracelet: 18K pink gold with integrated clasp.

PIAGET POLO 32MM REF. G0A36223

Movement: quartz; Piaget 690P caliber.
Functions: hours, minutes.
Case: 18K white gold; Ø 32mm; bezel set with 36 brilliant-cut diamonds (approx. 0.5 carat).
Dial: silver; applied 18K white-gold Arabic numerals and hour markers.
Bracelet: 18K white gold with integrated folding clasp.

LIMELIGHT TONNEAU XL SHAPE REF. G0A36094

Movement: quartz; Piaget 57P caliber.
Functions: hours, minutes.
Case: 18K pink gold; 22x30mm; set with diamonds (approx. 0.3 carat); crown set with a diamond (approx. 0.1 carat).
Dial: silver-colored; gilded colored Arabic numerals and hour markers.
Bracelet: 18K pink gold with integrated folding clasp.

RALPH LAUREN
WATCH AND JEWELRY CO.

A TIMELESS TRADITION

Although he long desired to enter the world of haute horology, founder Ralph Lauren's passionate respect for fine timepieces led him to wait until he could create models that would respond in every way to his standards of design and expertise.

SLIM CLASSIQUE SQUARE WATCH
This timepiece's sleek design is a debonair celebration of the intelligent and elegant geometry of the Art Deco era.

SLIM CLASSIQUE SQUARE WATCH
Housed in a rose-gold case just 5.75mm thick and 27.5mm wide, this elegant piece is powered by the RL430 caliber, made by Piaget for Ralph Lauren.

The Ralph Lauren Slim Classique collection, the Ralph Lauren Stirrup collection and the Ralph Lauren Sporting collection form a brand portfolio that translates the essence of the brand into the language of luxury, glamour and timelessness. The watches, produced in Switzerland, exemplify the greatest respect for watch-making tradition.

The Ralph Lauren Slim Classique collection, while still maintaining the delicate balance of sleek modernity and classical proportions, has been crafted and calculated as a modern tribute to the Art Deco style of the 1920s. The new square design is a celebration of the intelligent and elegant geometry of this grand early 20th-century era. Featuring genuine hand-guided guilloché craftsmanship and meticulous gem setting, the Slim Classique collection offers sophistication with a superbly slender silhouette.

At just 5.75mm thick and 27.5mm wide, the Ralph Lauren Slim Classique square watch is true to the implications of its name and the proportional principles of the iconic dress watch and of the era it honors. The square case frames a dial composition of concentric squares with a combination of Roman and Arabic numerals. The debonair Ralph Lauren Slim Classique square watch is equipped with the RL430 caliber, made by Piaget for Ralph Lauren, offering a 40-hour power reserve. This distinguished Art Deco marriage of classicism and modernity is available in rose or white gold, including a guilloché reference that conveys Ralph Lauren's devotion to the exquisite and rarefied art form.

LARGE STIRRUP WATCH

Ralph Lauren Stirrup collection captures the iconic equestrian heritage of Polo Ralph Lauren with a unique silhouette that is immediately identifiable.

STIRRUP DIAMOND LINK WATCH

Over 1,500 diamonds decorate this timepiece, with diamonds of 12 different sizes used to create a smooth, uninterrupted surface of gemstones for maximum sparkle.

The Ralph Lauren Stirrup collection is a bold encapsulation of the iconic equestrian heritage of Polo Ralph Lauren and the unique silhouette that expresses the designer's philosophy. These additions complement the current collection with the introduction of stainless steel and fully diamond-pavé timepieces.

As part of the SIHH novelties, the Ralph Lauren Large Stirrup watch in stainless steel is a synergic contrast of masculine black dial with off-white Roman numerals. This self-winding piece is powered by the automatic column-wheel chronograph caliber RL750, produced by Jaeger-LeCoultre. The case and dial find their perfect complement in a black calf strap that completes its journey with a unique loop around the top of the case.

Joining these watches is the Ralph Lauren Stirrup Diamond Link timepiece. The latter combines a white-gold and diamond-pavé case with ingeniously supple white gold and diamond-pavé chain link bracelet designed with both comfort and beauty in mind. Ralph Lauren achieves maximum sparkle through the use of over 1,500 diamonds that decorate this timepiece, including diamonds of 12 different sizes that create an uninterrupted surface of gemstones.

Completing the designer's watch introductions is the Ralph Lauren Sporting collection. This collection's philosophy of style and performance, of purpose and beauty, is exemplified by the unveiling of the Ralph Lauren Automotive watch with wood dial. This passionate piece is nothing short of the designer's homage to his love of fine automobiles, in this case his 1938 Bugatti Type 57SC Atlantic Coupé. The warmly handsome dial made of loupe d'orme, or elm burlwood, pays honor to the car's iconic wooden dashboard and trim detail. Prized for its highly figured patterns and rarity, each piece of elm burlwood has unique grain, and has found a purpose in both sculpture and in the consoles of the finest luxury cars. The dial's matte black galvanic center and the watch's black calf leather strap offer a refined and calculated contrast to the warmth of the wood, reminiscent of the juxtaposition of the wooden dashboard and black leather seating in Lauren's prized vintage automobile. True to the designer's philosophy, the Ralph Lauren Automotive watch showcases the balance of beauty and functionality, combining bygone motoring elegance with the precision of a manual-winding mechanical movement.

AUTOMOTIVE WATCH

The combination of wood dial, gauge-inspired indexes and manual-winding movement brings together the worlds of fine watches and cars—two worlds of detailed craftsmanship and optimal performance.

Guilloché is the art of using a rose engine to create ornamental patterns of the finest intricacy and exact regularity. Authentically performed only by highly skilled artisans, this craft requires extraordinary dedication.

Genuine guilloché has historically been found only on the metal dials and cases of the highest quality timepieces from the most renowned watch manufactures. Pioneered in the 18th century, engine turning is both time-consuming and unforgiving. The piece to be engraved is carefully mounted in the rose engine so that rosettes, the guide templates from which the machine's name is derived, can direct the engraving across the watch dial or case to be decorated. Since both the speed of rotation and amount of pressure are manually controlled, complete concentration and an absolutely steady hand are vital to the regularity of the pattern and exact depth of the engraving.

Such an utter lack of a margin for error partly explains the current rarity of this noble art. Not only do few skilled artisans remain who carry on this Old World craft, but rose engines themselves have not been produced since the middle of the last century. As a matter of fact, the rose engine used to create the "barleycorn" pattern on the Ralph Lauren Slim Classique and Ralph Lauren Sporting Chronograph watches is a museum piece itself, dating back to the late 1800s. While guilloché was once a thriving art, with more than a thousand craftsmen in the Swiss Jura alone, only a handful of guillocheurs can be found in Switzerland who are still full time practitioners of this craft.

The beauty of guilloché guidé à la main, hand-guided guilloché, is truly unique. While it is often imitated by metal stamping, an experienced eye can clearly distinguish the authentic art from the pretender. Stamping flattens the crystalline structure of the metal as the impression is struck, creating a dull surface. Genuine guilloché, on the other hand, exposes the grain of the metal and leaves it intact, resulting in an almost silken brilliance.

Ralph Lauren watches decorated with guilloché craftsmanship feature a distinct pattern. A spiral "barleycorn" guilloché pattern is executed in the central portion of the dial, with 80 waves gently snailing in a series of compact spirals from the outer to the inner circle. The central intersections are so fine as to be invisible to the naked eye. The Roman numerals are delineated with a subtle guilloché track while the "barleycorn" pattern of the dial is repeated on the bezel as well. This is a particularly challenging execution as the guillocheur must follow a complex convex curved surface.

Ralph Lauren's commitment to preserving the art of guilloché finishing truly breathes new life into one of the most beautiful decorative techniques of traditional horology.

SLIM CLASSIQUE COLLECTION

Housed in a rose-gold case with a diameter of 42mm, the Slim Classique boasts a hand-guilloché dial and bezel.

RAYMOND WEIL

GENEVE

A TIMEKEEPING SYMPHONY

Re-inventing itself as the conductor of a Swiss watchmaking orchestra, RAYMOND WEIL expands its collection with an enchanting interpretation of lines, colors, and vivid architecture.

The celebration of RAYMOND WEIL's 35th anniversary marks the manufacture's continuous devotion to reinventing itself while preserving the DNA of its original success.

Founded in 1976 by the innovator of the same name, RAYMOND WEIL has, for more than three decades, not only upheld its principles of creativity, expertise, accessibility and independence, but has successfully done so as a genuine family affair. As Olivier Bernheim, RAYMOND WEIL's son-in-law, welcomed his sons Elie and Pierre Bernheim to the team, the manufacture's family structure grew stronger in its quest to maintain its exceptional Genevan horological heritage. This saga of three generations continues to integrate the sincere human quality of the family spirit into a highly competitive marketplace.

With every new generation, the evolution of the RAYMOND WEIL brand expands the width of its visionary pursuit without sacrificing the equilibrium that propelled it from its very inception in the middle of a watch industry crisis. Five years ago, as the Swiss watchmaker celebrated its 30th birthday, the youthful ambition of Elie and Pierre Bernheim injected new blood into the company's veins. The exclusive RW Club was created to provide a unique, privileged service to the members of the RAYMOND WEIL client family.

Today, in celebration of its ruby anniversary in the world of haute horology, the Genevan house presents an exclusive complication wristwatch of timeless elegance. Joining a collection whose very name is a proud declaration of the manufacture's passion for the arts, the Maestro 35th Anniversary Edition timepiece is a prestigious toast to a symbolic and precious anniversary. The intricate texture of the silver dial draws immediate attention to the delightful use of vivid colors as a complement to the watch's classical spirit. Just as the alluring blued hands in the most classical watchmaking style complement the moonphase at 12 o'clock, the day and month counters at 4 and 8 o'clock add harmony through contrast to the Roman numerals and Arabic date indicators on the outer ring of the dial. Housed within an 18-karat yellow-gold case, this anniversary timepiece adorns the wrist with an inebriating choreography of lines, colors, and luxurious texture, and proudly expresses the values of RAYMOND WEIL's sophisticated collection.

MAESTRO 35TH ANNIVERSARY EDITION

RAYMOND WEIL celebrates its ruby anniversary with a visionary homage of exquisite geometry.

Joining this special anniversary timepiece, the Maestro Automatic Phase de Lune draws its inspiration from the ultimate master of proportion: Leonardo da Vinci. Just as his Vitruvian Man illustrated the glory of dimensional geometry, the Maestro Phase de Lune's delicate, pure silvered hands conduct a symphony that echoes the moon's 29-day revolution around the earth. The silvered numerals play off the depth of the black dial's Clou de Paris craftsmanship, setting the stage for the royal blue moonphase to emerge from the calmness of night and energize the elegant design of this automatic timepiece. The clever positioning of the date counter at 6 o'clock provides an asymmetrical harmony, and hypnotizes the owner as he dives into the illusions of the dial. Powered by the RW4500 mechanical movement with 38-hour power reserve, and housed in a perfectly round 39.5mm polished steel case, this elegant play on the vitality of night adds a poetic note of modernity to the spirit of the Genevan brand's legacy.

MAESTRO AUTOMATIC PHASE DE LUNE
This moonphase timepiece plays off the luster of the night's mysterious illuminator.

In honor of women who dream of the romance of the Orient, RAYMOND WEIL's new Jasmine collection embodies the beauty of the Bengal lights, within a design as delicate as the flower that inspires its name. In consideration of the RAYMOND WEIL woman, each version of this delightfully feminine timepiece embraces a common symbolism of exotic charm. Framed within a voluptuously curved case, each model illuminates the wrist with the full-bodied radiance of a Far East sunset. The blue-tinted leaf-shaped hands rise from the dazzling silver dial and initiate a dance with the blue Indian tone of the lacquered crown. A discreet date indicator at 3 o'clock finds its place along the black Roman numerals and gracefully interrupts the intricate center of the design. With its models submerged in a river of diamonds, the brilliance of the bezel invigorates the rhythmic beat of the movement. In more discreet versions, a classical elegance lets the subtle aesthetic dialogues speak for themselves. Available with a 29 or 35mm diameter, with or without diamonds, in stainless steel, pink gold, or dual tone, and with a leather strap, or bracelet in stainless steel or two-tone steel and gold, the Jasmine collection gently wraps a stunning emblem of faraway romanticism around the feminine wrist.

As the RAYMOND WEIL family celebrates its 35th watchmaking anniversary, the Genevan manufacture continues to express its vision of graceful classicism. Keeping true to a passionate love of the artistic spirit, the manufacture unveils its newest timepieces with tremendous regard for the symphony of fine Swiss watchmaking.

JASMINE COLLECTION

Alluding to the seductive aura of the Far East, the Jasmine is available in a variety of models, powered by automatic or quartz movements.

REBELLION®
SWISS EXCLUSIVE TIMEPIECES

RACING FOR PERFECTION

While Rebellion's name communicates the brand's rejection of the established boundaries of fine watchmaking, it is a philosophy of unyielding passion that has, since its inception in 2008, driven the Lonay manufacture to establish itself as a leading creator of precision-engineered timepieces that declare a spirit of fierce independence.

Bound only by a devotion to technical excellence and a decisive commitment to quality, Rebellion puts its sophisticated expertise at the service of audacious timekeeping perfection. The manufacture's use of such advancements as state-of-the-art precision lasers, for example, fits right in line with the founders' fervent involvement in the world of motor racing. This vibrant marriage of haute horology and high-performance competition is at the very heart of the brand's development of the T-1000, a standout masterpiece with an incredible 1000-hour power reserve.

Inspired during the running of the famous 24 Hours of Le Mans, founders Steve Clerici and Alexander Pesci decided to honor the spirit of high-speed racing's truest test of stamina with a watch of unparalleled endurance. Joining forces with a master of horological design, Eric Giroud, Rebellion took on the challenge of creating a timepiece that would evoke the visceral impact of an engine pushed to the limit of innovation. Ensuring the perfect integration of the watch's every component, the exclusive manual-winding REB T-1000 movement was developed in parallel to the designing efforts. Six barrels, set on a patented energy-transmission device as two trios on either side of the case, provide the power required for the unprecedented endurance of the timepiece. The commanding titanium case provides a dynamic frame for a large aperture showcase of the watch's splendid engineering. Combining the 39°-inclined double-hairspring balance, visible at 6 o'clock, with a vertical roller time display in the center of the dial, the T-1000 exudes a mesmerizing balance of performance and suspension. The embodiment of roaring masculinity, this 1000-hour power reserve timepiece honors the wrist of its owner like the mighty engine of a racecar honors the pavement on which it destroys the boundaries of speed.

T-1000

Using an ingenious arrangement of six vertical mainspring barrels, the T-1000 features a colossal 1000-hour power reserve.

RE-1 CHRONOGRAPH

This revitalized racing emblem boasts an automatic movement that beats at a frequency of 28,800 vph.

The rebirth of Rebellion's RE-1 Chronograph is a statement of refinement and extraordinary power. With uncompromised attention to detail, Eric Giroud's reinvention of the functional aesthetics of this Rebellion opus provides the perfect setting for the watch's virile determination to shine. The RE-1 self-winding mechanical movement finds a home within a robust 46 by 56mm case in red gold, stainless steel, black steel or titanium. A growing signature of the manufacture, this timepiece's chassis features helical screw heads that gracefully complement the high-performance racing concept of the watch. On the case middle at 3 o'clock, two new ergonomic triangular pushers evoke cylinder covers, and offer rapid and optimal control of the watch's chronometric function. Separating them, the generous crown is shaped like the robust nut of a racing hubcap. The dial is no stranger to the essence of a high-powered engine, exhibiting a finely crafted arrangement of turbines, wheels and competition dials and gauges. While each distinctive version offers the wearer a medium for self-expression, the black rubber strap furthers the mechanical allure of the overall design. Possessing the sensuality of a missile-like racecar that slices the air with surgical precision, the RE-1 exemplifies the future of the high-end chronograph.

Eternally determined to challenge the establishment, Rebellion takes its daring expertise to the field of high-performance motor racing. With two innovative timepieces that capture the dynamic essence of refined masculinity, the young Swiss watchmaker declares its valiant commitment to writing the future of haute horology.

REB-5 TOURBILLON MANUFACTURE — REF. REB5TIDLC

Movement: manual-winding REB-5 caliber; 38.25x36.7mm; 7-day power reserve, from two mainspring barrels; 23 jewels; 21,600 vph; galvanic black-gold plates; gold-plated wheels; blue- and black-gold screws, wolf-teeth barrels.
Functions: hours, minutes, seconds; one-minute tourbillon.
Case: black titanium DLC; 46x56.7mm, thickness: 19.6mm; modular construction; compound curved; beveled edges; antireflective sapphire crystal caseback; water resistant to 5atm.
Strap: natural rubber; double folding buckle in matching case metal.
Note: limited to 12 pieces.
Suggested price: $186,000

REB-7 SKELETON REGULATOR MANUFACTURE — REF. REB7TIDLC

Movement: automatic-winding regulator REB-7 caliber; 30x6mm; 42-hour power reserve; 45 components; 23 jewels; 28,800 vph; galvanic black-gold plates; black-gold date ring; gold-plated wheels.
Functions: off-centered hours; minutes, seconds; large date at 6.
Case: black titanium DLC; 46x56.7mm, thickness: 19.6mm; modular construction; compound curves; beveled edges; antireflective sapphire crystal caseback; water resistant to 5atm.
Strap: natural rubber; double folding buckle in matching case metal.
Note: limited to 36 pieces.
Suggested price: $38,500
Also available: titanium.

RE-1 CHRONOGRAPH — REF. RE1DLC

Movement: automatic-winding RE-1 caliber; 13¼ lines; 50-hour power reserve; 45 components; 28,800 vph.
Functions: hours, minutes; small seconds at 9; date; chronograph: 12-hour counter at 6, 30-minute counter at 3 and central seconds hand; start/stop at 2 and return-to-zero at 4.
Case: black titanium DLC; 46x56.7mm, thickness: 19.6mm; modular construction; compound curves; beveled edges; antireflective sapphire crystal caseback; water resistant to 5atm.
Strap: natural rubber; double folding buckle.
Suggested price: $34,100
Also available: red gold; steel; steel/DLC.

T-1000 TIME MACHINE — REF. T1000TIT

Movement: manual-winding REB T-1000 caliber; aluminum; 1,000-hour power reserve; 693 components; 22 jewels; 18,000 vph.
Functions: hours, minutes.
Case: titanium; 46.7x46.9mm, thickness: 19.5mm; crown with patented pushbutton clutch system; water resistant to 5atm.
Strap: black alligator leather; patented folding clasp with micrometric pushbutton regulation.
Note: limited to 50 pieces.
Suggested price: $115,500
Also available: titanium/black; titanium DLC.

PREDATOR 3 HANDS GOLD REF. 48.REB3.2A0

Movement: automatic-winding RE-9 caliber; 50-hour power reserve; 28,800 vph.
Functions: hours, minutes; sectorial seconds at 9; date at 3.
Case: red gold; Ø 48mm; rose-gold crown; water resistant to 10atm.
Dial: black DLC honeycomb; rose-gold hour markers with SuperLumiNova.
Strap: black rubber; deployment buckle.
Suggested price: $34,000
Also available: steel; steel/ceramic; gold/ceramic.

PREDATOR CHRONO SECTORIAL SECOND STEEL/CERAMIC REF. 48.REB6.1B0

Movement: automatic-winding RE-1 caliber; 50-hour power reserve; 28,800 vph.
Functions: hours, minutes; sectorial seconds at 9; date at 4; chronograph: 12-hour counter at 6 and 30-minute counter at 3.
Case: steel and ceramic; Ø 48mm; steel crown; water resistant to 10atm.
Dial: black DLC honeycomb; steel hour markers with SuperLumiNova.
Strap: black rubber; deployment buckle.
Suggested price: $20,300
Also available: gold; gold/ceramic; steel.

PREDATOR CHRONO MONO-PUSHER STEEL/CERAMIC REF. 48.REB5.2A0

Movement: automatic-winding RE-8 caliber; 50-hour power reserve.
Functions: hours, minutes; sectorial seconds at 9; chronograph: 30-minute counter at 3 and 60-second counters at 9.
Case: steel and ceramic; Ø 48mm; water resistant to 10atm.
Dial: black DLC honeycomb.
Strap: black rubber; deployment buckle.
Suggested price: $21,200
Also available: steel; gold; gold/ceramic.

ICED DIAMOND BEZEL

Note: This is the bezel only (set with 72 WWSI diamonds, 2.3 carats), available separaty to complement the Predator Collection.
Suggested price: $19,300
Also available: gold and steel.

RICHARD MILLE

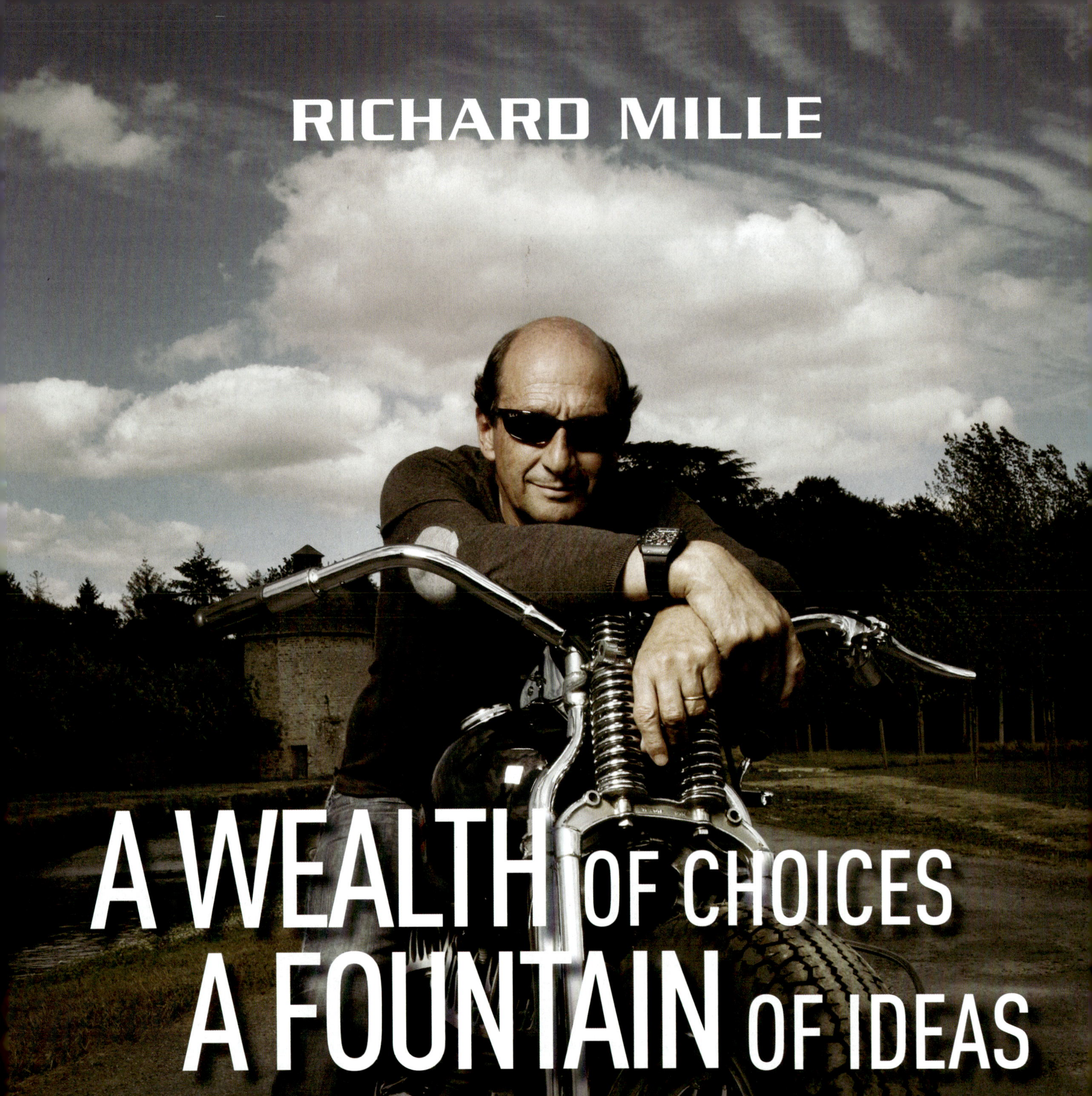

A WEALTH OF CHOICES A FOUNTAIN OF IDEAS

Par for the course at Richard Mille Watches, 2012 is yet another bonanza year with a total of nine new watch models being presented, each an epitome of advanced design and haute horology. One of the exceptional aspects of Richard Mille's vision must be his uncanny ability to transform the very essence of classical watchmaking tradition and fuse it with futuristic materials and techniques—with every model remaining true to the brand identity in a totally coherent fashion, whether sports watch, jewelry watch, ultra thin tourbillon or automatic. Just when you think he cannot go a step further, he does, continuously challenging everyone to look, enjoy, and look again.

RM 037

With its elongated case design, Roman numerals and beautifully shaped pushers for date change and function selection, the new RM 037 with its in house designed automatic movement breaks the mold and brings a subtle new direction of refinement to the brand.

One of the first models to be presented, the culmination of several years' development is the new RM 037 Automatic fitted with the new caliber CRMA1. It represents an original in-house construction by the Richard Mille movement designers in Les Breuleux, Switzerland. This automatic-winding caliber created from skeletonized grade-5 titanium sports an oversize date at 12 o'clock and a function window between 3 and 4 o'clock that indicates the movement's state of activity: Winding, Neutral and Handsetting (W-H-N). Two subtly shaped pushers, with organic and rounded profiles reminiscent of natural forms, are located at 4 and 10 o'clock. The pusher at 4 o'clock controls the watch's functions as mentioned above, while the pusher at 10 o'clock controls date changes, for instance when one is traveling or needs to correct the date for months with 29, 30 and 31 days. A simpler method of correcting the date would be impossible to imagine.

The specially patented and newly designed crown is a pinnacle of invisible and artful engineering. Its special design allows for the integrity of the movement to be fully guaranteed and protected from external influences, since it does not use a classical crown attachment going into the depth of the movement's heart. This means that the crown is virtually impossible to dislodge and yet it is easily inserted and removed under the skillful hands of the watchmaker when needed; a typical view towards longevity that typifies the brand's philosophy. If all this were not enough, the case design brings new visual elements into play: look closely and you will see that the case has been subtly elongated, defining a new appearance that at first glance recalls a wristwatch that has taken on the mood of a bracelet with its deeper curves and lines that would be at home on any wrist in any situation.

THE SKY HAS NO LIMITS: RM 039 E6B AVIATOR TOURBILLON CHRONOGRAPH

The world of aviation and aeronautics has been a part of Richard Mille's world virtually since its inception. Many materials such as titanium, carbon nanofiber, honeycombed titanium alumide, ARCAP and tungsten carbide have found their way into the collection from aerial worlds to the domain of horology—once they were finally recognized for their special potential in watchmaking.

Now, for the first time, Richard Mille continues the challenge by presenting a new tool for pilots with the introduction of the RM 039 E6B Aviator Tourbillon Chronograph. Unlike any other pilot watch on the market, the RM 039 offers the complement of functions from the well-known E6B slide rule calculator, including fuel consumption, time en route, ground speed, density altitude and much more, complemented with the full functionality of a specially designed Flyback chronograph with subdial. The possibilities of the E6B can be used real time within the time recording utility of a chronograph. By uniting these functions, the applications for the E6B are greatly enriched and made even more useful for pilots.

In the pre-flight check phase, the E6B slide rule calculator is still considered the most reliable tool for reviewing the projected fuel consumption, the density altitude (critical for take-off and landing maneuver's) and ground speed as well as many other functions. The fact that it requires no batteries makes it totally reliable and a necessity for many pilots even today. In this way, the RM 039 E6B Aviator Tourbillon Chronograph represents a real marriage of horology and aeronautics in the creation of a supremely useful tool for pilots.

Furthermore, this new Richard Mille timepiece respects all aspects and demands of haute horology, with extreme attention to the fine details of hand finishing and the challenges presented by a tourbillon-driven flyback chronograph movement. The complex case design with its turning bezel, combinations of finishes and special lug attachment also incorporates five different pushers that work in combination with the fixed and moving scales of the watch.

FLIGHT INSTRUMENT
RICHARD MILLE
TACHYMETER
RATE 60
DENSITY ALTITUDE
RM039
SWISS MADE
COUNT DOWN

HAUTE HOROLOGY AT THE SUMMIT: LIMITED EDITION RM 031

Cutting-edge horology, the pursuit of excellent timing characteristics combined with new concepts and materials, has always been a passion of Richard Mille. For the new RM 031 High Performance caliber, these issues form a key aspect in every single detail and decision behind its design principles, starting with the use of the AP direct-impulsion escapement. This new escapement design forms a brilliant symbiosis of a detent escapement with a Swiss lever escapement and was originally developed by Renaud & Papi for Audemars Piguet. The accuracy of the escapement is improved by the fact that it is the escapement wheel that directly drives the balance, unlike the Swiss lever escapement where the anchor indirectly activates the escapement wheel. Beating at 36,000 vph with two Elinvar hairsprings placed in opposition, the performance results of +/- 30 seconds per month are proof of this attention to ultimate movement design. To provide perfect power transfer, the entire going train consists of wheels using a new gear tooth profile with a pressure angle of 20°, very similar to that used in car transmissions, thus allowing for a highly sustainable and continuous transfer of power through the going train to the high performance escapement. The baseplate and bridges are created from ARCAP, a material first used extensively in watchmaking with the realization of the RM 002. It is a material commonly used in aerospace, automotive and advanced electronics industries today.

These extreme horological attributes, combined with ultimate hand finishing in which every part is given hours of attention, is enclosed within a new round Richard Mille case of Ø 50x13.90mm. This extremely complex case design combines beveling, polishing and brushing with unique expressivity. In a typical example of extreme attention to detail, the lugs are meticulously designed to flow from the case and directly follow the contours of the matching strap.

THE RM 052 SKULL TOURBILLON

Throughout history the human skull has been manifested in many forms and uses, sometimes purely visual, sometimes within different beliefs and ideologies. For Latin Americans, it was the symbol of life, yet for Europeans, it was perhaps an image more likely to be associated with death, the short time span of our lives and the need to use our time wisely. Damian Hurst's famed bejeweled skull transformed this emblem into a new artistic and fashion statement. Through the course of centuries, the skull has become the emblem of rebellion and insubordination, its previously macabre associations having been usurped by those of freedom and nonconformity.

The RM 052 Skull Tourbillon visualizes these precepts in timekeeping. The baseplate and bridges take the form of a titanium skull, indeed the tourbillon movement itself is built inside these skull plates. The entire movement is connected to the case by four bridges that are inspired by the crossed bones from a pirate ship's flag. The new case design, with its opened flanks, continues this visual allegory to the human skeleton. Where others may have been content to exploit the purely visual aspect of the skull, Richard Mille has taken the concept further by integrating it into the complete timepiece. This new caliber from Richard Mille represents the fullest expression of liberty and nonconformity and as such, very much typifies the philosophy of the brand: the creation of exceptional watches that stand on a pinnacle within the world of haute horology.

RICHARD MILLE
TACHYMETER
RM050
SWISS 120 MADE

REVISION OF A MODERN CLASSIC: TOURBILLON SPLIT SECONDS COMPETITION CHRONOGRAPH RM 050 FELIPE MASSA

The newly designed manual winding tourbillon movement caliber RMCC1 with hours, minutes, chronograph, split seconds, power reserve, torque indicator and function indicator represents a new progression and development at Richard Mille. The flagship RM 008 Tourbillon Split Seconds model has for more than 8 years been a landmark in the world of watchmaking and now the new RM 050 Chrono Competition Felipe Massa represents a new movement that takes all the best characteristics of the first new split seconds design of the 21st century and takes it even further. The new caliber for the RM 050 was not a simple exercise of merely reviewing the existing RM 008 movement. The engineers at Richard Mille began by researching every possible manner to lower the weight, and brought the total movement weight down to a mere 9.5 grams. Further development of the caliber with its skeletonized baseplate and bridges as well as novel movement designs meant the creation of more than 400 new parts for the new RMCC1 caliber.

In parallel to this, the engineers have optimized the movement to the maximum, notably the precision and calculations of the long-term timekeeping aspects. The result is a beast of a watch at the cutting edge of the possible. The case is composed of composite injected with carbon nanotubes. Carbon nanotubes are extremely resistant to stress (two hundred times more than steel) and very light. They have the ability to absorb violent shocks significantly better than carbon fibers due to their structure, unique geometry and high surface-volume ratio.

TOURBILLON SPLIT SECONDS COMPETITION CHRONOGRAPH RM 056 FELIPE MASSA SAPPHIRE

As a special creation to celebrate the release of this new caliber, the RM 056 has been created in a limited edition with a case created from a block of sapphire. This is the first time that such a complex case design has been realized in this material. As one of the hardest materials on the Earth, with a Mohs rating of 9.0, just below diamond, sapphire is very difficult to work with. The cutting tools to work with it must be specially designed and tipped with diamond; the wear and tear on the machines during its production is extreme. The creation of just the case takes more than 1,000 hours of machining, fraction of a millimeter by fraction of a millimeter. The end result is something unique and hitherto unknown in the watchmaking industry, with a transparent case allowing a full view of the fabulous new RMCC1 movement design.

A UNIQUE COMBINATION OF SPORTIVE AND COMFORTABLE: RM 055 BUBBA WATSON

The new RM 055 Bubba Watson continues many of the concepts presented by the RM 038 Bubba Watson Tourbillon presented last year. It sports a highly skeletonized movement created from components in grade-5 titanium, with black PVD coating for the baseplate and Titalyt® for the bridges. This ensures that the whole assembly will have perfect rigidity as well as precise surface flatness—an essential for the perfect functioning of the watch's going train. After treatment with Titalyt®, the movement is lightly ground to create the visible lines on the movement plate, providing dynamic visual interest to the intricate detailed view of the caliber floating in the case.

Keeping with a high standard of escapement design, the movement uses a free sprung balance with variable inertia. The regulator index is eliminated and a more accurate and repeatable adjustment is possible thanks to four small adjustable weights located directly on the balance. Its double-barrel system helps improve torque stability over a longer period by utilizing more turns of each barrel, thereby reducing pressure and wear on the teeth, bearings and pivots, resulting in improved long-term performance. Typical for all Richard Mille creations, the RM 055 Bubba Watson makes extensive use of spline screws for the case and movement. This permits better control of the torque applied to the screws during assembly. These screws are therefore unaffected by physical manipulation during assembly or disassembly and age well.

The case of the RM 055 is a special construction, with great attention to the demands of sportsmen. The ATZ bezel is cut and milled from a ATZ block made from tubes of powdered aluminum oxide injected at a pressure of about 3000 bar. This high-pressure injection gives 20% to 30% more rigidity compared to a conventional ceramic injection. The resulting ATZ material is known for its high scratch resistance and permanent color. ATZ is, after diamond, one of the hardest materials in the world. A long and difficult work of machining and grinding will be necessary for the creation of the highly complex, curved shape of this upper bezel. At the final stage, the material is worked to give it a matte finish instead of the polished and shiny surface look usually associated with conventional ceramic.

The case band and back bezel are made of grade-5 titanium, which is later injection molded with a rubber surround. This isolates the movement from vibration by inducing a progressive deformation, and is additionally extremely comfortable to wear on the wrist. The RM 055 combines a fashionable sporting look with haute horology and total comfort on and off the course.

A TOUGH WATCH FOR A TOUGH SPORT: RM0 53 POLO TOURBILLON PABLO MAC DONOUGH

Polo must be one of the toughest sports for any watch to have to deal with; sudden turns, wild swings, the clash of horses and riders—these are forces far different from the norms found in other sports disciplines. The first known record of a polo match dates back to 600 B.C., making Polo the oldest team sport in the world. Eventually Polo was brought to the West via India during the course of the 19th century when officials of the British Army began playing the game. Known as the "King of Sports," polo is a uniquely elegant, highly exclusive and dangerous game.

For this reason, Richard Mille created a totally new case design, an "armored" case with a viewing window and movement design tilted at 30° and created for a new partner of the brand, the celebrated polo sportsman Pablo Mac Donough World Number One. The seconds run with the tourbillon cage in the left viewing window and on the right the hours and minutes are shown. This angled view is ideal when seen from the rider's position in the saddle. The highly compact, totally new tourbillon movement design utilizes a highly skeletonized baseplate and bridges with a compact going train- winding barrel arrangement. Since the movement itself is ultra light and tightly unified, it is less susceptible to the centrifugal and centripetal forces generated during a game.

RM 057 DRAGON-JACKIE CHAN TOURBILLON

2012 marks the start of the Year of the Dragon, beginning on January 23, 2012 and ending on February 9, 2013. The dragon is a uniquely auspicious creature of myth and legend. In ancient China, the celestial dragon embodied a visual representation of the emperor and power, whereas today it is the ultimate propitious symbol signifying success and happiness. A Sung Dynasty manuscript once described the dragon as having the head of an ox, muzzle of a donkey, eyes of a shrimp, horns of a deer, body of a serpent covered with fish scales and the feet of a phoenix. Invariably accompanied by thunder and rain, dragons move like lightning and whirlwinds—all powerful yet totally unpredictable.

People born in the Year of the Dragon share innovative, enterprising, self-assured, brave, passionate and quick-tempered characteristics. Dragons are the extroverted free spirits of the Chinese Zodiac and they do not have patience for restrictions limiting their creative spark that is ready to flame into life. So they search for freedom and space. Because they are confident, fearless in the face of challenge, they are almost inevitably successful.

For such an auspicious occasion and animal, the RM 057 Dragon Tourbillon embodies all that is worthy of a dragon's attention. On the movement baseplate of pure, deep black Onyx—considered a stone of protection against negative thoughts and the stone of equilibrium and inspiration—the golden dragon covered in jewels, engraving and colored scales grips the bridge the tourbillon bridge in one of his claws. The dragon's five-toed claw is proof of its Imperial status. Adding a refined visible touch, the round, engraved Jackie Chan signature set into the black Onyx baseplate side turns once every 60 seconds in time with the tourbillon's rotation.

RICHARD MILLE
SWISS MADE

SPLIT SECONDS CHRONOGRAPH — RM 004-V2

Movement: manual-winding RM004-V2 caliber; approx. 70-hour power reserve; carbon nanofiber baseplate; titanium column wheels, gear wheels and lever; split-seconds mechanism with improved and patented functions; fast rotating barrel; function indicator; variable inertia balance with overcoil hairspring; newly designed three-tiered titanium bridge with lever escapement; spline screws in grade-5 titanium for the bridges and case; winding barrel and third pinion's teeth with central involute profile.

Functions: hours, minutes, seconds; split-seconds chronograph; power reserve; torque indicator; function indicator.
Case: anatomically curved three-piece case; 48x39.7mm, thickness: 14.95mm; assembled with 20 spline screws in grade-5 titanium; sapphire crystal front and back with double-sided antireflective coating; water resistant to 50 meters.
Dial: sapphire crystal with double-sided antireflective treatment; protected with eight silicon braces in grooved edges.
Strap: leather, crocodile or rubber; attached via titanium screws to the case; matching buckle.
Available in: 18K red gold; 18K white gold; titanium; platinum.

AUTOMATIC (TITANIUM VERSION) — RM 007

Movement: automatic-winding RM007 caliber; approx. 38-hour power reserve; rotor fitted with a patented auto-reverse system integrated into the rotor ball bearing; grade-5 titanium screws; teeth with central involute profile.
Functions: hours, minutes; date at 6.
Case: anatomically curved three-piece case with Titalyt® surface treatment; 45x31mm, thickness: 10.95mm; crown with double-seal O-ring and collar in Alcryn; assembled with 12 spline screws in grade-5 titanium; sapphire crystal front and back with double-sided antireflective coating; water resistant to 50 meters.

Dial: sapphire crystal with double-sided antireflective treatment; sapphire crystal calendar disc treated with double-sided antireflective coating; protected with eight silicon braces in grooved edges.
Strap: leather, crocodile or various fabrics; attached via titanium screws to the case; matching buckle.
Available in: titanium.

AUTOMATIC — RM 007 TITALYT®

Movement: automatic-winding RM007 caliber; approx. 38-hour power reserve; rotor fitted with a patented auto-reverse system integrated into the rotor ball bearing; grade-5 titanium screws; teeth with central involute profile.
Functions: hours, minutes; date at 6.
Case: anatomically curved three-piece case with Titalyt® surface treatment; 45x31mm, thickness: 10.95mm; crown with double-seal O-ring and collar in Alcryn; assembled with 12 spline screws in grade-5 titanium; sapphire crystal front and back with double-sided antireflective coating; water resistant to 50 meters.

Dial: sapphire crystal with double-sided antireflective treatment; sapphire crystal calendar disc treated with double-sided antireflective coating; protected with eight silicon braces in grooved edges.
Strap: leather, crocodile or various fabrics; attached via titanium screws to the case; matching buckle.
Available in: titanium.

AUTOMATIC — RM 010

Movement: automatic-winding skeletonized RMAS7 caliber; approx. 55-hour power reserve; rotor with variable geometry via white-gold wings adjustable to six positions; ceramic rotor ball bearings; PVD-coated titanium baseplate, bridges and balance cock; double-winding barrel; spline screws in grade-5 titanium for the movement and case.
Functions: hours, minutes, seconds; date.

Case: anatomically curved three-piece case; 48x39.3mm, thickness: 13.84mm; crown in sandblasted grade-5 titanium with double-seal O-ring and collar in Alcryn; assembled with 12 spline screws in grade-5 titanium; sapphire crystal front and back with double-sided antireflective coating; water resistant to 50 meters.
Dial: sapphire crystal with double-sided antireflective treatment; protected with eight silicon braces in grooved edges.
Strap: leather or crocodile; attached via titanium screws to the case; matching buckle.
Available in: 18K red gold; 18K white gold; titanium.

FELIPE MASSA FLYBACK CHRONOGRAPH — RM 011 ALL CARBON

Movement: automatic-winding skeletonized chronograph RMAC1 caliber; approx. 55-hour power reserve; rotor with variable geometry via white-gold wings adjustable to six positions; ceramic rotor ball bearings; PVD-coated titanium baseplate, bridges and balance cock; double-winding barrel; titanium column wheel, gear wheels and lever; split-seconds mechanism with improved and patented functions; spline screws in grade-5 titanium for the movement and case.

Functions: hours, minutes, seconds; oversize date; month; annual calendar; flyback chronograph: 12-hour and 60-minute counters.

Case: central case ring; anatomically curved three-piece case; 50x40mm, thickness: 16.15mm; crown in sandblasted grade-5 titanium with double-seal O-ring and collar in Alcryn; assembled with 20 spline screws in grade-5 titanium; sapphire crystal front and back with double-sided antireflective coating; water resistant to 50 meters.

Dial: sapphire crystal with double-sided antireflective treatment; protected with eight silicon braces in grooved edges.

Strap: rubber; attached via titanium screws to the case; matching buckle.

Available in: all carbon case.

AUTOMATIC FLYBACK CHRONOGRAPH — RM 011 TITALYT®

Movement: automatic-winding skeletonized chronograph RMAC1 caliber; approx. 55-hour power reserve; rotor with variable geometry via white-gold wings adjustable to six positions; ceramic rotor ball bearings; Titalyt®-coated titanium baseplate, bridges and balance cock; double-winding barrel; titanium column wheel, gear wheels and lever; split-seconds mechanism with improved and patented functions; spline screws in grade-5 titanium for the movement and case.

Functions: hours, minutes, seconds; oversize date; month; annual calendar; flyback chronograph: 12-hour and 60-minute counter.

Case: central case ring; anatomically curved three-piece case with Titalyt® surface treatment; 50x40mm, thickness: 16.15mm; crown in sandblasted grade-5 titanium with double-seal O-ring and collar in Alcryn; assembled with 20 spline screws in grade-5 titanium; sapphire crystal front and back with double-sided antireflective coating; water resistant to 50 meters.

Dial: sapphire crystal with double-sided antireflective treatment; protected with eight silicon braces in grooved edges.

Strap: leather or crocodile; attached via titanium screws to the case; matching buckle.

Available in: titanium.

AUTOMATIC FLYBACK CHRONOGRAPH — RM 011 RED GOLD

Movement: automatic-winding skeletonized chronograph RMAC1 caliber; approx. 55-hour power reserve; rotor with variable geometry via white-gold wings adjustable to six positions; ceramic rotor ball bearings; titanium baseplate, bridges and balance cock; double-winding barrel; titanium column wheels, gear wheels and lever; split-seconds mechanism with improved and patented functions; spline screws in grade-5 titanium for the movement and case.

Functions: hours, minutes, seconds; oversize date; month; annual calendar; flyback chronograph: 12-hour and 60-minute counters.

Case: anatomically curved three-piece case; 50x40mm, thickness: 16.15mm; crown in sandblasted grade-5 titanium with double-seal O-ring and collar in Alcryn; assembled with 20 spline screws in grade-5 titanium; sapphire crystal front and back with double-sided antireflective coating; water resistant to 50 meters.

Dial: sapphire crystal with double-sided antireflective treatment; protected with eight silicon braces in grooved edges.

Strap: leather, crocodile or rubber; attached via titanium screws to the case; matching buckle.

Available in: full 18K red gold.

AUTOMATIC — RM 016 TITALYT®

Movement: automatic-winding skeletonized RMAS7 caliber; approx. 55-hour power reserve; rotor with variable geometry via white-gold wings adjustable to six positions; ceramic rotor ball bearings; Titalyt®-coated titanium baseplate, bridges and balance cock; double-winding barrel; spline screws in grade-5 titanium for the movement and case.

Functions: hours, minutes, seconds; date.

Case: anatomically curved three-piece case with Titalyt® surface treatment; 49.8x38mm, thickness: 8.25mm; crown in sandblasted grade-5 titanium with double-seal O-ring and collar in Alcryn; assembled with 12 spline screws in grade-5 titanium; sapphire crystal front and back with double-sided antireflective coating; water resistant to 30 meters.

Dial: sapphire crystal with double-sided antireflective treatment; protected with eight silicon braces in grooved edges.

Strap: leather or crocodile; attached via titanium screws to the case; matching buckle.

Available in: titanium.

AUTOMATIC RM 016

Movement: automatic-winding skeletonized RMAS7 caliber; approx. 55-hour power reserve; rotor with variable geometry via white-gold wings adjustable to six positions; ceramic rotor ball bearings; PVD-coated titanium baseplate, bridges and balance cock; double-winding barrel; spline screws in grade-5 titanium for the movement and case.
Functions: hours, minutes, seconds; date.

Case: anatomically curved three-piece case; 49.8x38mm, thickness: 8.25mm; crown in sandblasted grade-5 titanium with double-seal O-ring and collar in Alcryn; assembled with 12 spline screws in grade-5 titanium; sapphire crystal front and back with double-sided antireflective coating; water resistant to 30 meters.
Dial: sapphire crystal with double-sided antireflective treatment; protected with eight silicon braces in grooved edges.
Strap: leather or crocodile; attached via titanium screws to the case; matching buckle.
Available in: 18K red gold; 18K white gold; titanium.

EXTRA FLAT TOURBILLON RM 017

Movement: manual-winding extra-flat tourbillon RM017 caliber; approx. 70-hour power reserve; black PVD-treated titanium baseplate; fast rotating barrel; variable inertia balance with overcoil; ceramic tourbillon endstone; spline screws in grade-5 titanium for the bridges and case; winding barrel and third pinion's teeth with central involute profile; safety system blocking gear.
Functions: hours, minutes; power reserve; function indicator.

Case: anatomically curved three-piece case; 49.8x38mm, thickness: 8.7mm; assembled with 12 spline screws in grade-5 titanium; sapphire crystal front and back with double-sided antireflective coating; water resistant to 30 meters.
Dial: sapphire crystal with double-sided antireflective treatment; protected with eight silicon braces in grooved edges.
Strap: crocodile; attached via titanium screws to the case; matching buckle.
Available in: 18K red gold; 18K white gold; titanium; diamond set.

TOURBILLON POCKET WATCH RM 020

Movement: manual-winding tourbillon RM020 caliber; approx. 10-day power reserve via two winding barrels; carbon nanofiber baseplate; fast rotating barrel; function indicator; variable inertia balance with overcoil hairspring; ceramic tourbillon endstone; central bridge in rigidified ARCAP; spline screws in grade-5 titanium for the bridges and case; winding barrel and third pinion teeth with central involute profile; jewels set in gold chatons.

Functions: hours, minutes; power reserve; torque indicator; function indicator.
Case: central case ring with both front and back bezels; 62x52mm, thickness: 15.6mm; assembled with 20 spline screws in grade-5 titanium; sapphire crystal front and back with double-sided antireflective coating; water resistant to 50 meters.
Dial: sapphire crystal with double-sided antireflective treatment; protected with eight silicon braces in grooved edges.
Note: supplied with specially designed titanium chain with quick-release mechanism.
Available in: 18K red gold and titanium; 18K white gold and titanium; titanium and titanium.

TOURBILLON AERODYNE RM 021

Movement: manual-winding tourbillon RM021 caliber; approx. 70-hour power reserve; baseplate of titanium and honeycombed orthorhombic titanium aluminide with carbon nanofiber core; fast rotating barrel; function indicator; variable inertia balance with overcoil hairspring; ceramic tourbillon endstone; central bridge in rigidified ARCAP; spline screws in grade-5 titanium for the bridges and case; winding barrel and third pinion's teeth with central involute profile; jewels set in gold chatons.

Functions: hours, minutes; power reserve; torque indicator; function selector.
Case: anatomically curved three-piece case; 48.18x39.7mm, thickness: 13.85mm; assembled with 12 spline screws in grade-5 titanium; sapphire crystal front and back with double-sided antireflective coating; water resistant to 50 meters.
Dial: sapphire crystal with double-sided antireflective treatment; protected with eight silicon braces in grooved edges.
Strap: leather, crocodile or rubber; attached via titanium screws to the case; matching buckle.
Available in: 18K red gold; 18K white gold.

TOURBILLON AERODYNE SECOND TIME ZONE — RM 022

Movement: manual-winding tourbillon RM022 caliber; approx. 70-hour power reserve; baseplate of titanium and honeycombed orthorhombic titanium aluminide with carbon nanofiber core; fast rotating barrel; function indicator; variable inertia balance with overcoil hairspring; ceramic tourbillon endstone; central bridge in rigidified ARCAP; spline screws in grade-5 titanium for the bridges and case; winding barrel and third pinion's teeth with central involute profile; jewels set in gold chatons.
Functions: hours, minutes; second time zone; power reserve; torque indicator; function selector.
Case: anatomically curved three-piece case; 48.18x39.7mm, thickness: 13.85mm; assembled with 20 spline screws in grade-5 titanium; sapphire crystal front and back with double-sided antireflective coating; water resistant to 50 meters.
Dial: sapphire crystal with double-sided antireflective treatment; protected with eight silicon braces in grooved edges.
Strap: leather, crocodile or rubber; attached via titanium screws to the case; matching buckle.
Available in: 18K red gold; 18K white gold.

AUTOMATIC — RM 023

Movement: automatic-winding partially skeletonized RMA02 caliber; approx. 55-hour power reserve; rotor with variable geometry via white-gold wings adjustable to six positions; ceramic rotor ball bearings; PVD-coated titanium baseplate, bridges and balance cock; double-winding barrel; spline screws in grade-5 titanium for the movement and case.
Functions: hours, minutes, seconds; date.
Case: anatomically curved three-piece case; 45x37.8mm, thickness: 11.25mm; crown in sandblasted grade-5 titanium with double-seal O-ring and collar in Alcryn; assembled with 12 spline screws in grade-5 titanium; sapphire crystal front and back with double-sided antireflective coating; water resistant to 50 meters.
Dial: sapphire crystal with double-sided antireflective treatment; protected with eight silicon braces in grooved edges.
Strap: leather or crocodile; attached via titanium screws to the case; matching buckle.
Available in: 18K red gold; 18K white gold; titanium.

TOURBILLON CHRONOGRAPH DIVER'S WATCH — RM 025

Movement: manual-winding RM025 caliber; approx. 70-hour power reserve; carbon nanofiber baseplate; titanium column wheel; gear wheels and lever; chronograph mechanism with improved and patented functions; fast rotating barrel; function indicator; variable inertia balance with overcoil hairspring; newly designed in-line lever escapement; spline screws in grade-5 titanium for the bridges and case; winding barrel and third pinion's teeth central involute profile.
Functions: hours, minutes, seconds; chronograph: 30-minute counter; power reserve; torque indicator; function indicator.
Case: anatomically curved three-piece case; Ø 50.7mm, thickness: 19.1mm; unidirectional turning timing bezel; screw-down crown; assembled with 22 spline screws in grade-5 titanium; screw-in crown; sapphire crystal front and back with double-sided antireflective coating; water resistant to 300 meters (according to ISO 6425).
Dial: sapphire crystal with double-sided antireflective treatment protected with silicon braces in grooved edges.
Strap: made of perfluoroelastomer Kalrez®; matching buckle.
Available in: titanium with 18K red-gold lugs.

TOURBILLON — RM 026

Movement: manual-winding tourbillon RM026 caliber; approx. 48-hour power reserve; black onyx baseplate; variable inertia balance with overcoil hairspring; ceramic tourbillon endstone; spline screws in grade-5 titanium for the bridges and case; winding barrel and third pinion's teeth with central involute profile; jewels set in chatons.
Functions: hours, minutes; power reserve.
Case: anatomically curved three-piece case; 45x39.7mm, thickness: 12.6mm; assembled with 12 spline screws in grade-5 titanium; sapphire crystal front and back with double-sided antireflective coating; water resistant to 50 meters.
Dial: sapphire crystal with double-sided antireflective treatment; protected with eight silicon braces in grooved edges.
Strap: leather or crocodile; attached via titanium screws to the case; matching buckle.
Note: limited edition of 15 numbered unique pieces.
Available in: 18K white gold.

AUTOMATIC DIVER'S WATCH — RM 028

Movement: automatic-winding partially skeletonized RMAS7 caliber; approx. 55-hour power reserve; rotor with variable geometry via white-gold wings adjustable to six positions; ceramic rotor ball bearings; PVD-coated titanium baseplate, bridges and balance cock; double-winding barrel; spline screws in grade-5 titanium for the movement and case.
Functions: hours, minutes, seconds; date.

Case: anatomically curved three-piece case; Ø 47mm, thickness: 14.6mm; unidirectional turning and locking three-piece bezel fastened with 22 special spline screws; crown in sandblasted grade-5 titanium with double-seal O-ring and collar in Alcryn; sapphire crystal front and back with double-sided antireflective coating; water resistant to 300 meters (according to ISO 6425).
Dial: sapphire crystal with double-sided antireflective treatment; protected with eight silicon braces in grooved edges.
Strap: special rubber; attached via screws to the case; matching buckle.
Available in: 18K red gold; titanium.

AUTOMATIC OVERSIZE DATE — RM 029

Movement: automatic-winding skeletonized RMAS7 caliber; approx. 55-hour power reserve; rotor with variable geometry via wings adjustable to six positions; ceramic rotor ball bearings; PVD-coated titanium baseplate, bridges and balance cock.
Functions: hours, minutes, seconds; oversize date.
Case: anatomically curved three-piece case; 48x39.7mm, thickness: 12.6mm; crown in sandblasted grade-5 titanium with double-seal O-ring and collar in Alcryn; assembled with 12 spline screws in grade-5 titanium; sapphire crystal front and back with double-sided antireflective coating; water resistant to 50 meters.

Dial: sapphire crystal with double-sided antireflective treatment; protected with eight silicon braces in grooved edges.
Strap: leather or crocodile; attached via titanium screws to the case; matching buckle.
Available in: 18K red gold; 18K white gold; titanium.

AUTOMATIC WITH DECLUTCHABLE ROTOR — RM 030

Movement: automatic-winding skeletonized RMAR1 caliber; approx. 55-hour power reserve; special declutching mechanism; rotor with variable geometry via white-gold wings adjustable to six positions; ceramic rotor ball bearings; PVD-coated titanium baseplate, bridges and balance cock; double-winding barrel; spline screws in grade-5 titanium for the movement and case.
Functions: hours, minutes, seconds; date; power reserve indicator; rewinding indicator.

Case: anatomically curved three-piece case; 50x42.7mm, thickness: 13.95mm; crown in sandblasted grade-5 titanium with double-seal O-ring and collar in Alcryn; assembled with 20 spline screws in grade-5 titanium; sapphire crystal front and back with double-sided antireflective coating; water resistant to 50 meters.
Dial: sapphire crystal with double-sided antireflective treatment; protected with eight silicon braces in grooved edges.
Strap: leather or crocodile; attached via titanium screws to the case; matching buckle.
Available in: 18K red gold; 18K white gold; titanium.

HIGH PERFORMANCE — RM 031

Movement: manual-winding RM031 caliber; approx. 50-hour power reserve; baseplate and going train of ARCAP; grade 5 titanium barrel bridges and balance; double-winding barrels; fast rotating barrels; variable inertia balance with two overcoil hairsprings; direct impulsion AP escapement; spline screws in grade-5 titanium for the bridges and case; going train teeth with 20° central involute profile; completely hand-finished movement.

Functions: hours, minutes, seconds; function indicator.
Case: anatomically curved three-piece case; Ø 50mm, thickness: 13.9mm; assembled with spline screws in grade-5 titanium; sapphire crystal front and back with double-sided antireflective coating; water resistant to 50 meters.
Dial: sapphire crystal with double-sided antireflective treatment; protected with eight silicon braces in grooved edges.
Strap: special composite; attached via titanium screws to the case; matching buckle individually engraved with model number.
Note: limited edition of 10 pieces.
Available in: platinum caseband with titanium bezels.

AUTOMATIC CHRONOGRAPH DIVER'S WATCH — RM 032

Movement: automatic-winding skeletonized chronograph RMAC2 caliber; approx. 55-hour power reserve; titanium column wheels, gear wheels and lever; split-seconds mechanism with improved and patented functions; rotor with variable geometry via white-gold wings adjustable to six positions; ceramic rotor ball bearings; PVD-coated titanium baseplate, bridges and balance cock; double-winding barrel; spline screws in grade-5 titanium for the movement and case.
Functions: hours, minutes, seconds; large date; month; annual calendar; flyback chronograph: 12-hour, 30-minute and 60-seconds counters; running indicator.
Case: anatomically curved three-piece case; Ø 50mm, thickness: 17.8mm; locking crown in sandblasted grade-5 titanium with double-seal O-ring and collar in Alcryn; assembled with 22 spline screws in grade-5 titanium; sapphire crystal front and back with double-sided antireflective coating; water resistant to 300 meters (according to ISO 6425).
Dial: sapphire crystal with double-sided antireflective treatment; protected with eight silicon braces in grooved edges.
Strap: special composite; matching buckle.
Available in: 18K red gold; titanium.

RAFAEL NADAL CHRONOFIABLE® CERTIFIED — RM 035

Movement: manual-winding skeletonized chronofiable® certified RMUL1 caliber (4.3g); approx. 55-hour power reserve; certified Chronofiable® under extensive and extreme testing conditions; PVD-coated titanium baseplate, bridges and balance cock; double-winding barrel; spline screws in grade-5 titanium for the movement and case.
Functions: hours, minutes, seconds.
Case: anatomically curved three-piece case; 48x39.7mm, thickness: 12.25mm; crown in sandblasted grade-5 titanium with double-seal O-ring and collar in Alcryn; assembled with 12 spline screws in grade-5 titanium; sapphire crystal front and back with double-sided antireflective coating; water resistant to 50 meters.
Dial: sapphire crystal with double-sided antireflective treatment; protected with eight silicon braces in grooved edges.
Strap: special composite; matching buckle.
Availablein:alumagnesium with miarox® treatment.

AUTOMATIC — RM 037

Movement: automatic-widing skeletonized CRMA1 caliber; approx. 50-hour power reserve; rotor with new adjustable geometry; ceramic rotor ball bearings; PVD-coated titanium baseplate, bridges and balance cock; teeth profile of 20° pressure angle for the entire going train; spline screws in grade-5 titanium for the movement and case.
Functions: hours, minutes, seconds; oversize date; function selector.
Case: anatomically curved three-piece case; 52.2x34.4mm, thickness: 12.5mm; new, patented crown design in sandblasted grade-5 titanium with double-seal O-ring and collar in Alcryn; assembled with 12 spline screws in grade-5 titanium; sapphire crystal front and back with double-sided antireflective coating; water resistant to 100 meters.
Dial: sapphire crystal with double-sided antireflective treatment; protected with eight silicon braces in grooved edges.
Strap: leather, crocodile or rubber; attached via titanium screws to the case; matching buckle.
Available in: titanium, 18K red and white gold.

TOURBILLON — RM 038 BUBBA WATSON

Movement: manual-winding skeletonized tourbillon RM038 caliber; approx. 48-hour power reserve; skeletonized grade 5 titanium baseplate and bridge; fast rotating barrel; spline screws in grade-5 titanium for the movement and case.
Functions: hours, minutes.
Case: anatomically curved three-piece case; 48x39.7mm, thickness:12.8mm; crown with double-seal O-ring and collar in Alcryn; assembled with 12 spline screws in grade-5 titanium; sapphire crystal front and back with double-sided antireflective coating; water resistant to 50 meters.
Dial: sapphire crystal with double-sided antireflective treatment; protected with eight silicon braces in grooved edges.
Strap: special composite; matching buckle.
Available in: magnesium WE 54 with miarox® treatment.
Note: limited numbered edition of 38 pieces.

TOURBILLON CHRONOGRAPH — RM 039 E6B AVIATOR

Movement: manual-winding tourbillon flyback chronograph RM039 caliber; approx. 50-hour power reserve; full E6B functionality including density altitude and temperature; titanium column wheels, gear wheels and lever; fast rotating barrel; variable inertia balance with overcoil hairspring; spline screws in grade-5 titanium for the bridges and case; going train teeth with central involute profile.
Functions: hours, minutes, seconds; split-seconds chronograph: 30-minute counter; power reserve; torque indicators; function indicator.

Case: anatomically curved three-piece case; Ø 50mm, thickness: 17.8mm; assembled with spline screws in grade-5 titanium; sapphire crystal front and back with double-sided antireflective coating; water resistant to 50 meters.
Dial: sapphire crystal with double-sided antireflective treatment; protected with eight silicon braces in grooved edges.
Strap: rubber; attached via titanium screws to the case; matching buckle individually engraved with model number.
Note: limited to 30 pieces.
Available in: full titanium.

TOURBILLON SPLIT SECONDS COMPETITION CHRONOGRAPH — RM 050 FM

Movement: manual-winding tourbillon RMCC1 caliber (9.5g); approx. 70-hour power reserve; skeletonized grade-5 titanium baseplate; titanium column wheels, gear wheels and lever; split-seconds mechanism with improved and patented functions; fast rotating barrel; variable inertia balance with overcoil hairspring; in-line lever escapement; spline screws in grade-5 titanium for the bridges and case; going train teeth with central involute profile.

Functions: hours, minutes, seconds; split-seconds chronograph: 30-minute counter; power reserve; torque indicators; function indicator.
Case: anatomically curved three-piece case; 50.5x42.7mm, thickness: 16.3mm; assembled with 20 spline screws in grade-5 titanium; sapphire crystal front and back with double-sided antireflective coating; water resistant to 50 meters.
Dial: sapphire crystal with double-sided antireflective treatment; protected with eight silicon braces in grooved edges.
Strap: leather or crocodile; attached via titanium screws to the case; matching buckle individually engraved with model number.
Note: limited edition of 10 pieces.
Available in: carbon nanotube injected composite.

TOURBILLON — RM 051 PHOENIX-MICHELLE YEOH

Movement: manual-winding tourbillon RM051 caliber; approx. 48-hour power reserve; black onyx baseplate; variable inertia balance with overcoil hairspring; fast rotating barrel; ceramic tourbillon endstone; spline screws in grade-5 titanium for the bridges and case; winding barrel and third pinion's teeth with central involute profile; jewels set in white-gold chatons; torque-limiting crown.
Functions: hours, minutes; power reserve.

Case: anatomically curved three-part case; 48x39.7mm, thickness: 12.8mm; assembled with 12 spline screws in grade-5 titanium; sapphire crystal front and back with double-sided antireflective coating; water resistant to 50 meters.
Dial: sapphire crystal with double-sided antireflective treatment; protected with eight silicon braces in grooved edges.
Strap: leather or crocodile; attached via titanium screws to the case; matching buckle.
Note: limited to 18 pieces.
Available in: titanium; 18K red and white gold.

SKULL TOURBILLON — RM 052

Movement: manual-winding tourbillon RM052 caliber created from grade-5 titanium; approx. 48-hour power reserve; fast rotating barrel; variable inertia balance with overcoil hairspring; ceramic tourbillon endstone; spline screws in grade-5 titanium for the bridges and case; winding barrel and third pinion's teeth with central involute profile; jewels set in chatons.
Functions: hours, minutes; power reserve.

Case: anatomically curved three-part case; 50x42.7mm, thickness: 15.95mm; assembled with 20 spline screws in grade-5 titanium; sapphire crystal front and back with double-sided antireflective coating; water resistant to 50 meters.
Dial: sapphire crystal with double-sided antireflective treatment; protected with eight silicon braces in grooved edges.
Strap: leather or crocodile; attached via titanium screws to the case; matching buckle.
Note: limited edition of 15 pieces in titanium and 6 unique pieces in 18K red gold.
Available in: titanium; 18K red gold.

TOURBILLON — RM 053 PABLO MAC DONOUGH

Movement: manual-winding tourbillon RM053 caliber (30° inclined); approx. 48-hour power reserve; variable inertia balance with overcoil hairspring; ceramic tourbillon endstone; spline screws in grade-5 titanium for the bridges and case; winding barrel and third pinion's teeth with central involute profile; jewels set in chatons; torque-limiting crown.
Functions: hours, minutes, seconds.
Case: anatomically curved three-piece case; 50x42.7mm, thickness: 20mm; assembled with spline screws in grade-5 titanium; sapphire crystal front and back with double-sided antireflective coating; water resistant to 50 meters.
Dial: sapphire crystal with double-sided antireflective treatment; protected with eight silicon braces in grooved edges.
Strap: composite; attached via titanium screws to the case; matching buckle.
Note: limited edition of 15 pieces.
Available in: titanium carbide/titanium combination.

AUTOMATIC — RM 055 BUBBA WATSON

Movement: manual-winding skeletonized chronometer RMUL2 caliber (4.3g); approx. 55-hour power reserve; PVD-coated titanium baseplate, bridges and balance cock; double-winding barrel; spline screws in grade-5 titanium for the movement and case.
Functions: hours, minutes, seconds.
Case: anatomically curved three-piece case; 49.9x42.7mm, thickness: 13.05mm; crown in sandblasted grade-5 titanium with double-seal O ring and collar in Alcryn; assembled with 20 spline screws in grade-5 titanium; sapphire crystal front and back with double-sided antireflective coating; water resistant to 30 meters.
Dial: sapphire crystal with double-sided antireflective treatment; protected with eight silicon braces in grooved edges.
Strap: special composite; matching buckle.
Available in: rubberized grade-5 titanium caseband and back with ATZ front bezel.

TOURBILLON SPLIT SECONDS COMPETITION CHRONOGRAPH — RM 056 FM SAPPHIRE

Movement: manual-winding tourbillon RMCC1 caliber (9.5g); approx. 70-hour power reserve; skeletonized grade-5 titanium baseplate; titanium column wheels, gear wheels and lever; split-seconds mechanism with improved and patented functions; fast rotating barrel; variable inertia balance with overcoil hairspring; in-line lever escapement; spline screws in grade-5 titanium for the bridges and case; going train teeth with central involute profile.
Functions: hours, minutes, seconds; split-seconds chronograph: 30-minute counter; power reserve; torque indicators; function indicator.
Case: anatomically curved three-piece case; 50x42mm, thickness: 18.85mm; created in synthetic sapphire during 1,000 hours of machining; assembled with 20 spline screws in grade-5 titanium.
Dial: sapphire crystal with double-sided antireflective treatment; protected with eight silicon braces in grooved edges.
Strap: special composite; attached via titanium screws to the case; matching buckle.
Note: limited edition of five numbered unique pieces worldwide.
Available in: sapphire.

TOURBILLON — RM 057 DRAGON-JACKIE CHAN

Movement: manual-winding tourbillon RM057 caliber; approx. 48-hour power reserve; black onyx baseplate; variable inertia balance with overcoil hairspring; ceramic tourbillon endstone; spline screws in grade-5 titanium for the bridges and case; winding barrel and third pinion's teeth with central involute profile; jewels set in chatons; torque-limiting crown.
Functions: hours, minutes; power reserve.
Case: anatomically curved three-part case; 50x42.7mm, thickness: 14.55mm; assembled with 12 spline screws in grade-5 titanium; sapphire crystal front and back with double-sided antireflective coating; water resistant to 50 meters.
Dial: sapphire crystal with double-sided antireflective treatment; protected with eight silicon braces in grooved edges.
Strap: leather or crocodile; attached via titanium screws to the case; matching buckle.
Note: limited edition of 36 pieces.
Available in: 18K red and white gold.

ROGER DUBUIS

HORLOGER GENEVOIS

RAISE THE STAKES

Founded by a duo of horological superstars in 1995, Roger Dubuis's swift rise through the ranks of fine Swiss watchmaking is the result of a determination to innovate at every stage of the creative process.

Less than two decades after the brand's inception, a strict adherence to a set of rooted principles put in place by co-founders Carlos Dias and Roger Dubuis has allowed the manufacture to transform the sphere of haute horology with a code of excellence reflected by the distinction of the Geneva Seal on every produced timepiece.

With the presentation of La Monégasque collection, Roger Dubuis boldly reflects its founding principles of innovative design, cutting-edge style, absolute exclusivity, and high-end technical proficiency. Honoring the dazzling spirit of Monaco's Monte Carlo Casino, the line of timepieces embodies the elegant audacity of the high-stakes player who wears it. Comprised of five principal versions, and a total of eight models, La Monégasque combines the deep tradition of sophisticated watchmaking with strength of character that unmistakably trumpets the glory of modernity. Round dials, stretching the refined curves of the bezels, are home to dramatic expressions of the brand's very own high-stakes temperament. Behind the daring dials, Roger Dubuis's latest mechanical masterpieces provide the heartbeat of the timepieces' intricate choreographies.

Upon a rhodium-plated sunburst dial center, La Monégasque Perpetual Calendar delivers a timeless complication that evokes the grandeur of time. This supreme feat of miniaturization is contained within a 44mm pink-gold case with a black DLC-coated titanium bezel, embodying refined luxury with ultimate precision.

LA MONÉGASQUE PERPETUAL CALENDAR

With pink-gold applied Arabic numerals and a comprehensive perpetual calendar dial, this Roger Dubuis timepiece captures the essence of precise continuity.

LA MONÉGASQUE FLYING TOURBILLON

Armed with an exposed one-minute tourbillon, the manual-winding RD540 caliber that powers this splendid wristwatch is finely adjusted in six positions and features a 60-hour power reserve.

Much as the card counter subverts the challenges of the casino's most emblematic game, the Monégasque Flying Tourbillon defies the effects of gravity to ensure a performance envied by all who witness its brilliance. Cased in platinum, with a gray rhodium-plated theme, the dial creates a shining stage upon which the large date at 12 o'clock, power reserve indication at 4 o'clock and flying tourbillon ring at half past 7 o'clock shine with pride and elegance.

La Monégasque Limited Edition Chronograph's vibrant color combination of red, black, and green, alludes to the exhilarating world of chance—prosperity or despair in the spin of a roulette wheel. La Monégasque Limited Edition Chronograph evokes the dimly lit ambience of the casino's private room, where revealing the value of each card is a pleasure worth taking one's time, as the brown leather strap with Chesterfield pattern completes the timepiece's luxurious arrangement. On both models, two black snailed counters at 3 and 9 o'clock join the central seconds hand to complete the double-pusher chronograph function of the 4-Hertz RD78 mechanical movement.

The 42mm La Monégasque Automatic, in pink gold or stainless steel, possesses all the exclusive luster of the collection, in two understated variations that let the cool elegance of their design dictate the virtue of their appeal. With a snailed small seconds subdial at 6 o'clock, these two Monégasque Automatic models let the exceptional precision of the RD821 caliber speak for itself.

Finally, La Monégasque Chronograph, presented in either a pink-gold case with black PVD-coated titanium bezel, or in vibrant stainless steel, is a veritable master of time's shortest expressions. Specifically developed for this Monégasque event, the RD680 self-winding chronograph movement that powers these watches features a classic Dubuis self-winding micro-rotor, semi-instant 30-minute counter at 3 o'clock, small seconds at 9 o'clock, and a central chronograph hand that permits the measurement of time at a frequency of 28,800 vph. Finely adjusted in five positions, and distinguished with both the prestigious Geneva Seal and the COSC precision certification, this 261-component exploit of technical excellence boasts a power reserve of 48 hours and a daring vertical clutch that ensures smooth chronometric operation with no loss of amplitude. Under the governance of the house's guiding principles, the RD680 caliber integrates the distinguishing shaping of its bridges, springs, and levers, in combining timeless allure with the most innovative technological expertise of the Genevan manufacture.

With La Monégasque collection, the illustrious Roger Dubuis team unveils a line of wristwatches worthy of the high-stakes players in Monaco's exclusive casinos. Powered by an array of high-performance mechanical movements, the eight models that make up this line of chance equip the wrist with an elegance that exclaims the cutting-edge spirit of a house founded on courage and bold creativity.

LA MONÉGASQUE
LIMITED EDITION CHRONOGRAPH

LA MONÉGASQUE AUTOMATIC

LA MONÉGASQUE CHRONOGRAPH

LA MONEGASQUE AUTOMATIC — REF. MG42-821-90-00/0ER01/B

Movement: automatic-winding RD821 caliber; 48-hour power reserve; 33 jewels.
Functions: hours, minutes; small seconds at 6.
Case: stainless steel; Ø 42mm; water resistant to 5atm.
Dial: dark gray satin center; charcoal snailed small seconds counter; charcoal circular satin exterior; black flange with white transfer and number 60 in red.
Strap: hand-stitched black alligator leather; stainless steel adjustable folding buckle.
Suggested price: $14,700

LA MONEGASQUE AUTOMATIC — REF. MG42-821-59-00/0RR01/B

Movement: automatic-winding RD821 caliber; 48-hour power reserve; 33 jewels.
Functions: hours, minutes; small seconds at 6.
Case: pink gold; Ø 42mm; black PVD-coated titanium bezel; water resistant to 5atm.
Dial: rhodium-plated satin center; rhodium-plated snailed small seconds counter; rhodium-plated circular satin exterior; black flange with white transfer.
Strap: hand-stitched black alligator leather; pink-gold pin buckle.
Suggested price: $25,200

LA MONEGASQUE CHRONOGRAPH — REF. MG44-680-90-00/0ER01/B

Movement: automatic-winding RD680 caliber; 48-hour power reserve; 42 jewels.
Functions: hours, minutes; small seconds at 9; chronograph: 30-minute counter at 3 and central seconds hand.
Case: stainless steel; Ø 44mm; water resistant to 5atm.
Dial: dark gray satin center; charcoal circular satin exterior; charcoal chronograph counters; black flange with red transfers.
Strap: hand-stitched black alligator leather; stainless steel adjustable folding buckle.
Suggested price: $24,200

LA MONEGASQUE LIMITED EDITION CHRONOGRAPH — REF. MG44-78-59-00/0IR01/B

Movement: automatic-winding RD78 caliber; 48-hour power reserve; 33 jewels.
Functions: hours, minutes; small seconds at 9; chronograph: 30-minute counter at 3 and central seconds hand.
Case: pink gold; Ø 44mm; black PVD-coated titanium bezel; sapphire crystal caseback; water resistant to 5atm.
Dial: pink gold color satin center; black intermediate section; black snailed chronograph counters; pink gold color circular satin exterior; black flange with green, red and white transfers.
Strap: hand-stitched black alligator leather; pink-gold pin buckle.
Note: limited edition of 128 pieces.
Suggested price: $38,900

LA MONEGASQUE FLYING TOURBILLON REF. MG44-540-80-00/03R01/B

Movement: manual-winding RD540 caliber; 60-hour power reserve; 28 jewels.
Functions: hours, minutes; flying tourbillon; power reserve indicator.
Case: platinum; Ø 42mm; water resistant to 5atm.
Dial: silver satin center; rhodium-plated satin sunburst intermediate section; charcoal circular satin exterior; rhodium-plated flying tourbillon ring; snailed silver power reserve; white flange with black transfers.
Strap: hand-stitched black alligator leather; platinum pin buckle.
Note: limited edition of 28 pieces.
Suggested price: $157,500

LA MONEGASQUE PERPETUAL CALENDAR REF. MG44-821J-59-00/0RR01/B

Movement: automatic-winding RD821J caliber; 48-hour power reserve; 33 jewels.
Functions: hours, minutes; perpetual calendar.
Case: pink gold; Ø 44mm; black PVD-coated titanium bezel; sapphire crystal caseback; water resistant to 5atm.
Dial: rhodium-plated satin center, black ROGER DUBUIS transfer; rhodium-plated snailed date; rhodium-plated circular exterior; black flange with white transfers.
Strap: hand-stitched black alligator leather; pink-gold pin buckle.
Suggested price: $62,900

EASY DIVER CHRONOGRAPH REF. SED46-78-91-00/09A01/A

Movement: automatic-winding RD78 caliber; 42-hour power reserve; 36 jewels.
Functions: hours, minutes; small seconds at 9; double-pushbutton column-wheel chronograph.
Case: stainless steel; Ø 46mm; molded runner on the bezel, crown and caseback; water resistant to 30atm.
Dial: black; applied rhodium-plated numerals at 12 and 6; black chronograph counters; white Arabic numerals; white-gold hour markers; black flanges; white transferred minute-circle.
Strap: black rubber; stainless steel adjustable folding buckle with black molded rubber.
Note: limited edition of 280 pieces.
Suggested price: $34,000

EASY DIVER AUTOMATIC REF. SED46-821-93-00/09A01/A2

Movement: automatic-winding RD78 caliber; 48-hour power reserve; 33 jewels.
Functions: hours, minutes; small seconds at 6.
Case: stainless steel; Ø 46mm; black ceramic bezel; sapphire crystal caseback; water resistant to 30atm.
Dial: black sunburst; black sectors at 3 and 9; white SuperLumiNova; applied rhodium-plated numeral 12; black small seconds counters at 6; white Arabic numeral transfers; black flange; white motion-work transfers.
Strap: black rubber; stainless steel adjustable folding buckle with black molded rubber.
Note: limited edition of 88 pieces.
Suggested price: $16,300

EXCALIBUR AUTOMATIC LADY — REF. EX36-821-90-10/09R01/F

Movement: automatic-winding RD821 caliber; 48-hour power reserve; 168 components; 28,800 vph.
Functions: hours, minutes; small seconds at 6.
Case: stainless steel; Ø 36mm; bezel set with 48 diamonds (0.99 carat); water resistant to 3atm.
Dial: black satin; mirror-polish applied Roman numerals; black satin small seconds counter.
Strap: black satin-finish fabric; stainless steel adjustable folding buckle.
Suggested price: $16,800

EXCALIBUR AUTOMATIC LADY — REF. EX36-821-50-10/0RR01/F

Movement: automatic-winding RD821 caliber; 48-hour power reserve; 168 components; 28,800 vph.
Functions: hours, minutes; small seconds at 6.
Case: pink gold; Ø 36mm; bezel set with 48 diamonds (0.99 carat); water resistant to 3atm.
Dial: rhodium-plated satin; black Roman numerals; rhodium-plated satin small seconds counter.
Strap: gray satin-finish fabric; pink-gold adjustable folding buckle.
Suggested price: $26,300

EXCALIBUR AUTOMATIC FLYING TOURBILLON — REF. EX45-520-20-00/0ER01/B

Movement: automatic-winding RD520 caliber; 60-hour power reserve; 30 jewels.
Functions: hours, minutes; flying tourbillon.
Case: white gold; Ø 45mm; water resistant to 5atm.
Dial: charcoal; white Roman numerals; black onyx plates; black bottom flange; black top flange.
Strap: hand-stitched black alligator leather; white-gold adjustable folding buckle.
Note: limited edition of 88 pieces.
Suggested price: $149,000

EXCALIBUR DOUBLE FLYING TOURBILLON — REF. EX45-01-50-00/09R01/B

Movement: manual-winding RD01 caliber; 48-hour power reserve; 61 jewels.
Functions: hours, minutes; double flying tourbillon.
Case: pink gold; Ø 45mm; water resistant to 5atm.
Dial: black; gray Roman numerals; pink-gold engraved Arabic numerals and retrograde minute-circle.
Strap: hand-stitched black alligator leather; pink-gold adjustable folding buckle.
Note: limited edition of 88 pieces.
Suggested price: $250,000

EXCALIBUR MINUTE REPEATER TOURBILLON REF. EX45-08-50-00/VER00/B

Movement: automatic-winding RD08 caliber; 60-hour power reserve; 42 jewels.
Functions: hours, minutes; flying tourbillon at 5:30; minute repeater.
Case: pink gold; Ø 45mm; water resistant to 5atm.
Dial: charcoal gray and sapphire crystal; engraved gray Roman numerals; gray bottom flange; black top flange with white minute-circle.
Strap: gray alligator leather; pink-gold adjustable folding buckle.
Note: limited edition of 28 pieces.
Suggested price: $550,000

EXCALIBUR WORLD TIME REF. EX45-1448-50-00/09R01/B

Movement: automatic-winding RD08 caliber; 48-hour power reserve; 69 jewels.
Functions: hours, minutes; three time zones.
Case: pink gold; Ø 45mm; water resistant to 5atm.
Dial: black with plates; white Roman numerals; globe decoration in the center; black time zone displays at 3 and 9; green and red at 9.
Strap: black alligator leather; pink-gold adjustable folding buckle.
Suggested price: $66,000

EXCALIBUR SKELETON FLYING TOURBILLON REF. EX45-505SQ-20-00/0E000/B

Movement: automatic-winding RD505SQ caliber; 60-hour power reserve; 19 jewels.
Functions: hours, minutes; flying tourbillon.
Case: white gold; Ø 45mm; water resistant to 3atm.
Dial: skeleton; flange set with black diamonds; red minute-circle transfer.
Strap: hand-stitched black alligator leather; white-gold adjustable folding buckle.
Note: limited edition of 88 pieces.
Suggested price: $139,000

EXCALIBUR SKELETON DOUBLE FLYING TOURBILLON REF. EX45-01SQ-20-00/0E000/B88

Movement: manual-winding RD01SQ caliber; 48-hour power reserve; 28 jewels.
Functions: hours, minutes; double flying tourbillon.
Case: white gold; Ø 45mm; water resistant to 5atm.
Dial: skeleton; charcoal flange; white minute-circle and ROGER DUBUIS transfers; white-gold screws.
Strap: hand-stitched black alligator leather; white-gold adjustable folding buckle.
Note: limited edition of 88 pieces.
Suggested price: $250,000

ROLEX

THE SPEED OF LIGHT

Adding the creation of innovative alloys to its legendary tradition, Rolex presents two watches that exude passion and refinement.

Fit for a man who dares to experience the drive of life with zeal and conviction, the new Oyster Perpetual Cosmograph Daytona is a state-of-the-art timepiece that pays homage to the collection's legendary heritage. Every component of this elegant and sporty wristwatch is an emblem of speed, elegance, and superior performance.

Certified by the Contrôle Officiel Suisse des Chronomètres (COSC), the high-precision chronograph of the Cosmograph Daytona allows the measure of time to the eighth of a second. Entirely designed and manufactured by Rolex, the 4130 caliber with column wheel and vertical clutch features a revolutionary architecture that provides reduced complexity and increased reliability. The values of high-performance racing exert an influence throughout the watch's engineering. The blue Parachrom hairspring with Breguet overcoil is a feat of innovation that demands attention. Through a fusion of the metals niobium and zirconium, Rolex answers an age-old challenge for the watchmaking industry, by developing an alloy that is both extremely resistant to shocks and immune to magnetic fields.

Obtained by the deposition of finely layered pink gold via magnetron cathode sputtering, the graduations on the black Cerachrom bezel offer perfect readability, complementing the phosphorescent quality of the pink-gold hands and hour markers. The Oyster case in Everose gold houses a chocolate-brown or ivory-colored dial, and is corrosion-resistant, non-fading, and virtually impervious to scratches. A tachometric scale on the bezel allows the wearer to instantly measure the speed of a moving object over a given distance. For example, if a driver wearing the Cosmograph Daytona is driving at 180 miles per hour, he immediately knows that a mile will have been traveled in exactly 20 seconds. The name Daytona, in red lettering, is a finishing touch that pays tribute to the most prestigious racing circuit in America.

With its cutting-edge technology and powerful aesthetics, the Oyster Perpetual Cosmograph Daytona boasts the finest principles of high-performance racing while echoing the understated elegance of its owner.

OYSTER PERPETUAL COSMOGRAPH DAYTONA

Worn with a black Alligator Mississippiensis leather strap, this 28,800 vph chronometer takes a racing collection born in 1963 to new heights of innovation.

Continuing the Oyster Perpetual theme, Rolex presents the DateJust Special Edition—a dazzling feminine wristwatch that uses light as a playground of seduction.

With a case, bezel, and bracelet made of 18-karat Everose gold, Rolex's own exclusive alloy creation, this self-winding timepiece immediately sets a lustrous tone of nobility. Twelve brilliant-cut diamonds in 18-karat white-gold settings adorn the bezel and contribute to the enchanting quality of the luminous and dynamic design of the watch. The Goldust Dream dial, in white or black mother-of-pearl, however, is the splendid centerpiece of this work of art. Through a patented PVD process that preserves the mother-of-pearl's natural structure while giving it a superb metallic sheen, finely layered pink-gold dust creates a subtle yet exquisite design to complement the nature-inspired motif of the dial. As a result of this delicate process, the embellished mother-of-pearl shimmers sensually with every ray of light, creating unique displays of splendid illumination. A large gem-set numeral at 6 o'clock adds to the graceful audacity of the watch and brings together the intricacy of the face and the vitality of the bezel.

The date at 3 o'clock is subtly magnified by a Cyclops lens with double antireflective coating, proposing a sophisticated element of perspective to this 34mm chronometer. A magical play on luminosity, the DateJust Special Edition offers the woman who wears it an unmistakable aura of majesty.

With the Cosmograph Daytona and DateJust Special Edition, Rolex adds to its legacy two stunning spectacles of elegance and intensity, brilliantly capturing the inebriating essence of speed and the glory of light.

OYSTER PERPETUAL DATEJUST SPECIAL EDITION

Highly technical processes and craftsmanship make this ladies' timepiece a veritable light show.

COSMOGRAPH DAYTONA REF. 116515LN

Movement: automatic-winding 4130 caliber; Rolex manufactured; bidirectional automatic-winding via perpetual rotor on ball bearings; 72-hour power reserve; 44 jewels; 28,800 vph; non-magnetic blue Parachrom hairspring; Breguet overcoil; large balance wheel with variable inertia; high-precision regulating via four gold Microstella nuts; traversing balance bridge; high-performance Paraflex shock absorbers; COSC-certified chronograph.
Functions: hours, minutes; small seconds at 6; column-wheel chronograph: 12-hour counter at 9, 30-minute counter at 3 and central seconds hand; tachometric scale.

Case: 18K Everose gold; Ø 40mm; polished finish; monobloc black Cerachrom bezel with engraved pink-gold numerals; screw-down winding crown; scratch-resistant sapphire crystal; screw-down caseback with Rolex fluting; water resistant to 10atm.
Dial: chocolate brown; 18K pink-gold subdials; gold Arabic numerals with black PVD coating; phosphorescent hour markers at 3, 6 and 9; 18K pink-gold hands filled with phosphorescent material.
Strap: black alligator Mississippiensis leather; 18K Everose gold Oysterlocking folding clasp with safety catch.
Price: available upon request.

OYSTER PERPETUAL SUBMARINER DATE REF. 116613 LN

Movement: automatic-winding; 31 jewels; COSC-certified chronograph.
Functions: hours, minutes, seconds; date at 3.
Case: stainless steel and yellow gold; Ø 40mm; black ceramic rotating bezel; sapphire crystal; water resistant to 30atm.
Dial: black; luminescent hour markers.
Bracelet: 18K Oyster; Oysterlock with Easylink comfort extension link.
Price: available upon request.
Also available: stainless steel with black dial (ref. 16610); stainless steel and yellow gold with blue dial (ref. 116613LB).

OYSTER PERPETUAL SUBMARINER DATE REF. 116610 LN / 97200

Movement: automatic-winding perpetual rotor 3135 caliber; 48-hour power reserve; 28,800 vph; Parachrom hairspring with Breguet overcoil; COSC-certified chronograph.
Functions: hours, minutes, seconds; date at 3; instantaneous change and rapid setting.
Case: 904L steel; Ø 40mm; unidirectional rotating bezel with black Cerachrom insert, platinum graduations; Triplock winding crown, shoulders to protect the crown; sapphire crystal, Cyclops lens with antireflective coating; water resistant to 30atm.

Dial: black; luminescent Chromalight hands and hour markers.
Bracelet: 904L steel; Rolex Glidelock clasp.
Price: available upon request.

OYSTER PERPETUAL SUBMARINER DATE REF. 116610 LV / 97200

Movement: automatic-winding perpetual rotor 3135 caliber; 48-hour power reserve; 28,800 vph; Parachrom hairspring with Breguet overcoil; COSC-certified chronograph.
Functions: hours, minutes, seconds; date at 3; instantaneous change and rapid setting.
Case: 904L steel; Ø 40mm; unidirectional rotating bezel with green Cerachrom insert, platinum graduations; Triplock winding crown, shoulders to protect the crown; sapphire crystal, Cyclops lens with antireflective coating; water resistant to 30atm.

Dial: green gold; luminescent Chromalight hands and hour markers.
Bracelet: 904L steel; Rolex Glidelock clasp.
Price: available upon request.

OYSTER PERPETUAL DATEJUST SPECIAL EDITION — REF. 81315-7284

Movement: automatic-winding 2235 caliber; Rolex manufactured; bidirectional automatic-winding via perpetual rotor on ball bearings; 48-hour power reserve; 31 jewels; 28,800 vph; hairspring with Breguet overcoil; large balance wheel with variable inertia; high-precision regulating via two gold Microstella nuts; traversing balance bridge; high-performance Paraflex shock absorbers; COSC-certified chronograph.
Functions: hours, minutes, seconds; date at 3.
Case: 18K Everose gold; Ø 34mm; polished finish; monobloc case middle; bezel set with 12 brilliant-cut diamonds (0.39 carat); screw-down winding crown; scratch-resistant sapphire crystal; screw-down caseback with Rolex fluting; water resistant to 10atm.
Dial: mother-of-pearl; 18K gold Roman numerals, large gem-set VI hour marker; 18K pink-gold hands.
Bracelet: 18K Everose gold, polished finish; 18K Everose gold folding clasp with invisible crown clasp.
Price: available upon request.

OYSTER PERPETUAL LADY-DATEJUST — REF. 179383–63133

Movement: automatic-winding 2235 caliber; Rolex manufactured; bidirectional automatic-winding via perpetual rotor on ball bearings; 48-hour power reserve; 31 jewels; 28,800 vph; hairspring with Breguet overcoil; large balance wheel with variable inertia; high-precision regulating via two gold Microstella nuts; traversing balance bridge; high-performance paraflex shock absorbers; COSC-certified chronograph.
Functions: hours, minutes, seconds; date at 3.
Case: yellow Rolesor (904L stainless steel superalloy and 18K yellow gold); Ø 26mm; polished finish; monobloc case middle; 18K yellow-gold bezel set with 46 brilliant-cut diamonds (0.67 carat); 18K yellow-gold screw-down winding crown; scratch-resistant sapphire crystal; screw-down caseback with Rolex fluting; water resistant to 10atm.
Dial: 18K yellow-gold and gray Rolex Jubliée motif; 18K gold bezel settings; set with 10 diamond hour markers; 18K yellow-gold hands.
Bracelet: three-piece links; Oyster clasp with invisible crown clasp.
Price: available upon request.
Also available: ivory colored with sunbeam guilloché decoration.

OYSTER PERPETUAL EXPLORER II — REF. 216570-77210

Movement: automatic-winding 3187 caliber; Rolex manufactured; bidirectional automatic-winding via perpetual rotor on ball bearings; 48-hour power reserve; 31 jewels; 28,800 vph; non-magnetic blue Parachrom hairspring; Breguet overcoil; large balance wheel with variable inertia; high-precision regulating via four gold Microstella nuts; traversing balance bridge; high-performance Paraflex shock absorbers; COSC-certified chronograph.
Functions: hours, minutes, stop seconds; date at 3; 24-hour hand; GMT.
Case: 904L stainless steel superalloy; Ø 42mm; polished and satin finished; 24-hour graduated, sun satin-finished fixed bezel polished with beveled edges; screw-down crown; scratch-resistant sapphire crystal; screw-down caseback with Rolex fluting; water resistant to 10atm.
Dial: white lacquered; wide, hollowed, black lacquered white-gold hands; orange 24-hour hand; black, satin-finished Chromalight display with long-lasting luminescence; applied white-gold hour markers.
Bracelet: three-piece solid links; 904L steel superalloy, satin finished, polished edge; Oysterlock folding clasp with safety catch.
Price: available upon request.

OYSTER PERPETUAL YACHT-MASTER II — REF. 116681-78211

Movement: automatic-winding 4160 caliber; Rolex manufactured; bidirectional automatic-winding via perpetual rotor on ball bearings; 72-hour power reserve; 42 jewels; 28,800 vph; non-magnetic blue Parachrom hairspring; Breguet overcoil; large balance wheel with variable inertia; high-precision regulating via four gold Microstella nuts; traversing balance bridge; COSC-certified chronograph.
Functions: hours, minutes; small seconds at 6; column-wheel chronograph; retrograde minute hand and on-the-fly synchronization of the countdown seconds and minute hand to the nearest minute.
Case: Everose Rolesor (combination of 904L stainless steel superalloy and 18K Everose gold); Ø 44mm; monobloc case middle; 18K Everose gold winding crown; 18K Everose gold bidirectional 90° rotatable bezel; blue Cerachrom insert with engraved numerals filled with pink gold via magnetron cathode sputtering; scratch-resistant sapphire crystal; screw-down caseback with Rolex fluting; water resistant to 10atm.
Dial: white lacquered; snailed pink-gold small seconds counter; twelve applied pink-gold hour markers; pink-gold hands with blue.
Bracelet: three-piece solid links; Everose Rolesor; polished center links and satin-finished outer links with polished edges; Oysterlock folding clasp with safety catch.
Price: available upon request.

STÜHRLING
ORIGINAL

RESPECTING ART AND TRADITION

Stührling Original is dedicated to offering fine timepieces made in the artful tradition of Swiss heritage.

The meticulous details of Stührling Original timepieces are key: movements are decorated with Cotes de Genève, perlage and Damier treatments, screws are blued, cases are blanked from solid 316L surgical grade stainless steel and dials are hydraulically guilloché with vintage machines and produced one at a time to offer distinct impressions and appeal.

Stührling Original timepieces cover a broad spectrum, ranging from the casual, everyday wear of the brand's Lifestyles and Sportsman's Collections to the most formal and sophisticated dress pieces of the Special Reserve and Boardroom lines.

Models range from stylistic Art Deco-inspired timepieces, such as the Gatsby Series, to the more traditional designs of the watchmaker's Heritage Series, from Old World designs such as their signature Emperor line, to the contemporary styles of the Metro and Epiphany Collections.

Continuing the expansion of the brand, 2011 has spawned an entirely new collection: Stührling Prestige. This luxury line is comprised of all Swiss Made models featuring the highest-quality movements (ETA Valjoux 7750), and its models feature the finest components and craftsmanship upon which the Swiss label has built its reputation.

Whether Stührling Original or Stührling Prestige, all of the fine timepieces in Stührling's gallery of more than 1,200 models are made with respect for the art and tradition of the Swiss watchmaking legend.

EMPEROR'S TOURBILLON

Individually hand-crafted in Switzerland, Stührling Original's Emperor's Tourbillon marks a first in the watchmaker's rich history—it is its first completely skeletonized tourbillon model ever created. The 18-jewel mechanical ST-93351 tourbillon movement beats at 28,800 vph, and has been masterfully skeletonized and decorated with deeply engraved scrollwork. Harkening back to an earlier age of watchmaking, the round 46mm Emperor case design, with the crown and bow at 12 o'clock, recalls a time when pocket watches were first strapped to the wrist. A subtle mother-of-pearl dial ring accents the whirlwind motif on the Emperor's face. A 24mm-wide genuine crocodile strap adorns the Emperor's Tourbillon, which is available in a limited edition of 333 pieces (111 each in silvertone, rose-tone and goldtone).

EMPEROR'S GLORY

One of Stührling Original's crowning achievements, the Emperor's Glory makes its mark as a stunning example of design and engineering. The 46mm case is constructed from solid stainless steel, and pays homage to its pocket watch roots with a bow and crown at 12 o'clock. Powered by the 22-jewel ST-91015 caliber, this beautifully skeletonized timepiece features a dual-time complication, AM/PM indicator, flywheel and bridge at 3 o'clock, and dual barrel with two mainsprings for up to 72 hours of power reserve. The minute track is accented with diamond hour markers for a truly scintillating finish.

PHANTOM TOURBILLON

The concept of a ceramic case and bracelet with a carbon-fiber dial and a genuine tourbillon movement displays a brilliant execution in Stührling Original's Phantom Tourbillon. Unlike Stührling Original's previous tourbillon models, the design of the Phantom shows more versatility with a clean look that is equally suited to a formal dress event or more casual sporty look. The 47mm ceramic case houses the ST-93301 caliber, an 18-jewel tourbillon movement which beats at 28,800 vph and features a custom tourbillon assembly accented with a triple "S" design denoting Stührling Original. The Limited Edition Phantom Tourbillon is completely hand assembled in Switzerland and the entire edition consists of 400 pieces (320 in black and 80 in white).

ACCOLADE

The Accolade is a member of Stührling Original's Prestige Collection, a special line of timepieces made with the finest materials by the most talented and capable hands. Within the beautifully constructed 42mm case beats the 25-jewel ETA Valjoux 7750 Swiss Made automatic chronograph movement. Its complications include a chronograph minute counter, 12-hour totalizer, small seconds, and day and date indications. Its polished design extends to the dial, which is home to the individually hand-applied Roman numerals.

COMMANDER

Within the bold and sporty exterior of the Commander is the Swiss Ronda Startech 5030-D chronograph movement. Its complications include add-and-split functionality, chronograph minute counter, 12-hour totalizer, small seconds and a quick-set date. The 47mm case is constructed of solid 316L stainless steel and is framed with a beautifully polished dodecagonal bezel. Individually hand-applied hour markers rest atop a dial with a hydraulically embossed starburst design. The Commander is finished with a fully integrated high-grade silicon rubber strap with tire tread and wave design.

MAVERICK

From Stührling Prestige's entirely Swiss Made lineup comes the Maverick. Its rugged stainless steel construction is home to the automatic-winding ETA Valjoux 7750 movement. With 25 jewels, its complications include a chronograph minute counter, 12-hour totalizer, small seconds, and day and date indications. This timepiece's wild, energetic personality is enhanced by its high-rising unidirectional ratcheting bezel, which features the same gear-edge design as the pushers and screw-down crown. The deep-set dial is decorated with a hydraulically embossed starburst pattern and accented with individually hand-applied markers. The Maverick is finished with a high-grade silicon rubber strap with tire tread design.

LAUREL

Stührling Prestige's Laurel is powered by the self-winding Swiss Made ST-80003 caliber. With 27 jewels and 42 hours of power reserve, the Swiss engine provides hours, minutes, small seconds and a quick-set date complication. The Laurel represents the quintessential boardroom style with its Clous de Paris dial design in concert with Breguet-style hands, individually hand-applied Roman numerals and a brilliantly polished case.

TAG HEUER FORMULA 1
LADY STEEL AND CERAMIC PAVEE

The cycle of time in women's lives, this constant flow we all would like to suspend for a minute, an hour or a year is inflexible. As immutable and unalterable as ceramic. Forever is diamonds' unique shine. Both meet in the Formula 1 Lady Steel and Ceramic, the highly successful feminine timepiece launched in 2010. With this new Pavée edition, TAG Heuer's fashion icon takes dazzle to its most generous expression: a mysterious and feminine timepiece set with 136 diamonds that personifies the myriad richness of the TAG Heuer woman and that exudes one of the prestigious brand's most distinctive creations, the Formula 1.

CARRERA CALIBRE 1887 CHRONOGRAPH REF. CAR2012.FC6235

Movement: automatic-winding TAG Heuer Calibre 1887.
Functions: hours, minutes; small seconds at 9; date at 6; chronograph: 12-hour counter at 6, 30-minute counter at 12 and central seconds hand.
Case: polished stainless steel; Ø 43mm; polished bezel, crown and pushbuttons; antireflective scratch-resistant curved sapphire crystal; scratch-resistant sapphire caseback; water resistant to 10atm.

Dial: silver; protruded polished rose-gold-colored Arabic numerals; polished rose-gold-plated hour and minute hands with luminescent markers; chronograph counters with azurage and black polished hands; protruded and polished rose-gold-colored TAG Heuer logo and "Carrera" lettering; Minuterie on the flange; "Cal. 1887" and "Swiss Made" lettering on the dial.
Strap: black alligator.
Price: available upon request.
Also available: silver dial with brown alligator strap or steel bracelet; black dial with black alligator strap or steel bracelet.

CARRERA CALIBRE 16 DAY-DATE CHRONOGRAPH REF. CV2A10.BA0796

Movement: automatic-winding TAG Heuer Calibre 16.
Functions: hours, minutes; small seconds at 9; day and date at 3; chronograph: 12-hour counter at 6, 30-minute counter at 12 and central seconds hand.
Case: polished stainless steel; Ø 43mm; aluminum bezel with black tachometer scale; polished oversized crown and pushbuttons; antireflective scratch-resistant domed sapphire crystal; scratch-resistant sapphire crystal caseback; water resistant to 10atm.

Dial: black; hand-applied Arabic numerals; polished steel hour and minute hands with luminescent markers; silver-ringed chronograph counters with polished hands and small seconds hand with red tip; hand-applied monochrome TAG Heuer logo.
Bracelet: five-row alternate fine-brushed and polished steel; solid steel folding clasp with safety pushbuttons.
Price: available upon request.
Also available: black dial with black alligator strap; silver dial with black alligator strap or steel bracelet.

CARRERA CALIBRE 16 RACING CHRONOGRAPH REF. CV2014.FT6014

Movement: automatic-winding TAG Heuer Calibre 16.
Functions: hours, minutes; small seconds at 9; date at 3; chronograph: 12-hour counter at 6, 30-minute counter at 12 and central seconds hand.
Case: polished stainless steel; Ø 41mm; aluminum bezel with black tachometer; polished oversized crown and pushbuttons; antireflective scratch-resistant domed sapphire crystal; screw-down caseback with a specific FANGIO decoration; water resistant to 10atm.

Dial: black; sunray center and spiral outer band; hand-applied hour and minute markers; polished steel hour and minute hands with luminescent markers; silver-ringed chronograph counters with red hands; monochrome TAG Heuer logo.
Strap: thick black perforated rubber embossed with TAG Heuer; polished steel folding clasp with safety pushbuttons.
Price: available upon request.
Also available: five-row alternate fine-brushed and polished steel bracelet; solid steel folding clasp with safety pushbuttons.

AQUARACER AUTOMATIC CHRONOGRAPH CALIBRE 16 REF. CAP2110.BA0833

Movement: automatic-winding TAG Heuer Calibre 16.
Functions: hours, minutes; small seconds at 9; date at 3; chronograph: 12-hour counter at 6, 30-minute counter at 12 and central seconds hand.
Case: polished and fine-brushed stainless steel; Ø 42mm; unidirectional turning bezel in fine-brushed steel with polished studs with engraved black lacquered numerals and luminescent dot at 12; polished screw-down crown; scratch-resistant sapphire crystal; screw-down caseback with special diver decoration; water resistant to 30atm.

Dial: black with horizontal streak effect; hand-applied hour markers with polished facets and luminescent coating; diamond-shaped hour and minute hands with polished facets and luminescent coating; monochrome TAG Heuer logo.
Bracelet: three-row alternate fine-brushed steel with polished edges; folding buckle with diving extension and safety pushbuttons.
Price: available upon request.
Also available: black dial and rubber strap; silver dial and rubber bracelet or steel bracelet; blue dial and rubber bracelet or steel bracelet.

AQUARACER AUTOMATIC WATCH CALIBRE 5 — REF. WAP2011.BA0830

Movement: automatic-winding TAG Heuer Calibre 5.
Functions: hours, minutes, seconds; date at 3.
Case: polished and fine-brushed stainless steel; Ø 41mm, thickness: 11.6mm; unidirectional turning bezel in fine-brushed steel with engraved black lacquered numerals and luminescent dot at 12; polished screw-down crown; scratch-resistant sapphire crystal; screw-down caseback with special diver decoration; water resistant to 30atm.
Dial: silver with horizontal streak effect; hand-applied hour markers with luminescent coating; diamond-shaped hour and minute hands with polished facets and luminescent coating; monochrome TAG Heuer logo; "Aquaracer", "Calibre 5" and "300 Meters" lettering on the dial at 6.
Bracelet: three-row alternate fine-brushed steel with polished edges and pushbuttons.
Price: available upon request.
Also available: black dial.

TAG HEUER FORMULA 1 CHRONO — REF. CAU1115.BA0869

Movement: quartz; RONDA 5040.
Functions: hours, minutes; small seconds at 3; date at 4; chronograph: 1/10th of a second and hour counter at 6, 30-minute counter at 9 and central seconds hand.
Case: fine-brushed stainless steel; Ø 42mm; polished steel and brushed black ceramic fixed bezel with silver tachometer scale; polished steel easy-grip screw-down crown with raised fine-brushed TAG Heuer shield and steel crown protectors; polished steel pushbuttons; circular fine-brushed screw-down caseback with special checkered decorations; water resistant to 20atm.
Dial: anthracite sunray brushed; curved and polished hand-applied numeral 12 and hour indicators with luminescent markers; polished rhodium-plated hour and minute hands with luminescent markers; black azurage chronograph counters; monochrome TAG Heuer Logo; "Tag Heuer Formula 1" and "Swiss Made" lettering; "Minuterie" on the flange.
Bracelet: five-row alternate steel and brushed black ceramic; fine-brushed steel double safety clasp and extension system.
Price: available upon request.
Also available: steel bracelet.

LINK AUTOMATIC CHRONOGRAPH CALIBRE 16 — REF. CAT2010.BA0952

Movement: automatic-winding TAG Heuer Calibre 16.
Functions: hours, minutes; small seconds at 9; date at 3; chronograph: 12-hour counter at 6, 30-minute counter at 12 and central seconds hand.
Case: polished and fine-brushed stainless steel; Ø 43mm; polished and fine-brushed cushion-shaped fixed bezel with black tachometer scale; polished steel screw-down crown and pushbuttons; antireflective scratch-resistant curved sapphire crystal; scratch-resistant screw-down caseback with engraved decoration and TAG Heuer logo; water resistant to 10atm.
Dial: black with vertical streak effect; hand-applied curved, faceted and polished hour markers; faceted polished rhodium-plated hour and minute hands with luminescent coating; oversized subcounter (running seconds) at 9; "Calibre 16" and "Swiss Made" lettering on the dial; hand-applied monochrome TAG Heuer logo.
Bracelet: fine-brushed with polished edges; solid steel folding clasp with safety pushbuttons.
Price: available upon request.
Also available: silver dial.

MONACO V4 TITANIUM & CERAMICS — REF. WAW2080.FC6288

Movement: automatic belt-driven transmission; tungsten ingot linear mass; two pairs of barrels in series, set in parallel and linked by belts.
Functions: hours, minutes; small seconds at 4.
Case: bi-material: polished grade 5 titanium and fine-brushed ceramic; Ø 41mm; titanium crown; beveled sapphire crystal with double sided antireflective treatment; sapphire caseback in three sections; water resistant to 5atm.
Dial: seven fine-brushed bridges coated with black ruthenium with Côtes de Genève and haute horology hand-finishings; escapement and belt-driven transmission visible from the front; faceted rhodium-plated hour and minute hands with luminescent coating; faceted rhodium-plated small seconds hand; engraved white "V4"; white TAG Heuer logo at 10.
Strap: hand-sewn anthracite alligator leather with soft-touch effect; titanium folding buckle with safety pushbuttons; engraved with "V4".
Note: limited edition of 200 pieces (engraved and numbered on the linear mass).
Price: available upon request.

AQUARACER LADY REF. WAF1313.BA0819

Movement: quartz.
Functions: hours, minutes, seconds; date at 3.
Case: polished stainless steel; Ø 32mm, thickness: 9.55mm; unidirectional turning bezel with polished steel base set with 42 Top Wesselton diamonds (0.567 carat); polished screw-down crown; scratch-resistant sapphire crystal; screw-down caseback with stamped diver decoration; water resistant to 30atm.
Dial: white mother-of-pearl; hand-applied curved numeral 12; hour markers set with 10 Top Wesselton diamonds (0.098 carat); polished finished hour and minute hands with luminescent coating; polished and protruded TAG Heuer logo.
Bracelet: five-row alternate fine-brushed and polished steel; solid steel folding clasp with safety pushbuttons.
Price: available upon request.
Also available: without diamond bezel.

AQUARACER LADY REF. WAF1450.BB0825

Movement: quartz.
Functions: hours, minutes, seconds; date at 3.
Case: polished stainless steel; Ø 27mm; 2N 18K gold-plated polished unidirectional turning bezel set with 35 Top Wesselton diamonds (0.48 carat); 2N 18K gold-plated polished screw-down crown; scratch-resistant sapphire crystal; screw-down caseback with stamped diver decoration; water resistant to 30atm.
Dial: white mother-of-pearl; gold-plated numeral 12; hour markers set with 10 Top Wesselton diamonds (0.07 carat); gold-plated hour and minute hands with luminescent coating; polished and protruded monochrome TAG Heuer logo.
Bracelet: three-row steel and 2N 18K gold plated; solid steel clasp with diving extension system and safety pushbuttons; alternately finished with polished central 2N 18K gold-plated row, fine-brushed steel lateral rows, and polished edges.
Price: available upon request.
Also available: without diamond bezel.

TAG HEUER FORMULA 1 LADY STEEL & CERAMIC REF. WAH1315.BA0868

Movement: quartz; ETA F03.111.
Functions: hours, minutes, seconds; date at 3.
Case: polished stainless steel; Ø 32mm; polished fixed steel and white ceramic bezel engraved with black minute indicators; polished steel screw-down crown with protectors; sapphire crystal; polished screw-down caseback; water resistant to 20atm.
Dial: white; hour markers set with 12 Wesselton diamonds (0.09 carat); rhodium-faceted hour and minute hands with luminescent markers; protruded monochrome TAG Heuer logo; "TAG Heuer Formula 1" and "Swiss Made" lettering on the dial.
Bracelet: five-row alternate steel and white ceramic; polished steel butterfly folding clasp and safety pushbuttons.
Price: available upon request.
Also available: black version.

TAG HEUER FORMULA 1 LADY STEEL & CERAMIC REF. WAH1312.BA0867

Movement: quartz; ETA F03.111.
Functions: hours, minutes, seconds; date at 3.
Case: polished stainless steel; Ø 32mm; polished fixed steel and black ceramic bezel engraved with black minute indicators and set with 48 Wesselton diamonds (0.35 carat); polished steel screw-down crown with protectors; sapphire crystal; polished screw-down caseback; water resistant to 20atm.
Dial: black; hour markers set with 12 Wesselton diamonds (0.09 carat); rhodium-faceted hour and minute hands with luminescent markers; protruded monochrome TAG Heuer logo; "TAG Heuer Formula 1" and "Swiss Made" lettering on the dial.
Bracelet: five-row alternate steel and black ceramic; polished steel butterfly folding clasp and safety pushbuttons.
Price: available upon request.
Also available: white version.

TAG HEUER FORMULA 1 LADY STEEL & CERAMIC CALIBRE 5 REF. WAU2210.BA0859

Movement: automatic-winding TAG Heuer Calibre 5.
Functions: hours, minutes, seconds; date at 6.
Case: polished stainless steel; Ø 37mm; polished fixed steel and black ceramic bezel engraved with black minute indicators; polished steel screw-down crown with protectors; sapphire crystal; sapphire caseback; water resistant to 20atm.
Dial: black; hour markers set with 11 Wesselton diamonds and middle circle set with 38 Wesselton diamonds (total: 0.18 carat); rhodium-faceted hour and minute hands with luminescent markers; protruded monochrome TAG Heuer logo; "TAG Heuer Formula 1 Automatic" and "Swiss Made" lettering on the dial.
Bracelet: five-row alternate polished steel and black ceramic; polished steel butterfly folding clasp and safety pushbuttons.
Price: available upon request.
Also available: white diamond-set dial with diamond-set bezel and steel and ceramic bracelet.

TAG HEUER FORMULA 1 LADY STEEL & CERAMIC CHRONOGRAPH REF. CAH1212.BA0862

Movement: quartz; RONDA 5021D.
Functions: hours, minutes; small seconds at 3; date at 4:30; chronograph: 30-minute counter at 9 and central seconds hand.
Case: polished stainless steel; Ø 41mm; polished fixed stainless steel and black ceramic bezel engraved with black minute indicators and set with 60 Wesselton diamonds (0.44 carat); polished stainless steel screw-down crown and pushbuttons; sapphire crystal; polished screw-down caseback; water resistant to 20atm.
Dial: black; hour markers set with 12 Wesselton diamonds (0.09 carat); polished hour and minute hands with luminescent markers; protruded monochrome TAG Heuer logo; "TAG Heuer Formula 1" lettering on the dial.
Bracelet: five-row alternate polished steel and black ceramic; polished steel butterfly folding clasp and safety pushbuttons.
Price: available upon request.
Also available: white diamond-set dial with diamond-set bezel and steel and ceramic bracelet.

CARRERA LADY ROSE GOLD REF. WV1440.FC8179

Movement: quartz; ETA F03.111.
Functions: hours, minutes, seconds; date at 3.
Case: polished solid 5N 18K rose gold; Ø 27mm; polished 5N 18K rose-gold bezel and crown; antireflective scratch-resistant sapphire crystal; water resistant to 5atm.
Dial: white mother-of-pearl with external spiral effect; hand-applied 5N 18K solid rose-gold hour indicators; polished 5N 18K solid rose-gold hour and minute hands with luminescent markers; printed rose-gold colored TAG Heuer logo and "Carrera" lettering on the dial.
Bracelet: white glossy alligator leather; solid 5N 18K rose-gold pin buckle.
Price: available upon request.
Also available: black alligator leather strap.

TAG HEUER FORMULA 1 LADY STEEL & CERAMIC PAVEE REF. WAH121D.BA0861

Movement: quartz; ETA F05.111.
Functions: hours, minutes, seconds; date at 3.
Case: polished stainless steel; Ø 37mm; polished stainless steel and ceramic bezel set with 72 Wesselton diamonds (0.48 carat); polished stainless steel screw-down crown and protectors; sapphire crystal; polished screw-down caseback; water resistant to 20atm.
Dial: white; hour markers set with 10 Wesselton diamonds and middle circle set with 54 Wesselton diamonds (total: 0.175 carat); polished rhodium-plated hour and minute hands with luminescent markers; protruded TAG Heuer logo.
Bracelet: five-row alternate polished steel and ceramic; polished steel butterfly folding clasp and safety pushbuttons.
Price: available upon request.
Also available: black version.

URWERK®

BAUMGARTNER & FREI / GENEVE

TIME IN ORBIT

United by a fascination for the communication of time in never-before imagined ways, Felix Baumgartner and Martin Frei have shaken the world of haute horology with such excellence that traditionalists have no choice but to stand back in admiration.

UR-110 TORPEDO

Counter-rotating satellites mounted on planetary gears permit the sophisticated modules to remain parallel to one another, providing a fluidity of motion that fits right in line with the Torpedo's modus operandi of optimal time-telling simplicity.

Since 1995, Urwerk has fascinated with rebellious eccentricity and genuine horological pedigree, thriving on the right side of the line between genius and insanity. Drawing from a vast cultural heritage, with visions that belong in the future's future, the dynamic pair continuously reinvents the reading of time.

The UR-110, known as the Torpedo, embodies Urwerk's radical tradition of time telling. While the asymmetry of the grade 5 titanium case provides an immediate visual appeal, the design was in fact ingeniously conceived with the convenience of the wearer in mind. The placement of the graded indicator line on the right of the dial permits a discreet viewing of the time without the need to adjust one's sleeve or cuff. Three torpedo-shaped satellites orbit the expressive dial, taking turns to indicate the time as they traverse the 60-minute track. However, the simplicity of the affair is the result of an extremely sophisticated concept and equally complicated construction.

The silent and subtle journey of the satellites through the dial is a story of fascinating mechanical choreography. Upon a central carousel, the hour modules are mounted on three planetary gears, and conduct a constant counteracting revolution to maintain their parallel alignment throughout the continuous centrally driven orbit. In conjunction, while time is being indicated with optimal clarity, the modules that await their turn rotate on an additional axis, delivering the appropriate upcoming numeral to the visible side of their architecture. A large panoramic sapphire crystal reveals the astounding technology of the Torpedo. The three-dimensional metallic theme of the dial smoothly integrates a day/night indicator, "oil change" gauge that alerts the owner of needed servicing, and small seconds on a subdial.

As the watch is turned over, the titanium caseback shields the innovative UR 9.01 automatic caliber that powers the Torpedo at a frequency of 28,800 vph. A testament to Urwerk's boundless genius, the UR-110 achieves astonishing simplicity through the groundbreaking complexity of its perfectly executed mechanical concept.

UR-110
TURBINE
AUTOMATIC
URWERK
1/55
SWISS MADE
TITANIUM
DAY
NIGHT
OIL
CHANG
min
URWERK
UR-110

UR-1001 ZEIT DEVICE ÜBER COMPLICATION

Along with its dual equation of time displays, ellipsoidal cam, and perpetual calendar complete with moonphase indication, this limited edition timepiece features a finely decorated gold winding rotor.

With the UR-1001 Zeit Device Über Complication, Martin Frei and Felix Baumgartner allow themselves carte blanche in developing a large playground for a constellation of indications, on a dial that places no constraints on the creators' imagination. The eight-piece limited edition, housed within a case coated with super-resistant Aluminum Titanium Nitride (AlTiN), is a decisively modern take on the complicated calendar timepiece. The epoch-defining Zeit Device puts Urwerk's mastery of precision at the service of the measurement of time, from seconds all the way to a monumental millennium. As the chosen of the three orbiting hour satellites makes its passage from zero to 60 minutes, a white pointer, seemingly attached to the module, indicates the passing of minutes in a way only Urwerk could imagine.

The dance, however, lacks no spectacular feats. Over the course of the time-telling journey, the two other modules revolve on their own vertical axis, preparing their respective Arabic numeral for its time of demonstration. Once the pointer has completed the 60-minute interval, the magnificent illusion is revealed. Fixed to a sprung ring around the circumference of the satellite complication, the retrograde pointer separates from its associated module and is launched with flawless accuracy back to zero, where it joins the following hour indicator.

Above the time-telling complication, the UR-1001 Zeit Device boasts a revolving satellite calendar that brings the innovative genius of Urwerk to the realm of the day and month indication. While it is driven by a similar concept to the hours complication, three Maltese crosses intervene, at the end of shorter months, to make the date advance accordingly to the next interval. The smallest units of time measured by the watch also enjoy an innovative display: a three-handed indication displays 3 x 20 seconds on a 120° segment. Appropriately for this limitless playground of Frei and Baumgartner, the caseback reveals an alternative way of thinking about of time. Advancing in five-year increments, the 100-year indicator acts as the watch's precision odometer. In a play of horological wit, Urwerk places a register of the high-performance movement's total running time. When the circular dial reaches 100, the 1,000-year scale to its left takes an imperceptibly slow yet important leap toward the next millennium. As a final touch, the 5-year "oil change" gauge lets its wearer know when the timepiece should be serviced for optimal functioning.

With a visionary approach to the calendar interface and a time-keeping registry that extends to a titanic 1,000 years, the UR-1001 Zeit Device is an avant-garde masterpiece that understands its place in the universe of time.

Finally, Urwerk gives its UR-202, aka The Hammerhead, a full-metal rebirth in collaboration with high-end bracelet manufacture Maspoli.

The Hammerhead's revolving hour satellites feature a twist on the spectacular Urwerk mechanism. Following three vector intervals that mark the minutes, the module's hands adjust their length to allow for optimal clarity when extended, and a comfortably sized case when retracted. This ingenious design is achieved through a patented carousel of microscopic precision. Transporters, which control the hands' variable length, contain separately operating ends. One follows a cam—calculated from 380 reference points—while the other designates the precise length of the indicator. The UR-202S, where the S stands for "stripe" (three-dimensional lines running along the dial, achieved with the newly acquired five-axis CNC machine) is the result of a joint resurgence effort with bracelet specialist Maspoli, an integral player in haute horology since 1951. Aiming to create the Rolls-Royce of bracelets, the Swiss company embarked on an 11-step process that drew on its wealth of expertise. The result is a supremely refined bracelet that contains 22 links, of which only six are identical.

The new UR-202S, in gold, AlTiN, or polished stainless steel, with matching bracelet, is powered by the UR 7.03 caliber. With its rebirth as The Hammerhead – Full Metal Jacket, the UR-202S provides a futuristic home fit for the telescopic minute hands and orbiting satellite complication that dictate its precise telling of the time.

As has always been the house's trademark, Urwerk once again sends shockwaves through the world of haute horology. With three watches of exclusive time-telling eccentricity, the Genevan manufacture recalibrates the notion of the wristwatch with a measure of excellence and imagination that furthers watchmaking's ancient spirit of relentless innovation.

UR-202S THE HAMMERHEAD

Telescopic variable-length minute hands extend for optimal clarity on the three-vector 60-minute scale, then retract within the case, mounted on a bracelet by Maspoli.

VACHERON CONSTANTIN

Manufacture Horlogère. Genève, depuis 1755.

A LEGENDARY PATRIMONY

An esteemed leader in the world of haute horology for more than two and a half centuries, Vacheron Constantin proudly pays tribute to the 125th anniversary of the Poinçon de Genève—the Geneva Seal.

Established in 1886 by the legislative body of the Grand Council of the Republic and Canton of Geneva, the emblematic guarantee of origin, craftsmanship, durability, and expertise celebrates an extension of its certification to the watch in its entirety, and no longer merely the movement that powers it. An avid supporter of this standard of excellence since its creation, Vacheron Constantin unveils three brilliant timepieces stamped with the privileged distinction.

The first Vacheron Constantin watch to meet the newly appointed standards of the Geneva Seal, the Patrimony Traditionnelle 14-Day Tourbillon, is a symbol of unequalled performance housed within a framework of absolute purity. Endowed with an exceptional 14-day power reserve, the newly developed hand-wound 2260 tourbillon caliber provides this watch with optimal precision and enhanced long-term stability. Four barrels, mounted in pairs, unwind simultaneously at an impressively reduced rate, and supply the requisite energy for a full two weeks of power reserve. Inspired by the brand's signature Maltese Cross, the tourbillon cage with small seconds at 6 o'clock (whose bar alone demanded 11 hours of delicate craftsmanship) is a splendid exhibition of the manufacture's exquisite finishing, and features the intricate hand-beveling of several interior angles. Countering the positioning of the tourbillon cage on the lower half of the silver-toned opaline dial, the 280° power reserve indication at 12 o'clock draws inspiration from the architecture of several of the brand's 20th-century pocket watches. A faithful reflection of the collection's rigorous standards and elegant purism, the Patrimony Traditionnelle 14-Day Tourbillon is anchored by rose-gold dauphine hands, housed within an 18-karat rose-gold case. The refinement of the timepiece's details and slender bezel reminds us that the graceful balance of timeless tradition and intelligent modernity continues to define Vacheron Constantin's heritage.

PATRIMONY TRADITIONNELLE 14-DAY TOURBILLON

A masterful blend of tradition and modern expertise, this is Vacheron Constantin's first watch honored with the newly redefined Geneva Seal.

PATRIMONY CONTEMPORAINE SMALL MODEL

Sixty-two brilliant-cut diamonds on the case middle brilliantly testify that aesthetic simplicity, when perfected, can also be a symbol of luxury.

Adorning the feminine wrist with a tone of understated sensuality, the Patrimony Contemporaine Small Model is powered by the 1400 caliber, an entirely in-house hand-wound movement that bears the prestigious Geneva Seal. Embellishing the slender purity of the 6.7mm profile, 62 brilliant-cut diamonds accentuate the seductive elegance of the watch's case middle. Lean hour and minute hands sweep the gold-beaded minute circle with long applied hour markers, in pursuit of distinguished simplicity. The gently-curved 36mm case, in 18-karat rose or white gold, frames a sober silver-toned opaline dial that finds beauty in the bare honesty of mechanical rhythm. While the movement echoes a design imbued with the authenticity of the house's rich tradition, the entirely hand-crafted finishing is matched by a degree of technical sophistication worthy of the recognition that has been bestowed upon it. A picture of supreme feminine elegance, the Patrimony Contemporaine Small Model embodies the nobility of Vacheron Constantin's profound horological expertise.

With the development of the Patrimony Contemporaine Self-Winding, part of the Collection Excellence Platine, the Genevan watchmaker rewards the purity of the collection's lines with the prestigious refinement of 950 platinum. Powered by the legendary ultra-thin self-winding 1120 caliber, this 150-piece limited edition emblem of unassuming luxury fittingly boasts the Geneva Seal. The new 42mm platinum case exhibits the virtues of a slim silhouette and broad dial opening, setting the stage for platinum to star in a show of unostentatious character. Found in only a few deposits scattered around the world and 20% purer than 18-karat gold, the precious metal's density and weight make it extremely durable while its immunity to oxidation ensures a lifelong conservation of its distinctive merits. Baring the inscription "PT950" between 4 and 5 o'clock, the finely-grained sandblasted 950 platinum dial sets a perfect tone upon which the 18-karat white-gold beaded minute circle and applied hour markers reflect the brilliant simplicity of the watch's design. Vacheron Constantin does not stop there. Not only are the hands, crown, and pin buckle made of the prized material, but the dark blue alligator leather strap is hand-stitched with silk and 950 platinum threads. Combining the elegance of its understated design with the luxurious appeal of the finely finished precious metal, the Patrimony Contemporaine Self-Winding grants distinguished connoisseurs entry into an elite horological society.

PATRIMONY CONTEMPORAINE SELF-WINDING COLLECTION EXCELLENCE PLATINE

An elegant showcase of platinum and delicate craftsmanship, this limited edition timepiece brings the prestige of the precious metal to the wrist of the watchmaking connoisseur.

OVERSEAS CHRONOGRAPH PERPETUAL CALENDAR BOUTIQUES EXCLUSIVE

This highly technical addition to the sporty Overseas collection is delivered with two straps: one in black vulcanized rubber and the other in dark gray alligator leather.

Limited to 80 pieces and reserved for Vacheron Constantin's 27 worldwide boutiques, the Overseas Chronograph Perpetual Calendar Boutiques Exclusive represents the innovative future of a technical collection. The Swiss manufacture's integration of a perpetual calendar chronograph into the Overseas line makes this impressive dual-complication timepiece a worthy new ambassador to the world of fine sporty watchmaking. Inspired by the emblematic Maltese Cross, the titanium bezel eases the wearer's eye into the sunburst slate-gray dial where the watch's technical spectacle awaits its audience. Powered by the 228-part 1136 QP self-winding mechanical movement, the perpetual calendar ingeniously displays months on a 4-year cycle, complete with leap years, date, day of the week, and a moonphase upon which the small seconds is cleverly positioned. This exceptional caliber, featuring a 40-hour power reserve, also contributes the driving force for a chronograph function that has been perfectly designed for optimal legibility. Along with the house's employment of a luminescent substance in the 18-karat white-gold hour markers, Vacheron Constantin instills a dynamic accent into the dial with its use of yellow in the three chronograph hands, ensuring excellent readability and vibrant personality. Protecting the timepiece from unwanted magnetic fields, the 42mm stainless steel case incorporates a soft iron cage. A signature of the Overseas collection, the watch's caseback features a medallion, intricately engraved with the legendary Amerigo Vespucci three-masted ship of the Italian navy. With two highly regarded complications under its belt, the Overseas Chronograph Perpetual Calendar Boutiques Exclusive propels Vacheron Constantin's sporting collection to an unprecedented height of technical complexity, all while capturing the elegant design code of the Genevan watchmaker.

Vacheron Constantin's presentation of four exceptional new timepieces makes a powerful statement of the Swiss manufacture's 255-year expertise in all facets of watchmaking. Appropriately named, the Patrimony line of timepieces joins the groundbreaking innovations of the Overseas collection in proving once again why this legendary house remains a celebrated leader of haute horology.

HISTORIQUES ULTRA-FINE 1955 — REF. 33155/000R-9588

Movement: manual-winding Vacheron Constantin 1003 caliber; Ø 21.1mm, thickness: 1.64mm; approx. 30-hour power reserve; 117 components; 18 jewels; 18,000 vph; Geneva Seal.
Functions: hours, minutes.
Case: 4N 18K pink gold; Ø 36mm, thickness: 4.1mm; antireflective convex sapphire crystal; screw-down transparent sapphire crystal caseback; water resistant to 3atm.
Dial: silvered opaline; 4N mirror-polished hour markers.
Strap: black Mississippiensis alligator leather, stitched-tip, large square scales; 4N 18K pink-gold buckle with polished half Maltese cross.
Suggested price: $30,600

HISTORIQUES ULTRA-FINE 1968 — REF. 43043/000R-9592

Movement: automatic-winding Vacheron Constantin 1120 caliber; Ø 28.4mm, thickness: 2.45mm; approx. 40-hour power reserve; 144 components; 36 jewels; 19,800 vph; Geneva Seal.
Functions: hours, minutes.
Case: 4N 18K pink gold; 35.2x35.2mm, thickness: 5.5mm; antireflective convex sapphire crystal; screw-down solid caseback; water resistant to 3atm.
Dial: metal; silvered vertical satin finish; applied 18K gold hour markers.
Strap: black Mississippiensis alligator leather, stitched-tip, large square scales; 4N 18K pink-gold buckle with polished half Maltese cross.
Suggested price: $37,400

HISTORIQUES ARONDE 1954 — REF. 81018/000R-9657

Movement: manual-winding Vacheron Constantin 1400 AS caliber; Ø 20.65mm, thickness: 2.6mm; 40-hour power reserve; 98 components; 20 jewels; 28,800 vph; Geneva Seal.
Functions: hours, minutes; small seconds at 6.
Case: 5N 18K pink gold; 31.2x44.5mm; antireflective convex sapphire crystal; screw-down transparent sapphire crystal caseback; water resistant to 3atm.
Dial: silvered opaline; hand-guilloché; applied 18K gold hour markers.
Strap: brown Mississippiensis alligator leather, hand-stitched, saddle finish, large square scales; 5N 18K pink-gold buckle with polished half Maltese cross.
Suggested price: $30,500

HISTORIQUES AMERICAN 1921 — REF. 82035-000R-9359

Movement: manual-winding Vacheron Constantin 4400 AS caliber; Ø 28.6mm; thickness: 2.8mm; 65-hour power reserve; 106 components; 21 jewels; 28,800 vph; Geneva Seal.
Functions: hours, minutes; small seconds at 3.
Case: 5N 18K pink gold; 40x40mm; off-centered crown; antireflective convex sapphire crystal; screw-down transparent sapphire crystal caseback; water resistant to 3atm.
Dial: silvered sand-blasted; black painted Arabic numerals and minute track; black oxidized 18K gold hands.
Strap: black Mississippiensis alligator leather, hand-stitched, saddle finish, large square scales; 5N 18K pink-gold buckle with polished half Maltese cross.
Suggested price: $34,900

PATRIMONY TRADITIONNELLE SQUELETTE — REF. 43578/000G-9393

Movement: hand-engraved automatic-winding Vacheron Constantin 1120 SQ caliber; Ø 28mm, thickness: 2.45mm; 40-hour power reserve; 144 components; 36 jewels; 19,800 vph; Geneva Seal.
Functions: hours, minutes.
Case: 18K white gold; Ø 38mm; bezel set with 82 brilliant-cut diamonds (0.46 carat); antireflective convex sapphire crystal; screw-down transparent sapphire crystal caseback; water resistant to 3atm.
Dial: openworked; twelve applied 18K white-gold hour markers; black painted exterior minute track.
Strap: black Mississippiensis alligator leather, large square scales; 18K white-gold buckle with polished half Maltese cross.
Suggested price: $82,000

PATRIMONY TRADITIONNELLE WORLD TIME — REF. 86060/000R-9640

Movement: automatic-winding Vacheron Constantin 2460 WT caliber; Ø 36.6mm, thickness: 7.55mm; 40-hour power reserve; 255 components; 27 jewels; 28,800 vph; Geneva Seal.
Functions: hours, minutes, seconds; world-time indication with day/night zone (37 cities).
Case: 5N 18K pink gold; Ø 42.5mm; antireflective convex sapphire crystal; screw-down transparent sapphire crystal caseback; water resistant to 3atm.
Dial: three dials; inner ring: sapphire with day/night indication and inked and engraved 24-hour indications; middle ring: metal with "Lambert Projection" map and transferred city names; external ring: metal with transferred minute-track and gold applied hour markers.
Strap: brown Mississippiensis alligator leather, hand-stitched, saddle finish, large square scales; 5N 18K pink-gold triple-blade folding clasp with polished half Maltese Cross.
Suggested price: $48,900

PATRIMONY CONTEMPORAINE RETROGRADE DAY & DATE — REF. 86020/000G-9508

Movement: automatic-winding Vacheron Constantin 2460 R31R7 caliber; Ø 27.2mm, thickness: 5.4mm; approx. 40-hour power reserve; 283 components; 27 jewels; 28,800 vph; Geneva Seal.
Functions: hours, minutes; retrograde day of the week at 6; retrograde date on an arc between 9 and 3.
Case: 18K white gold; Ø 42.5mm, thickness: 10.1mm; polished finish; antireflective convex sapphire crystal; transparent sapphire crystal caseback, snap-on; water resistant to 3atm.
Dial: silvered opaline; convex external zone; circular-grained minute track.
Strap: black Mississippiensis alligator leather, hand-stitched, saddle finish, large square scales; 18K white-gold buckle with polished half Maltese cross.
Suggested price: $45,900
Also available: pink gold.

PATRIMONY TRADITIONNELLE — REF. 82172/000R-9382

Movement: manual-winding Vacheron Constantin 4400 AS caliber; Ø 28.6mm, thickness: 2.8mm; approx. 65-hour power reserve; 106 components; 21 jewels; 28,800 vph; Geneva Seal.
Functions: hours, minutes; small seconds at 6.
Case: 18K pink gold; Ø 38mm; antireflective convex sapphire crystal; screw-down transparent sapphire crystal caseback; water resistant to 3atm.
Dial: silvered opaline; twelve applied 18K pink-gold hour markers; black painted minute tracks; internal zones painted in white; snailed small seconds counter.
Strap: brown Mississippiensis alligator leather, hand-stitched, saddle finish, large square scales.
Suggested price: $19,900
Also available: 18K pink gold with diamond-set hour markers; 18K white gold with or without diamond-set hour markers.

PATRIMONY CONTEMPORAINE SELF-WINDING REF. 43150/000P-9684

Movement: automatic-winding Vacheron Constantin 1120 caliber; Ø 28.4mm, thickness: 2.45mm; 40-hour power reserve; 144 components; 36 jewels; 19,800 vph; Geneva Seal.
Functions: hours, minutes.
Case: platinum 950; Ø 42mm, thickness 7.3mm; antireflective convex sapphire crystal; transparent sapphire crystal caseback, snap-on; water resistant to 3atm.
Dial: platinum 950; sandblasted; "PT 950" hallmark between 4 and 5; convex external zone; circular grained minute track; applied 18K white-gold hour markers; platinum 950 hour and minute hands.
Strap: dark blue Mississippiensis alligator leather, hand-stitched with platinum 950 and silk, saddle finish, large square scales; platinum 950 buckle with polished half Maltese cross.
Suggested price: $57,300
Note: Collection Excellence Platine; limited edition of 150 individually numbered pieces.

PATRIMONY CONTEMPORAINE PERPETUAL CALENDAR REF. 43175/000R-9687

Movement: automatic-winding Vacheron Constantin 1120 QP caliber; Ø 29.6mm, thickness: 4.05mm; 40-hour power reserve; 276 components; 36 jewels; 19,800 vph; Geneva Seal.
Functions: hours, minutes; perpetual calendar: day of the week at 9, date at 3, 48-month counter with leap year cycle at 12; moonphase.
Case: 5N 18K pink gold; Ø 41mm; sapphire crystal; transparent sapphire crystal caseback, snap-on; water resistant to 3atm.
Dial: silvered opaline; convex external zone; circular-grained minute track; applied 5N 18K pink gold hour markers.
Strap: brown Mississippiensis alligator leather, hand-stitched, saddle finish, large square scales; 5N 18K pink-gold triple blade folding clasp with polished half Maltese cross.
Suggested price: $79,000

PATRIMONY TRADITIONNELLE CALIBRE 2253 REF. 88172/000P-9495

Movement: manual-winding Vacheron Constantin 2253 caliber; Ø 32mm, thickness: 9.6mm; approx. 336-hour power reserve; 457 components; 30 jewels; 18,000 vph; Geneva Seal.
Functions: hours, minutes; small seconds on tourbillon at 6; equation of time; sunset/sunrise time; perpetual calendar: date at 3, day of the week at 9 and 48-month counter with leap year cycle at 12; power reserve indicator on the back of the watch.
Case: platinum 950; Ø 44mm, thickness: 15.7mm; antireflective convex sapphire crystal; transparent sapphire crystal caseback; water resistant to 3atm.
Dial: platinum 950; sandblasted; black-painted minute tracks; snailed counters.
Strap: dark blue Mississippiensis alligator leather, hand-stitched with platinum 950 and silk, saddle finish, large square scales; platinum 950 triple blade folding clasp with polished half Maltese cross.
Suggested price: $464,000
Note: limited to 10 pieces.

PATRIMONY TRADITIONNELLE CALIBRE 2755 REF. 80172/000P-9505

Movement: manual-winding Vacheron Constantin 2755 caliber; Ø 33.9mm, thickness: 7.9mm; approx. 58-hour power reserve; 602 components; 40 jewels; 18,000 vph; Geneva Seal.
Functions: hours, minutes; small seconds on tourbillon at 6; minute repeater; perpetual calendar: date at 3, day of the week at 9 and month at 12; power reserve indicator on the back of the watch.
Case: platinum 950; Ø 44mm; antireflective convex sapphire crystal; screw-down transparent sapphire crystal caseback.
Dial: slate-colored opaline; white-painted minute and seconds tracks; snailed counters.
Strap: black Mississippiensis alligator leather, hand-stitched, saddle finish, large square scales.
Suggested price: $760,000
Also available: platinum with silvered opaline dial and pink gold with silvered opaline dial.

PATRIMONY TRADITIONNELLE CHRONOGRAPH PERPETUAL CALENDAR REF. 47292/000P-9510

Movement: manual-winding 1141 QP caliber; Ø 27.5mm, thickness: 7.37mm; approx. 48-hour power reserve; 324 components; 21 jewels; 18,000 vph.
Functions: hours, minutes; small seconds at 9; date at 6; day and month in aperture at 12; column-wheel chronograph: 30-minute counter at 3 and central chronograph hand; moonphase.
Case: platinum 950; Ø 43mm, thickness: 12.9mm; antireflective convex sapphire crystal; screw-down transparent sapphire crystal caseback; water resistant to 3atm.
Dial: slate-colored opaline; white-painted indications; snailed counters.
Strap: black Mississippiensis alligator leather, hand-stitched, saddle finish, large square scales.
Suggested price: $151,200
Also available: platinum with silvered opaline dial and pink gold with silvered opaline dial.

PATRIMONY TRADITIONNELLE CHRONOGRAPH REF. 47192/000R-9352

Movement: manual-winding 1141 caliber; Ø 27.5mm, thickness: 5.6mm approx. 48-hour power reserve; 164 components; 21 jewels; 18,000 vph.
Functions: hours, minutes; small seconds at 9; column-wheel chronograph: 30-minute counter at 3 and central chronograph hand.
Case: 18K pink gold; Ø 42mm, thickness: 10.6mm; antireflective convex sapphire crystal; screw-down transparent sapphire crystal caseback; water resistant to 3atm.
Dial: silvered opaline; black-painted indications; snailed counters.
Strap: brown Mississippiensis alligator leather, hand-stitched, saddle finish, large square scales.
Suggested price: $55,900
Also available: white gold and white gold with 5N 18K gold crown, pushbuttons, hour markers and hands.

QUAI DE L'ILE RETROGRADE ANNUAL CALENDAR REF. 86040/000G-M936R

Movement: automatic-winding Vacheron Constantin 2460 QRA caliber; Ø 26.2mm, thickness: 5.4mm; 40-hour power reserve; 326 components; 27 jewels; 28,800 vph; special Quai de l'Ile 22K gold rotor with ruthenium finishing and decorated with five embossed fillets; Geneva Seal.
Functions: hours, minutes; small seconds at 9; annual calendar: retrograde date at 3 and month at 7; precision moonphase.
Case: 18K white gold; cushion-shape; 43x54mm; screw-down transparent sapphire crystal caseback; water resistant to 3atm.
Dial: slate-colored opaline external ring; slate-colored soft vertical satin-finishing center; opaline moonphase, day and date indication zones; UV ink sun; chamfered hour markers and counters; matte ebony opaline-metal moonphase disc and circular satin-finished moon figure.
Strap: black Mississippiensis alligator leather, hand-stitched, saddle finish, large square scales; 18K white-gold triple-blade folding clasp; delivered with an additional black natural rubber strap.
Suggested price: $68,000

QUAI DE L'ILE RETROGRADE ANNUAL CALENDAR REF. 86040/000R-I0P29

Movement: automatic-winding Vacheron Constantin 2460 QRA caliber; Ø 26.2mm, thickness: 5.4mm; 40-hour power reserve; 326 components; 27 jewels; 28,800 vph; special Quai de l'Ile 22K gold rotor with ruthenium finishing and decorated with five embossed fillets; Geneva Seal.
Functions: hours, minutes; small seconds at 9; annual calendar: retrograde date at 3 and month at 7; precision moonphase.
Case: 5N 18K pink gold; cushion-shape; 43x54mm; screw-down transparent sapphire crystal caseback; water resistant to 3atm.
Dial: silvered opaline external ring; silvered soft vertical satin-finishing center; opaline moonphase, day and date indication zones; UV ink sun; chamfered hour markers and counters; matte ebony opaline-metal moonphase disc and circular satin-finished moon figure.
Strap: brown Mississippiensis alligator leather, hand-stitched, saddle finish, large square scales; 5N 18K pink-gold triple-blade folding clasp; delivered with an additional brown natural rubber strap.
Suggested price: $68,000

OVERSEAS CHRONOGRAPH PERPETUAL CALENDAR REF. 49020/000W-9656

Movement: automatic-winding 1136 QP caliber; Ø 28mm, thickness: 7.9mm; 40-hour power reserve; 228 components; 37 jewels; 21,600 vph; antimagnetic protection.
Functions: hours, minutes; small seconds at 6; chronograph: 12-hour counter at 9, 30-minute counter at 3 and central chronograph hand; perpetual calendar: day of the week at 9, date at 3, 48-month counter with leap year cycle at 12; moonphase.
Case: stainless steel; Ø 42mm, thickness: 12.9; titanium bezel; screw-down crown and pushbuttons; antireflective sapphire crystal; closed, screw-down solid caseback stamped with the "Overseas" medallion; water resistant to 15atm.

Dial: slate-colored; sunray satin finish; twelve applied 18K white-gold hour markers with luminescent coating;
Strap: black vulcanized rubber; stainless steel triple-bladed deployant buckle with double security pushbuttons; polished half Maltese cross; delivered with an additional dark gray Mississippiensis alligator leather, hand-stitched, saddle finish, large square scales.
Suggested price: $67,000
Note: limited to 80 pieces; model only available through the Vacheron Constantin Boutiques.

OVERSEAS DUAL TIME REF. 47450/B01J-9228

Movement: automatic-winding 1222 SC caliber; Ø 26.6mm, thickness: 4.85mm; approx. 40-hour power reserve; 153 components; 34 jewels; 28,800 vph; antimagnetic protection.
Functions: hours, minutes, seconds; date at 2; second time zone with day/night indication at 6; power reserve indicator at 9.
Case: 3N 18K yellow gold; Ø 42mm, thickness: 12.4mm; screw-down crown and pushbutton; antireflective sapphire crystal; closed, screw-down solid caseback stamped with the "Overseas" medallion; water resistant to 15atm.

Dial: silvered "Overseas" pattern; black-painted indications; snailed counters; twelve applied 3N 18K yellow gold hour markers with luminescent coating.
Bracelet: 3N 18K yellow gold; 18K yellow-gold triple-bladed deployant buckle with double security pushbuttons; polished half Maltese cross; .
Suggested price: $59,300
Also available: pink gold; stainless steel and stainless steel with titanium bezel and pushbutton ring.

OVERSEAS CHRONOGRAPH REF. 49150/000R-9454

Movement: automatic-winding 1137 caliber; Ø 26.2mm, thickness: 6.6mm; approx. 40-hour power reserve; 183 components; 37 jewels; 21,600 vph; antimagnetic protection.
Functions: hours, minutes, seconds; large date at 12; column-wheel chronograph: 12-hour counter at 9, 30-minute counter at 3 and central chronograph hand.
Case: 18K pink gold; Ø 42mm, thickness: 12.4mm; screw-down crown and pushbutton; solid caseback closed with screws stamped with the "Overseas" medallion; water resistant to 15atm.

Dial: silvered "Overseas" pattern; black-painted indications; snailed counters; twelve applied 5N 18K pink-gold hour markers with white luminescent coating.
Strap: brown Mississippiensis alligator leather, hand-stitched, saddle finish, large square scales; 5N 18K pink-gold triple-bladed deployant buckle with double security pushbuttons; polished half Maltese cross; delivered with an additional dark brown vulcanized rubber strap.
Suggested price: $46,200
Also available: yellow gold; stainless steel; with either silvered or dark dials, and stainless steel with titanium bezel and pushbuttons rings.

OVERSEAS DATE SELF-WINDING REF. 47040/B01A-9093

Movement: automatic-winding 1226 caliber; Ø 26.6mm, thickness: 3.25mm; 40-hour power reserve; 143 components; 36 jewels; 28,800 vph; antimagnetic protection.
Functions: hours, minutes, seconds; date at 4:30.
Case: stainless steel; Ø 42mm, thickness: 9.7mm; screw-down crown; solid caseback closed with screws stamped with the "Overseas" medallion; water resistant to 15atm.

Dial: black "Overseas" pattern; twelve applied 18K white gold numerals and hour markers with white luminescent coating.
Bracelet: stainless steel; stainless steel triple-bladed deployant buckle with double security pushbuttons; polished half Maltese cross.
Suggested price: $14,300
Also available: pink gold; stainless steel with silvered dial and stainlesss steel with titanium bezel.

METIERS D'ART LA SYMBOLIQUE DES LAQUES TURTLE AND LOTUS REF. 33222/000R-9548

Movement: utlra-thin manual-winding Vacheron Constantin 1003 SQ caliber; Ø 21.1mm, thickness: 1.64mm; 30-hour power reserve; 117 components; 18 jewels; 18,000 vph; open-worked; 18K gold rotor with ruthenium finishings; Geneva Seal.
Functions: hours, minutes.
Case: 4N 18K pink gold; Ø 40mm, thickness: 7.5mm; water resistant to 3atm.
Dial: 18K gold lacquered using the Japanese *maki-e* technique on both sides.
Strap: black Mississippiensis alligator leather, large square scales; 4N 18K pink-gold buckle with polished half Maltese cross.
Suggested price: $103,300
Note: limited edition to 20 sets of 3 watches (Turtle & Lotus, Frog & Hydrangea and Carp & Waterfall).

METIERS D'ART LA SYMBOLIQUE DES LAQUES FROG AND HYDRANGEA REF. 33222/000R-9546

Movement: utlra-thin manual-winding Vacheron Constantin 1003 SQ caliber; Ø 21.1mm, thickness: 1.64mm; 30-hour power reserve; 117 components; 18 jewels; 18,000 vph; open-worked; 18K gold rotor with ruthenium finishings; Geneva Seal.
Functions: hours, minutes.
Case: 4N 18K pink gold; Ø 40mm, thickness: 7.5mm; water resistant to 3atm.
Dial: 18K gold lacquered using the Japanese *maki-e* technique on both sides.
Strap: black Mississippiensis alligator leather, large square scales; 4N 18K pink-gold buckle with polished half Maltese cross.
Suggested price: $103,300
Note: limited edition to 20 sets of 3 watches (Turtle & Lotus, Frog & Hydrangea and Carp & Waterfall).

METIERS D'ART LA SYMBOLIQUE DES LAQUES CARP AND WATERFALL REF. 33222/000G-9550

Movement: utlra-thin manual-winding Vacheron Constantin 1003 SQ caliber; Ø 21.1mm, thickness: 1.64mm; 30-hour power reserve; 117 components; 18 jewels; 18,000 vph; open-worked; 18K gold rotor with ruthenium finishings; Geneva Seal.
Functions: hours, minutes.
Case: 18K white gold; Ø 40mm, thickness: 7.5mm; water resistant to 3atm.
Dial: 18K gold lacquered using the Japanese *maki-e* technique on both sides.
Strap: black Mississippiensis alligator leather, large square scales; 18K white-gold pin buckle with polished half Maltese cross.
Suggested price: $103,300
Note: limited edition to 20 sets of 3 watches (Turtle & Lotus, Frog & Hydrangea and Carp & Waterfall).

METIERS D'ART KALLA HAUTE COUTURE A PAMPILLES REF. 17626/S13G-9479

Movement: manual-winding 1005 caliber; 6.2x17.9mm, thickness: 3.6mm; 35-hour power reserve; 89 components; 17 jewels; 19,800 vph.
Functions: hours, minutes.
Case: 18K white gold; 40x56mm, thickness: 10mm; fully-paved with 58 flame-cut diamonds (approx. 16.20 carats) and 54 brilliant-cut diamonds (approx. 0.18 carat).
Dial: 18K white gold; fully-set with 130 brilliant-cut diamonds (approx. 0.32 carat).
Bracelet: 18K white gold fully-set with 29 flame-cut diamonds (approx. 4 carats) and 39 princess-cut diamonds (approx. 8.2 carats); 18K white-gold jewelry clasp.
Suggested price: $735,000

Van Cleef & Arpels

REDISCOVER THE WORLD

Van Cleef & Arpels's affectionate connection to Jules Verne's tales of wondrous travels is a poetic symbol of the most fundamental core of horology—the determination to discover the world.

With its Extraordinary Journeys collection, or les Voyages Extraordinaires, Van Cleef & Arpels passionately recaptures the reasons for the very creation of modern watchmaking, when the need to measure longitude at sea gave birth to the art of timekeeping.

Closely inspired by the works of the 19th-century French author, whose relentless imagination and passion for exploration led him to become a science fiction pioneer, the Extraordinary Journeys collection expresses time in its most magical form.

The Poetic Complication Five Weeks in a Balloon watch is an homage to the first novel in Jules Verne's series of 68 tales of exceptional travel. The dial of this timepiece is decorated with champlevé enamel and mother-of-pearl inlays, and portrays a balloon at its center that has just lifted off from the island of Zanzibar. The JLC 846 mechanical movement boasts a unique retrograde module, specially developed for Van Cleef & Arpels, and provides an ingenious method for telling the time. The retrograde minute, on the right side of the dial, is indicated by the balloon's anchor, which descends from zero to sixty, and subsequently returns to its starting point at the top of the function. On the left side, a bird in flight moves upward to specify the hours, before returning to its starting point at the bottom every 12 hours. While the anchor is an emblem of stability, keeping the memory of a precious moment, the bird symbolizes hope in perpetuity, constantly rising in its flight toward the central balloon.

POETIC COMPLICATION FROM THE EARTH TO THE MOON

The dial and space capsule are adorned with an inlay of jade, agate, meteorite stone and champlevé enamel.

FIVE WEEKS IN A BALLOON

Based on the 1863 book of the same name, this white-gold limited edition timepiece uses a unique time-telling module.

Joining the From the Earth to the Moon line of the Voyages Extraordinaires collection, the High Jewelry Timeless From the Earth to the Moon watch takes on Jules Verne's vision of a spaceship taking to the sky. The design's creative audacity shows the engines leaving behind them a trail of diamonds and sapphires. Meanwhile, the multi-colored gold rocket soars through a star-filled sky, sparkling with diamonds that were rigorously selected for their purity, shine and carat by Van Cleef & Arpels' master stone setters. Inside the cabin, passengers gaze at the pearly reflection of the pursuit of infinity. The lower half of the dial displays the earth with delicately crafted mother-of-pearl inlay, as the constantly changing reflections breathe life into this timekeeping jewel. Over the course of three months, white, black and gray mother-of-pearl, as well as jasper, quartz and a variety of hard stones, are carved and assembled with meticulous precision. The remarkable mastery of the technique and a white-gold case set with the finest diamonds give this watch a fittingly glowing aura. As a finishing touch to this luxurious numbered edition tribute to Jules Verne's genius, the satin strap is secured with a white-gold pin buckle set with diamonds.

Whether through elaborate adorning techniques or innovative engineering, Van Cleef & Arpels captures the essence of Jules Verne's endlessly imaginative quest. The Timeless From the Earth to the Moon and Poetic Complication Five Weeks in a Balloon timepieces join a complete collection of whimsical watches meant to ignite the everlasting curiosity of their owners.

TIMELESS FROM THE EARTH TO THE MOON

The artistic intricacy of this High Jewelry watch creates a precious miniature backdrop for the golden hour and minute hands.

LADY ARPELS FEERIE REF. VCARF80600

Movement: Swiss mechanical.
Functions: retrograde hours and minutes.
Case: white gold; Ø 38mm; set with diamonds (2.82 carats); scratch-proof sapphire crystal; water resistant to 3atm.
Dial: blue enamel; hand engraved guilloché; diamond-set fairy.
Strap: deep blue satin; white-gold buckle set with diamonds.

PONT DES AMOUREUX REF. VCARN9VI00

Movement: Swiss mechanical.
Functions: retrograde hours and minutes.
Case: white gold; Ø 38mm; set with round diamonds.
Dial: backlit enamel; white-gold bridge; engraving on the back.
Strap: alligator; white-gold buckle set with diamonds.
Note: numbered edition.

Also available: checkered links.

FROM THE EARTH TO THE MOON REF. VCARO24800

Movement: JLC 846 caliber; exclusive module for Van Cleef & Arpels; 30-hour power reserve.
Functions: bi-retrograde hours and minutes: hours displayed on the left, through the course of the star and minutes on the right hand side, following the Lunar capsule's trajectory.
Case: white gold; Ø 42mm; agate cabochon.
Dial: mother-of-pearl and Champlevé enamel; black jade and agate meteorite.
Strap: black alligator leather.
Note: numbered edition.

POLAR WHALE REF. VCARO22K00

Movement: manual-winding.
Functions: hours, minutes.
Case: white gold; set with diamonds.
Dial: white gold; sculpting set with diamonds; mother-of-pearl marquetry; glass sculpting Champlevé enamel.
Strap: dark gray alligator leather.

Note: limited to 22 pieces.

CHARMS PAVE — REF. VCARM95400

Movement: Swiss quartz.
Functions: hours, minutes.
Case: white gold; Ø 38mm; set with three rows of diamonds (3.16 carats).
Dial: white Alhambra guilloché; sunburst effect; white-gold Roman numerals.
Strap: interchangeable black satin strap; buckle set with diamonds.
Also available: pink gold or white gold.

CHARMS MINI — REF. VCARN9UX00

Movement: Swiss quartz.
Functions: hours, minutes.
Case: pink gold; Ø 25mm set with two rows of diamonds.
Dial: Alhambra guilloché motif; sunburst effect.
Strap: black satin; pink-gold buckle set with diamonds.
Also available: white gold; fully paved with diamonds; alligator strap; white-gold buckle set with diamonds.

PIERRE ARPELS — REF. VCARO23Y00

Movement: Piaget 830 P caliber; 60-hour power reserve; 19 jewels; 21,600 vph.
Functions: hours, minutes.
Case: polished white gold; white-gold bezel; white-gold crown set with diamonds; brushed white-gold caseback with English letter.
Dial: white lacquered with Van Cleef & Arpels hallmark.
Strap: green anthracite varnished; white-gold pin buckle.

ALHAMBRA VINTAGE BRACELET — REF. VCARF53500

Movement: Swiss quartz.
Functions: hours, minutes.
Case: yellow gold; scratch-proof sapphire crystal; water resistant to 3atm.
Dial: mother-of-pearl.
Bracelet: seven Alhambra motifs.

ZENITH

SWISS WATCH MANUFACTURE

SINCE 1865

TAKE FLIGHT

With its El Primero Stratos Flyback and El Primero Stratos Flyback Striking 10th, Zenith pushes the limits of watchmaking mastery in its effort to put a fighter jet on the wrist of a man.

EL PRIMERO STRATOS FLYBACK STRIKING 10TH

This virtual cockpit is limited to 1969 pieces, to honor the birth year of the El Primero movement.

This limited edition wristwatch dares to be the fastest, strongest, and most accurate of all timepieces, while achieving a visual effect that evokes the cockpit of these stealthy beasts of the sky.

Inspired by Zenith's Rainbow Flyback, which the watchmaker designed in accordance with the standards of the French Ministry of Defense, the El Primero Stratos Flyback Striking 10th is more than an homage to the tradition of military chronographs. Whereas pilots once had to recalculate a new route using a three-step process, the flyback function that equips this Zenith wristwatch allows them to stop, reset, and restart the chronograph with a single button. Such a demonstration of pure speed and ingenious efficiency is a fitting attribute for this military-grade chronograph.

Having remained faithful to the vision of its founder that all its timepieces must be produced entirely in-house, it is no surprise that Zenith armed this watch with its legendary El Primero caliber. As the integrated column-wheel movement vibrates at 36,000 beats per hour, the Striking 10th function visibly displays time to the tenth of a second, as the red seconds hand completes one revolution of the dial every ten seconds.

The design of this stainless steel watch is inspired by the perfect efficiency of aero-navigational instruments, while also honoring the first El Primero chronograph, launched in 1969. Zenith has raised the rhodium faceted hands off the dial's surface to enhance legibility, and has stayed true to the three counter colors laid out in a 3-6-9 configuration: the cockpit is comprised of a 60-second counter at 3 o'clock, a 60-minute counter at 6 o'clock, and a small seconds at 9 o'clock.

EL PRIMERO STRATOS FLYBACK

This military chronograph is designed with Alchron, providing strength worthy of the world's finest air forces.

Zenith's El Primero Stratos Flyback introduces a model in black Alchron and red gold. Specifically developed for the aeronautical and auto racing industries, Alchron possesses a magnetic permeability 50 times lower than that of steel, protecting the movement from magnetic fields. The high-tech alloy, which boasts a Vickers hardness number of 210 HV, is especially resistant to corrosion.

The battery of tests that preceded Alchron's integration into the El Primero Stratos Flyback is a testament to the brand's ambition to provide the high-precision caliber with the best high-strength alloy technology available. Zenith tested Alchron's corrosion resistance with saline mists, simulated tropical climates and artificial perspiration, and examined its impact resistance with a hammer-like pendulum striker that hits the case at full force.

The El Primero 405B automatic caliber, which also beats at a highly precise 36,000 beats per hour, powers this watch, a picturesque balance of strength and precision. The red-gold case and bezel with gold-plated hands set a frame for a black dial displaying three subdials in the 3-6-9 arrangement. The date indicator sits beneath a 12-hour counter at 6 o'clock, while small seconds at 9 o'clock and a 30-minute counter at 3 o'clock complete the aesthetic cockpit experience of this timepiece.

Zenith's El Primero Stratos Flyback Striking 10th and El Primero Stratos Flyback are culminations of Zenith's commitment to produce the finest timepieces in-house, benefiting from expertise that has been handed down

ACADEMY CHRISTOPHE COLOMB EQUATION OF TIME REF. 18.2220.8808/01.C631

Movement: manual-winding El Primero 8808 caliber; Ø 37mm, thickness: 5.85mm; 50-hour power reserve; 359 components; 28 jewels; 36,000 vph; gyroscopic system that ensures perfect horizontal positioning of the regulating organ (167 components).
Functions: small hours and minutes at 12; power reserve indicator at 3; self-regulating gyroscopic module at 6; equation of time at 9.

Case: 18K rose gold; Ø 45mm; sapphire crystal with antireflective treatment on both sides with excrescent domes that cover zero-gravity module; water resistant to 3atm.
Dial: gold with handmade silver rounded "Grain d'Orge" guilloché; black lacquered numerals and markers; blued steel hands.
Strap: brown alligator leather; 18K rose-gold triple-folding buckle.
Note: limited to 75 pieces.

EL PRIMERO TOURBILLON REF. 65.2050.4035/91.C714

Movement: automatic-winding El Primero 4035 D caliber; Ø 37mm, thickness: 7.66mm; 50-hour power reserve; 381 components; 35 jewels; 36,000 vph; 18K gold oscillating weight with Côtes de Genève pattern.
Functions: hours, minutes; small seconds and date in the tourbillon at 11; chronograph: 12-hour counter at 6, 30-minute counter at 3 and central seconds hand; tourbillon at 11.

Case: 18K white gold; Ø 44mm; sapphire crystal with antireflective treatment on both sides; sapphire crystal caseback; water resistant to 10atm.
Dial: slate-gray sunray; rhodium faceted hands and markers with SuperLumiNova C1 coating.
Strap: black alligator leather; 18K white-gold triple-folding buckle.

EL PRIMERO TOURBILLON REF. 03.2051.4035/51.C715

Movement: automatic-winding El Primero 4035 D caliber; Ø 37mm, thickness: 7.66mm; 50-hour power reserve; 381 components; 35 jewels; 36,000 vph; heavy metal oscillating weight with Côtes de Genève pattern.
Functions: hours, minutes; small seconds and date in the tourbillon at 11; chronograph: 12-hour counter at 6, 30-minute counter at 3 and central seconds hand; tourbillon at 11.

Case: stainless steel; Ø 44mm; sapphire crystal with antireflective treatment on both sides; sapphire crystal caseback; water resistant to 10atm.
Dial: blue sunray; rhodium faceted hands and markers with SuperLumiNova C1 coating.
Strap: blue alligator leather; stainless steel triple-folding buckle.
Note: limited edition to 250 pieces; tribute to Charles Vermont.

EL PRIMERO RATTRAPANTE REF. 51.2050.4026/01.C713

Movement: automatic-winding El Primero 4026 caliber; Ø 30mm, thickness: 9.35mm; 50-hour power reserve; 370 components; 32 jewels; 36,000 vph; heavy metal oscillating weight with Côtes de Genève pattern.
Functions: hours, minutes; small seconds at 9; date at 6; split-seconds chronograph: 30-minute counter at 3 and central split seconds and seconds hands.
Case: stainless steel and rose gold; Ø 44mm; sapphire crystal with antireflective treatment on both sides; sapphire crystal caseback; water resistant to 10atm.

Dial: silver sunray; nickel circular satined zones; rhodium gold-plated hands and markers with SuperLumiNova C1 coating.
Strap: brown alligator leather; stainless steel triple-folding buckle.

EL PRIMERO CHRONOMASTER OPEN — REF. 18.2080.4021/01.C494

Movement: automatic-winding El Primero 4021 caliber; Ø 30mm, thickness: 7.85mm; 50-hour power reserve; 248 components; 39 jewels; 36,000 vph; heavy metal oscillating weight with Côtes de Genève pattern.
Functions: hours, minutes; small seconds at 9; power reserve indicator on an arc between 5 and 8; chronograph: 30-minute counter at 3 and central chronograph hand.
Case: 18K rose gold; Ø 42mm; sapphire crystal with antireflective treatment on both sides; sapphire crystal caseback; water resistant to 10atm.
Dial: silver sunray; rhodium gold-plated hands and markers with SuperLumiNova C1 coating.
Strap: brown alligator leather; 18K rose-gold pin buckle.

EL PRIMERO CHRONOMASTER OPEN — REF. 03.2080.4021/21.M2040

Movement: automatic-winding El Primero 4021 caliber; Ø 30mm, thickness: 7.85mm; 50-hour power reserve; 248 components; 39 jewels; 36,000 vph; heavy metal oscillating weight with Côtes de Genève pattern.
Functions: hours, minutes; small seconds at 9; power reserve indicator on an arc between 5 and 8; chronograph: 30-minute counter at 3 and central chronograph hand.
Case: stainless steel; Ø 42mm; sapphire crystal with antireflective treatment on both sides; sapphire crystal caseback; water resistant to 10atm.
Dial: black sunray; rhodium-plated hands and markers with SuperLumiNova C1 coating.
Bracelet: metal with triple-folding buckle.

EL PRIMERO 36,000 VPH — REF. 03.2040.400/21.C496

Movement: automatic-winding El Primero 400 B caliber; Ø 30mm, thickness: 6.6mm; 50-hour power reserve; 326 components; 31 jewels; 36,000 vph; heavy metal oscillating weight with Côtes de Genève pattern.
Functions: hours, minutes; small seconds at 9; date at 6; chronograph: 12-hour counter at 6, 30-minute counter at 3 and central chronograph hand; tachometric scale.
Case: stainless steel; Ø 42mm; tachometric scale on the flange; sapphire crystal with antireflective treatment on both sides; sapphire crystal caseback; water resistant to 10atm.
Dial: black sunray; nickel zones around the counters; rhodium-plated hands and markers with SuperLumiNova C1 coating.
Strap: black alligator leather; stainless steel pin buckle.

EL PRIMERO 36,000 VPH — REF. 03.2041.400/51.C496

Movement: automatic-winding El Primero 400 B caliber; Ø 30mm, thickness: 6.6mm; 50-hour power reserve; 326 components; 31 jewels; 36,000 vph; heavy metal oscillating weight with Côtes de Genève pattern.
Functions: hours, minutes; small seconds at 9; date at 6; chronograph: 12-hour counter at 6, 30-minute counter at 3 and central chronograph hand; tachometric scale.
Case: stainless steel; Ø 42mm; tachometric scale on the flange; sapphire crystal with antireflective treatment on both sides; sapphire crystal caseback; water resistant to 10atm.
Dial: blue sunray; nickel zones around the counters; rhodium-plated hands and markers with SuperLumiNova C1 coating.
Strap: black alligator leather; stainless steel pin buckle.

EL PRIMERO STRATOS REF. 03.2060.4057/69.C714

Movement: automatic-winding El Primero 4057 B caliber; Ø 30mm, thickness: 6.6mm; 50-hour power reserve; 326 components; 31 jewels; 36,000 vph; heavy metal oscillating weight with Côtes de Genève pattern.
Functions: hours, minutes; small seconds at 9; date at 6; chronograph: 60-minute counter at 6, 60-second counter at 3 and 1/10th of a second central chronograph hand.

Case: stainless steel; Ø 45.5mm; sapphire crystal with antireflective treatment on both sides; sapphire crystal caseback; water resistant to 10atm.
Dial: silver sunray; three-color counters; rhodium-plated hands and markers with SuperLumiNova C1 coating.
Strap: black alligator leather; stainless steel folding buckle.

EL PRIMERO STRATOS REF. 86.2060.405/23.C714

Movement: automatic-winding El Primero 405 B caliber; Ø 30mm, thickness: 6.6mm; 50-hour power reserve; 331 components; 31 jewels; 36,000 vph; heavy metal oscillating weight with Côtes de Genève pattern.
Functions: hours, minutes; small seconds at 9; date at 6; chronograph: 12-hour counter at 6, 30-minute counter at 3 and central chronograph hand; tachometric scale.
Case: rose gold; Ø 45.5mm; black alchron bezel, pushers and crown; sapphire crystal with antireflective treatment on both sides; sapphire crystal caseback; water resistant to 10atm.
Dial: black; rose-gold-plated hands and markers with SuperLumiNova C1 coating.
Strap: black alligator leather; black triple-folding buckle.

CAPTAIN WINSOR REF. 03.2070.4054/02.C711

Movement: automatic-winding El Primero 4054 caliber; Ø 30mm, thickness: 8.3mm; 50-hour power reserve; 341 components; 29 jewels; 36,000 vph; heavy metal oscillating weight with Côtes de Genève pattern.
Functions: hours, minutes; small seconds at 9; day and month at 3; date at 6; chronograph: 60-minute counter at 6 and central chronograph hand.
Case: stainless steel; Ø 42mm; sapphire crystal with antireflective treatment on both sides; sapphire crystal caseback; water resistant to 5atm.
Dial: silver guilloché in the center and silver circular satined on the exterior; rhodium-plated hands and markers with SuperLumiNova C1 coating.
Strap: brown alligator leather; stainless steel pin buckle.

CAPTAIN CHRONOGRAPH REF. 51.2112.400/01.M2110

Movement: automatic-winding El Primero 400 B caliber; Ø 30mm, thickness: 6.6mm; 50-hour power reserve; 326 components; 31 jewels; 36,000 vph; heavy metal oscillating weight with Côtes de Genève pattern.
Functions: hours, minutes; small seconds at 9; date at 6; chronograph: 12-hour counter at 6, 30-minute counter at 3 and central chronograph hand.
Case: stainless steel; Ø 42mm; 18K rose-gold bezel, pushers and crown; sapphire crystal with antireflective treatment on both sides; sapphire crystal caseback; water resistant to 5atm.
Dial: silver sunray; rhodium faceted markers and hands with gold plating.
Bracelet: stainless steel and 18K rose gold with triple-folding buckle.

CAPTAIN CHRONOGRAPH — REF. 03.2116.400/51.C700

Movement: automatic-winding El Primero 400 B caliber; Ø 30mm, thickness: 6.6mm; 50-hour power reserve; 326 components; 31 jewels; 36,000 vph; heavy metal oscillating weight with Côtes de Genève pattern.
Functions: hours, minutes; small seconds at 9; date at 6; chronograph: 12-hour counter at 6, 30-minute counter at 3 and central chronograph hand.
Case: stainless steel; Ø 42mm; sapphire crystal with antireflective treatment on both sides; sapphire crystal caseback; water resistant to 5atm.
Dial: blue sunray; rhodium faceted markers and hands.
Strap: blue alligator leather; stainless steel pin buckle.
Note: limited edition of 1975 pieces.

CAPTAIN MOONPHASE — REF. 18.2140.691/02.C498

Movement: automatic-winding Elite 691 caliber; Ø 25.6mm, thickness: 5.67mm; 50-hour power reserve; 228 components; 27 jewels; 28,800 vph; heavy metal oscillating weight with Côtes de Genève pattern.
Functions: hours, minutes; small seconds at 9; date at 1; moonphase at 6.
Case: 18K rose gold; Ø 40mm; sapphire crystal with antireflective treatment on both sides; sapphire crystal caseback; water resistant to 5atm.
Dial: silver guilloché; rhodium faceted markers and hands with gold plating.
Strap: brown alligator leather; 18K rose-gold pin buckle.

CAPTAIN POWER RESERVE — REF. 16.2120.685/02.C498

Movement: automatic-winding Elite 685 caliber; Ø 25.6mm, thickness: 4.67mm; 50-hour power reserve; 179 components; 38 jewels; 28,800 vph; heavy metal oscillating weight with Côtes de Genève pattern.
Functions: hours, minutes; small seconds at 9; date at 6; power reserve indicator on an arc between 12 and 3.
Case: stainless steel; Ø 40mm; set with 74 brilliant-cut VS diamonds (0.8 carat); sapphire crystal with antireflective treatment on both sides; sapphire crystal caseback; water resistant to 5atm.
Dial: silver guilloché; rhodium faceted markers and hands.
Strap: brown alligator leather; stainless steel pin buckle.

CAPTAIN CENTRAL SECOND — REF. 03.2020.670/01.C498

Movement: automatic-winding Elite 670 caliber; Ø 25.6mm, thickness: 3.47mm; 50-hour power reserve; 144 components; 27 jewels; 28,800 vph; heavy metal oscillating weight with Côtes de Genève pattern.
Functions: hours, minutes, seconds; date at 6.
Case: stainless steel; Ø 40mm; sapphire crystal with antireflective treatment on both sides; sapphire crystal caseback; water resistant to 5atm.
Dial: silver sunray; rhodium-faceted hands and markers with gold plating.
Strap: dark brown alligator leather; stainless steel pin buckle.

CAPTAIN CENTRAL SECOND REF. 03.2020.670/21.M2020

Movement: automatic-winding Elite 670 caliber; Ø 25.6mm, thickness: 3.47mm; 50-hour power reserve; 144 components; 27 jewels; 28,800 vph; heavy metal oscillating weight with Côtes de Genève pattern.
Functions: hours, minutes, seconds; date at 6.
Case: stainless steel; Ø 40mm; sapphire crystal with antireflective treatment on both sides; sapphire crystal caseback; water resistant to 5atm.
Dial: black; rhodium-faceted hands and markers with gold plating.
Bracelet: stainless steel with triple-folding buckle.

PILOT CHRONOGRAPH REF. 03.2117.4002/23.C704

Movement: automatic-winding El Primero 4002 caliber; Ø 30mm, thickness: 6.6mm; 50-hour power reserve; 307 components; 31 jewels; 36,000 vph; heavy metal oscillating weight with Côtes de Genève pattern.
Functions: hours, minutes; small seconds at 9; date at 6; chronograph: 30-minute counter at 3 and central chronograph hand.
Case: stainless steel; Ø 42mm; sapphire crystal with antireflective treatment on both sides; sapphire crystal caseback; water resistant to 5atm.
Dial: black; markers with SuperLumiNova C1 coating; white varnished hands with SuperLumiNova C1 coating.
Strap: camel brown alligator with beige stitching; stainless steel pin buckle.

HERITAGE ULTRA THIN REF. 18.2010.681/01.C498

Movement: automatic-winding Elite 681 caliber; Ø 25.6mm, thickness: 3.47mm; 50-hour power reserve; 128 components; 27 jewels; 28,800 vph; heavy metal oscillating weight with Côtes de Genève pattern.
Functions: hours, minutes; small seconds at 9.
Case: 18K rose gold; Ø 40mm; sapphire crystal with antireflective treatment on both sides; sapphire crystal caseback; water resistant to 5atm.
Dial: silver sunray; rhodium faceted hands and markers with gold plating.
Strap: brown alligator leather; 18K rose-gold pin buckle.

HERITAGE ULTRA THIN REF. 18.2010.681/11.C498

Movement: automatic-winding Elite 681 caliber; Ø 25.6mm, thickness: 3.47mm; 50-hour power reserve; 128 components; 27 jewels; 28,800 vph; heavy metal oscillating weight with Côtes de Genève pattern.
Functions: hours, minutes; small seconds at 9.
Case: 18K rose gold; Ø 40mm; sapphire crystal with antireflective treatment on both sides; sapphire crystal caseback; water resistant to 5atm.
Dial: white; black transferred numerals; rhodium faceted markers and hands with gold plating.
Strap: brown alligator leather; 18K rose-gold pin buckle.